The *Connoisseur's Guide to* **BEER**

An early example of Stroh print advertising

The Connoisseur's Guide to
BEER

By James D. Robertson
Introduction by Bob Abel

Jameson Books

Ottawa, Illinois 61350

10 9 8 7 6 5 4

Copyright © 1984 by James D. Robertson

Printed in the United States of America

All inquiries should be addressed to Jameson Books, Inc., 722 Columbus St., Ottawa, Illinois 61350. (815) 434-7905.

Distributed to the trade by Kampmann and Company, New York. Orders and returns accepted by Kampmann.

ISBN: 0-915463-05-9

CONTENTS

The Miss Budweiser U-1.... Defending the national championship of the American Power Boat Association's Unlimited Hydroplane Racing circuit is the powerful Miss Budweiser, which stormed to victory in the first five races of the 1980 season, smashing the record for consecutive heat victories and extending that mark to 20. The Miss Budweiser team has won national championships in 1969, '70, '71, '77 and 1980 and has claimed victory in every race on the Unlimited Hyrdroplane circuit.

BEER BATH—August A. Busch III bungs gold-plated keg to celebrate Anheuser-Busch, Inc. becoming the first brewer in history to produce 50 million barrels of beer in one year. Busch, chairman and chief executive officer of the company, is flanked by his father, 81-year-old August A. Busch Jr., the company's honorary chairman of the board.

PREFACE

Beer has been around for approximately eight thousand years. During that time, it was mainly produced by small, family operations serving a limited marketing area. Although there have been large brewing companies in existence for the past one hundred years, they also were run as family businesses serving a relatively small marketing area, that is, until the middle of this century.

Throughout the world, economic pressures have created giant multibrewery corporations which compete with each other to improve or maintain their share of the market. The competition is such that the small breweries, capable of serving only local regional tastes, are swallowed up by the giants. This small brewery mortality is a by-product of the competition rather than a part of any plan to monopolize the industry.

Despite the continual loss of small indepen-

11

dent breweries throughout the world, there are literally thousands of beer brands still being produced (over one thousand available in the United States and Canada alone). While this may seem like an inordinately large number, three reasons can be cited. First, the United States is still the most important market in the world (despite what you may have heard since the 1973 oil crisis), and with increased American interest in imported beer, Europeans and Asians are eager to trade their brew for dollars. Second, when a small brewery is taken over by a larger one, many of the small brewery's brands are continued lest the regional market be lost to the competition. Sometimes these brands are continued for years and even become a permanent part of the product line. Last, there is a growing number of very small breweries appearing on the scene. Complaining that the giant, national brewers don't make a brew worthy of their palates, they are transforming their home-brewing operations into commercial enterprises.

As the brewing industry consolidated, many predicted that there would eventually be only a handful of beer brands to choose from. Instead, there are now more beer brands available to the American consumer. We are in a period which should bring joy to the life of a beer connoisseur; however, it may be a fairly short period. If a product does not turn a profit, it will disappear. So, if beer drinkers are not selective about which brands they buy, they may quickly find that beer stores are offering only a half dozen or so national brands.

In *The Connoisseur's Guide to Beer,* over 1,350 brands are described and rated. At the time this book went to press, I know of no packaged brew produced in or exported into the United States that eluded my search. A few obscure Canadian labels could not be obtained; they may not be in current production. New beers appear all of the time and old ones disappear. With that in mind, this book is as up to date as it could possibly be.

As you read this book, try some of the brands and compare your responses with my descriptions. I do not believe that any brewer in the world makes a bad beer, but some are very fragile and highly susceptible to the environment and

age. The brew you taste may be better than the one I tasted, or it may be worse. If you are disappointed, try again at a different store, or wait until a new batch comes in. The payoff for you comes in finding a new and better beer, improving the quality of your life, and expanding your connoisseur's consciousness.

COURTESY THE STROH BREWERY COMPANY

An early example of Stroh beer tray

COURTESY ALL BRANDS IMPORTERS, INC.

"Let's Toast Them." A Foster's poster of the 1890s

ACKNOWLEDGMENTS

This book could not have been written without the assistance of a great many people.

First, I want to thank Sheldon and Pauline Wasserman for encouraging me to write and for their continuing support and guidance. I also wish to thank Art Ballant for arranging the contact with my publisher, Jameson Campaigne Jr., with whom I have had the most amiable relationship and who has provided me with a steady stream of factual data for use in this book.

For all around assistance, I wish to recognize Bill Geiger of Middletown, New Jersey. Bill served as a regular panel member for the tastings, wandered far and wide seeking elusive brands of beer and searched libraries all over for reference material.

For their diligence in combing the package stores of North America looking for new beers to taste, I am grateful to Margot Smith, Corey Adams, Brownell Salomon, Lynn Parry, Shirley and Andrew Gabriel, Bill Cowperthwaite, Lud Bilow, Art Rathgen, Peter Iserloth, Lou Prusinovski and Steve Elsen. In this regard, the superhero award goes to Jim Peabody of Simi Valley, California. He roamed up and down the West Coast chasing down brews that I might otherwise have missed. Without the 250-plus brands that he located, this book would still be far from complete. Also, special thanks goes to Charles Finkel and J. Elizabeth Purser of Merchant du Vin, who provided a wealth of samples and technical information.

Special recognition, for spartan duty as taste panel regulars for over six years, goes to Don and Vivian Lambrecht, Bill Geiger, and Ken Orey. Others who served whenever they were able were Art Rathgen, George Hessel, Erin Clark, Bill and Suzanne Cowperthwaite, Bob Dening, Dick Roleke, Stan Freeny, Ken Nelson, Corey Adams, Paul Geiger, Madeline Geiger, Tom Weathers, Trevor and Ann Richards, Lt. Col. and Mrs. Brian Simons, Bob Farrell, Richard and Jean Ackermann, Thom and Anne Leidner, Ron Polkowsky, Mike Stevenson, Sid Martin, Robert and Barbara Scott, Larry and Barbara Carton, Hollis Morris, Walter Duschka, Ray Belanger, Bob Kent, Bill Kelly, Ellis and Jo Grace, Phil Skelton, Lud Bilow, Steve Elsen, John O'Brien and Ellen and Ben Perchik.

For his gracious cooperation and most helpful technical assistance, I wish to thank Mr. Don Brumsted of the Carling National Breweries of G. Heileman Brewing Co., Inc. The assistance of many brewers in the United States, Canada, and abroad, who responded to my requests for taste samples, information, and illustration material, is gratefully acknowledged. Labels (and other photographic material) used as illustrations in this book were provided by the brewers and by various brewing or brewer associations. They are used with the permission of the brewing companies and associations; the reader is advised that the labels are registered trademarks of the companies and permission for their reproduction must be secured in advance.

I also wish to thank Mr. Ross Heuer, editor of *Brewers Digest,* and Mr. Harry Foulds, for background information on some of the small American breweries, and Mr. Henry B. King, president of the United States Brewers Association, for allowing me to use the library of that organization for my research.

Finally, I want to thank the members of my family: my wife Maryana (who frequently served on the taste panel) and my beautiful daughters Suzanne, Kathleen, Sheila, and Bonnie, who lived in a house that was wall-to-wall beer, and who spent many hours helping to prepare for beer tastings and to clean up afterward.

Interior Brew-House — Seventeenth Century

INTRODUCTION

I stand in awe of Jim Robertson. No, I *sit* in awe of Jim Robertson. This implies no diminishment of awe on my part. It's just that I take no pleasure in either my awe or my drinking from an upright position. I feel, both anatomically and spiritually, that imbibing is a civilized activity that requires—no, demands—a civilized physical posture. Ergo, my sitting in awe of Jim Robertson because this is also a civilized activity.

However, lest you think that there is a lot of genuflecting going on here, let me promptly rid you of that notion. Everything has its time and place including awe. And I resolutely decline to dispense any awe in Robertson's direction unless I also happen to be imbibing with him, because this awe business becomes burdensome unless you're in good company. And, properly administered, awe does best when you're in the company of the awed object.

Now in the case of our James, this means being in the company of someone who is personable, witty, well-traveled, a good storyteller and intrepid explorer of things gastronomic. These are, to be sure, estimable qualities but do not advance him from Ordinary Mortal into the awe category from where I'm sitting. No, the awe which, by the way, Robertson is learning about for the first time right here, stems from specific areas of his expertise. Most impressive, I guess, is his palate. When I grow up thirty or forty years from now, I hope to have developed as sophisticated a palate as our James has. And may *my* nose know the things *his* does. Consider his commentary in this book on Yugoslavia's Union Export Stout: "...austere pine needle and celery seed malt aroma." Or Robertson on Canada's Black Horse Ale: "...nice well-hopped nose with perfumy soap powder and talcum background." Or his less flattering observations on Old Chicago Light Lager Beer: "skunky aroma with motor oil overtones, flabby semisweet flavor with a bitter finish." This book will also inform you that in addition to the smells and palate effects I've just mentioned, there are such charmers as nail polish remover, rubber boot and wet basement odors, hints of leather, paper and cardboard, as well as green apple-acetylaldehyde-dehydrogenerated alcohol, which I do not believe should be discussed in mixed company. And, on the positive side, "pleasant herbal aromas—aromatic hops which may give sensations of clover, verbena, sage, parsley, orange or orange peel."

Okay, okay, I can already hear some of you mumbling to yourselves, "Gee, I'm glad to know about these things, but I don't want to sit and drink beer with some guy who talks that way." You're right. Neither do I. But our James *doesn't* talk that way. This chemical stuff is awe-inspiring because you know it's *there*, inside his head, part of all the knowledge he has to share with us. As he notes in his section entitled "The Sensory Perception of Beer": "While the information below may be difficult to work into a conversation while having a brew at your local watering hole, it is at least of interest to some and required for completeness."

I think that last word—completeness—is the real key to Jim Robertson. Assuming the task of identifying, locating and then procuring every brew either made in America or imported here is both unprecedented and, being logistically logical, impossible to accomplish. One just doesn't call up importers or domestic brewers and say, "Send me all your beer brands, kid, I'm writing this terrific book..." Even presuming an attitude of complete generosity and cooperation on their part—and I assure you this is no small presumption—these folks cannot always get their beer to you. Alcoholic beverages cannot be sent through the mail. And a brewer any distance away is not about to ship, truck or otherwise haul beer samples to Robertson's abode in Fair Haven, New Jersey. But our James got his beers—an astounding 1150-plus of them!—and here they are for you to read about. I don't know how he accomplished this—I suspect he isn't sure either—but there is no truth to the rumor that he has his own underground railroad system.

What he does have, of which there can be no disputation, is a vast knowledge of beer, not only how it smells and tastes, but how it's made, and knowledge about the workings of an industry that does not usually think that Americans have much taste. Robertson thinks otherwise. That, in essence, is the point and the metaphor of this remarkable book. Either beer in America will have one homogenized taste, most notable for its blandness, or else we can have a wide diversity of beer styles and a delicious range of flavors. There are scores of fine beers, some domestic and many, many imports, available to almost anyone reading this book, but they can't remain on the market if there isn't a growing, increasingly knowledgeable audience for them. Robertson's done his job, and then some. Now, you beer lovers, as soon as you're done reading this book or even before, since good reading and good drinking are hardly incompatible, go out there and taste some of these good brews he's telling you about. Maybe next time, har, har, there will be two or three thousand-plus beers for him to scribble about. That'll serve Robertson right for having done such a good job *this* time out!

BOB ABEL

New York City

An early example of Schlitz print advertising

Ancient Municipal Brewery of Nürnberg, Bavaria, Germany

1. THE HISTORY OF BEER

All vegetable material, given sufficient moisture, appropriate temperature range, and the proper yeasts (with which our atmosphere abounds), will undergo some kind of decomposition or fermentation. It is therefore not surprising that prehistoric man knew of foods and beverages that tasted pleasant, provided nourishment, and, if taken in sufficient quantities, brought on an exhilarated condition of mind.

These beverages differed widely according to climate and available flora. Tree sap, berries, fruit juices, tree bark, plant stems, and leaves were all used to make intoxicating beverages. Beers made from cereal grains were known long before history recorded the fact, but these were vastly different brews from today's product.

The oldest document known to man, a clay tablet inscribed in Babylonia around 6000 B.C., depicts the preparation of beer for sacrificial purposes. By 4000, the Babylonians had made sixteen different types of beer from barley, wheat, and honey. Bittering agents (to add character to the taste and a degree of shelf life) have been used in beer making since 3000. For almost three thousand years, beer was important to the daily life and religion of ancient Egypt. It was in common use in China about 2300 B.C., and the ancient Incas used a corn-based beer for centuries before America was discovered.

The *Rig-Veda* of India (circa 1000 B.C.) contains a prayer to Indra, offering an intoxicating beverage, *soma,* made from the juice of a creeping plant, *asclepas.* In India the

17

common people of that time drank *sura,* a more intoxicating brew made from panicum—an Indian grass—honey, water, curds, melted butter, and barley. According to the sacred book *Zend-Avesta,* the Persians had similar beverages in 1000 B.C. Though drunkenness was a violation of the religious tenets of Zoroaster, he included intoxicating beverages among the offerings to be made at religious rites. According to ancient Egyptian fables, beer had been present at the Creation.

In premedieval Europe, wherever there was no significant viticulture, beer or beerlike beverages (like barley wine) became deeply ingrained into the culture, both in religion and in everyday life. Even in Spain, where viticulture was widespread, the districts without wine made a beer from barley called *celia* and one from wheat named *ceria.* The Celts brewed something called *Kurmi,* which Doiscorides (about 25 B.C.) said brought on headaches, tired blood, and weak knees. History does not record how much *Kurmi* was required to bring on these effects. The Gauls, who were also not without wine grapes, brewed a beer, *cervisia,* and the Romans, who spread viticulture throughout Europe, had their *cerevisia* (in Latin: *Ceres,* the goddess of agriculture, and *vis,* strength). The word *beer* may have multiple origins: the Latin word *bibere*

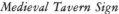

Medieval Tavern Sign   *Medieval Cellarer*

means to drink and the Saxon word *baere* means barley.

The Romans introduced wine to the Saxons, who quickly adopted its use and it was drunk thereafter on all great occasions but ale and meth remained the national beverages of the ancient people at all times. In the oldest epic of modern

languages, *Beowulf* tells us of the mead hall, ale carvuse, and the beer hall. *Meth,* or mead, made from honey and water, originated in the remotest days and may have preceded any wines or beers used by man. Its popularity spans thousands of years. The ales of that time were cereal beverages and seem to have been of fairly high quality by modern standards, since clarity and mildness were deemed desirable features. Other beverages of that time were cider and *piment,* a mixture of wine, honey, and spices.

In his work *Germania* (A.D. 99), the Roman historian Tacitus reports that the ancient Teutons' daily activity was as likely to be a drinking bout as anything else. The drinking of a

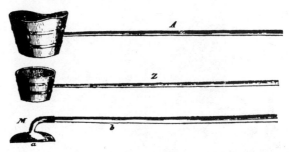

Ancient Brewers tools — A: Ladle for thick mash. Z: Dipper for wort. M: Stirrer for thick mash.

barley and wheat brew was an important part of all marriages, meetings, elections, decisions, and day to day living.

The great book of Northern mythology, *The Edda,* describes at length the part played by beer among the gods. *The Edda* also reported on the German beer conventions, describing violations and penalties, which were mainly drinking large quantities of beer in one draught. Some of these conventions have carried into the twentieth century in such tradition-steeped establishments as Heidelberg University and in modern U.S. college fraternities.

Until the Middle Ages, the brewing of beer was left to the women, as was everything except drinking, warring, and carousing (where did we go astray?). In medieval times the brewing of beer shifted from the family to the brewhouses of the monasteries, convents, and villages. Brewing was believed to be a very important part of monastery life and the staples of diet were bread and beer. Large monasteries often had a

Brew-House Interior — Sixteenth Century

number of functioning breweries since the daily ration for a monk could be as much as a gallon.

The nobility had an interest in maintaining a ready supply of brew for their community and guests; all the larger courts and castles had their own brewhouses. Charlemagne took a great interest in brewing and in 812 listed, in his *Capitulare de Villis Imperialibus,* beer brewers among the artisans and laborers to be employed by district public administrators.

Although bittering agents had been used in very early times, the first clear indication of the use of hops (and with it the early beginnings of modern beer) occurs in 768, when, in the record of a gift by Pepin, a hop garden is mentioned. A public document from the year 822 certifies that hops were used in the production of beer, but the "official" creditation usually goes to the Abbess Hildegard (1079) of Rupertsberg, who wrote in her *Physica Sacia,* "If one intends to make beer from oats, it is prepared with hops, but is boiled with *grug* [herbs, most likely], and mostly with ash leaves."

By this time a beer trade was well established—and firmly in the hands of the clergy. Of course, since there were no "states" at this time, most cultural and economic activities were conducted by the clergy, as this class was the only tangible representation of society at that time. Christian clergymen were the wholesalers of beer and the Jews were the retailers, because the Christian clergymen were forbidden to make a profit. Beer was used in medieval Europe for tithing, trading, payment, and taxing; indeed, it was fully a part of the economics of the time.

As early as the eleventh century the larger cities began to press for freedom of action by acquiring privileges from their territorial and spiritual lords. Over the next two hundred years this became more of a reality with the formation of the trade guilds, each forming a corporation for itself. The guilds were represented on the councils, and commerce between the large cities flourished. In the fourteenth century great brewing houses were formed, especially in Germany. Since it had a wide reputation, there was even a substantial export of German beer. In 1376, the great brewing center of the Middle Ages, Hamburg, had over a thousand brewmasters.

Aside from the great beers of Hamburg, the most famous beer of the Middle Ages was that from the city of Einbeck, whose inhabitants were principally occupied with the making of beer and linen. It was on draught everywhere and exported as far as Jerusalem. Brewed only in winter, it was top-fermented, heavily malted, and strongly hopped, enabling it to keep its quality a very long time.

For almost two hundred years the growth of

Brew-House Cellar — Sixteenth Century

beer popularity and brewing continued unabated. Then suddenly the situation reversed. Brewing had long been a favorite object of taxation and more and heavier levies were laid on beer and grain as funds were required. Restrictions on trade appeared with the subsequent appearance of the usual counter-

Sixteenth Century Cooperage

restrictions. Brewers lowered the quality of the product to offset economic pressures and consumers reacted by switching to the new coffees, teas, and spirituous liquors. Although these effects caused a great contraction in the industry, it was a temporary situation. Man's preference for and use of malt beverages continued; he could still make a palatable brew at home.

In 1614 the brewers at Munich discovered that they could successfully imitate the great beers of Einbeck and began a segment of the brewing trade that remains famous to this time. Many beer lovers today are grateful for the efforts of those Munich brewers. In 1602 Weiss (white) beer, which had been made locally and occasionally for several hundred years, attained

renewed favor, and that favor grew for over two hundred years. Today, Weiss beer is still made by a few Munich brewers, but it is usually referred to as Berliner Weiss.

As for early Celtic brews, the beer of the Britons was alelike in nature; the British preference for ale continues to the present, with pale lager-style beers making serious inroads into the British markets only in the large cosmopolitan areas. The ale of Britain's past and presently available brews are not the same. Hops were not introduced there until about 1500. Even then, there is evidence that the hops were not used in the ale for some time. Ale was made of malt and water and drunk new, with great pride taken in avoiding "unnatural" ingredients. The hops were used only for beer, in place of preserving it with various leaves and barks. Before the introduction of hops into Britain, the word *ale* was meant to indicate pure malted liquor and the word *beer* meant imported German brew. When hops were finally added to the venerable ale (late in the sixteenth century), *ale* came to mean a stronger malted drink, which contained a greater quantity of unfermented extract than beer.

Although the end of the sixteenth century saw a softening of the brewing trades in Germany, it was the beginning of the heyday of Britain's fledgling industry. London was the center of this rapidly growing industry and considerable amounts of beer were being exported to France. The product of the British brewers was as lusty a brew as had ever been placed on the market. It was very strong and could be stored for several years without spoiling.

The prosperity and growth continued through the seventeenth and into the eighteenth century when porter was introduced (by Harwood in 1722). It had become popular in public houses to drink half-and-half (half ale and half "twopenny") or "three shreads" (ale, beer, and twopenny). Porter combined the taste of the various beers and eliminated the need to draw from different casks. By this time the growth of brewing was so great that the country had a general problem with drunkenness and the attendant pauperism and rowdyism. Steps were taken to stem the tide of drunkenness, but no effective measures were devised until the tax man, who regarded the brewing industry as another source of income, took an interest in matters.

The colonies in America never suffered a problem of widespread drunkenness. Even though the Pilgrims may have made landfall at Plymouth because they had run out of beer, alcoholic beverages in the colonies were regulated from the start. Breweries were born in America almost with the communities. The first brewery was built in New Amsterdam in 1612. Twenty years later Peter Minuit established the first public brewery in America. Taxes on malt liquors appeared in 1644. Director General Peter Stuyvesant, a crusader in regulating public morals, leaned heavily on brewers and tavern-keepers. William Penn built the first brewhouse in Philadelphia in 1685. Most of the famous figures of colonial New England began or participated in brewing ventures beginning early in the seventeenth century, but the industry did

Filling Beer Casks — Seventeenth Century

not flourish there as barley could not be raised in that climate. Perhaps, a more important reason for the failure was that a brewhouse was regarded as an essential part of a homestead. The few cities were seaports and had ready access to imports from England and thus did not offer much of a market for a local brewing industry. This changed with the taxation that led to the Revolution, and after independence was achieved, the brewing industry thrived there for over a century.

The founding fathers of the new republic were kindly disposed toward beer and cider (but not to distilled spirits) and the popular bodies of the States viewed the subject similarly; in doing so, they believed they were upholding the cause of temperance. They even encouraged the brewing industry by withholding taxes on brewery property. Such leading citizens as Adams, Jefferson, and Madison either owned or promoted breweries and George Washington himself maintained a small brewery at Mt. Vernon.

About 1820, German immigrants began to arrive in large numbers. Since immigrants tended to settle in ethnic "colonies," wherever Germans settled there was an instant market for beer. With them came young men already educated and experienced in the field of brewing. Breweries sprang up by the hundreds and many flourished in the benign atmosphere of the new country. At this time, the beers were mostly ales and porter. There were also a considerable number of breweries, especially in the New York City area, devoted to making Weiss beer.

The new chill-brewed lager first appeared in the United States in Philadelphia in 1840, manufactured by a man named John Wagner. Shortly thereafter, most of the German brewers began to produce malt beverages made in accordance with the new recipe from the old country. The lager enjoyed immediate public acceptance. And although it caused difficulties for brewers because it required the use of refrigeration facilities for brewing and storage, more and more brewers built plants to handle the rapidly growing market for the new lager beer.

The conquest of the American market by this pale lager (more appropriately called Dort-munder or pilsener) beer is so complete that the number of true ales still brewed in America is quite small; there are no Weiss beers, few dark beers, and even less porter. One truly American phenomenon in brewing was the steam beer of the Pacific Coast. Because ice was prohibitive in

San Francisco in the mid-nineteenth century, there was a great demand for malt liquor that could not be satisfied by imports. A technique of beer making developed that employed bottom fermentation in the 60°-68°F. range and cellaring at 60°-70°F. This beer too disappeared for a time, and only one brewery producing this uniquely American product remains in operation today.

Fraunces' Tavern, New York City (Built in 1730)

Fraunces' Tavern, New York (Interior)

The above is the famous Long Room of Fraunces' Tavern, in which the merchants and brewers of New York often met for consultation and action. Here, in 1768, was organized the New York Chamber of Commerce and it was in this historic room that Washington, in 1783, delivered his farewell address to his officers.

*A worker at an Anheuser-Busch brewery pushes fabled beechwood chips into
a huge, stainless steel beer aging tank.*
*The company is the only U.S. brewer to age its beers on beechwood chips. Fermented beer is aged in
these tanks on beechwood chips, which are deposited and removed from the tanks in special
"torpedoes," such as the one shown here. A small amount of freshly yeasted wort is added during this
long aging process to cause secondary fermentation or "krausening."*

2. THE ART OF MAKING BEER

The making of beer, or any fermented beverage, simply involves the conversion of sugar to alcohol by the action of yeast. The prime ingredient, and the oldest used in malt beverages, is barley. Barley was originally used in beer making because, of all the available grains, it was the least suitable for making bread. Fortunately for us beer lovers, it proved to be best suited for the making of beer. The Chevalier, or two-rowed barley, is preferred by European brewers, particularly in Germany where it has been used since the earliest times.

Much of it is grown in America, but is largely exported since it has a thin husk and a high percentage of albuminoids, a disadvantage in the American method of mashing. The common four-rowed barley is also used predominantly in Europe. The most popular strain of barley in the United States is the six-rowed barley, considered unsuitable by most of the big European brewers. The *row* refers to the number of rows of fertile flowers, and therefore the number of rows of barleycorn that are produced. Six-rowed barley is that in which all the flowers are fertile and

Corn is the most commonly used adjunct for pilseners; it makes a pale, brilliant, light-bodied beer. Rice is a close second as it produces the palest of possible brews, a big selling point with American beer drinkers today.

All have the important advantage to the brewer competing in the U.S. today of being cheaper than barley. They do, however, produce an inferior beer to one made only with finest barley malt. Many of the lower-priced beers, and most home-brewed beer, use malt extract. It is usually carried by grocery stores in rural areas. Another advantage of these adjuncts is that they are all high in starch, and fewer are required to provide the malt sugar needed during fermentation. Beers made with a heavy use of adjuncts may be higher in alcoholic content and less costly to make than barley beers, but suffer in comparison because they lack greatly in flavor. Wheat malt is often used to stimulate yeast growth, improve stability, and promote body and flavor, but it is expensive to use and is mainly

produce three barleycorns, which result in six rows. Two-rowed barley is generated from the type wherein only one of each of the three flowers is fertile. The six-rowed variety gathers more sunlight and has a higher protein content, which makes it less suitable for brewing, although it is more productive, which makes it less expensive to use. Understand? Well, if you find this barley doubletalk confusing, you are in good company.

The barley gives beer its flavor, its head, its body (in the form of maltodextrins and protein), and its color, but in modern brewing, barley is not the only cereal grain used. Properly malted barley, once the only grain used, is not suitable for making the pale beers preferred by most beer drinkers today—and is very expensive, compared to other grains. To make pale, light lager beer, the percentage of barley used is reduced and high-starch malt adjuncts are substituted. The list of adjuncts normally used includes corn, rice, unmalted barley, malt syrups, and tapioca starch.

COURTESY OLYMPIA BREWING COMPANY

Brew Kettle at the Olympia Brewery, Olympia, Washington

used today in making Berliner Weiss. Oat and rye malt is used in making certain stouts.

The starches in the cereal grains are not readily fermentable without special preparation. The yeast (and in beer making it is always brewer's yeast, *Saccharomyces cerevisiae*) cells need something good to "eat" and to metabolize, so that as they feed and reproduce themselves they will manufacture alcohols and tiny bubbles of carbonation. This process of preparing the barley (and other grains) for fermentation is called malting.

The first step in the malting process is to sort the grains of barley so that they are nearly the same size and weight to ensure equal and uniform growth in the same batch of malt. Sorted, the barley is steeped, or soaked, in water to receive the necessary moisture to start germination. At this time, the dead grains can be removed and certain coloring and extractive matter eliminated. The barley is allowed to grow a limited amount during which time the natural enzyme systems of the barley are released to break down the membranes of the starch cells. This is the process that requires the maltster's greatest skill; timing is crucial. When germination has progressed sufficiently, the grains are kiln-dried to stop the growth and to partially caramelize. The dried, sprouted barley resulting from this process is called malt.

The first main stage of the actual brewing process is called mashing. In mashing, heated water is added to the prepared malt and the starches in the grains are converted into soluble, fermentable sugars—maltose and dextrins. The temperature and chemical composition of the water are strictly controlled; they activate the amylolytic enzymes that convert the starches. The proteins are also partly modified during mashing. It is here that some brewers have to use additives (like salts, softeners, or dealkalinizers) to adjust or "condition" their water, or to add amylolytic enzymes to produce fermentable sugars if they are not supplied by their excuse for malt. If adjuncts, like corn or rice, are employed, they are milled and then boiled in a "cooker" before being added to the malt in the "mash kettle." The temperature and acidity of the mash are strictly controlled, for the outcome of the final product is highly dependent on the success of this stage. A high temperature, for example,

COURTESY ANHEUSER-BUSCH, INC.

Some 360 kegs of beer are filled and bunged (sealed) hourly on this draught line; it is typical of the draught lines at all ten Anheuser-Busch breweries throughout the U.S.

will produce a beer with less alcohol, but with greater flavor. In America, a quick-mashing method is used, where two mashes are employed, one at 145° and one at 172°F. The European method involves four temperature stages, ranging from 100° to 170°F., which gives the proteolytic enzymes a chance to convert the proteins into more soluble states. From the mash kettle, the mash is filtered and the resulting malt extract is sent to the brew kettle. The filter is called a Lauter tub and the spent grains are removed for use as livestock feed. The remaining highly fermentable liquid is called the wort.

In the brew kettle, the hops are added to the wort and they are boiled together. The finest hops are grown in central European countries, with the finest of all attributed to Czechoslovakia. This may be because the Czech hops (Saaz variety) are ideally suited to the now very popular pilsener-type brews. Most of the

Munich beers use the German-grown Hallertau variety, and the popular strains in England are Golding for light ales and Fuggle for brown ales. Until recently, Bullion, the American-grown variety of hop, was our only commercially useful hop produced. It is a hop noted for its marked bitterness, and was favored only by foreign brewers for making stouts and long-aged beers, few of which are made in America today. For the usual American brews, domestic hops had to be

Bottles and cans of beer are filled with lightning speed and efficiency at Anheuser-Busch, Inc. breweries coast to coast

blended with milder, imported varieties. In the past year, however, experiments with milder varieties of hops in the Yakima Valley of Washington have yielded some successes and there is some hope that American-produced hops may, in the near future, yield the same quality of brews as the finest of European hops, all other things being equal. The use of hop extract by domestic brewers is becoming more

prevalent, but most of the world's finest and proudest breweries still use only whole, unrefined hops; to do less, they believe, is to compromise the quality of their product.

As the wort and hops boil together, the hop resins add flavor, aroma, and bitterness to the brew. The hops also act as a preservative and hop tannin aids in precipitating protein. During this boil, which lasts about two hours, the wort is concentrated to the desired specific gravity, sterilized, and rid of protein substances.

Next, the hops are removed in a hop separator or jack. Also removed is the protein precipitate (called trub) which results from the boiling. The wort now proceeds to the wort-collecting tank, or hot-wort tank, where the remaining trub is removed. The next step in the process is cooling the wort from a temperature just under boiling to about 50°F., which takes only a few seconds in the wort cooler.

Fermentation follows and is done in special tanks for the purpose. Jealously guarded "secret strains" of yeast are used. In all modern breweries, pure and unchanged yeast cultures are maintained so that a particular beer flavor is assured year after year. Throughout the fermentation period, which usually lasts about seven days in modern domestic breweries, strict temperature control is maintained, for if the fermenting wort were to become excessively warm, fermentation would cease.

With the fermentable material converted to alcohol, the "green" beer is transferred to the aging tanks in the storage cellars for the slow secondary fermentation. Protein and yeast settle out and more carbon dioxide is generated. As long as the beer is not exposed to oxygen, the flavor slowly improves and after several weeks to several months, depending on the sort of beer being produced, it is ready for final processing and packaging. Some brewers add enzymes in the storage phase to break down the complex proteins and to speed up clarification of the beer. This sometimes results in a loss of natural head and foaming agents are used to compensate for this loss. A commonly used example of a foaming agent is propylene glycol alginate, a modified seaweed extract called Kelcoloid. This action also tends to remove much of the distinction among individual brews, and a recipe so treated will essentially taste the same brew after brew.

The beer is filtered one more time and a few more adjustments may be made including the final carbonation. Some of the cheaper brews are simply charged with CO_2 just like soft drinks. An older method, krausening, calls for the addition of a younger beer, still in lively fermentation, to the beer that has been aged and is ready for packaging. This method has a slight disadvantage in that it is difficult to prevent changing the character of the aged brew when adding the young beer.

More recently, in 1978, the method of saving the natural carbonation from the fermenting brew and reinjecting it into the aged beer was developed. This is the method used today by most of America's leading brewers, though some, like Schaefer, still proudly assert that their beer is naturally carbonated through krausening. Natural carbonation results in smaller bubbles and is less likely to be overdone and offensive. Truly natural carbonation results from a very slow secondary fermentation where the carbonic gas is bound to the beer in very tiny bubbles. The result may be less "apparent" carbonation, but a smoother nongassy product.

Some brewers add a solution of invert sugar, caramel, or licorice to the brew after aging, when the beer is passed to final storage. This encourages some additional fermentation with resultant increased carbonation and some additional sweetness. Other brewers may use fining agents (such as gelatin, which aids in precipitating out suspended matter in a solution) in an effort to increase the clarity of the product, a brilliantly clear brew being the most desired achievement. Ever since some fifty people in Canada died from ingesting cobalt sulfate, placed in their beer to give it a head, there has been great and natural sensitivity with regard to additives in beer. The additives and processes used are under constant scrutiny by government agencies.

Oxidation is a major problem in the business and of great concern to brewers. The most effective antioxidant is potassium bisulfate ($KHSO_2$), but if this preservative is used in the U.S., the product cannot be advertised as "naturally brewed." Commercially safer and cheaper (but less effective) antioxidants like tannic acid and citric acid may be used if the

brewer asserts that they are for acid correction— and they still may be advertised as "natural." Actually, tight filtration and refrigeration with the use of sound materials, well-fermented in a scrupulously clean environment, is the most effective method, but also the most expensive.

In 1979 the U.S. Food and Drug Administration announced that twenty-eight of thirty beers tested contained cancer-causing nitrosamines and national interest in beer ingredients was aroused. The amounts ranged from 0.4 to 7.7 parts per billion, which for a moderate beer drinker would be as about as imperiling as having bacon for breakfast (bacon has long been known to contain nitrosamines).

Those brewers who had few or no nitrosamines were quick to advertise the fact. The others were equally quick to cast doubt on the findings or remained noticeably quiet, hoping that the whole thing would blow over and go away.

The nitrosamines were not additives, but byproducts of the brewing process. Changes were eventually effected by brewers that reduced or eliminated the problem. The net effect on the industry was small, much less than the famous cranberry scare of almost twenty years ago. The FDA set a limit of 5 ppb and in 1980 FDA tests showed that all domestic brews were at less than 1 ppb. Most showed no detectable levels. Only three imports failed to meed FDA standards.

Much beer advertising seems to center on the source of water. We are led to believe that the purest water makes the best beer. Mountain streams are depicted on labels universally and it is their water, or that from crystal clear springs, that makes their beer so good.

It sure sounds good, but it isn't necessarily so. Most brewers use the local tap water or deep wells on the premises because it is cheaper. Lake Michigan water makes a perfectly respectable beer. There are, however, some waters that are more suitable to beer making than others. Newark, New Jersey, for instance, has wells that are considered excellent for brewing and whose waters require little "adjustment." Other sites are not so well suited, lacking some necessary "secret ingredient."

There is nothing secret about the ingredient today, but before analytic chemistry was around to tell us what was going on, there were mysteries in brewing. The ales of Burton-on-Trent, England, had become world famous for their quality. With their successful recipes in hand, the Burton brewers sought to establish brewhouses in London, their greatest market. Unfortunately, the brews made in London were dismal failures. Only those made in Burton (using the waters of the Trent River) could satisfy their patrons. Years later, chemists found that the waters of the Trent contained a significant quantity of calcium sulfate, called "Burton Salts." All you had to do to transfer a Burton beer operation to another area was to match the concentration of the waters of the Trent as found at Burton, a process which was called "Burtonizing."

Today, much more is known about the desired constituents of the water used for brewing and if a perfect source of water is not available, it can be adjusted, standardized, dealkalinized, deacidified, etc. Of course, if a source is found that needs no adjustment, the brewer does not bear the obvious added expense—and he can proudly point to how "pure" his water is. Again, most of it is just hyperbole or, in the vernacular, "hype."

Beer that is to be packaged in bottles or cans is usually pasteurized at a temperature of 140°F. for fifteen minutes (Coors is one very notable exception; it uses a sterile technique and end-to-end refrigeration in its distribution). Beer that is to be kegged for draught service is not pasteurized, but is placed in aluminum or stainless steel barrels which must be kept refrigerated until used. Some brews are now subjected to very fine filtration and meet purity standards without pasteurization. The shelf life may be less than pasteurized beer but brewers feel that filtration is less harmful to the taste of their product than is pasteurization, and filtered beer is easier to handle than unpasteurized beer.

A recent development in the brewing industry is "heavy brewing," where beer is made in concentrated form and then diluted with water. The major advantage is to derive maximum output from the brewing facilities. It also means that a premium, regular, or local beer can be produced from the same equipment and recipe simply by adjusting the dilution.

COURTESY OLYMPIA BREWING COMPANY

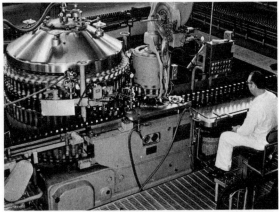

Beer Bottling at Olympia Brewery, Olympia, Washington

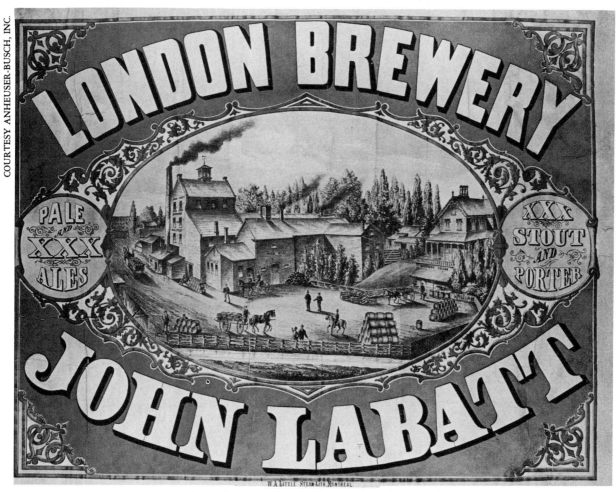

An early example of Labatt's print advertising

3. THE TYPES OF BEER

Until the middle of the nineteenth century, the form of fermentation generally applied was top fermentation, so called because the yeast rose to the top of the fermenting vat during the process. The yeast of the previous brew was added to the cooled beer wort, which was then pitched and put up for fermentation in open tubs placed in a cellar with as low a temperature as possible. The chief object of the brewmaster at this time was to protect the beer against acidification, a condition vey likely in view of the high temperatures that might be reached within the fermenting mixture. This method was in general use in the United States until 1850 and its use continued in England well into the twentieth century.

It was in Germany where brewers first began to pay more attention to the temperature of fermentation and to the length of fermentation. The thermometer and the saccharometer were to become the brewmaster's most important tools, as it was found that acidification could be best prevented by not allowing the wort temperature to exceed 75°F. Further, it was found that the best temperature range for producing the desired taste of the beer was 55°-60°F. in winter and 60°-65°F. in summer. Actually, it was difficult in those times to maintain a temperature that low at all ambient temperatures, since a fermenting mass generates

29

large amounts of heat.

The principal fermentation of ales usually lasted about forty-eight hours, that of porter somewhat less, and the Scots beers required fermentation of eleven to eighteen days or more.

Around 1850 bottom fermentation began to gain favor in the United States and has since been almost universally adopted. This method originated in Bavaria about 1830 and its introduction has been credited to Gabriel Sedlmayr of Munich and Anton Dreher of Vienna. Bottom fermentation takes place at a lower temperature (about 40°-50°F.) and the yeast settles to the bottom, instead of rising to the top. This method is now used exclusively for so-called lager beers. While Sedlmayr took Munich to the heights by bottom-fermenting luscious dark brews, Dreher brought Vienna to the forefront of brewing with his magnificent light bottom-fermented beverages. When Liebig published his theory of fermentation in 1843, with a carefully developed list of the disadvantages of top fermentation, bottom fermentation was greatly promoted throughout the world.

Two principal forms of beer were produced by the new method. Winter beer was brewed in October, November, March, April, and the summer months. Lager beer was brewed only during the months of December, January, and February. In Bavaria the seasons for brewing were fixed by law; lager beer could be brewed only from Michaelmas (29 September) to St. George's Day (23 April). During the rest of the year, only top-fermentation brews were allowed.

Around 1870 this situation changed in America as a result of improved refrigeration techniques. Brewers were able to operate during the entire year without regard to the outside temperature, and the distinction between summer and winter beer disappeared.

The principal fermentation of lager beer is conducted somewhat more slowly, mainly because it allows the beer to retain a sufficient amount of unfermented substances for the long secondary fermentation in the aging cellars.

Lager Types

The term *lager* is derived from a German word that means to store or stock. It refers to the long period of lagering, wherein the beer is stored in cellars to undergo the slow second fermentation. It is bottom-fermented and "long" aged. The aging of a better lager will last for several months, but all too many of our domestic products see little more than a week of cellar time, so great is the rush to the marketplace.

In America fermentation takes place at temperatures of 45°-55°F. (and sometimes higher) and proceeds slowly, over a period of five to eight days. European lager brewers usually ferment at a slightly lower temperature and less vigorous fermentation occurs over a longer period of time, often as long as ten to fourteen days. Better domestic beers may also be brewed according to European practice. The aging is done very near the freezing temperature for water and proceeds very slowly. The longer the beer is aged, the more "complete" will be the flavor and the resultant brew will have more body and a longer shelf life.

Alcoholic content of lager is usually 3.0-4.0 percent by weight (3.4-4.5 percent by volume) as opposed to ales, which are usually 4-5 percent. In the United States malt beverages with an alcohol content higher than 5 percent must be called malt liquor, stout, porter, or ale. They cannot be labeled beer. Individual states may have stricter rules.

Light lagers are pale gold in color, light in body, flavored with a medium to light hop taste and are fairly high in carbonation. They generally have a soft, mellow, dry taste. They are best served cold, at around 40°-45°F. The two most popular types, pilsener and Dortmunder, make up the major volume of U.S. beer production. These two styles, which differ only slightly, best match the definition of light lager given above, with the malt having more influence in aroma and taste than the hops. The term *pilsener* is used interchangeably with the word *lager* in most of the world today, whereas the use of *Dortmunder* has almost disappeared as a beer adjective in the U.S. With the utilization of corn or rice as an adjunct to the barley malt, the appearance of many domestic beers is becoming paler and paler, with some already nearly as pale as water.

The Vienna type is characterized by an amber color and a very mild hop taste. It is usually brewed with less hops than the Dortmunder or pilsener type, but is not less flavorful because the malt contribution is increased by this particular brewing method.

The Munich type, or dark lager, has a dark brown color, is full-bodied with a sweet malt flavor and slight hop taste. It is more aromatic and "creamy" than a light lager. The color of a true dark lager comes from the addition of roasted barley. Imitation dark lagers are made with caramel or with a roasted barley malt extract, a much less expensive process. The alcohol content in these dark lagers approaches 5 percent by weight. Light Munich beers are Dortmunder types and, like many of the current Dortmunder brews, have more of a hop flavor. The color of these German light lagers is darker than the corresponding American brews because of the slower fermentation. They can be likened to the Bohemian beers with their fine and strongly noticeable hop flavor, pronounced bitter taste and vinous character.

Oktoberfest beer was once brewed only for the autumn festivals (usually held in September). Originally a light lager of high alcoholic content available only on draft for serving at the festival, it is now readily found year round in bottles. Packaged Oktoberfest beer differs very little from the regular export lager, including its alcoholic content.

In Germany, *festbier* (festival beer) is produced by many brewers, large and small, in conjunction with Christmas, Easter, local folk festivals, and for *Kirchweihen,* the celebration for the patron saint of the local church. These beers are usually brewed the month before the festival, mostly only draft, but sometimes packaged. For example *Märzen* and *Ostern*

Open ale fermentation at Labatt's, London, Ontario.

(March beer and Easter beer) are brewed in January, lagered outside in winter and tapped (traditionally by the mayor) when it is very cold, so that some of the water is frozen and the beer is higher in alcohol.

The origins of *festbier* are less romantic than practical. Before refrigeration, brewing could only be carried out in winter. Because the beer produced in March had to last throughout the entire summer (before the first batch of next winter's beer could be made), it was made a little stronger than usual. If any of this beer was left over at the end of summer, it was ceremonially consumed. Since this also was the time of the traditional country fairs, the celebration of the harvest in a predominantly agrarian economy and culture, the beer was used at the Oktoberfest. When Sedlmayr completed work on refrigeration, the brewing of beer could take place year long. Sedlmayr wisely continued the tradition by specially brewing a stronger beer to be drunk at the end of summer, a gem of inspiration that many have appreciated over the years.

Bock beer is believed to have originated in the once famous beer capital of Einbeck. A heavy dark beer with a slightly sweet malt flavor and strong hop background, bock is brewed in the winter for consumption in the spring. True bock derives its color from the heat treatment given to the barley in the malting process and may have as much as 10 percent alcohol by weight. Many artificial bocks produced today are colored and flavored with a prepared syrup containing caramelized sugar.

Throughout Europe, many local breweries produce beer with high density and high alcoholic content, often in excess of 10 percent. This is done by various means such as extended fermentation and freezing. The beer with the greatest reputation is EKU Kulminator from Kulmbach, Germany, which is reported to have an alcoholic content of 13.2 percent. While this figure may be disputed by brewers in the U.S. (and elsewhere), there is no doubt that there are beers with very high alcoholic levels.

Steam beer, another bottom-fermented brew, originated on the West Coast of the United States as a direct result of the desire for malt beverages and the extreme shortage of ice. It is a development in beer brewing that is peculiar to America. Fermentation proceeds at a relatively high temperature (60°-68° F.) and barley malt is used exclusively. Within twelve to eighteen hours after the yeast has been added to the wort in the fermenting tubs, the beer comes into "krausen," where it is kept from six to eight hours. It is then run into the clarifier for two to three days (depending on the ambient temperature) for completion of fermentation. If fermentation has been proper, at the end of this stage the beer will undergo a reduction of 50-60 percent and will be quite clear in appearance. From the clarifier, the beer is racked directly into barrels, where it receives an addition of about 20 percent of krausen, together with some fining. In four to six days the beer has raised a sufficient amount of "steam" in the barrels (some fifty pounds per square inch), and some bleeding of pressure is required. In olden times, these barrels were shipped to saloons, rested a few days, and then tapped for the trade. Steam beer is made today by only one West Coast firm and the product is bottled. Total refrigeration may not be necessary because of the strength of the brew, but it must be kept cool for it is not pasteurized. Steam beer has a golden brown color, sharp hoppy taste, full body, and a lingering malt finish.

Ale Types

Ale is more vinous in nature, possesses a greater percentage of alcohol (four to five percent by weight) and extract than a lager, is more aromatic, more full-bodied, and has a more pronounced hop flavor and tartness.

Prior to the rise of lager beers in the mid-nineteenth century, all brewing was done with top-fermenting yeast and the beers so made were commonly called ale. Early ales were unhopped and low in carbonation. Ale types have retained their great popularity only in Britain and in parts of the British Commonwealth, particularly in Canada and Australia. Even in the latter countries, lagers are gradually supplanting the top-fermented brews, and soon Britain will be the last stronghold of great ales in the world.

Ale is fermented at a higher temperature than lager for a lesser period of time and, when maturing, is stored at temperatures in the range of 40°-45° F. (as opposed to lager, which matures at temperatures near 32°F.). Ale requires additional aging in the bottle to develop its best strength and flavor.

There are a number of different types of ale produced today. Common or stock ales are characterized by lower levels of carbonation. Cream ales and sparkling ales have relatively

An early example of Labatt print advertising

high levels of carbonation, resulting in a rich foam and strong effervescence. The "bitter" of England is brewed from pale-ale malts, with corn and rice added in small amounts to make the beer clear and brilliant. It is more heavily hopped than "mild," the other staple of British pubs, a brown-hued smooth ale beverage with a dominant malt flavor.

The strong or brown ales are quite dark and may be tawny brown, ruby red, or brown with a reddish tinge in their coloring. Some are highly carbonated; others have just the slightest touch

of bubble. The alcohol level is usually quite high, some approaching the equivalent of a wine. These will keep for several years in a bottle, just like a wine. All have the characteristic full malt flavor and a vinous character, and some are hopped quite heavily. Included in this type are the barley wines, which are notably vinous and well hopped. These may be matured for up to eighteen months, often in oak casks, which imparts a tannin to the brew, making it seem even more like a wine.

A recent and popular addition to the ranks of widely available top-fermented brews is Altbier from Germany. Originally found only in the Düsseldorf–lower Rhine region, Altbier is now being produced to a limited extent by major German brewers. Altbier is supposed to remind you of olden times (before bottom fermentation became feasible)˙and is a more highly hopped, more heavily malted brew, with a specific gravity nearly the same as a lager, but slightly more bitter and aromatic in taste. It is a welcome addition for those who are dismayed by the trend to lighter and more innocuous brews.

Stout and Porter

Stout has a dark color (some are almost black), a rich malty flavor usually combined with a rather strong bitter hop taste, and a high alcohol content (5-6.5 percent by weight). Stout usually has low to medium carbonation and is best served at temperatures above 45°F. Stout is a heavy beer with barley added as its main ingredient. Although rarely seen today, milk stout was once popular with the sick and elderly for its reputed restorative properties. It is a sweet stout so named from the lactose used as a nonfermentable sugar in the brew.

Porter originated in England about 1722 to satisfy the market that had arisen from a public demand for a brew that was drawn equally from casks of ale and beer. Originally it was a heavy beverage, but is more lightly brewed today and has a more bitter and dry taste than it had in the eighteenth century. Porter is made with charcoal or colored malt and is a dark brown, heavy-bodied, malty-flavored brew with a slightly sweet taste and a less pronounced hop flavor than ale. It is usually about 5 percent alcohol by weight. All early porter was top-fermented and many of the better ones still are; a few domestic American ones are bottom-fermented.

Malt Liquor

In America, as in the rest of the world, the term *malt liquor* is a loosely defined term with no legal or accepted definition. In general, malt liquor has higher alcohol and warmer fermentation. An average American malt liquor has 4.5-5 percent alcohol by weight (compared to 3.6-3.8 percent for lagers); 12-13 percent original gravity, strength of wort before fermentation in percent solids (lagers are 11-11.5 percent); and 65-75 percent real degree of fermentation, the percentage of original gravity lost during fermentation to alcohol (lagers are 60-64 percent). In many American states and in some foreign countries, a brew cannot be called beer or ale if its alcoholic content exceeds specified limits. Malt liquor is one of the allowed terms and it is hung on many higher alcohol brews, particularly imports, just to satisfy local labeling laws.

The major producers of malt liquor in the United States are convinced that its market is predominantly black and much of the malt liquor marketing is clearly oriented in that direction. Some malt liquor is designed to compete with "pop" wines and there are beer and wine and beer and soda combinations offered as malt liquor. Others are dry, malty, and very beerlike. There are many good malt liquors and they come in a wide variety of styles and flavors.

The first American malt liquor was Colt .45, developed by the Altes Brewery in Detroit. It was later sold to the National Brewery of Baltimore, who promoted it into a national brand.

Light Beer (Low-calorie)

The term *light* has been used for many years by brewers to distinguish its pale pilseners from its dark pilseners and ales. Even though the term is being used more and more to indicate a low-calorie brew, the usage is not universal. Some companies use the term to describe both their pale beers and their low-calorie beers. Pale light beers have become the epitome of pilsener style brews and various means have been used to create paler and paler examples. Corn and rice adjuncts help to create pale brews, but do little for calorie reduction.

It has long been known that longer fermentation (more time in the mash tub) yields a greater level of alcohol at the expense of the fermentable sugars. Beers so brewed, like Straub Beer from St. Mary's, Pa., have higher alcohol and lower carbohydrate content and were, in a sense, the forerunner of the low-calorie beers of today.

Some brewers simply dilute their regular beer. This does indeed reduce the calories and carbohydrates, but it also reduces the aroma, flavor, body, and everything else that makes beer a worthwhile drink. Others add an enzyme, alpha amylase, to the fermenter, which converts some of the dextrins to alcohol, but, as with extended fermentation, this only works to a limited degree as the dextrins are not completely converted. Still others use glucose as an adjunct in place of some of the barley malt (or adjuncts), but while the desired level of alcohol is achieved with some carbohydrate reduction, the brews are not very successful in the marketplace.

In 1964, true low-calorie beer became possible with the development and commercial availability of an enzyme called amyloglucosidase. This enzyme completed the work of the malt amylases and rendered all the dextrins in beer completely fermentable. All the starchy content could be converted to alcohol. The real extract of a beer made with amyloglucosidase in the fermenter consists only of protein, minerals, by-products of fermentation (e.g., lactic acid) and some pentose sugars which are neither fermentable nor caloric.

The alcohol level resulting from the amyloglucosidase fermentation is greater than for regular beer. The higher alcohol comes from the dextrins that are broken down by the enzyme to fermentable sugars and which are then fermented by the yeast that is already present. The level of alcohol is usually about 1 percent higher than that for regular beer, but there is an interesting effect concerning it. Because this low-calorie beer has no dextrins remaining, the alcohol in it can be more rapidly absorbed by the bloodstream significantly increasing its intoxicating potential. To mitigate this undesired fringe benefit, the brewer adjusts the light beer to an alcohol level slightly below that of regular beer by adding water. This low-calorie beer, when packaged, will have about 0.3 percent less alcohol than regular beer, but will have the same potential for intoxication.

So, a true light low-calorie beer has fewer calories, no carbohydrates, and as much intoxicating effect as regular beer. There is a loss of body because the dextrins are no longer there. Because of the need for alcohol reduction by dilution, there also may be less aroma and flavor. This loss of flavor and aroma can be avoided to a great degree by the brewer's use of high-quality ingredients that would make a brew with character sufficient to stand out even with the dilution to reduce alcohol.

Imperial Russian Stout

This richly flavored brew, with its powerful bouquet, is a stout in name only. With its fruity taste, it is more properly termed a barley wine. Originally made for the Russian market in St. Petersburg, this English brew is bottle-aged for one full year before it is released. It is then good for another five years, but aficionados store them for decades in cool dark cellars like fine wines and claim they continue to improve with further aging. They are still brewed by Courage Ltd. of London.

Weissbier

White beer or wheat beer was first made in England but developed its major market in Germany. It came into prominence in Hamburg as Hamburg Wheat Beer in the sixteenth century. Made from wheat and barley malt, it has a distinctive sharp yeasty or bready aroma and a taste by itself. Berliner Weiss is usually served in bowl-shaped stemware with woodruff or with a fruit syrup, like raspberry, whereupon it becomes more like a lightly flavored, pleasant, effervescent liqueur. It is white colored and cloudy with a rich foam. In Munich, Weiss is served with a slice of lemon.

It is important when serving Weissbier, not to disturb or serve the yeast sediment. To that end, Weissbier should be stored standing in a refrigerator, not shaken when opened, and poured as you would heavily sedimented wine so that none of the white precipitate enters the glass. Pouring should be down the side of a clean glass, until near the end of the pour. At that time, the pour should be made into the center of the glass. This will give the most pleasing level of foam—a proper head.

Other Beers

There are a number of other types of beers or beerlike cereal beverages available which are favored locally or are for special diets. Some examples are faro and lambic beers of Belgium, which are fermented with wild yeasts and are very acidic; Malta, a popular beverage in Puerto Rico; and various malt tonics and near-beers that either have no alcohol or have alcohol of less

Mr. Graham Auton, export manager of Samuel Smith's Old Brewery Tadcaster (Taddy) of Yorkshire, England, and Jack Burton, head cooper, who is also pictured on the Samuel Smith Pale Ale six pack carrier, toast the first shipment of Samuel Smith The Famous Taddy Porter to leave the brewery. Bound for sales and distribution in the U.S. by Merchant du Vin Corporation.

than 0.4 percent. They are made in most countries of the world (e.g., Malzbier from Germany). Another brewed product is sake, the Japanese beverage that tastes more like a semi-dry white wine. To make sake, rice is steamed and fermented to produce germination, as in malting, with a yeast prepared from rice straw. Another term occasionally encountered is *small beer.* It is not a separate type at all, but rather a beer made from leftover or used grain and hops.

Fig. 1.   *Fig. 2.*

Fig. 3.   *Fig. 4.*

Fig. 5.   *Fig. 6.*

Early Bottling Methods
Figs. 1, 2 – Filling   Figs. 3, 4 – Cooking   Fig. 5, 6 – Later Devices

4. THE GREAT EXPERIMENT

Several wine tasters, sitting around after a tasting, were discussing various subjects of common interest, and the subject of the Schmidt's versus Coors TV commercial came up. This led to the idea of a beer tasting that would, of course, include the Schmidt's-Coors comparison. A few weeks later the event was held and was a tremendous success. It was such an entertaining feature, with unexpected educational benefits, that it was decided a second one should be held. The success of the second led to a third and a fourth. By this time, close to one hundred different beers had been tried and no one could say that any two were the same. Some eighty tastings later, over one thousand beers had been tried and rated by a panel of tasters.

The Taste Panel

The judging panel was a diverse group in occupation, background, and taste. There were lawyers, stockbrokers, real estate brokers, engineers, schoolteachers, salesmen, a chemist, administrators, career military men, housewives, and bluecollar workers. Ages ranged from mid-twenties to late fifties. There were twice as many men as women. A wide representation of regional tastes was involved; tasters from New England, the Northwest, the Middle Atlantic states, the Midwest, the Plains states, the Deep South, and the West Coast were on hand. Also involved were foreign nationals from Canada and Australia. In all, some forty-five tasters participated in the trials.

Each taster was requested to provide background information on himself, including data on beer-drinking experience, and general and specific beer preferences. Tasting schedules were adjusted so that these avowed preferences could be challenged and tested.

Serving the Beer

Beers were served in pairs at all times, the items being matched as closely as possible with regard to color, aroma, and flavor (in that order of priority). Only one person knew which beers were being served and by transferring the beers to a decanter and having the second person pour them into the tasting glasses, no one present knew what beer was in which glass. Beers were poured down the side of the glass for uniformity and to retain head control. Some brewers recommend that their beer be poured straight into the center of the glass, claiming that the beer tastes different otherwise. To pour in this fashion could result in a glass full of foam. If a head is desired, the last ounce can be poured into the center of the glass.

French pilsener stemware was used exclusively so that serving and tasting temperature could be maintained. A mug would have been too time-consuming. A standard "beer glass" allows the heat of the hand to warm the fluid too easily. Only stemware—which can be held by the stem if the drinker wishes to keep the beer cool or by the bowl if the beer needs to be warmed up slightly to fulfill its potential—gave the required personal control. Also, these glasses have a slightly closed opening, which gathers aroma and bouquet, even from beers that are not particularly well-endowed with those features. Glasses were rinsed and air-dried because the

slightest trace of detergent will ruin the head.

The beers were refrigerated at 36°-40°F., which is actually a bit too cold for serving (although the National Brewing Co. has always recommended a serving temperature of 38°F.). With the two-step decanting and pouring, this low temperature was required so that the test items would be in the appropriate temperature range (40°-45°F.) when served (as recommended by Heineken and many other brewers). Some items, such as the English brown ales, were served at slightly higher temperatures (50°-55°F.) since they are brewed according to that custom and their flavor is severely lacking when served 10° cooler.

After trying several variations, it was found that the tasters preferred testing a variety of flavors spread over twelve pairs of beers, instead of testing just one style for the entire evening. The palates became dulled after more than a dozen similar beers; one beer became indistinguishable from another. Likewise, only a very few of the heavy or flavorful beers, like the dark English ales, could be appreciated in one sitting.

Tasters had to be exposed to the beers in a very specific manner to avoid confusing their palates. The lightest styles of beers had to be tasted first, followed by increasingly flavorful beers. The heaviest or strongest flavored items had to be tasted last since anything of lesser flavor tasted subsequently resulted in an invalid reaction. There had to be a respite in between each major change of style as well, to allow the tasters to clear their palates.

The Criteria Used

The tasters were asked to make their judgment on appearance, "nose" (the bouquet and aroma), taste, and aftertaste.

The appearance of the beverage had to be attractive, with color and color density appropriate to type and style, and reasonably devoid of particulate matter. Cloudiness or haze can be a good omen (when it is the presence of high malt content and therefore large protein molecules, as in some imports like Hansa Fjord, which imparts an excellent flavor), a bad sign (when it is caused by lactic acid bacteria, which is detrimental to flavor), or have little to do with the product (served too cold).

Dark beer should be a rich gold brown or amber, but reddish-brown hues can be equally attractive. Stouts may be almost opaque. The dark color usually comes from roasting the malt, but there are other techniques, such as adding color or licorice. Light beers (lightly colored, not low-calorie) come in various intensities of yellows and golds, separately, and in combination, sometimes with a greenish cast.

The nose of the beverage consists of two elements, aroma and bouquet. The aroma is the nasal sensation produced by the ingredients of the product and the bouquet results from the by-products of fermentation. The aroma should be characteristic of the type and style of beverage being judged. For example, a pilsener beer should have a subtle hop aroma, whereas an English brown ale should have an aroma that is predominantly malt.

Positive features are related to cleanness, purity, "beeriness," appropriate presence of hops, malt, etc. Negative features are excessive yeastiness, sourness, lactic acid, staleness, and skunkiness (believed caused by exposure to light—photosynthesis).

As to flavor, tasters judged on the first sensation, the middle taste (while swallowing), and the aftertaste (once swallowed). Ideally, the taste is present all the way through, start to finish. A beer that lacks any taste feature deprives the drinker of much of the potential enjoyment and must be deemed faulty. Likewise, a watery or unpleasant taste leaves the drinker with an unpleasant memory of the brew, especially if the fault is reflected in the aftertaste.

The beer should have sufficient body. Too little is to be watery, lifeless, and unsatisfying. Too much may be cloying or prematurely filling. If you are enjoying beer with a meal, you don't want the beer to fill you up before you have stopped enjoying the food.

Sweetness in a beer is best appreciated at the beginning of the taste. The sweet-sensing buds are located on the tip of the tongue and one of the impressions a beer drinker expects when he takes that first tiny, trial sip is given by whatever unfermented sugar is in the brew. Too much sweetness on the palate at this point is a fault, and should the sweetness extend across the palate, the results may range from flabby to cloying. Sweetness adds to the impression of apparent body, while acid moderates that effect.

The bitter hop flavor should also be present at the first sip, but should gradually disappear as the beverage is swallowed. There should be only

A Colonial Ale-House

a little remaining in the finish. The degree of hop bitterness in the flavor will be good or bad according to personal taste. In beer, what to one is bitter gall, to another is a good, full-flavored brew. Even the type of hop can affect the flavor (and aroma) of beer. Some hops produce a clean pungent character, others give a spicy, musky nature.

Malt is the heart of the beer flavor and its distinctive characteristic taste will determine, to a great extent, the taster's overall evaluation of the beverage. Modern beer making uses barley malt, but to a lesser extent than in the past. Malt adjuncts, such as corn and rice, are becoming more and more common as prime ingredients. These adjuncts impart a flavor of their own, depending upon the amount used, but their main purpose, or effect, is to reduce aroma and flavor when used in place of barley. They are also cheaper to use, which fact speaks loudly as to why their use has become so prevalent.

Other flavor factors or palate sensations to consider are the degree of carbonation, style of carbonation, alcohol content, fermentation by-products, effects of mishandling, and brewery "house flavors."

If the beer is overcarbonated, like too many American beers (and some foreign beers brewed for the American market), the bubbles mask whatever subtleties of flavor may be present. Instead of the desired pleasant piquancy, the beer is gassy. Too little carbonation and the beer is flat, dull, and weak. The preferred condition is small bubble carbonation, as in fine champagne, a happy state which can be reached only by methods of natural carbonation. Large bubbles, as in soft drinks, are not half so pleasing and are the usual result of carbonic injection. Excess carbonation can sometimes be eased by pouring the brew into the center of the glass.

The amount of alcohol in a beer seems to be a factor that many tasters find difficult to assess. If there is too little alcohol, the beer will seem thin. If there is too much, it will be winy, which is not unbearable, unless it is obtrusive. So-called low-calorie beers necessarily will have less alcohol and must be judged accordingly.

Products of fermentation should not be present in the flavor. If they are, they are usually deemed faults. Similarly, mishandling almost never improves a beer. If it is too old, it gets stale, woody, or acidic. If it has been overheated, it may seem too old or may take on other unpleasant flavors, like metallic sensations. Beer that has been frozen is usually lifeless when served. Exposure to light may bring about photosynthesis resulting in a skunky aroma and taste. Beer bottles are colored deep green or brown to protect against this fault. Certain well-hopped beers, like Molson Golden Ale, seem to be particularly susceptible to skunkiness and it is so commonly encountered that one can suppose there are more reasons for this fault than simply exposure to light. Another fault is excess yeast cells disintegrating in the beer. This causes a "dirty" flavor, as opposed to the clean beeriness desired. Similarly, residual tannin from excessive malt extraction can cause the beverage to be rough or scratchy when swallowed.

Many brewers have their own house flavors, made according to their own recipes. Often the recipe has a secret ingredient (like juniper berries). The taster may or may not appreciate the house flavor. In many instances, use of such recipes tends to create something very unlike beer.

All of the aspects of flavor, taken together, are the taste of the beer. The relationship among the factors is called the balance. It is a very important aspect of the overall taste impression and where all other factors are equal but different, the discerning beer drinker will invariably select the better balanced brew.

The last part of the taste is the finish, the consideration of how well it ends and what taste is left in the mouth thereafter. If the beer has no aftertaste or a very brief one, it finishes poorly. If the aftertaste is sour, metallic, or bitter, it finishes badly. As you swallow, the palate sensation should be mostly of malt, with some faint sweetness, and even fainter bitterness from the hops. An ideal brew has balance throughout, with a taste remaining in the mouth that is pleasant in all respects. It may be the only recollection of the entire experience.

Rating the Beers

Tasters were asked to comment upon each of the beers sampled. Each gave his impressions of the aroma and taste, particularly when the effects were not obvious or when choice of words was difficult. Tasters were also required to provide a numerical score as follows:

13–15 **Excellent.** Characteristic of the best of type. No faults. No offensive features. All components of aroma and flavor in harmony. Aroma, flavor, and aftertaste all present to the appropriate degree. You would be willing to pay a premium price for this beer and go far out of your way to get it.

10–12 **Very good.** True to type. No significant faults. No offensive features. Well balanced. Aroma, flavor, and aftertaste all present to the appropriate degree, but short of excellent. You would be willing to pay some premium for this beer and even go out of your way to find it.

7–9 **Good.** Typical of type. Faults are small and forgivable. Good balance for the most part. Pleasant and enjoyable. Good serviceable beer for thirst quenching and casual enjoyment, if obtainable at a good price.

4–6 **Fair.** May not be true to type. Some noticeable faults but not unpleasantly so. Poorly balanced. May have bitterness or sourness in the aftertaste, or no finish at all. May be thirst quenching and nothing more. Not a beer you would normally purchase a second time.

0–3 **Poor or bad.** Atypical of type. Has definite unpleasant features. Flawed aroma or taste or both. Badly mishandled. Gone off with age. Improperly made. Contains unforgivable features. Undrinkable, or tastes like nothing more than carbonated water or a soft drink. A beer you would not purchase again.

To ensure that there would be no bias from unusually high- (or low-) scoring groups of tasters, scores were normalized. The highest single score and the lowest single score for each item were discarded. The total of the remaining scores was adjusted to an equivalent score for six

raters, and the midrange score set to 45, the middle value of the scoring range. The remaining scores were then adjusted accordingly. Extreme scores were further subjected to inspection for any remaining bias, and adjusted or retried, if appropriate.

A final score of 73–90 could thus be adjudged excellent, 55–72 very good, 37–54 good, 19–36 fair, and 0–18 poor, based on the taster's scoring criteria. In Appendix I, all brews are listed and rated.

Foods at Tastings

Beer tasters, like wine tasters, need some means of clearing their palates after sampling their subjects, and a wide variety of food was tried. We found very early that greasy foods, like potato chips, have an extremely deadening effect on the palate. It took a bit longer to realize that pretzels, because of their saltiness, also impaired taste sensitivity. Some other traditional beer foods, like liverwurst, produced a mixed reaction, enhancing the taste of some beers and clashing with others.

The best devices we found for clearing beer palates in a tasting situation were unbuttered and very lightly salted popcorn, unsalted saltine crackers, and French bread. From this, one can draw useful conclusions. If you are going to enjoy a few beers and intend to eat some oily or salty foods, save some money by drinking good inexpensive beverages rather than some high-priced brew, at least after the first one. The potato chips, pretzels, corn chips, and salted nuts will so dull your taste that, to you, one good beer will taste about the same as any other good one.

COURTESY ANHEUSER-BUSCH, INC.

Brewmasters at all Anheuser-Busch breweries daily taste packaged, filtered and unfiltered beers to assure maximum taste quality and uniformity. Their expert palates have the final say on whether a batch of beer measures up to the company's strict taste standards and is good enough for consumers.

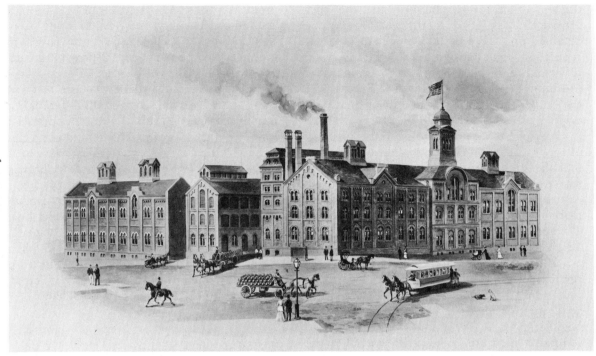

Jos. Schlitz Brewing Company 1869

5. THE BEERS

In the following pages you will find the sensory descriptions of most of the beers available in North America. To be sure, the list is not 100 percent complete; there are obscure regional brews only marketed locally. Some cannot be found more than twenty miles from the brewery. Until recently an effort to gather the brands listed herein was fairly impossible. Thousands of labels existed, but most were marketed in tiny geographical areas. By the time a reasonably complete set of such labels could have been gathered, many of them would have been obsolete, what with the reduced number of breweries and marketed brands.

The advent of beer-can collecting, however, has made some small brands available in large metropolitan areas, thereby giving them a public exposure not otherwise available.

Some of the beers listed herein may not now be available. Domestic brands that sell poorly upon introduction may be discontinued after a few months. They may appear later or may

appear under the banner of another brewing firm. Some imports are in short supply, especially those brought in for can collectors. One label, I heard, was brought in by a Washington, D.C., liquor store in a quantity of six dozen.

The sensory descriptions given include all features worthy of note. The impression on the eye, nose, and palate of the drinker is recorded. The nose of the brew includes the aroma and bouquet, the factors detected by the sense of smell. In the mouth the palate sensations usually indicate the total effect, including the change in sensation as the brew crosses the sweet, sour, and bitter detectors located in different sections of the tongue. "Textural" notes are provided when meaningful. Particular attention has been given to the ending sensation (finish) and the aftertaste.

Whenever it was suspected that a sample had been mishandled or was otherwise different from what the manufacturer intended, addi-

43

tional samples were obtained and the beer retasted. If a "good" sample could not be obtained after three separate efforts to do so, the report of such may be regarded as a valid reflection of the beer as you can expect to find it in America, but not necessarily of that beer under the proper conditions or in its city or country of origin.

Beers are reported according to their country of origin and, within that classification, listed by manufacturer. If information on the company was available, it is provided in brief. Corporate names are given when known, as well as data on marketing area, distribution, and brand history. Where alcohol percentage is given, it is percent alcohol by volume unless otherwise specified.

With very few exceptions, all the beers reported herein were tasted in packaged form, that is, in can or bottle. Some beers are known to be far inferior when packaged than on draft. One notable example of this is Iron City. Even company literature makes that note. On the other hand, I know of no beer that is better in a can or bottle than on draft. We, who like to enjoy a beer at home, should be grateful that there are recipes and techniques for beermaking that enable brewers *very nearly* to produce a beer in package that equals the same product on draft. My home is so much more comfortable than most of the dingy bars we have available in this country that I am more than willing to put up with the slight loss of flavor.

In reaching out to the far corners of the country for the obscure regional brands, it could be that many brands were tasted under circumstances to their disadvantage. Brewers know that each recipe has a limited shelf life and, for most of the light pilseners, the generally agreed figure is three months. For some of the very light brews, however, the viable peak performance period may be as short as a few weeks. Thus, many of the beers that performed so poorly in our trials could be quite good if tasted from a fresher source. The fault conceivably could lie in the length of time it took for me to obtain the beer and subject it to the taste panel. Also, poor performance could mean that the beer is very fragile and it is not uncommon to obtain "defective" samples even close to origin. Probably the day will come when the can or label of your beer will bear a

production date so that you can be reasonably assured of freshness; very few do it now. Coors does and in doing so qualifies for my vote as the brewer with the most conscience and greatest pride in the quality of product.

If, in performing your own taste tests, you come up with results substantially different from those reported herein, I would appreciate learning of them. Although alteration in recipes is relatively rare, brewers do adjust them to the ideas of marketing personnel. And brewing techniques are in a constant state of flux. A change in the master brewer at a facility can have a significant effect on the entire product line.

In the future, I hope to continue the testing effort until every product available in North America is scrutinized. And there is no reason why everyone interested cannot participate. Please write me in care of my publisher.

United States of America

The earliest settlers in America brought with them a thirst for malt beverages and as soon as there were communities, there were brewhouses. Since they also brought with them the Puritan ethic, the production and the dispensing of malt beverages were highly regulated from the very start.

As the first arrivals were English, the first brews were ales and brewing in America closely followed the evolution of malt brewing in the United Kingdom. Early in the nineteenth century, immigrants from the European continent began to arrive in great numbers. They thirsted for the beers of their tradition. As might be expected, among them were men who had the know-how to produce these brews. These new Americans tended to settle in ethnic pockets and thus instantly created a viable market for the brews they favored. Pennsylvania and Wisconsin still contain such pockets, having their own regional tastes satisfied by small independent brewers.

In the beginning, the brews were all top fermented and of four basic styles: ale, porter, stout, and Weiss (for rapidly growing German population). By 1840, the majority of American brewers were of German origin and were closely following the development of their art as practiced in their native land. When bottom-fermented brews were introduced, American brewers were quick to join in. Always at the forefront of the technology of the time, the American brewers converted their plants or built new facilities to produce the new lager. They were also the first to employ artificial refrigeration on a grand scale.

Except for the West Coast, where ice and refrigeration were unavailable (and where steam beer was developed as a workable and popular alternative), the new lager caught on rapidly. It soon began to supplant the traditional ales in the American culture. The popularity of the brews gave the industry a tremendous boost. With the rapidly growing population, over four thousand breweries were operating in the United States by the centennial 1876.

As an outgrowth of the Puritan ethic (which was big on denial), there had always been a strong temperance movement in America. Since all aspects of alcoholic beverages had been regulated from the very beginning, widespread drunkenness had never been a problem in the U.S. as it had elsewhere, but this did not deter the zeal of the temperance folk.

That some states would vote for Prohibition was inevitable, for even today there are large pieces of "dry" real estate in the country. It is doubtful, however, if national Prohibition would have occurred without the shortage of grain, and more importantly, the strong anti-German sentiment resulting from World War I.

National Prohibition became effective on 16 January 1920, one year after the thirty-sixth state legislature ratified the Eighteenth Amendment to the Constitution. States usually went dry, however, as they ratified the amendment, some as early as 1918. The Eighteenth Amendment banned the manufacture and sale of intoxicating beverages and the Volstead Act, passed by Congress, declared that any beverage containing more than one-half percent alcohol was intoxicating.

Prohibition lasted 13 years and history records it as a disaster. It was unpopular, unworkable, and unenforceable. It established a financial base for organized crime in America that guaranteed its existence unto perpetuity.

During Prohibition more people were involved in the manufacture and sale of alcoholic beverages than in any other period in the history of the world. Some breweries stayed alive throughout the 13 years by producing the malt, yeast, and ice needed by the millions of home brewers.

When the nation had had enough, 3.2 percent beer was legalized by the Cullen-Harrison Act, which simply raised the definition of *nonintoxicating* to that level. This bill was passed by Congress and signed by President Roosevelt in April, 1933. It essentially ended Prohibition for breweries, which reopened, producing "3.2" for an eager public. But of the thousands shut down by Prohibition, only some

THE VERY HIGHEST POINT
known to the Art of Modern Brewing is found within every bottle of

Budweiser
"The Old Reliable"

Brews will come and brews will go — have their little day — then vanish — but *Budweiser* goes on forever — everlasting *Quality, Purity and Mildness* is the reason.

COURTESY ANHEUSER-BUSCH, INC.

An early example of Budweiser print advertising

seven hundred fifty breweries reopened and many of those rested on badly weakened financial foundations.

Following World War II, there was a drastic change in American beer drinking habits. Whereas most beer drinking before the war had taken place at the neighborhood taproom, Americans now wanted their beer at home. In 1948 television was introduced to the public at large and by 1952 most families had a set. For the

Massacre made military and advertising history — Custer's last fight, the Sioux massacre of the 7th Cavalry at Little Big Horn, took place June 25, 1876. The same year, Adolphus Busch introduced Budweiser, the brew that would go on to become the largest selling beer in the world. By coincidence and uncanny marketing instinct, Busch acquired the right to this now-classic painting of the slaughter. In 1895, Busch commissioned F. Otto Becker, a Milwaukee artist, to copy the work for lithographic reproduction. Anheuser-Busch made one million prints of the painting. Most of them were displayed in American saloons, and were credited as an early breakthrough in mass marketing and product merchandising — one of many that paralleled the rise of Budweiser.

next ten years, few of them left their homes except to work or obtain provisions. Movie theaters died by the scores and taprooms survived only because of the regulars who would watch their TV from the bar. The packaged-beer industry followed and was here to stay. The beer can, which appeared in 1935 but was deemed only a fad item for ten years, came into its own and soon was augmented by the nonreturnable bottle, which first showed up in quantity in 1953.

Television's impact on American beer drinking went beyond the packaging considerations, however. National advertising gave an edge to those who chose to take the expensive gamble. Packaged beer had become a supermarket item and the housewife who included beer on the shopping list tended to buy the more familiar well-advertised national brand than the local regional brew. Regional brewers were less efficient in production, had higher distribution costs and were, in general, less well known to this new beer customer.

The formula for success in the industry was clear to many and the brewing giants of today made their well-considered moves. They increased their advertising budgets to all media with advertising costs often exceeding beer production and distribution costs. They expanded nationally to reduce distribution expenses and thus were able to offer their brands at or below the prices of local competitors. Regional independent breweries folded or were absorbed at a furious rate. Fortunately, many of the better regional labels were continued by their new owners.

One aspect of this upheaval, one of great

Budweiser

At the Top
Because of Quality and Purity

*Bottled with crowns or
corks only at the Home
Plant in St. Louis*

The Anheuser-Busch Brewery

Covers an area of 140 acres of ground, equal to 70 city
blocks, upon which are located 110 individual buildings.

CAPACITY		TRANSPORTATION FACILITIES	
Brewing Capacity	2,500,000 barrels per year	Refrigerator freight cars	1,500
Malting Capacity	2,000,000 bushels per year	Horses at home plant	143
Bottling Works	1,000,000 bottles daily	Wagons at home plant	78
Grain Storage Elevators	1,750,000 bushels	Auto Trucks at home plant	74
Stockhouses (for lagering)	600,000 barrels	Horses at Branches	483
Steam Power Plant	12,000 horse power	Wagons at Branches	430
Electric Power Plant	4,000 horse power	Auto Trucks at Branches	47
Refrigerator Plant	4,000 horse power		
Ice Plants	1,200 tons per day	EMPLOYES	
Coal used	325 tons per day		
FREIGHT		At St. Louis Plant	6,000 people
Inbound and outbound	50,000 cars per year	At 36 Branches	1,500 people

Total Sales, 1911—1,527,832 Barrels
Budweiser Bottled Beer Sales, 1911—173,184,600 Bottles

The King—even then

concern to the true lover of beer in America, is that mediocrity has been steadily overtaking the product line of most U.S. brewing firms. More and more, corn and rice adjuncts are being used to produce brews that cost less to make, while more and more money is being spent to convince the public that these tasteless beers are not only good, but a virtue as well. The American taste, used to soft drinks, a habit arising from a generation of Prohibition, accepts the products under the constant urging of the TV, which promotes lightness and mediocrity as a virtue in malt beverages.

The beers introduced in the past decade are very pale, have fewer and fewer calories, and less and less flavor. They are beers for people who really don't like beer. They would really prefer soda pop in a container labeled beer. Since so many don't care which beer they drink, many stores now offer generic beer at a price 25–40 percent below national brands. Sales reports show generics outselling some name brands and

over a half-dozen companies have hopped on the generic bandwagon.

Despite the trend, excellent beers are still available in America today. The standard bearers of the giants are usually, at least, acceptable as beers. Some, like Budweiser and Michelob, are very good, and scattered about the country are excellent regional brews like Augsburger from Huber, Straub from Straub, and Maximus Super from F.X. Matt. These should be tasted by all serious beer drinkers and, if enjoyable, supported by their trade lest they should disappear from the scene.

Anchor Brewing Co.
(San Francisco, Calif.)

The roots of this brewery go back to the 1860s and it operated under at least two different names until 1896, when it became known as the Anchor Brewing Co., which name it carries today. (For several years Anchor was called the Steam Beer Brewing Co., but has been Anchor since 1977.)

The most significant event in Anchor history was the arrival of the energetic Fritz Maytag in 1965 who, as president and brewmaster, took a foundering concern and built it into a successful specialty brewery with a large and dedicated following.

Up to 1971 Anchor produced its brews only in draught, but it is now bottled and available in twenty states. In 1982, over 28,000 barrels were produced. Based in a new brewery, a rebuilt coffee factory, since 1979, Anchor continues to grow, and Fritz Maytag expects to reach a

35,000–40,000-barrel annual capacity in the next few years.

Anchor produces all-malt brews without adjuncts or preservatives: these are well deserving of their fine reputation, and some of the special brews are spectacular treats.

ANCHOR STEAM BEER—deep bright orange-copper with red hues, foamy texture, small bubbles, rich malt aroma with good hops in back, sweet creamy flavor that starts out with malt and becomes hoppy as it crosses palate, full-bodied, complex, very flavorful and very satisfying.

OUR SPECIAL ALE 1982—bright yellow-orange, sweet perfumy fruity ale aroma, nicely balanced malt and hop flavor, big-bodied and richly flavored, extremely long on the palate.

ANCHOR PORTER—deep brown, creamy texture, very faint aroma of malt, big creamy malt flavor, extremely complex character of malt, licorice, molasses, etc., very long on the palate, a magnificent porter.

OUR SPECIAL ALE 1978—issued for the 1978 Christmas and New Year holiday season, this brew should satisfy "real ale" advocates. Pale cloudy yellow, orange, unusual canned lychee nut aroma, intense palate, perfumy sweet ale taste, big malt, oaklike bite in finish, but too much bitterness for good balance.

OLD FOGHORN BARLEYWINE STYLE ALE—copper-red brown, caramel, roasted malt and molasses aroma, rich intense flavor of orange, caramel, and roasted malt, big and complex, sweet sipping beer, long on palate, well balanced.

OUR SPECIAL ALE 1979—cloudy orange, unusual canned-fruity-lychee nut nose and palate, strong sweet ale hop flavor, oaklike bite in finish, very bitter and long aftertaste. A little too harsh.

OUR SPECIAL ALE 1980—cloudy tawny orange-gold, highly hopped ale aroma, bit intense "sweet ale" flavor, some oaky character, big body, beautiful balance, lots of hops, lots of malt, long long aftertaste. A spectacular brew; Anchor's greatest achievement.

LIBERTY ALE—opaque coffee brown, intense malty aroma, huge body, big malt flavor all the way through to the lingering roast malt aftertaste. Made in April, 1975, and still may be good, it was that big!

LIBERTY ALE—more recent version than above; found in Massachusetts and California regularly in 1984; pale orange, flowery hop-ale aroma, extremely complex, palate of oranges, apricots, and spices; very flavorful, long long aftertaste. A brew with pizzazz; as good as, or better than, the earlier version.

OUR SPECIAL ALE 1981—pale orange, good sharp hop aroma, small bubble carbonation, huge body, big flavor mostly bitter hops, but with some sweetness in the middle, complex and interesting, a fine brew of its style.

OUR SPECIAL ALE 1983—bright deeply colored reddish caramel, mild malt and hop aroma, small bubble carbonation, smooth dry malt flavor, faint sweetness in back most noticeable in the finish, very complex, slightly sour aftertaste.

Anheuser-Busch, Inc.
(St. Louis, Mo.; Newark, N.J.; Los Angeles, Calif.; Tampa, Fla.; Houston, Tex.; Columbus, Ohio; Jacksonville, Fla.; Merrimack, N.H.; Williamsburg, Va.; Fairfield, Calif.; Baldwinsville, N.Y.)

In 1850 a primitive brewery was established in St. Louis by a Mr. Schneider. He was succeeded shortly after by the firm of Hammer & Urban. This business failed in 1857 and the principal creditor, Eberhard Anheuser, bought the plant and continued the business with moderate success. In 1865 Anheuser's son-in-law, Adolphus Busch, bought an interest in E. Anheuser & Co. In 1873 the firm was incorporated as the E. Anheuser & Co. Brewing Association. Anheuser was president and Busch was secretary and general manager.

Ten years later the name was changed to the Anheuser-Busch Brewing Association. When Anheuser died in 1880, Busch became president. Under Busch the business developed very rapidly. Year after year, new structures were added to keep pace with ever-increasing sales. By the turn of the century, the brewing plant covered sixty acres, the equivalent of some six city blocks in St. Louis. Annual production stood at one million barrels by 1900 and the company operated its own railroad and had forty-two branches in various cities.

Today Anheuser-Busch is the world's largest brewer with a record 60-plus million barrels in sales during 1983, and for the twenty-fifth consecutive year, led the brewing industry in sales. Under the continuing leadership of the Busch family, the company continues to expand and modernize. Its current shipping capacity exceeds that of the next largest brewer by some fifteen million barrels.

Since 1951 Anheuser-Busch has developed a coast-to-coast system of breweries which has worked great economies through their expansion across the American market. The expansion began in 1951 with construction of the Newark, New Jersey, plant. Later, Los Angeles (1954) and Tampa (1959) were added. The late 1960s saw a rapid expansion with Houston (1966), Columbus (1968), and Jacksonville (1969) being added. New England obtained an Anheuser-Busch facility (and the famous Budweiser Clydesdales) in 1970 with the opening of the Merrimack (N.H.) plant. The latest additions have been Williamsburg in 1972 and Fairfield (Calif.) in 1976, the latter not reaching full production capability until 1977, and in 1980 Anheuser-Busch purchased the Schlitz plant in Baldwinsville, N.Y. where a substantial expansion is planned before the facility will be opened. The largest plant is still the St. Louis facility (the original but greatly expanded plant), which has an annual production capacity in excess of ten million barrels.

Anheuser-Busch commands about twenty percent of the American market and a great deal of that is because of the popularity of its primary brand, Budweiser—the king of beers. Budweiser was introduced in 1876, but Anheuser-Busch did not obtain the rights to the name until 1891. Until that time the label belonged to Carl Conrad, who, with Adolphus Busch, had developed the formula. Anheuser-Busch brewed Budweiser, but Conrad bottled and sold it.

Anheuser-Busch has never compromised the quality of the original Budweiser formula. Only the purest of natural ingredients are used and they were listed on the label long before it was popular to do so or required by law. The recipe calls for the more expensive Western two-row barley, pure hops (rather than extract), rice adjunct, natural carbonation through krausening, and "beechwood chip aging" for a full month. Beechwood chip aging is a process of lagering in tanks containing a lattice of beechwood strips to clarify the brew and to absorb bitterness. All this means a more costly but better-brewed product, one that is famous the world over. Budweiser is brewed in all Anheuser-Busch plants and production of draft Budweiser in quarter barrels has recently resumed.

Another product of Anheuser-Busch is the famous Michelob, introduced as a draft beer in 1896. It was originally a high malt beer, but since

COURTESY ANHEUSER-BUSCH, INC.

Public tours of 70-block Anheuser-Busch, Inc. brewery are offered daily and are considered a must for visitors to St. Louis. Dominant building in this photo is the Brew House, which has been in operation since 1892. It is one of three officially designated National Landmark buildings within the brewery complex.

1961, when it became available in bottles, rice has been used as a means of lightening the flavor. The quality of Michelob is no less than that of Budweiser; only the choicest ingredients, including only imported hops, are used. The bottled and canned product is different from the unpasteurized brew kegged for draft service, being lighter and having less zest. Many feel that draft Michelob is the finest beer produced in America and to an earlier generation, it enjoyed a mystique much as Coors does today. The youthful beer drinkers of the late 1940s and the 1950s would often travel to another town where Michelob was available. Today Michelob is produced in all Anheuser-Busch plants except Tampa. Michelob Light was introduced in 1978. With about a 20 percent reduction in calories, it is remarkably similar to Michelob.

Anheuser-Busch has recently entered the international market with Budweiser being produced in a 5 percent version by Labatt's in Quebec and Ontario, test marketing of an "Anheuser-Busch" brand in Germany by Berliner Kindl, and export of Budweiser to Sweden, England (with Allied Breweries), France (with Société Européenne des Brasseries), and Japan (Suntory, Ltd.).

Other Anheuser-Busch products include Busch Beer (originally called Busch Bavarian) and the new Natural Light and Classic Dark beers. Busch, popular in the South, was introduced in 1955 as Busch Bavarian. It became simply Busch in 1979. It is made with corn grits as an adjunct but is otherwise brewed like Budweiser. It is produced in St. Louis, Los Angeles, Tampa, Jacksonville, Merrimack, and Columbus. Natural Light was introduced in early 1977 in several test markets to compete in the low-calorie segment of the market. As with the other products, only natural ingredients and processes are employed in making Natural Light. It is made in St. Louis, Williamsburg, Columbus, Los Angeles, Houston, and Tampa. The Classic Dark draft beer was introduced in 1976. It is produced in all plants except Tampa and Merrimack. It is only available on draft. Budweiser Light was introduced in a test market in Tucson, Arizona in May, 1981.

In 1979 Anheuser-Busch began importing the light beer of Würzburger Hofbräu A.G. The beer is brewed in Germany, shipped to the U.S.

in specially insulated 5100-gallon barrels, and bottled in the Newark, N.J., facility. After being introduced in a three-city test market, distribution was expanded in early 1980. This lasted until 1983, when the arrangement with Würzburger was terminated. Anheuser-Busch introduced an economy-priced beer named Eagle, L-A reduced alcohol beer, and a malt liquor in 1984 test markets.

Anheuser-Busch has a long history of successful advertising that has made its mark on American life. Most Americans are familiar with the Budweiser Clydesdales and earlier generations sang the words "come, come, drink some Budweiser, under the Anheuser bush." In 1976 a theme, developed for a commercial on radio and TV, became a hit recording. In this decade family memories of many Americans include Anheuser-Busch from days spent at Busch Gardens amusement parks in Tampa (the "Dark Continent"), Williamsburg (the "Old Country"), and Los Angeles.

Anheuser-Busch also produces baker's yeast, syrups, and starches (for the paper industry), and whereas many breweries may support local professional athletic teams, Anheuser-Busch owns the St. Louis Cardinals baseball team. Number One is a big, big company.

BUDWEISER LAGER BEER—pale, light but good malty hop aroma, good hop and malt flavor, very balanced, a dry, good-tasting finish. Certainly one of the best of the big national brands, if not the best. There is a lot of opinion regarding the merits of St. Louis-brewed Budweiser. We obtained samples from several plants and tasted them "in the blind." All were clearly recognized as being the same brew (even though the tasters did not know they were) and interestingly enough, St. Louis Bud was a unanimous choice.

BUDWEISER LIGHT BEER—108 calories, brilliant pale gold, lovely malty aroma, good malt and hop flavor, light but pleasant, not much finish or aftertaste, foamy but not overly carbonated on the palate.

MICHELOB BEER—brilliant golden color, hops notable in the aroma, smooth and beautifully balanced, good body, fine dry, malt-hop taste, finely balanced aftertaste with hops remaining only faintly. An excellent beer and worthy choice for serious beer drinkers. The draft version is similar but better. Until 1961, the Michelob recipe was that of an all-barley malt brew. Since that time rice has been used as an adjunct.

MICHELOB LIGHT—134 calories, rather high for a lo-cal, light color, fragrant malty aroma, highly carbonated but the bubbles are small, good-tasting light malty flavor with plenty of character, good finish of medium duration. Maybe

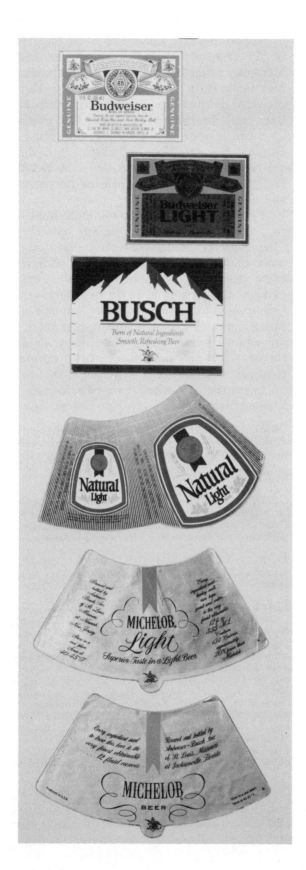

it is the calories that make a beer taste good.

BUSCH PREMIUM BEER—originally labeled Busch Bavarian, pale, yellow color, faintly sweet apple-malt aroma, highly carbonated, medium malt-hop flavor, taste all up front and fades rapidly across the palate, slight hop aftertaste. Good for hot weather thirst quenching, but stick to "Bud" for flavor and depth. Busch made in the Merrimack plant is inferior to that brewed elsewhere (Tampa, for instance).

ANHEUSER NATURAL LIGHT—pale gold, grainy aroma, dry and refreshing, well balanced, long on palate, quite good. 110 calories.

WÜRZBURGER HOFBRÄU (Brewed in Germany by Würzburger Hofbräu, A.G., imported and bottled by Anheuser-Busch at Newark, N.J.)—brilliant gold, visibly carbonated, faint hops in delicate nose, light malty flavor that seems to be somewhat muted by the carbonation; to replace Würzburger Hofbräu brewed and bottled in Germany. See Würzburg Hofbräu, under Germany for comparative description.

MICHELOB CLASSIC DARK BEER—medium deep bright copper brown, faint malt nose, faint malt and hop flavor, CO_2 dominates, little flavor, faint malt aftertaste.

Boulder Brewing Co.
(Longmont, Colo.)

Boulder Beer was issued its federal brewery license in September 1979 and since that time University of Colorado physicist David Hummer and electrical engineer Al Nelson have been running test brews under the guidance of brewmaster Otto Zavatone. Their credentials are mainly a great love of beer and the brewery is the outgrowth of a home-brewing hobby.

Devising its own recipes, Boulder plans to market a line of naturally brewed bitter, stout, and porter. With a capacity of about one hundred cases per week, its output is enough only to supply a few taverns and one retail outlet in Boulder. Production in 1980 reached 170 barrels.

Its bitter made its appearance in July, 1980 and the porter and stout appeared later the same year. The beers are masterpieces of the brewer's art and harken to the preference of beer lovers of almost two centuries ago when Britain produced the world's leading brews; robust brews that brought your senses to attention with each sniff and sip.

In late 1983, construction of a new facility began. When completed, Boulder intends to expand production capacity from the present 600-barrel figure.

51

BOULDER EXTRA PALE ALE—medium pale orange, reasonably clear unless the sediment has been disturbed in which case it will appear cloudy, huge head, big alelike nose with a citrus-kumquat background, very different and very pleasant, intense mouth-filling flavor, strong and zesty with an oaklike-citrus character, good brew, in a class by itself. If you like the type, you will be wild about it. Previously labeled Boulder Bitter.

BOULDER STOUT—deep brown, almost opaque, huge complex malty aroma, complex well-balanced flavor

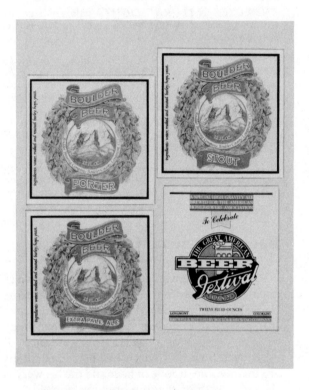

dominated by roasted malt, good malty finish, complex aftertaste with sour licorice component.

BOULDER PORTER—deep copper, natural small bubble carbonation, rich roasted malt aroma with hop and citrus background, strong alelike flavor, fair balance, a real sipping beer, starts out strongly on the palate and seems to soften as you drink it and become inured to the strength.

Champale, Inc.
(Trenton, N.J. and Norfolk, Va.)

Champale, America's most widely advertised malt liquor, is produced in New Jersey by Champale, Inc., on the site of the former premises of Peoples Brewing Co. of Trenton, and by Champale Products Corp. of Norfolk, in the old Jacob Ruppert (and Century Brewing Co.) plant. When Champale was first introduced, the corporate name of the brewery was the

Metropolis Brewing Co. of Trenton, New Jersey.

At Trenton, Champale, Pink Champale, Metbrew (a near-beer from Metropolis renamed Metbrau in early 1981) and Black Horse Ale are produced. Former products included Cherry Hill Beer and Trenton Old Stock Ale, Olbrau, Gaybree, Copenhagen Castle, and Pilser's Original, but according to Champale, Inc., these are no longer in its product line. The Norfolk facility produces only Champale for the southern and southeastern markets.

Champale is designed to minimize head and to appeal to a sweeter palate. All three Champales are intended to resemble champagne more than beer in appearance and taste. It is even packaged in splits to further this image. Golden Champale is a fruitier version of Champale with more body. Pink Champale very closely imitates a pink champagne, a touch of grenadine serving to enchance the color and flavor. The products successfully emulate champagnes and are cost-effective in that role.

Champale is a wholly owned subsidiary of Iroquois Brands, Ltd.

ORIGINAL SPARKLING EXTRA DRY CHAMPALE MALT LIQUOR—pale gold color, grapelike aroma much like an American charmat process champagne, light body, champagnelike bubbles, slightly sweet, grapelike finish. Good cost-effective alternative to champagne.

GOLDEN CHAMPALE FLAVORED MALT LIQUOR—bright golden color, aroma like Juicy Fruit gum, fruit pop flavor like Barr's Irn-Bru of Scotland (Iron Brew in Canada), fairly sweet and very clean taste. Interesting and worth a try.

PINK CHAMPALE FLAVORED MALT LIQUOR—colored a pale pink, aroma like a Cold Duck, mildly flavored sweet taste, slides down easily, very pleasant, good balance.

BLACK HORSE ALE (Black Horse Brewery of New Jersey, Champale, Inc., Trenton N.J., a subsidiary of Iroquois Brands, Ltd.)—cloudy deep yellow-brown color, robust English style, excellent burnt caramel flavor, excellent balance, long pleasing finish. A smooth beer yet one with great character. Best domestic ale tasted and a low-priced bargain. This label sells quite well in the New England and Middle Atlantic states. A Black Horse Ale is also made in upstate New York by the Koch Brewery. A Black Horse Ale was originally seen in Canada and today's U.S. Black Horse may be a descendant of the Black Horse of Dow's of Montreal and Toronto. The Black Horse of Canada was widely marketed in the Northeastern U.S. in the 1940s, and in the 1950s a Black Horse Ale was made at the Diamond Springs Brewery of Lawrence, Massachusetts.

CHERRY HILL PREMIUM BEER (Metropolis of Trenton, N.J.)—dusty vegetal nose, lots of flavor with a good hop-malt balance in the middle, flawed at the end with a bitter finish.

METBREW PREMIUM LIGHT NEAR BEER (Metropolis Brewery of New Jersey, Trenton)—pale gold aroma like the salty edge of the sea, very little flavor, touch of malt and carbonation only, no finish or aftertaste. Nonalcoholic.

METBREW NEAR BEER (Metropolis Brewery of New Jersey, Trenton)—Non alcoholic. Yellow, smoky, sour aroma, high carbonation, sharp malt flavor. Probably a spoiled sample. Renamed *METBRAU* and repackaged in early 1981.

Cold Spring Brewing Co.
(Cold Spring, Minn.)

"Ist Das Nicht Ein Schnitzel Bank? Ja, Das ist Ein Schnitzel Bank!" Or Schweiger Mutter, Grosse Stein, and (of course) Kegle Brau—and so goes the Cold Spring promotional piece.

The Cold Spring Brewing Co. had its origins in a plant constructed by a George (or Michael) Sargel, who began brewing lager beer there in 1874. The business was incorporated by John Oster, Ferdinand Peters, and a Canadian brewmaster named Eugene Hermanutz in 1900. It was reincorporated in 1930, still under the control of the Peters and Oster families. In 1942 Myron C. Johnson was brought in to run the company and two years later he acquired it.

The Cold Spring annual production capacity has grown to 350,000 barrels and its market is primarily in Minnesota, Wisconsin, northern Illinois and Indiana, Iowa, and the Dakotas. The primary brand is Cold Spring Beer, available in both cans and bottles. Another premium beer, Kegle Brau, is marketed in cans and returnable bottles. Kegle, the German word for bowling, ties in with a major Cold Spring promotional effort, "Johnson's Cold Spring 'Kegle' Handicap Bowling Tournament."

Popular-priced brands include Western, White Label, Fox de Luxe, North Star, Karlsbrau, and Gemeinde Brau. Gemeinde (meaning community) is a German-style beer brewed according to an old formula supplied by the Amana Colony of Amana, Iowa. It is a private label owned by Paul Zimmerman of Amana and it is brewed especially for the community. By special arrangement, Gemeinde Brau does have some limited "outside" availability.

In 1979, Cold Spring began producing Kolonie Brau, "brewed for Gemeinde Brau Inc. from an old Amana, Iowa formula." In early 1980 Cold Spring began brewing Cold Spring Export, a highly hopped, pure malt premium lager beer

for national distribution through Merchant du Vin, a national marketing firm specializing in marketing super-premium "boutique" beers.

A number of Cold Spring brands have recently been discontinued. These include Minnesota 13, Northern, Billy, Arrowhead, and Gluek.

In accordance with Minnesota law, beer is available in 3.2 percent and regular (called Strong) alcoholic content. All Cold Spring products sampled were in the Strong category.

COLD SPRING BEER—pale gold, fragrant beery malty aroma, fresh and clean, good malt-hop flavor, carbonation more noticeable in finish than up front.

KEGLE BRAU, THE CLASSIC BEER—gold with a touch of brown, lovely malt and hop aroma, good carbonation level, good flavor, long on the palate, tart finish and aftertaste, lots of character, good complexity, sipping beer.

WHITE LABEL QUALITY LIGHT BEER—medium gold, faint malty apple aroma, clean refreshing malt flavor, like North Star but with less carbonation, touch of sweetness in the finish. White Label was produced previously by White Label Co., Minneapolis, Storz of Omaha, and Kiewel Brewing Co. of Little Falls, Minnesota.

FOX de LUXE BEER—pale gold, nice rich clean beery aroma, carbonation is a bit high and dominates the palate, tangy flavor with a touch of apple peel, long pleasant finish. This label has knocked around the Midwest for some time, made by Fox de Luxe Brewing Co. of Marion, Indiana, and Grand Rapids, Michigan; Fox Head of Waukesha, Wisconsin; Peter Fox Brewing Co. of Chicago; and the Fox head division of G. Heileman, LaCrosse, Wisconsin.

GEMEINDE BRAU—aroma of slightly fermented apples with a pilsenerlike background, very good malty hop, classic pilsener flavor up front but after several sips the taste tends to flatten out and the brew finishes a bit watery.

NORTH STAR XXX BEER—medium gold, clean rich beery aroma, highly carbonated, small bubbles, refreshing, lightly hopped, light body, short finish, a bit watery. North Star is another well-known Midwest label, previously produced by Jacob Schmidt of St. Paul, G. Heileman Co., Mathie Huber Brewing Co. of Wausau, Wisconsin, and Northern Brewing Co. of Superior, Wisconsin.

WESTERN PREMIUM BEER—pale gold, sprightly beery fresh aroma, high carbonation but the flavor comes through, mellow, good malty finish. Western previously was a brand of the Sioux City Brewing Co. and Dakota Brewing Co. of Bismarck, North Dakota.

COLD SPRING EXPORT—medium gold, complex aroma, clean hop flavor with much complexity, like an India Pale Ale without the sharpness, nice tart backtaste, citruslike finish. Tasters found it difficult to describe, but all agreed it was good brew. This product is being marketed nationally by Merchant du Vin, boutique beer specialists.

BILLY BEER—bright gold, sweet malt aroma, light sweet

flavor, a bit like a slightly malty spring water, neutral spring water finish. Tastes like a typical Cold Spring product and certainly a recipe different from that of either the Falls City or the F.X. Matt Billy Beer. Introduced in 1978, discontinued in 1979.

COLD BRAU EASTERN PREMIUM BEER—pale yellow color, light fresh malty aroma, refreshing spring water taste, pleasant, very drinkable, low in hops. This brand belonged to Drewry's of South Bend, Indiana.

GLUEK, FINEST PILSENER BEER—pale gold color, nice "beery" aroma with noticeable hops, well-carbonated, sour flavor with a tangy astringent finish. This was a brand of the Gluek Brewing Co. of Minneapolis (see G. Heileman Brewing Co., Inc.).

NORTHERN BEER (also seen as Northern Premium Beer)—pale gold, faint sweet malt aroma, light sweet malt flavor with a faint sense of hops, a little too sweet. A former

label of the Northern Brewing Co., Superior Wisconsin.

KARLSBRAU OLD TIME BEER—pretty bright gold appearance, sour malt aroma, strong sour flavor, heavily carbonated, lingering sour finish. This label belonged to the Karlsbrau Brewing Co. of Duluth, Minnesota, went to G. Heileman, and thence to Cold Spring (in 1974).

ARROWHEAD BEER—very good sour typical pilsener aroma, good hops and malt, medium dry, clean tasting with a good balanced flavor, pleasant and very drinkable, brief finish.

KOLONIE BRAU (Brewed for Gemeinde Brau, Inc., Amana, Iowa, from an old Amana formula by the Cold Spring Brewing Co.)—pale gold, lovely complex malty aroma, complex flavor of malt and hops, good balance, more malt than hops but the hops show well in the finish and aftertaste.

Adolph Coors Co.
(Golden, Colo.)

If ever a beer had a mystique, it is Coors. The proponents of the beer will go to great lengths (and distances) to obtain it; the opponents sneer derisively and call it Colorado Kool-Aid. Whether you like it or not, the American brewing industry is impressed, for this one product gives Coors the sixth-ranking in sales in the country and is the leading beer in sales in eleven western states.

Coors was founded in Golden in 1873 when the original Adolph Coors and Jacob Schueler converted an old tannery into a brewing plant. When Schueler sold out seven years later, the firm became Adolph Coors Golden Brewery. In 1913 the company was incorporated and today is a very large brewery. Coors had to survive seventeen years of Prohibition as Colorado was the first state to vote dry in 1916. During that period Coors made near-beer, malted milk, buttermilk, and skim milk crystals.

Coors is manufactured using pure Rocky Mountain spring water, Coors' proprietary two-row Moravian III brewing barley, which Coors malts itself, rice (for a lighter body), and hops. The hops are used more for flavoring than for bittering; Coors has been importing a fragrant variety from Germany for that purpose. It hopes eventually to convert to domestic hops because of recent successes in the quality of home-grown hops. Absolutely no additives or corrective salts are used.

Coors' main product is Coors Banquet, packaged in kegs, cans, and bottles. Coors plans to be the first to package beer in plastic bottles if it can develop a method suitable for beer and conducive to high-speed production. A 3.2 percent Coors is also produced for states so regulated. Herman Joseph's 1868 Premium Beer was introduced in 1980 to compete in the super-premium market.

Coors is no longer pasteurized. In 1959 Coors began filling in aseptic conditions, even to the point of sterilizing the air entering the room. The operators of the equipment observe the sterilization technique of a hospital and sterile garments are worn in the filling room. These techniques obviate the need for pasteurization.

The beer, aged for an average of forty-nine days, is chilled throughout the entire production process and emerges in its package very near the freezing point, which aids the distributors in keeping it cold on its way to market.

Coors, however, claims that the brewing and packaging in an aseptic environment, the assurance of refrigeration all the way through until delivery to retail stores and restaurants, tight inventory control on distributors and retailers to ensure fast turnover, and removal of stock more than two months old allow you the confidence to buy Coors beer warm or cold. This "Coors Drinkability Process" supposedly retains brewery fresh taste and Coors says that short periods of warming or chilling and rewarming will not noticeably harm its brews. It does, however, recommend that Coors beers be kept refrigerated "to preserve all the freshness and drinkability."

For many years Coors was available only west

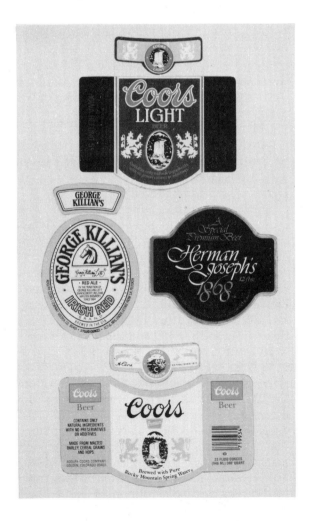

55

of the Mississippi. The company felt it could not profitably market Coors so far from the plant because of the need to maintain a refrigerated condition. In the early 1970s entrepreneurs decided to take advantage of the Coors mystique and truckloads of refrigerated Coors headed for the East Coast where the beer would be sold at unprecedented prices. Eager East Coast buyers gladly laid down $4 or more for a sixpack, many times the price in Colorado; in many instances, the beer was mishandled.

It is understood that Adolph Coors took the matter to court and won his suit to limit the market of Coors to boundaries determined by the company. I view the case and victory for Coors as evidence that it is greatly concerned with making the finest product it can and with assuring its customers that each purchase of Coors is a worthwhile one.

Coors has continued to expand its market to offset sagging sales in the western states where it long held sway. In 1983, eight southeastern states were added, bringing the total to twenty-eight, and increasing sales by 21 percent. In order to more readily reach the vast East Coast markets, Coors has long planned a second brewery in the East. Coors is presently sixth in sales in the nation.

The market expansion appears to be limited to Coors Banquet and Coors Light. Distribution of Herman Joseph's 1868 is still limited. A new full-bodied premium called Golden Lager 1873 was test-marketed in 1983.

COORS BANQUET—very pale color, lovely fresh clean aroma, hops barely noticeable, light-bodied, slightly sweet flavor, very refreshing, very lightly flavored, very quaffable.

COORS LIGHT—pale yellow, very clean aroma, good head, small bubbles, perky clean taste. Very little flavor, slightly salty, like seltzer, very drinkable but not much of a beer, 110 calories.

HERMAN JOSEPH'S 1868 PREMIUM BEER—tawny gold, rich malty talcum aroma with nice hops, light body, clean, fresh and well-balanced flavor of hops and malt, no harsh or unpleasant notes, light but lingering aftertaste. This is definitely going to be a beer to reckon with in the super-premium market. A very fine brew that you must try, introduced in a San Diego test market in 1980-81.

GEORGE KILLIAN IRISH RED ALE—copper red color on the pale side, light toasted malt nose, roasted malt flavor, light body, slightly sweet palate with little duration, fades out at the finish and there is little aftertaste. The recipe for this brew is owned by George Killian Lett of Ireland. It was brewed by his family, the firm of Lett's, at Enniscorthy, County Wexford, Ireland, until 1956. Lett's was the last of the small independent breweries in Ireland. Since that time, it has licensed other brewers to produce its famous red ale (see Pelforth). The Coors version is much lighter than the Pelforth version. It appeared on the market in mid-1981.

GOLDEN LAGER—yellow-gold color, clean malt aroma, very light malt flavor, highly carbonated, fruity-berry tartness in back of palate, light malt aftertaste.

Dixie Brewing Co.
(New Orleans, La.)

Founded in 1903, Dixie maintained a major share of the New Orleans market and was the only independent brewer in New Orleans to survive the onslaught of the large national brewers in the 1960s. Times were tough, however, and Dixie's share of the market was becoming smaller and smaller.

Part of the Dixie plan for the '70s was to renovate its equipment, and in 1975, while a new floor was being laid in the brewhouse as part of the renovations, some phenol leaked into cooling vats in the cellars below contaminating water waiting to be brewed into beer. While not toxic, the contaminated beer was impossible to drink—and it reached stores and taverns for the Fourth of July weekend.

Dixie was slow to recognize and trace the problem and for three weeks replaced bad beer with bad beer. Sales dropped 55 percent and the Dixie image was shattered.

Since that time, Dixie has taken extraordinary measures to prove to stores, taverns, and consumers that the poor image was not deserved. An improved recipe was devised, new equipment installed, old equipment repaired and renovated, and the biggest giveaway campaign in brewing history was launched. First, 60,000 sixpacks were given away on a single weekend, then six months later another 94,000 sixpacks were given away via a newspaper coupon. In 1978 sales began to pick up. Dixie continued to offer "cents off" coupons and sales are booming. In 1982, 139,000 barrels were sold to meet increasing demand.

Dixie produces Beer, Lager, and Light and a number of private labels under the corporate name of the Royal Brewing Co. Most of these are grocery store brands like K&B, Schwegmann, Mr. Thrifty, and Golden Brau. All are marketed in the vicinity of New Orleans and rarely seen elsewhere. Dixie brews good beers and consumers in its marketing area should give them a try. They are bargains.

DIXIE BEER—medium gold, hop and sour malt aroma, hop flavor with metallic finish.

DIXIE LAGER—pale copper gold, lightly hopped sour malt aroma, light body, very tasty smooth hoppy flavor, neutral finish. A good brew and leads one to suspect that the Dixie Beer sample was not a good one.

DIXIE LIGHT BEER—brilliant pale gold, fragrant yeasty-malty aroma, salty malt flavor, small bubble carbonation, slight hops in the finish.

DIXIE LIGHT LIGHT LIGHT BEER—pale gold, yeasty aroma, faintly salty beer flavor, small bubble carbonation, light but not watery, touch of sour metal in the finish. Probably the same as Dixie Light.

K&B PILSENLAGER BEER (brewed exclusively for Super Distributors, New Orleans, by Royal Brewing Co.)—billed as a "special blend of Pilsner and Lager Beer" (an interesting concept since they have the same definition), pale gold, yeasty-beery-malty aroma, pleasant, a bit watery, sweet malt flavor, slightly salty, small bubble carbonation, virtually no finish and aftertaste.

SCHWEGMANN PREMIUM LIGHT LAGER BEER (brewed exclusively in New Orleans for Schwegmann Brothers Giant Super Markets by Royal Brewing Co.)—pale gold, yeasty-malty-beery aroma, similar to K&B but less flavor, small bubble carbonation, faint sweet finish, no aftertaste.

ROCK & ROLL BEER (Brewed for Rock & Roll Beer Co., St. Louis)—yellow, beautiful clean sweet malt aroma, creamy head, light-flavored but very tasty, no aftertaste.

Eastern Brewing Corp.
(Hammonton, N.J.)

If brewery size was based on the number of brands produced rather than by annual sales, Eastern would be somewhere high in the top ten. Located in the southern New Jersey pine barrens, this company produces a wide variety of brands obtained from defunct brewing firms over a wide area, plus many of the private labels marketed today. Some are marketed in Eastern's home state, but many are also marketed elsewhere and rarely seen in New Jersey. Should you try to seek them out, your task will be further complicated by their use of various corporate names on the packages.

ABC PREMIUM BEER (Garden State Brewing Co.)—fresh clean malty aroma, very light flavor but with some hop

character, yeasty finish, a delightful beer at a very low price. Previously produced by the August Wagner Brewing Co. of Columbus, Ohio, and the Gold Brau Brewing Co. of Chicago, this product appears now to be made for the ABC chain of liquor stores in Florida. It has been seen only in Florida, except for outlets specializing in sales of "odd" brands, perhaps for can collectors. The can design of ABC is identical to Gold Brau Brewing's 905 brand of twenty years ago, with the ABC replacing the 905. It is possible that it may be the same recipe as well.

ABC PREMIUM EXTRA DRY ALE (Garden State Brewing Co.)—supposedly slow-brewed according to the label, this is a pale clear brew, highly carbonated with small bubbles, with a faint applelike aroma and a light sweet malty flavor, totally harmless. Again, only seen in Florida. The Garden State name may have originated with the Garden State Brewing Co. of Belleville, New Jersey.

BILOW GARDEN STATE LIGHT BEER (Garden State Brewing Co.)—a cereal noselike Pablum (does anybody remember Pablum?), grainy cereal-barley taste with a very brief finish and no aftertaste. This beer was originally produced for the Bilow Liquor Stores chain in Monmouth County, New Jersey, but is no longer.

BLANCHARD'S QUALITY PRODUCT BEER (Waukee Brewing Co.)—light malty nose, clean and light malty taste and finish, maybe with some hops if you think about it hard enough; no zest, no character. This must be what people mean when they speak of computerized beer—no zest, no faults, no anything. Made for Blanchard's Liquor Stores of

the Greater Boston area. There was also an Eastern product made for the Kappy's chain of liquor stores in Massachusetts that tasted like this brew, called Kappy's Premium Light Beer. Both are now being produced by Falstaff.

CANADIAN ACE BRAND PREMIUM BEER (Canadian Ace Brewing Co.)—very fragrant and malty, light sweet flavor, some hops noticeable in the finish. Reasonably good taste for an inexpensive beer. Seen recently only in half-gallon throwaway bottles with screw caps. This is the former product of Al Capone's Chicago brewery which operated as the Canadian Ace Brewing Co. of Chicago from 1948 to 1968, having succeeded the Chicago crime syndicate's famous Manhattan Brewing Co.

CANADIAN ACE DRAFT BEER (Canadian Ace Brewing Co.)—very fragrant aroma but virtually no flavor at all, very foamy. This has also only been seen in half-gallon NR bottles. Both Canadian Ace products have been seen in New York, New Jersey, and New England.

DAWSON LAGER BEER (Dawson Brewing Co.)—strange chemical aroma with an oily "off" flavor. Presuming a bad bottle, I obtained additional lots in both cans and bottles. The results were better but there was a chemical element to the nose and the taste was poorly balanced. This brew is marketed primarily in New England where it was originally produced by the Dawson Brewing Co. of New Bedford, Massachusetts, and taken over by Rheingold in 1967. Later, Dawson was produced under the Dawson corporate name in Willimansett, Massachusetts, at the Hampden-Harvard-Drewry's-Piels Bros. plant.

DAWSON SPARKLING ALE (Dawson Brewing Co.)—light gold, yeasty-bready, light malt aroma, light and watery, very little flavor, faintly yeasty finish.

FOXHEAD 400 BEER (Foxhead Brewing Co.)—pleasant malt aroma, good beery nose, good taste with zest and very good balance, an inexpensive good-tasting beer that is a super value. Very good with Chinese food. This product probably originated with the Fox-Head Waukesha Corp. of Waukesha, Wisconsin, then produced by Heileman at Sheboygan and by Wiedemann (for Heileman) at Newport, Kentucky.

FOXHEAD 400 DRAFT BREWED BEER (Foxhead Brewing Co.)—pale and clear, light clean malty aroma, very little flavor, mostly just light carbonation.

MILWAUKEE BRAND PREMIUM BEER (Waukee Brewing Co.)—a very cereal aroma, again like Pablum, but very light; flavor also cereallike and light in intensity, with a brief finish. A dull beer.

MILWAUKEE BRAND PREMIUM BEER (Waukee Brewing Co.)—5 percent version for export to Israel. Medium gold color, malty aroma, good snappy flavor, small bubble carbonation, well-balanced palate, dull finish, sweet aftertaste.

MILWAUKEE BRAND CREAM ALE (Waukee Brewing Co.)—pale gold, yeasty aroma, yeasty malty flavor, carbonation dominates finish. A little too sweet.

MILWAUKEE MALT TONIC (Waukee Brewing Co.)—cloudy gold, extremely faint aroma, slightly sweet applelike and carbonation taste like a French cider (but weaker), no finish or aftertaste. Nonalcoholic.

OLD BOHEMIAN BEER (Eastern Brewing Co.)—slightly sour vegetal malt aroma, slightly sweet taste, brief metallic finish and aftertaste. The Old Bohemia product line is available in New York, New Jersey, Pennsylvania, but its greatest market is in Maryland, Delaware, and the District of Columbia, where it is sold at a low price.

OLD BOHEMIAN ALE—clean malty aroma, light yeasty cardboard flavor, neutral watery finish.

OLD BOHEMIAN LIGHT BEER—pleasant sweet nose, too sweet, metallic flavor, dull finish, very foamy.

OLD BOHEMIAN BOCK BEER—tawny brown color without much saturation, faint burnt malt aroma, hardly any flavor at all, just brown colored water.

OLD GERMAN BRAND BEER (Eastern Brewing Corp.)—no aroma and no palate sensation other than carbonation. This is available in the greater New York–Philadelphia area at a low price, which is all that it is worth, if that. There used to be an Old German Brand Ale, but it is no longer available. At times, Old German Brand Beer was produced using the Colonial Brewing Co. corporate name.

OLD GERMAN MALT BEVERAGE (Eastern Brewing Corp.)—nonalcoholic. Pale yellow color, high carbonation, faint malty aroma, thin body, sour finish, no aftertaste. Could not tell that it was nonalcoholic.

MILWAUKEE BOCK BEER (Waukee Brewing Co.)—opaque brown, sourness briefly in an otherwise faint aroma, brief burnt malt flavor, and no follow-through.

HEDRICK LAGER BEER (Hedrick Brewing Co.)—cloudy tawny gold, faint malt aroma, light grainy flavor, little finish, less aftertaste. An old brand from the Albany area made by the Hedrick Brewing Co., Inc. (which closed in 1966), successor to J. F. Hedrick (1852-91). In the late 60s it was made by Piel Bros. at Willimansett, Mass.

FINAST BEER (Eastern)—tawny gold with age, faint grainy-yeasty aroma, more malt than hops, light grainy flavor, light finish and aftertaste. Produced for First National grocery stores.

GRAND UNION BEER (Eastern)—pale gold, malty yeasty aroma, light grainy malty flavor, light-bodied, light finish, faint grainy aftertaste. Made for Grand Union grocery stores.

STANDARD DRY ALE (Eastern)—cloudy yellow-gold, light body, woodpulp overrides the malt and hops of the aroma and flavor, oxidized, a brew that was overaged but which still showed some character. This brand was the mainstay of the Standard Brewing Co. of Rochester, New York, which was also called the Standard-Rochester Brewing Co. It closed in 1970.

POLAR CERVEZA PREMIUM QUALITY PILSNER (Polar Brewing Co.)—faint peppery aroma, coffee taste with a faint metallic background, a strange beer indeed. The *Cerveza* would indicate that this beer is marketed for a Hispanic area. The package resembles a popular

Venezuelan product with the same name.

SHOPWELL PREMIUM BEER (Colonial Brewing Co.)—unpleasant "wet-dog" aroma, flat with no taste. Thought to be the result of a bad can, several more samples were tried. Although none was as bad as the first, the poor aroma apparently is a regular feature. In better samples the flavor was slightly malty with faint sourness and a sense of metal, but the beer is definitely on the flat side and very dull. This beer is made for Daitch Crystal Dairies, Inc. of New York City, operators of the Daitch Shopwell grocery chain.

TOPPER LIGHT DRY PILSENER (Eastern Brewing Co.)—big malty aroma, water taste, "off" sour-tinny finish, tinny aftertaste. This was a brand of the Standard-Rochester Brewing Co., Rochester, New York, which shut down in 1970. The label has been seen in New York, Pennsylvania, and, occasionally, New Jersey.

NUDE BEER—pale gold, light sweet nose with a little yeast, light watery flavor, but not much to it. Label features a nude woman with a bra that can be scratched off. Introduced in Maryland, Tennessee, and Pennsylvania in early 1983.

STEINBRAU MALT BEVERAGE (Eastern Brewing Co.)—near-beer with a bready aroma and a sour taste.

STEINBRAU LIGHT MALT BEVERAGE (Eastern Brewing Corp.)—nonalcoholic, 58 calories, medium gold color, aroma of wood pulp and sour-decayed malt, flavor mostly carbonation, little more than carbonated water, brief malt taste at end.

CAPRUS AMERICAN MALT TONIC (Eastern Brewing Co. for AlJishi Trading and Development Stores, Damman, Saudi Arabia)—gold color, very grainy aroma, slightly skunky, very malty cereal taste, watery finish. Nonalcoholic.

HARRY'S WHITE LABEL MALTA (Colonial Brewing Co.)—nonalcoholic, vitamin B-complex added. Deep brown, deeply saturated with red tones, thick and foamy, heavy malty molasses aroma, heavy sweet malt flavor, flabby, long finish.

TRI-STAR NON-ALCOHOLIC BEVERAGE (Eastern Brewing Co.)—golden color, light perfumy rose water aroma, touch of skunkiness, malty rose water flavor, noticeable (obtrusive) carbonation, no aftertaste.

CAPE COD BEER—medium deep gold, faint sweet grainy aroma, slightly oxidized, palate same as aroma, little finish, no aftertaste.

Other Eastern products previously produced, but not seen lately, are: Cee Bee Pilsner Beer (Colonial), Dart Drug Gold Medal (Eastern) made for Dart Drugstores of Maryland and Virginia, Fischer's Old German Style Ale (Fischer) (see Duncan Brewing Co.), Markmeister (Eastern), and Wilco Premium Beer (Colonial) produced for the Roger Wilco liquor stores of the Camden, New Jersey area.

Falstaff Brewing Corp.
(Fort Wayne, Ind.; Omaha, Nebr.)

The Griesedieck family had been long identified with brewing, malting, and liquor industries in St. Louis and the Falstaff Brewing Co. has roots in two branches of the Griesedieck family.

"Papa Joe" Griesedieck purchased the Forest Park Brewing Co. in 1917 and formed the Griesedieck Brewing Co., which was to become the Falstaff Corporation during Prohibition. The

Falstaff name, from Shakespeare's comic character Sir John Falstaff, was obtained from the William J. Lemp Brewing Co., which had made the beer for many years (Lemp was an old company dating back to 1840 and was perhaps the first "national" brewer, being the first to ship its products outside its local regional market area).

Falstaff survived Prohibition making near-beer, soda pop, and smoked hams. When brewing was again legalized in 1933, the Falstaff Brewing Co. obtained Permit No. 1. Falstaff was one of the first brewers to expand, beginning in 1935 with the purchase of the Fred Krug Brewery in Omaha; in 1937 the National Brewery of New Orleans was obtained; World War II delayed further efforts. After the war the Berghoff Brewing Co. plant in Fort Wayne was purchased (with the Berghoff label going to the Walter Co. of Pueblo, Colo.), the Galveston-Houston Brewing Co. plant was acquired, and most recently (1965), the Narrangansett Brewing Co. of Cranston, R.I., was obtained, which thrust Falstaff firmly into the New England market. The Ballantine brands were obtained by Falstaff in 1972, but the Newark, New Jersey, plant was closed. The original St. Louis plant was closed in 1977, the New Orleans brewery closed in 1979, and the Cranston and Galveston plants were shut down in 1982.

Falstaff has operated other plants during the past decade; all are now closed. There were two plants in California, at San Francisco and San Jose. The San Francisco plant was the old Milwaukee Brewery, operated by the San Francisco Brewing Co. and the Burgermeister Brewing Co. before being obtained by Falstaff. The San Jose plant was formerly run by the Pacific Brewing Co., and later by the Wielands Brewing Co. Falstaff also operated the former Harry Mitchell Brewing Co. plant in El Paso, Texas.

Falstaff today is part of the "empire" of breweries owned by Paul Kalmanovitz of San Francisco, along with General and Pearl. Recently Falstaff has been supplying grocery store chains with "unbranded" beer. They may appear with a minimum descriptor like "Beer," which is as straightforward as you can get, Value Time Beer (for a grocery chain in California), or Scotch Buy (for Safeway stores). Falstaff also

produces low-calorie beers for these outlets. Additionally, Falstaff produces private labels, some competing with its own generics. Falstaff ranks ninth in sales among American brewers with a 3.2 million barrel annual output.

FALSTAFF BEER—light yellow color, fairly rich malty aroma, clean fresh malty flavor with some hops, a good average American beer, perhaps slightly better than average. Pleasant throughout with a good finish, but frequently overcarbonated.

FALSTAFF FINE LIGHT BEER—pale color, light dank swampy nose, slightly bitter flat taste, not very good at all.

FALSTAFF 96 EXTRA LIGHT BEER—96 calories, pale color, aroma of yeast and malt, flavor more yeasty than malty with a little sweetness in back, no noticeable hop flavor, watery-yeasty finish, very little aftertaste.

OLD HEIDEL BRAU LAGER (brewed for the Walgreen Co., Deerfield, Ill., by the Great Lakes Brewing Co., Fort Wayne, Ind.; a private label of Walgreen Drugs of the Washington, D.C., area)—vegetal-malt aroma, thin body, brief taste with no complexity, short finish, no aftertaste.

PULASKI PIVO (brewed fro Pulaski Pivo, Inc., Bay City, Michigan by Great Lakes Brewing Co., Ft. Wayne, In.)—supposedly "brewed in the Polish-American tradition," it is pale gold, has a sweet yeasty aroma, sweet malty flavor, and overall has little character.

DOUBLE K BEER (Great Lakes Brewing Co.)—pale color, yeasty malty aroma, slightly sweet and malty flavor, somewhat watery, little aftertaste. A Cincinnati private label.

GB LIGHT LAGER BEER (Griesedieck Bros. Brewing Co.)—pale gold, sweet yeasty aroma, malty flavor, fairly dry, little character.

TIME SAVER PREMIUM BEER (brewed in New Orleans exclusively for Time Saver by James Hanley Co., New Orleans)—clean pale gold, excellent malty nose with good hop balance, bright hoppy flavor, a little alelike taste but soft, salt-sweet finish, good complex brew, balance off just a touch. Time Saver was also brewed in recent times by Royal Brewing Co. (see Dixie).

KREWERS—pale gold, good malty-grainy-yeasty aroma, on the sweet side, medium body. Creamy malty flavor with some hops in back, hops show in the finish, a good-finish beer. Brewed exclusively for National Canal Villere Supermarkets by Falstaff in New Orleans.

KATZ PREMIUM BEER (James Hanley Co., St. Louis, Mo.)—pale gold, fairly clean malty aroma, clean sweet grainy flavor, highly carbonated, sweet malt finish and aftertaste.

SCOTCH BUY BEER—pale yellow, light malty and hop aroma, good hop flavor with some complexity, tasty hop and malt finish and aftertaste. Made for Safeway Stores.

SCOTCH BUY LIGHT BEER—pale yellow, light malt and hop aroma, lightly flavored, but hops are detectable, fairly clean and tasty with hops and malt showing in the finish, decent for an inexpensive low-calorie brew.

ULTRA-LIGHT PREMIUM BEER—brilliant pale yellow, fresh malt aroma, very little fresh malty flavor, creamy texture, small bubble CO_2; somewhat watery, grainy finish and aftertaste. Contains only 89 calories and 2.8 grams of carbohydrate. Logo very much like Pittsburgh brew of the same name. Disappeared from the market at the time Falstaff Lite appeared and since they have the same calorie and carbohydrate content, they may be the same beer.

FALSTAFF LITE BEER—pale yellow, fresh malty aroma, small bubble carbonation, light malt aroma, little zest beyond the CO_2; grainy, watery finish, little aftertaste. 89 calories and 2.8 grams of carbohydrate.

Lucky Lager Brewing Co. *(San Francisco et al.)*

Through its association with General, Falstaff produces a selection of the Lucky line of beers and several of General Brewing Company's other brands as well. Lucky products have seen many home breweries over the past years including ones in Ogden, Utah (the former Fisher Brewing Co. plant operated by Lucky), and Pueblo, Colorado (by the Walter Brewing Co.).

LUCKY LAGER BEER (since 1934)—complex and interesting, a sort of vanilla-cream soda nose that was reflected in the flavor, would be quite good except that it is a little too sweet. Although it would be better if it were drier, it is pleasant tasting and quite refreshing and will seem very good to some palates.

LUCKY BOCK BEER—dark brown color but with little saturation, malty sweet aroma, no faults or high points in the flavor, sweet dull finish, well carbonated.

BREW 102 PALE DRY BEER—supposedly perfected after 101 brews, this beer is very pale yellow, has a clean pleasant fresh aroma with a sweet background, a pleasant slightly sweet flavor and a pleasing aftertaste. Could be a little drier, but is quite good and very drinkable. This is a former brand of Maier of Los Angeles and is now owned by General.

LUCKY LITE—bright pale gold, very faint aroma, faint grainy taste, no finish, no aftertaste, mostly just CO_2.

Christian Feigenspan, Inc. *(Newark, N.J.)*

Feigenspan was a famous East Coast brewing name. A privately-owned corporation, Feigenspan began in Newark shortly before the turn of the twentieth century with the purchase of the old Charles Kolb brewery. Later, control was gained of the Dobler Brewing Co. of Albany, New York, and the Yale Brewing Co. of New Haven, Connecticut. By 1939 its lead brand, Pride of Newark, was the largest-selling ale in

New York City. In 1944 it was bought out by P. Ballantine & Sons. The Yale Brewery had not opened after Prohibition, but Dobler brand names continued into the 1960s, being produced by Piels at Willimansett, Massachusetts. Ballantine reactivated the Feigenspan name in the 1960s as the brewery of record for Munich beer. Falstaff continued the Feigenspan name on the Munich label with Galveston, Fort Wayne, and, most recently, Cranston as the origin.

MUNICH LIGHT LAGER BEER—pale color, light malty nose, very light barely hopped flavor, light body, no faults except for its lightness, inoffensive and could be consumed in quantity, better than average domestic lightweight beer, not noticeably like a Munich beer in style.

BLANCHARD'S PREMIUM QUALITY BEER—medium gold, dull-malty aroma, sour unbalanced taste, slightly bitter finish. Private label of Blanchard's liquor stores of the Boston area. Previously supplied by Eastern Brewing Corp.

KAPPY'S PREMIUM QUALITY BEER—bright gold, malty aroma, sour and sharp on palate, sour finish, sweet aftertaste. Private label of Kappy's liquor stores in the greater Boston area. Previously supplied by Eastern Brewing Corp.

P. Ballantine & Sons *(Newark, N.J.)*

Peter Ballantine started his brewing business in Albany, New York, in 1833 with a plant designed for making ale. In 1840 he moved the business to Newark where he leased (from Morton Bros. Brewers) the brewery founded by Gen. John N. Cumming in 1805. Recognizing that the new, lighter lager brew was rapidly becoming popular, Ballantine built a lager beer brewery nearby under the name of Ballantine & Company. By the 1880s Ballantine brewing plants had covered twelve acres.

Ballantine maintained its popularity in the greater New York City area and after Prohibition survived for many years. The Ballantine three-ring sign was widely seen and Ballantine beers sold well, probably because it was a major radio sponsor of the New York Yankees; no other team elicited more interest than the Yankees of the late 1940s and 1950s.

Ballantine produced beer, ale, bock beer, and a fine India pale ale. The last is an authentic India pale ale, made from a recipe used in the nineteenth century in England for beer sent to the military forces in India. Since this beer had to travel for many months on a sailing vessel in

61

equatorial waters, it had to be long-brewed and long-aged, otherwise it would perish before it reached its customers far away on remote Indian outposts. It is a strong beer with all the gusto that other beers only claim. It may be too intense for your palate, but you owe it to yourself to try it before it, like most others of its type, vanishes in favor of thin, watery, flavorless beers whose only noticeable feature is overcarbonation.

BALLANTINE PREMIUM LAGER BEER—light gold color, clean malty fresh aroma, clean fresh light flavor, medium body, pleasant tasting, lightly hopped, and quite refreshing.

BALLANTINE XXX ALE—deep gold color, yeasty-malty nose, big body, strong flavor with lots of bite, may be a bit much for those who aren't used to strong ale flavor. Those who like their beer strong will love this one, but for most palates there is an overabundance of hops for the level of malt.

BALLANTINE DRAFT BREWED BEER—pale color, flowery aroma of malt, hearty malty flavor, foamy, finish is mostly just carbonation, faint metallic aftertaste. Found in Florida, not seen elsewhere lately.

BALLANTINE BOCK BEER—brown color with little saturation, apple-teaberry aroma, dull taste with a fairly sweet finish and aftertaste, not very interesting.

BALLANTINE INDIA PALE ALE (since 1890)—deep brown gold, pungent aroma of hops, enormous body for a beer, powerful flavor yet with surprisingly good balance, taste very slightly on the sour side; long, long finish, lingering full-flavored aftertaste. This beer is unquestionably long-aged, maybe even in wood, and it shows in the flavor. It may be too intense for many people, but if you claim to be a beer drinker, you should at least try it.

BREWER'S GOLD PREMIUM ALE (P. Ballantine, Cranston, R.I.)—deep tawny gold, visible body, initially a skunky aroma, but this cleared quickly to sweet malt, strong well-hopped sweet ale flavor, very tangy with good duration, a hefty satisfying brew with a good hoppy finish and aftertaste.

BALLANTINE LIGHT LAGER BEER—89 calories, 2.8 grams of carbohydrate, bright gold, aroma is slightly grapy (wild Concord), palate is mostly CO_2, faint sweetness in back, pleasant but not exciting.

G. Krueger Brewing Co. (*Newark, N.J.*) In 1865 Gottfried Krueger and Gottfried Hill purchased the small brewery of Laibel & Adam and organized the firm of Hill and Krueger. By 1875, when Hill retired, the annual output of the brewery was 25,000 barrels. By 1889, when the firm was incorporated and sons John F. and Gottfried C. joined the business, annual production had reached 150,000 barrels.

Following Prohibition, Krueger reopened and gained the distinction of being the first firm to package beer in a can, a flat top Krueger Cream Ale issued in January, 1935. Krueger itself survived only a few short years after this achievement, however, with the Krueger brands being produced in Cranston, Rhode Island, license having been obtained by the Narrangansett Brewing Co.

KRUEGER BEER (since 1858)—pale color, good well-hopped nose, hops slightly dominate the flavor, medium body, quite a bit of character, sour malt in the middle, light finish. A good beer, better than average.

KRUEGER PILSENER BEER (during the period 1977–1980 this brew was renamed Krueger Light Beer)—very pale color, light flavor but good balance between the malt and the hops, no offensive features, pleasant, satisfying and clean tasting refreshing brew. One of the best lightly flavored beers. The 1977–1980 name change was apparently instituted to provide a means of competing in the "light" market without actually going to the trouble to put out a new beer.

KRUEGER CREAM ALE—sweet aroma, sour malty taste, bitter and perfumy. Not much to recommend this product. It has been seen only in large nonreturnable bottles, mostly in New England.

Narragansett Brewing Co. (*Cranston, R.I.*) With funds from his successful butterine (a predecessor of margarine) plant in Providence, Rhode Island, German immigrant John Fehlberg convinced Messrs Borchardt, Gerhard, Wertz, and Moeller to join with him to incorporate as the Narragansett Brewing Co. in 1890 and build a large brewery on a 23-acre tract in the Arlington section of Cranston. Following

Prohibition, Narragansett enjoyed modest success in New England. Narragansett began canning beer in June 1936 and was the first to do so in large volume. With its sponsorship of the Boston Red Sox, which became a New England institution in the 1940s, the Narragansett beers began to sell successfully all over the six-state area.

"Hi, neighbor, have a 'Gansett" and an accompanying song heralded the start of each Red Sox game on radio and TV and generations of New England youth waited until they would be old enough to do so. In the mid-1960s Narragansett purchased the Haffenreffer labels. Haffenreffer was an old Boston firm dating back to 1890, with a famous brewing family background. Falstaff bought out Narragansett in 1965.

NARRAGANSETT LAGER BEER—brilliant gold, malty aroma, medium body, flavor mostly malt, a little too light on the hops but still reasonably good, an average American pilsener-type beer.

NARRAGANSETT 96 EXTRA LIGHT BEER—96 calories, pleasant malty beery aroma, faintly sweet up front in the taste, at the end the sensation is like having just drunk a glass of spring water. Very light but refreshing and pleasant. One of the better low-calorie beers.

NARRAGANSETT EXTRA LIGHT CREAM ALE—medium gold, faint malty aroma with good hop balance, salty and harsh on the palate, unbalanced.

NARRAGANSETT PORTER—deep orange brown, clean light malty nose, very clean light flavor that is slightly sweet at the finish, hops show in the aftertaste.

CROFT PREMIUM QUALITY ALE (Croft Brewing Co.)—very light aroma of faint malt, sweet aromatic creamy taste. From 1937 to 1954 this brew has been named Croft Cream Ale, Champion Ale, and Banquet Ale.

BOH BOHEMIAN LAGER BEER (Haffenreffer Brewing Co.)—pale color, very faint malty aroma, almost no nose at all, no taste on the front of the tongue, lingering metallic finish. This label originated with the Enterprise Brewing Co. (Old Colony Brewery) of Fall River, Massachusetts. The Haffenreffer family had been the active force behind this business and when it closed in 1963 the brand was obtained by Haffenreffer.

HAFFENREFFER PRIVATE STOCK MALT LIQUOR (Narragansett Brewing Co.) (since 1870)—skunky aroma, lightly flavored for a malt liquor, very soft on the palate with a mostly malty flavor, light for a malt liquor.

HAFFENREFFER LAGER BEER (Haffenreffer Brewing Co.)—weak in aroma and body, very lightly flavored, has no real faults but also lacks zest, a slightly better than average light-flavored domestic brew.

PICKWICK ALE (Haffenreffer Brewing Co.)—intense yeasty aroma, soapy taste, creamy and foamy on the palate. This ale appeared in the late 1950s and was billed as "the only blend of lager beer, light ale, and malt liquor ever canned in the U.S." It is packaged only in returnable bottles today.

HANLEY LAGER BEER—gold, foamy, sweet yeasty aroma, medium body, sweet malty-yeasty flavor, CO_2 aftertaste, sweet finish, creamy and quaffable. This label originated with James Hanley & Co. of Providence, Rhode Island.

BEER—pale color, fairly pleasant malty aroma, faint touch of hops, lightly flavored with only a little hop background, medium to high CO_2, a little malty sweetness in the finish. This sample was a can from the Cranston Brewery (Narragansett Brewing Co.). It has also been seen on the West Coast with a similar logo on bottles produced by the General Brewing Co. of Vancouver, Washington, a Falstaff affiliate.

HOF-BRAU LAGER BEER—clear golden yellow, mild hops in the nose, pleasant malt and hop flavor, tinny sourness in the finish, long dry aftertaste not marred by the tinny nature of the finish.

4077TH MASH BEER (Hanley Brewing Co.)—pale gold, light but pleasant malt and hop aroma, bright slightly sweet flavor, finishes dry, brief aftertaste.

Franklin Brewing Co.
(Emeryville, Calif.)

TAMALPAIS PREMIUM DARK BEER—deep brown, almost opaque, natural small bubble carbonation, huge complex grainy aroma with a spicy background, good body, roast malt flavor with a smoky charcoal character (a lot like a Lapsang Suchong tea) and a complex sweetness, very long on the palate and finishes dry. Beautiful sipping beer. Tamalpais is not pasteurized.

General Brewing Co.
(Vancouver, Wash.)

The origins of this firm can be traced to 1858, to a small brewery in Victoria, Vancouver, Canada, from which evolved Lucky Lager Breweries, Ltd. of Canada and the Lucky Lager Brewing Co. in the United States with plants in Vancouver, San Francisco, and Azusa, California. Lucky Lager was a popular West Coast brew for over a half-century and a consistent winner of gold medals at international competitions.

The Lucky plant in Azusa was sold to the Miller Brewing Co. and the Los Angeles plant of the Maier Brewing Co. became part of the firm, renamed the General Brewing Co. in 1963. The old Maier plant is no longer included in General's operations, but most of the Maier labels are still marketed, mainly in California. The San Francisco plant was closed in 1979.

In 1958, when Labatt Breweries of Canada acquired Lucky Lager Breweries, it also acquired a 47 percent interest in Lucky Breweries, Inc. This interest was sold in 1971 to Paul Kalmanovitz. During Labatt ownership, General introduced California-brewed Labatt labels on the West Coast.

In recent years General has marketed a wide variety of brands, including Alpine, Amber Brau, Weiss Bavarian, Bohemian Pilsener, Brau Haus, Brown Derby, Bulldog Malt Liquor, Edelbrau, Fisher, Golden Crown, Golden Harvest, Hofbrau, Keg, Padre, Regal Select, Reidenbach, Spring, Steinbrau Beer, Velvet Glow, Brew 102, and the Lucky Lager line which is produced by General's associate, Falstaff, for the market east of the Rockies. Lucky Lager had earlier been produced by the Walter Brewing Co. of Pueblo, Colorado, and the Interstate Brewing Co., Lucky Lager Brewing Co., and Lucky Breweries, Inc. of Vancouver.

Can and label collectors can obtain items from the General product line (and some Falstaff) from ESP, Inc., 1629 Vancouver Way, Livermore, California 94550.

LUCKY LAGER BEER—pale gold, mild malt and hop aroma, grainy cereal taste that starts out slightly sour and ends sweet, clean aftertaste.

LUCKY DRAFT BEER—big malty nose with hops in the background, slightly sour grainy taste, high carbonation, a little sweetness in the finish, good balance, very drinkable. Label claims that freshness and clarity come from a double Swiss and Microfil filtration process.

LUCKY BOCK BEER—dark color, no aroma, thin body, slightly sweet flavor, but most of the palate sensation is carbonation.

LUCKY 96 EXTRA LIGHT BEER—foamy, lovely malt aroma, very light faint malty flavor, very little finish and aftertaste.

REIDENBACH PREMIUM PALE DRY BEER—faint perfumy malt aroma, overly sweet flabby weak taste, dull neutral finish.

ECONO BUY BEER—pale gold, pleasant grainy aroma, light grainy-malty flavor, clean and refreshing, slightly sour malty finish and aftertaste.

FISHER LAGER BEER—pale cloudy yellow, nice malty-beery aroma, light body, light malty flavor but mostly the palate is carbon dioxide, little finish, less aftertaste.

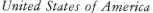

SPRING LAGER BEER—pale tawny yellow, slightly cloudy, a sensation of faint toasted malt in the nose, thin slightly sour vegetal background to a palate that is mostly CO_2, faint malt finish and aftertaste. This brand originated with the Silver Spring Brewing Co. of Tacoma, Washington, which closed in 1968.

BROWN DERBY LAGER BEER—clear pale gold, very little aroma, faint malt flavor, pleasant finish. Brown Derby is brewed for Safeway Food Stores in California. The brand has been produced by many brewers since it appeared in 1933. (See Pittsburgh.)

BROWN DERBY LIGHT BEER—96 calories, slightly cloudy gold, pleasant sweet hop and malt aroma, slightly flat, good pleasant hoppy flavor, touch of sour in the finish. One of the best lo-cal brews.

BOHEMIAN PILSNER LIGHT BEER—slightly cloudy golden yellow, lovely malt nose with slight vegetal background and good hop balance, pleasant malty-hop "beery" flavor with good character and complexity, soft and light but not dull, malty finish, fairly long aftertaste. Really good brew.

KEG BRAND NATURAL FLAVOR BEER—big malty nose, high carbonation, only quality in the middle is astringency, flavor is lacking until the finish, slight bitterness at the end. Originally a Maier label.

PADRE PALE LAGER BEER—pale gold, mild beery aroma, some slight hop character, low carbonation, light sour hop flavor, only slightly malty, lightly hopped finish. Originally a Maier label.

BREW 102 PALE DRY BEER—very pale gold, mild beery aroma, light malt flavor, well-carbonated, some zest, a little on the salty side, short finish. Another Maier label.

DE LIGHT BREW MALT BEVERAGE—55 calories, nonalcoholic, deep yellow, slightly cloudy, cereal aroma and flavor, weak and watery.

REGAL SELECT LIGHT BEER—gold color, malt aroma with a sweet background, apple peel flavor, medium dry, pleasant brew. When over age, it takes on a character of toasted malt that is quite good. Label says "Recognized as one of America's two great beers," a claim perhaps more humorous than pretentious when you consider the implication. Another former Maier brand.

LUCKY 50 EXTRA LIGHT BEER—64 calories, pale gold, lovely malt aroma, highly carbonated, light body, grainy finish, no hops on palate, light malty and yeasty aftertaste.

BEER—pale yellow, slight malt aroma, very light malt flavor, nothing much to it. Distributed by Ralph's Grocery Co., Los Angeles.

Pearl Brewing Co. *(San Antonio, Tex.)* In 1885 a group of leading San Antonio citizens purchased the City Brewery, a small brewing plant located on the site of the present Pearl Brewery. They formed the San Antonio Brewing Association and appointed Otto Koehler as manager.

An established beer formula was purchased from the Kaiser-Beck Brewery of Bremen, Germany, with rights to the product name. The actual name was *Perle,* a German word for the little pearllike bubbles, or *perlens* that would rise in a freshly poured glass of the brew.

By 1916 Pearl had become the largest brewery in Texas. Even though Prohibition did not become law until the 18th Amendment was ratified in 1920, Pearl had problems beginning with America's entry into World War I and the Food Control Act, which essentially cut off the brewer's supply of grain. Pearl survived until repeal as a creamery, ice plant, sign company, and soft drink bottler. Pearl was ready to go upon repeal and fifteen minutes after Prohibition officially ended, more than one hundred trucks and twenty-five boxcars loaded with Pearl Beer rolled out of the brewery's grounds, down a street loaded with cheering crowds.

Up to 1952 Pearl was known as the San Antonio Brewing Co. and labels bearing that name were seen throughout that decade. Pearl continued rapid growth through the 1950s and in 1961 acquired a famous old brewery, the Goetz Brewing Co. of St. Joseph, Missouri, and with it the Country Club Malt Liquor and Goetz Pale Near Beer labels. In 1970 Pearl merged with the Southdown Corp. of Houston and shortly thereafter, when the Jackson Brewing Co. of New Orleans closed, acquired the rights to Jax, a popular southern beer. In 1976 the St. Joseph Brewery was shut down and all Pearl operations were consolidated in San Antonio. In 1978 Pearl was obtained by Paul Kalmanovitz and added to his collection of breweries, which included Falstaff and General. Pearl is listed as a wholly-owned subsidiary of General.

Pearl Beer is made from the waters of the "Country of 1100 Springs" and corn is used to produce a pale-colored brew. In addition to cans and bottles, Pearl produces most of its main-line brews unpasteurized in kegs. Since the Kalmanovitz acquisition, Pearl has begun producing generics and a number of private labels, such as Slim Price, which is made for a California grocery chain. It also makes Texas Pride in an alcoholic form for Taiwan and in a nonalcoholic form (Texas Select) for Canada. Pearl Cream Ale is now widely available after being introduced in 1979. In 1980 a 68 calorie beer, Lucky Lite (note the General and Falstaff label already appearing) was released. This proliferation of labels is typical of a Kalmanovitz-owned brewing operation.

An interesting feature of the Pearl Brewery is its Jersey Lilly Hospitality Center with replicas of the San Antonio courthouse and saloon (circa 1886), reminiscent of the days when Judge Roy Bean dispensed Pearl XXX Beer (and occasionally justice, of a sort) from his original Jersey Lilly in Langtry, Texas. Believe me, Judge Roy never had it as good as you can at Pearl today.

Beginning in early 1981, Pearl started producing Coy International Private Reserve, a private label for a New Orleans beer distributor. This is the first distributor-marketed beer and the industry is viewing the experiment with interest. With reduced sales of the national brands they handle, distributors are particularly interested in anything that will fill empty trucks.

PEARL XXX FINE LAGER BEER—bright gold, good malt aroma, zesty flavor, somewhat alelike with a tangy citric touch, long on palate, good balance, very flavorful.

PEARL XXX LIGHT FINE LIGHT BEER—extremely pale color, faint yeasty nose, tart flavor, short slightly sweet finish, little aftertaste, faintly malty sweet.

PEARL XXX LIGHT LAGER BEER—pale color, good malty beery aroma, light-bodied, weak and watery. Label says 70 calories; may be a replacement for Pearl Light above.

JAX BEER (a New Orleans tradition since 1890)—yellow color with slight depth, pleasant mild malty aroma, highly carbonated, pleasant and mild flavor with a good hop-malt balance, slightly sweet aftertaste, a fairly good beer with some character and quite refreshing.

TEXAS PRIDE EXTRA LIGHT LAGER BEER—similar to Jax, slightly less aroma, good hop-malt flavor but mostly up front, flattens out in the middle and there is very little finish and aftertaste. Lacks the character of Jax.

COUNTRY CLUB MALT LIQUOR—medium dark gold color, faint grapish winelike nose, very little flavor (which came as a surprise in view of the aroma); most of the flavor comes as a faintly sweet sensation at the very end.

NOTE: in February, 1978 Pearl became the fourth brewer to produce and market Billy Beer, joining with Falls City, Cold Spring, and F.X. Matt in the Billy Carter venture. Pearl had the largest marketing area for Billy Beer, covering seventeen states throughout the South, Southwest, and West.

900 SUPER PREMIUM COUNTRY CLUB MALT LIQUOR—deep yellow, sweet winey alelike aroma, strong sweet palate, extremely good flavor up front, a bit flabby in the middle, long sweet aftertaste with a good hop bite. Unique and very interesting. Introduced in 1980.

SLIM PRICE BEER—medium pale yellow, lovely malty-beery aroma, highly carbonated, perky malt-hop flavor, good tasting, very drinkable, palate sags a bit toward the finish and there is little aftertaste. Found in California.

SLIM PRICE LIGHT BEER—96 calories, pale gold, lovely *clean* beery malty aroma, overall a bit watery, the beeriness is in the background on the palate, slightly sour finish, virtually no aftertaste.

GOLDEN CROWN EXTRA PALE DRY BEER—pale gold, light clean beery-malty nose, watery, a touch of a grainy flavor, a low level malty aftertaste. Can says "since 1875" but doesn't say what. Found in California.

STEINBRAU PALE DRY LAGER BEER—pale yellow, slightly cloudy, nice beery aroma, malty light flavor with little hops, slightly sweet finish and aftertaste.

STEINBRAU PALE DRY LIGHT BEER—96 calories, brilliant very pale gold, very faint malty aroma, some hops in the nose background, very light flavor, mostly CO_2, no aftertaste, just like a sparkling water.

GOETZ BEER—brilliant gold, creamy head, lovely malty aroma with good hops, small bubble carbonation, very pleasant fresh taste, clean malty finish. Very good quaffing beer.

PILSENER CLUB PREMIUM BEER—brilliant gold, obtrusive CO_2, subdued but good malt aroma, more hops in the taste but a vegetal background is noticeable, a complex good-tasting brew.

J.R. EWING'S PRIVATE STOCK—deep yellow, faint grainy malty aroma, touch of sweetness up front on the palate, balanced malt-hop middle; lightens a bit toward the finish, but the good flavor is still there, fairly good body. J.R. really has taste in beer.

PEARL CREAM ALE—bright clear gold, sweet malt aroma, soft ale flavor with good hop balance, good clean finish, medium to long pleasant dry aftertaste. Introduced in 1980.

Genesee Brewing Co., Inc.
(Rochester, N.Y.)

Genesee began in 1878 selling Liebotschaner Beer. It became part of the large Bartholomay Brewing Co. in 1889. Following Prohibition, a new Genesee was opened by Louis A. Wehle using the property and plant of the old firm.

Today Genesee is the third largest single-plant brewing operation in the United States and ranks eighth in the country with sales of 3.4 million barrels (1982). The bulk of its market is in upstate New York, but there is general availability of its popular-priced products in Pennsylvania, New Jersey, Ohio, Delaware, and New England. Genesee also can be found in parts of Florida, Maryland, Kentucky, and Indiana.

The primary product line includes Genesee Beer, Cream Ale, Bock, Fyfe & Drum Extra Lyte Beer, and Twelve Horse Ale, a robust brew heavier and stronger than the Cream Ale.

GOETZ PALE NEAR BEER—brilliant deep gold, light cereal grain aroma, flavor seems to be at least half carbonation, half cereal grain, light body, pleasant but not very interesting.

KASSEL BEER—medium pale gold, good beery aroma with more malt than hops, high CO_2, light but pleasant, light brief finish, faint malty aftertaste.

BROWN DERBY LAGER BEER—cloudy yellow, pleasant malty aroma with some hops, high carbonation, not much flavor beyond carbonation, slight malty aftertaste.

TEXAS SELECT—65-calorie nonalcoholic brew for Canadian markets, bright yellow, faint grainy aroma, light grainy flavor, slightly citrus aftertaste, a bit flat and not very flavorful. Not a very good way to repay Canadians for sending us V.O. and C.C.

HOF-BRAU PREMIUM BEER—bright pale gold, large bubbles, dry sharp hop nose that faded quickly, slight malty flavor, very little finish and aftertaste.

TEXAS PRIDE LITE LAGER BEER—89 calories, deep gold, clean malty nose, refreshing malty flavor, light-bodied, some sweet malt in the middle palate, light malty finish and aftertaste, good hot weather low calorie beer, very drinkable.

GENESEE BEER—good malty aroma, well-bodied, good malt flavor with a slight hop taste, good balance, very little aftertaste. Overall a fine beer, bargain-priced, worth a try.

GENESEE CREAM ALE—fully malty aroma with a slight hop background, good malt-hop balance, well-bodied, good taste, a bit weak on the finish, but one of the better ales, good value at its price.

GENESEE BOCK BEER—very much like Genesee Beer but more malty, medium dark color (like cognac), big roasted malt aroma, extremely good malt flavor, good body, good balance, pleasant aftertaste, a fine product, one of the best domestic bock beers tasted.

GENESEE LIGHT—pale color, mild malty yeasty aroma typical of many of the light beers, light body with a good dry flavor with some hops. One of the better low-calorie beers. 110 calories.

GENESEE CREAM LIGHT CREAM ALE—109 calories, medium gold, light talcum-malt aroma, good dry-malt and hop flavor, light but clean, refreshing, finishes well, dry aftertaste.

FYFE & DRUM EXTRA LYTE BEER—very faint malty aroma, light sweet grainy flavor, no hops evident, very foamy finish. Very light overall but not bad for type; one of the better low-calorie beers, probably 100 calories, but it is not given on the package.

TWELVE HORSE ALE—deep gold, rich and complex aroma with hops and apples, carbonation a bit high, but ale flavor comes through, rich flavor similar to a dark beer, good body, touch of sweet ale, top-fermentation taste, good balance, tart middle and finish, lots of character, you really know you have a beer in your mouth.

Geyer Bros. Brewing Co.
(Frankenmuth, Mich.)

The Cass River Brewery had been in operation for 12 years when John G. Geyer purchased it in 1874, and in 1902 the firm became known as Geyer Bros. It closed down during Prohibition but reopened immediately thereafter under the same name. The Geyers sold the business to the Matthean Investment Co. in 1969, but Walter Geyer remained as brewmaster until he retired in 1982. Brews bearing the Geyer and Frankenmuth names are produced. The plant has a brewing capacity of 30,000 barrels, but the most beer produced in a single year was 24,000 barrels in 1969. In recent years, annual production has been on the order of 4000 barrels.

FRANKENMUTH ORIGINAL DARK BAVARIAN BEER—dark amber color, teaberry aroma, malty teaberry flavor, very mild, a bit too sweet, heavily carbonated, inoffensive but lacks zest. Note: There was also a Frankenmuth beer produced by the International Brewing Co. of Buffalo, New York, in recent years, but with no apparent connection.

FRANKENMUTH ORIGINAL LIGHT BAVARIAN BEER—pale yellow, foamy, malty yeasty nose, rich yeasty malt flavor, long yeasty finish, all in a good sense. Yeastiness is usually not deemed a favorite feature in beers, but it comes off well in this one. A pleasant-tasting brew.

G. Heileman Brewing Co., Inc.
(LaCrosse, Wis.; St. Paul, Minn.; Evansville, Ind.; Newport, Ky.; Seattle, Wash.; Baltimore, Md.; Belleville, Ill.; Frankenmuth, Mich.; Phoenix, Az.; Auburndale, Fla.; Portland Ore.; San Antonio, Tx.; Perry, Ga.)

The Heileman story begins in 1850 with the firm of Gund and Witzel, which leased a small brewery in Galena, Wisconsin. Shortly thereafter, John Gund sold out and moved to LaCrosse, where he built a brewery on Front and Division Streets. He was joined by Gottlieb Heileman in 1858 and the partnership of Gund & Heileman continued to 1872, when Gund retired. When Gottlieb Heileman died in 1878, his wife, Johanna, assumed proprietorship and became president of the firm when it was incorporated in 1890.

The company survived Prohibition and slowly grew from a 160,000-barrel capacity at the turn of the century to one of about one million in 1966. When the great upheaval in the brewing industry came in the next decade with the onslaught of massive advertising campaigns by the large national brewing companies, Heileman set out to build a multibrand house of regional beer brands—each brand having the name, following, and quality to hold its own.

While hundreds of regional brewers were strangled by the national brands' inroads in their markets, Heileman's approach proved successful, even spectacular. By 1977 it had reached seventh in sales in the nation. With the late 1977 acquisition of Rainier in Seattle, the Falls City purchase in 1978, the purchase of Carling National Breweries in March-April 1979, and the addition of the Duncan Brewing Co. in mid-1980, Heileman moved from 32d place in the industry in 1959 to No. 6 in 1980. As a result of a successful takeover of Pabst-Olympia in 1982, Heileman acquired the Blitz-Weinhard Brewery and brands, the modern Perry, Ga., Pabst Brewery and Red White & Blue and Burgermeister brands, and the Lone Star plant in San Antonio with that brand and Buckhorn (Texas). A new Pabst Brewing Co. was spun-off minus these assets. Under special agreement, Heileman will continue to produce Pabst brands at these plants for five years.

With the new southern and southwestern markets Heileman has a firm grip on the 4th place among U.S. brewers. (See Pabst Brewing Co.).

HEILEMAN'S SPECIAL EXPORT BEER—tawny-gold color, hops dominate the nose, first taste is hop sweetness, subsequent sips yield a big hop flavor, smooth and complex, good character and zest, quite European in style, dry finish.

HEILEMAN'S OLD STYLE LIGHT LAGER BEER—gold, very perfumy and appetizing malt and hop aroma, bright hop flavor, with a complex slightly sweet nature, excellent balance, flavor constant throughout.

HEILEMAN'S LIGHT BEER—99 calories, brilliant pale gold, small bubbles, faint malty aroma, initial flavor hop sweetness, from middle palate on fairly dry, good balance, finely finished long aftertaste. One of the better low-calorie brews.

RED WHITE & BLUE SPECIAL LAGER BEER—extremely mild, light and clean nose and taste, very quaffable. First brewed in 1899, this product was originally marketed in the southeastern U.S., but in recent years has been widely available.

LIGHT RED WHITE & BLUE LAGER BEER—92 calories, bright gold, pleasant malty nose, very pleasant malty apple cider flavor, little finish, no aftertaste.

BURGIE! BURGERMEISTER BEER— pale yellow gold, subdued sour malt aroma, light body, dull flavor, sour metallic medicinal quality in the background. Burgermeister was a product of the San Francisco Brewing Co. until 1955, produced under the Burgermeister Brewing Co. label from 1955 to 1965, by Schlitz in San Francisco from 1966 to 1968, and by Hamm in San Francisco while that company was part of G. Heileman (to 1975), from which Pabst obtained the labels. The Burgie! usage on the label appeared in 1970 under the Burgermeister Brewing Co. name, a corporate name of Meister Brau, which had purchased the label from Schlitz when a court-ordered divestiture was effected. This is a brand different from the Burgermeister of Peter Hand and the Burgermeister of the Warsaw Brewing Co. of Warsaw, Illinois (now defunct).

BURGIE LIGHT GOLDEN BEER—deep gold, good beery aroma, light body, on the watery side, very little flavor, salty backtaste, unbalanced, bitter and slightly sour aftertaste.

Blatz Brewing Co. *(Milwaukee)* Founded in 1851 by Valentin Blatz in Milwaukee, the firm was incorporated in 1889 as the Valentin Blatz Brewing Co. In 1890 the firm was merged into the Milwaukee and Chicago Breweries, Ltd. Only Blatz emerged from the gloom of Prohibition and in 1958 was sold to Pabst. The U.S. Supreme Court ordered Pabst to divest itself of the firm and Blatz was sold to G. Heileman in 1969. Blatz has long been a favorite in many areas outside Milwaukee and is marketed in thirty-five states.

BLATZ, MILWAUKEE'S FINEST BEER—pale color, lightly scented, faintly malty, very light-bodied and very light-flavored, an ordinary beer that will offend no one and not satisfy real beer lovers.

BLATZ LIGHT CREAM ALE—medium yellow, sweet fruitlike aroma, pungent flavor with lots of hops, some sourness in back, aftertaste has some unpleasant components.

BLATZ LIGHT BEER (96 calories)—clear and pale, small bubble carbonation, lovely malty nose, you can taste the carbonation, slightly sour finish, little aftertaste, very drinkable, but could use more hops.

Blitz-Weinhard Co.
(Portland, Oreg.)

Henry Weinhard was born in Lindenbrom, Württemberg, Germany, in 1830. After learning the brewing trade in Stuttgart, he migrated to the U.S. in 1851. First employed in breweries in Philadelphia, Cincinnati, and St. Louis, he settled down as foreman of the Muench Brewery in Vancouver, Washington. In 1859 he purchased the brewery, which continued as the Henry Weinhard Brewery. In 1864 Weinhard had formed a brewing partnership with George Bottler in Portland. In 1866 Weinhard became sole proprietor.

Arnold Blitz appeared on the scene in 1909, when he purchased the Portland Brewery, a Weinhard competitor. The present company of Blitz-Weinhard was formed in 1928 when the two firms merged. Until 1979, when bought out by the Pabst Brewing Company, Blitz-Weinhard was the oldest continuously operating brewery west of the Mississippi. As a result of its successful takeover of Pabst and Olympia in 1982, G. Heileman acquired the Blitz-Weinhard plant and brands in early 1983 in exchange for the controlling interest in Pabst (see Pabst and Olympia).

ACME BEER (distributed by Acme Brewing Co., San Francisco, label of General Brewing Co. overprinted Blitz-Weinhard)—cloudy, tawny yellow, faint malt aroma, smoky flavor with salty-malt background, brief finish, no aftertaste.

BLITZ-WEINHARD BEER—dully malty aroma, highly carbonated, salty flavor.

BAVARIAN STYLE DARK BEER—deep reddish brown, roasted malt aroma with faint burnt background that had unpleasant tones, weak roasted malt flavor, sort of dull, carbonation accounts for most of the taste, very foamy.

TIVOLI LIGHT PREMIUM BEER—very pale color, faintly skunky-brackish aroma, brackish flavor, bitter in the finish, aftertaste weak and salty-sour, a poor performer. The Tivoli label originated with the Tivoli Brewing Co. of Denver and was made later by Falstaff of San Francisco.

BUFFALO PREMIUM LAGER BEER (made by Blitz-Weinhard for the Buffalo Brewing Co. of Sacramento)—aroma of brackish water, dull salty flavor. Label claims that Buffalo was established in 1890 in Sacramento. *One Hundred Years of Brewing* says that Buffalo was incorporated in 1888 and produced its first brew in 1890. Buffalo Beer was once a big seller in California and Nevada and enjoyed additional success as an export to Central America, China, and the Philippines. It has appeared under the Buffalo corporate name (1939) and that of the Southern Brewing Co. of Los Angeles (1950).

ALTA AMERICA'S EXTRA LIGHT PILSENER BEER—96 calories, yellow color, nose quite malty, light and pleasant, palate slightly sour up front, malty-vegetal, brief finish, little aftertaste.

HENRY WEINHARD'S PRIVATE RESERVE (Bottling No. 10)—medium to light gold, light hoppy aroma, hoppy flavor, light body, nothing after the initial burst of flavor.

HENRY WEINHARD'S PRIVATE RESERVE (Bottling No. 15)—light gold, light hoppy aroma but more than above, nose overall more intense, less hops in the flavor, a bit sweeter and lasts longer (a longer-lasting aftertaste and more flavor in the finish).

HENRY WEINHARD'S PRIVATE RESERVE (Bottling No. 49)—brilliant pale gold, swamp gas aroma, but the

palate was fine—a sweet alelike flavor with good hops, good clean finish but on the flat side, long pleasant aftertaste.

HENRY WEINHARD'S PRIVATE RESERVE (Bottling No. 70)—medium gold, lovely beery malt and hop aroma, tangy flavor, good balance, long on the palate.

HENRY WEINHARD'S PRIVATE RESERVE BEER (Bottling No. 73)—bright gold, faint malt and hop aroma, beautiful balance, light body, pleasant tasting, malt finish, slightly soapy aftertaste, good hops, good balance, refreshing and drinkable.

HENRY WEINHARD'S PRIVATE RESERVE DARK BEER—medium pale orange-brown, slightly smoky malt nose, light-bodied, slightly sweet malt flavor, dry up front, some complexity, pleasant and refreshing, more like a light

beer with dark coloring.

George Wiedemann Brewing Co. *(Newport, Ky.)* George Wiedemann founded this firm in 1870 and became sole proprietor in 1878. The present name of the company was adopted upon incorporation in 1890. Wiedemann's Bohemian Special is a strong regional favorite throughout the South and Midwest and is still brewed to the original Wiedemann recipe. Heileman has extended the market of this brew from coast to coast. I have seen it in Maine and California. Wiedemann is now the Wiedemann Division of

G. Heileman and the Newport facility is still operated as one of the Heileman plants.

WIEDEMANN BOHEMIAN SPECIAL FINE BEER—light color, fresh malty aroma with some hops, light but good flavor, finely balanced, a good-tasting fresh pilsener-type beer that has enough zest to give pleasure while it quenches thirst. A very fine beer whose only weakness is a slightly neutral finish. It should be more than satisfactory for most American palates. Recommended for everyday use.

ROYAL AMBER—deep gold color, lightly cabonated, beautifully balanced malt and hop nose, touch of sweetness at first on the palate, good hoppy middle, hop and malt flavors both well represented, big hop taste without obtrusive bitterness, a well-balanced excellent brew. One of America's truly fine beers that deserves wider distribution.

F.W. Cook Brewing Co./Cook's Brewing Co. *(Evansville, Ind.)* This company was founded in 1853 by Fred W. Cook and shut down in 1955. It was revived briefly in 1960 by the Associated Brewing Co. but closed in 1961. Sterling bought rights to its labels in 1964 and thus were acquired by Heileman. The most notable brands acquired were Cook's 500 Ale, distributed only for Indianapolis 500 races during the 1950s, and Cook's Goldblume, which is still marketed by Heileman in a few midwestern states.

COOK'S GOLDBLUME PREMIUM BEER—medium to light malt aroma, refreshing but watery, dank aftertaste.

John Hauenstein Brewing Co. *(New Ulm, Minn.)* A Sioux uprising in 1862 occasioned the establishment of this firm. John Hauenstein, a cooper employed at a New Ulm distillery, was put out of work when the Sioux attacked and destroyed the building. His solution to unemployment was to found the Hauenstein Brewery in 1864 with a partner named Andrew Betz. In 1881 a cyclone destroyed the newly remodeled plant, but the beer, stored underground, was saved and used to finance the rebuilding of the brewery. The firm was incorporated in 1900 as the John Hauenstein Brewing Co. Heileman obtained the rights to this label just prior to 1974 when it acquired Grain Belt, Inc. and closed down the New Ulm facility.

HAUENSTEIN NEW ULM BEER—medium to light color, clean malty aroma with some hops, clean bright taste, a little too heavily carbonated. Still, an enjoyable little brew.

Drewry's Ltd., U.S.A. *(South Bend, Ind.; St. Paul, Minn., et al.)* The Drewry firm began in 1860 with the partnership of Drewry & Scotten founding the North Star Brewery. The firm became Drewry & Grieg in 1864. Drewry left this partnership in 1867 and founded Drewry & Sons of St. Paul. In the 1950s Drewry's operated the old Edelweiss Brewing Co. plant in Chicago, and for a time owned the Hampden-Harvard plant in Willimansett, Massachusetts. In the early 1960s, Drewry's became part of the Associated Brewing Co. and then of Heileman. Heileman is beginning to market the Drewry label over a much wider area and in early 1978 the lead label, Drewry's Beer, appeared in New Jersey and New York.

DREWRY'S BEER—light sweet aroma, sweet taste with some hops faintly in the background, completely inoffensive, but lacks zest.

DREWRY'S BEER DRAFT FLAVORED—light brackish aroma, salty taste, very little aftertaste. This beer was obtained in Wisconsin in late 1977, at which time we heard that it was no longer being made. That has not been confirmed by Heileman, but it is not included in that firm's most recent product list.

Minneapolis Brewing Co. *(Minneapolis)* Since 1891 this firm has produced the very popular Grain Belt beers for the midwestern market. Over the years the Grain Belt Beer label has seen a great number of adjectives, including: special, friendly, golden, premium, and golden premium. When the firm was purchased by Heileman, it was renamed Grain Belt, Inc.

GRAIN BELT BEER—pale color, sweet aroma, lightly flavored, highly carbonated, harmless, and uninteresting.

GRAIN BELT PREMIUM (strong)—pale color, faint malty aroma, very lightly hopped, taste on the sweet side with vegetal overtones. Not a particularly good-tasting beer for one that supposedly sells very well in Minnesota where beer has been a favorite drink since early settlers continued their heritage of brewing fine European-style brews.

Jacob Schmidt Brewing Co. *(St. Paul)* In his younger days Jacob Schmidt had been employed by Miller, Best, Schlitz, Schell, and Blatz. When he bought out the Milwaukee Brewing Co. in 1884, he was foreman of the Hamm Brewery. His North Star Brewing Co. operated until 1901, when it was incorporated in the above name and the business was moved to the recently (1900) purchased St. Paul Brewing Co. facility. Billed as the "beer that grew with the great Northwest," this local Minneapolis-St. Paul brew has featured a series of labels that depict the fauna and activities of the area. Can collectors have been treated to moose, Canadian geese, antelope, pheasants, pike, ice fishing, bobsleds, and about a dozen other scenes. Schmidt became part of the Associated Brewing Co. complex shortly before its acquisition by Heileman in 1963 and the Schmidt plant operates as the Heileman St. Paul facility.

SCHMIDT BEER (3.2 percent by weight)—light color, fragrance of hops, medium body, good in the middle, some greenness typical of very youthful "3.2," watery finish.

SCHMIDT EXTRA SPECIAL BEER (labeled strong, denoting, in Minnesota where the sample was obtained, normal alcohol content instead of being 3.2 percent)—very pleasant fruitlike aroma, too sweet a taste, a bit cloying. A beer should be drier than this.

LIGHT SCHMIDT BEER—96 calories, pale gold, good hop

and malt aroma even if quite light, light but complex hop flavor, finish, and aftertaste, pretty good low-calorie beer.

SCHMIDT SELECT NEAR BEER—very pale, faint malty nose, watery, flat dusty flavor, also noticeable lack of alcohol.

Kingsbury Breweries Co. *Manitowoc and Sheboygan, Wis.)* The Kingsbury brands were obtained by Heileman early in its expansion program (1969); for a time Heileman operated the Sheboygan plant and produced the Heileman brands there. The primary labels obtained from this firm are Kingsbury Beer and Kingsbury Brew Near Beer. Interestingly, G. Heileman is the United States' largest manufacturer of near-beer, producing Kingsbury, Schmidt Select, and Zing.

WISCONSIN PREMIUM BEER—pale slightly cloudy yellow, good hop and malt nose, slightly oxidized but still good, light body, pleasant malt and hop flavor, malty finish, not much aftertaste.

KINGSBURY BREW NEAR BEER (60 calories)—very pale color, very faint malty nose, watery, grainy flavor, easy to recognize the absence of alcohol.

KINGSBURY WISCONSIN'S ORIGINAL BEER—bright gold, faint sweet aroma, very little flavor, little more than carbonation. Can notes the Kingsbury origin in 1847.

Gluek Brewing Co. *(Minneapolis)* This firm was founded in 1847 by Gottfried Gluek and operated as G. Gluek & Sons until 1894, when it was incorporated as the Gluek Brewing Co. Its products were Gluek's Beer or Gluek's Pilsener Beer and Gluek's Stite Malt Liquor, claimed to be America's first malt liquor, "the original malt liquor, pale and dry as champagne." After Gluek was purchased, it operated for a time as the Gluek Division of G. Heileman. Recent labels have dropped the Gluek name. (See Cold Spring.)

STITE SPARKLING MALT LIQUOR (Strong)—pale color, faint sweet pilsener-like aroma, medium body, pilsenerlike taste as well, but poorly balanced sour and sweet flavors. It is pale all right, but you can hardly call it dry.

Lone Star Brewing Co. In 1883 a number of prominent San Antonio citizens organized a stock company. The brewery was completed a year later. A new plant was completed in 1896 and in 1902 famed brewer Adolphus Busch of St.

Louis was named president. Lone Star operated a plant in Oklahoma City for a time, but closed it in the 1960s. Olympia acquired the company in 1976.

Lone Star operates a museum and hospitality center in San Antonio called the Buckhorn Bar. A set of TV commercials featuring a giant 12-ton armadillo has evoked considerable interest. The monster attacks, but the beer gets to safety.

LONE STAR BEER—pale gold, malt aroma with a vegetal background, decent malt and hop flavor, fairly dry, finish is a bit brief and the aftertaste is light and not long-lived.

BUCKHORN BEER—pale gold, pleasant sweet malty aroma, little hop flavor, pleasant, light, and inoffensive, slightly tart finish, very little aftertaste.

LONE STAR LIGHT BEER—96 calories, pale gold, pleasant malty aroma, there may be some hops, but they are light, slightly sweet flavor, the hops show a little better in the finish and aftertaste. Light and inoffensive. Lone Star Light was introduced in 1979.

LONE STAR DRAFT BEER—pale yellow and cloudy, lovely rising malt aroma, a beautiful nose, good malty flavor, slightly oxidized, but good nonetheless.

Pfeiffer Brewing Co. *(Detroit)* This brewery was established by Conrad Pfeiffer in 1890 and was operated by him in his name until he was succeeded by the Pfeiffer Brewing Co. in 1902. Sixty years later Pfeiffer merged with the E&B Brewing Co. of Detroit to form the beginnings of the Associated Brewing Co. At that time, the E&B plant was shut down and brewing continued at Pfeiffer. A Pfeiffer plant in Flint, Michigan, operated for a time but closed before the merger with E&B. The Pfeiffer labels of the 1960s indicate a South Bend facility, but it is likely that this was an Associated plant and not necessarily a producer of the Pfeiffer brands. The Pfeiffer label has been maintained since the purchase of Associated by Heileman, but the Detroit plant was closed.

PFEIFFER FAMOUS BEER—sweet malt nose, neutral taste, little character, unbalanced at the finish, also a bit "rough" after the initial palate sensation, some scratchiness in the throat on swallowing.

Sterling Breweries, Inc. *(Evansville, Ind.)* Sterling was merged into the Associated Brewing Co. complex during the 1960s and acquired by Heileman from there. The primary brands involved were Sterling Premium and Mickey's Fine Malt Liquor, the latter becoming a primary Heileman label.

STERLING PREMIUM PILSNER BEER—pale color, faint aroma that was barely noticeable, faint and nondescript taste, little more than thirst quenching. This beer could be served extremely chilled without impairing the flavor since there is so little to begin with. This is a popular beer in Kentucky, Indiana, and some southern states.

STERLING LIGHT BEER—96 calories, yellow gold, pleasant light malty aroma, very light flavor, light body, low carbonation, brief finish.

MICKEY'S FINE MALT LIQUOR—pleasant malty beery aroma, fresh and malty flavor, bittersweet and slightly perfumy taste like most U.S. malt liquors, some bitterness in the finish of some samples, but not in those that were fresh. Malt liquor drinkers should try this one, the number one choice of the rating panel. Available in a wide variety of packages, including 16-ounce cans.

Rainier Brewing Co. *(Seattle, Wash.)* This famous brewing company of the West Coast was obtained by Heileman in the spring of 1977 for $8 million, marking the passing of another big name from the ranks of the strong, independent regional brewers.

Rainier originated in 1878 with the Bayview Brewery on the site where today's Rainier Brewery is still located. From that time Rainier Beer was the premium brand produced at that place. In 1893 the Georgetown Brewery produced beer under the Rainier label and by 1916 the plant was the sixth largest brewery in the world.

Following Prohibition, the Bayview was purchased by Fritz Sick and his son, Emil, who, after converting it back from a feed mill (which it was throughout Prohibition), formed the Century Brewing Co. and obtained rights to the Rainier name in Washington and Alaska. In 1957, when the owners obtained rights to the Rainier name throughout the United States, the company name was changed from Sicks' Brewing and Malting Co. to Sicks' Rainier Brewing Company.

Although several smaller breweries were obtained along the way, all operations were eventually consolidated into the present brewery. With the formation of the Rainier Companies, Inc., in 1970, Rainier added an interesting property, the Robert Mondavi

Winery of Oakville, California, one of the foremost makers of fine wines in Napa Valley.

Rainier products include Rainier Beer, Ale, Light (a 96-calorie beer), Rheinlander Beer and, from the Heileman product list, Mickey's Malt Liquor. For can collectors and lovers of breweriana, Rainier has the largest assortment of goodies ever seen. Write for a price list to: Beeraphernalia, c/o Rainier, P.O. Box 24828, Seattle, WA 98124.

RAINIER ALE—beautiful amber color, slightly cloudy, lovely well-hopped aroma, big body, pungent yet sweet taste, pretty good as American ales go and a lot more authentic than most domestic brews so labeled. Locally called "Green Death" (the label is green), it is rated at over 7 percent alcohol by volume.

RAINIER MOUNTAIN FRESH BEER—pale gold, very hoppy aroma but there are very few hops in the flavor, taste is mostly just salty carbonation and the finish is light and brackish.

RHEINLANDER BEER—yellow, sour malt aroma with some character, good dry flavor, carbonation noticeable but with small bubbles, good flavor, good balance.

RAINIER LIGHT—good beery aroma, fairly flat, malty flavor with little hop character, touch of sourness in the background. May have been a bad sample.

Falls City Brewing Co. *(Louisville, Ky.)* This company was organized and incorporated in 1905 by citizens and tavern owners in the Louisville area. The name of the company was taken from the original (pre-1780) name of Louisville, so called because it is the site of the only large waterfall on the Ohio River south of Pittsburgh. In late 1906 the first draught beer was ready for delivery. Two years later Falls City marketed the first bottled beer in Louisville and spread its sales to nearby Indiana.

During Prohibition the plant continued to operate as the Falls City Ice and Beverage Company, producing soft drinks and near-beer. In 1933 Falls City reestablished itself as a successful regional brewery with its Falls City Premium Brew and produced up to one million barrels annually.

In 1972 Falls City introduced Drummond Bros. Preferred Beer, a light, mild beer directed at the twenty-one to thirty-five age group. In late 1977 Falls City introduced Billy Beer, "brewed expressly for and with the personal approval of one of America's all-time great beer drinkers— Billy Carter." The Billy Beer "hype" says that he

sampled about nine different recipes and selected this one each time. It was then brewed up specially for Billy, or at least for his endorsement. In early 1978 several other brewers began producing Billy Beer in an identical package for distribution in their marketing area. Two of these others were

1878 — Home of Rainier Beer

1900 — Rainier Brewery on Airport Way

1978 — Rainier Today

75

compared with the Falls City product, but it was clear that only the package was the same. The beers were from decidedly different recipes (see F. X. Matt Brewing Co. and Cold Spring Brewing Co.).

Billy Beer was discontinued in early 1979. Talk in the industry has it that the Billy Beer promotion was partly responsible for the closing of Falls City Brewery later that year. Shortly after closing, Heileman acquired the labels and began production of the Falls City and Drummond labels at the Evansville, Indiana, and Newport, Kentucky, plants.

FALLS CITY PREMIUM BREW—advertised as all-grain; aroma of sweet carbonation, malty flavor on the sweet side; faint yeasty finish, a light to medium beer, pleasant but without much zest.

DRUMMOND BROS. PREFERRED BEER—pleasant yeasty aroma, very pale color, pleasant refreshing taste, clean and very light finish, a very refreshing and quaffable brew. Since it is very lightly flavored, overchilling for hot weather refreshment does not seem to impair the flavor.

BILLY BEER—pale gold, foamy, heavy malty aroma with faint hops, sweet up front, brackish finish, weak aftertaste. Not worth all the publicity.

Carling National Breweries, Inc. *(Baltimore, Md.; Belleville, Ill.; Frankenmuth, Mich.; Phoenix, Ariz.; Tacoma, Wash.)* The Carling origins of this firm are found in London, Ontario, Canada, where Thomas Carling founded a brewery in 1840 (see Canada, Carling O'Keefe, Ltd.). Carling products appeared in the United States in 1933 with Black Label Beer and Red Cap Ale produced in Cleveland. Expansion began in 1954 with the addition of a plant in Belleville, Illinois. The International Breweries, Inc., plant in Frankenmuth, Michigan, was added in 1955. A plant was built in Natick, Massachusetts in 1956 and another erected in Atlanta in 1958. The West Coast was reached in 1958 with the acquisition of the Heidelberg Brewing Co. in Tacoma and a plant was established in 1961 in Baltimore.

The National Brewery was built in 1872 and was so named in 1885 when it became part of the firm of Joseph L. Straus & Brother. In 1899 it was one of sixteen breweries that formed the Maryland Brewing Co. with the then massive annual production capacity of 1.5 million barrels. In 1901 eight of the sixteen breweries were

Beercentennial Bottle—limited number produced during the summer of 1978. Authentic shape Circa 1890.

Of other historic Carling facilities, the Detroit plant (Tivoli Brewing Co. plant, 1897-1948, then Altes Brewing Co. and finally the National Detroit Brewery) was closed in 1973. The Miami facility (formerly the American Brewing Co.) closed in 1974 and Carling's plant in Natick, Massachusetts, closed its doors in 1977. The original Carling plant in Cleveland is now operated by C. Schmidt & Sons, Inc., of Philadelphia.

Carling Brewing Co. The Carling products, Black Label Beer and Red Cap Ale, date back to 1840 in their Canadian heritage. Although they had been available as imports, both appeared as U.S. domestic brews in the 1940s, being produced in Cleveland by the Brewing Corporation of America, which later became part of the Carling Brewing Co. Today Black Label is produced in four Carling National breweries in the United States, in ten Carling O'Keefe breweries across Canada, in England by Bass Worthington as Carling Black Label Lager, and in South Africa. Red Cap Ale is not sold as extensively, being made at only one U.S. plant and at three Canadian breweries.

CARLING'S BLACK LABEL BEER—pale gold color, big head, big malty-hop aroma, some hops in the flavor, dry, good balance, better than average, good beer at a reasonable price.

CARLING'S BLACK LABEL CANADIAN STYLE BEER—Bright gold, malt more noticeable than hops in the nose, hops show better on the palate, clean taste, highly carbonated, good balance, not complex. Likely, a new package for Black Label.

CARLING'S BLACK LABEL LIGHT BEER—96 calories, gold color, faint malty aroma, very light and dry, slightly malty flavor with a trace of hops, very little aftertaste.

CARLING 71 LIGHT PILSENER—pale gold, almost no aroma, light and watery, very little flavor, unbalanced, slightly bitter and sour aftertaste. Contains 71 calories, 3.2 percent alcohol.

CARLING'S ORIGINAL RED CAP ALE—deep gold color with tawny tones, big malt-hop aroma, strongly flavored, big body, bittersweet style, good of type, may be a bit too strongly flavored for those who are used to pilsener types of beer, similar to some of the true malt liquors.

STAG BEER (Stag Brewery)—clean fresh aroma, good body, big flavor at the start, family resemblance to Black Label quite noticeable, big head. Originally appeared in 1851 as a brand of Griesedieck-Western.

closed in a reorganization that renamed the syndicate the Gottlieb-Bauernschmidt-Straus Brewing Co. and one of the surviving plants was the National Brewery.

Before joining Carling, National had also begun an extensive expansion program with plants in Detroit, Phoenix, and Saginaw, Michigan. Until April 1979, Carling National was a subsidiary of Carling O'Keefe, Ltd. of Toronto, operating five plants, with an annual brewing capacity of 6.9 million barrels. At that time Carling was purchased by Heileman. Heileman closed down the old Columbia Brewery in Tacoma (the former plant of the Heidelberg-Columbia Brewing Co.), but re-opened the recently closed Stag Brewery in Belleville, Illinois, once the brewery of Griesedieck-Western.

The Carling National plants in Frankenmuth, Michigan, Baltimore and Phoenix (the former Arizona Brewing Co. and Dutch Treat Brewing Co. facility) have become part of the Heileman operation. The Baltimore-Highlandtown plant, the old National Brewery, was closed at the time of acquisition by Heileman.

COY INTERNATIONAL PRIVATE RESERVE BEER—"Cask No. 19," pale yellow, nice malt aroma, starts pleasantly but middle palate collapses, ends weakly and slightly sweet. Pleasant overall. A "distributor's beer" packaged by authority of Coy International Corp. of New Orleans.

COLUMBIA EXTRA MELLOW PALE BREW BEER—flowery malty aroma, foamy with small bubbles, watery weak body, not much flavor.

HEIDELBERG ALL NATURAL BEER—extremely faint nose, almost none at all, faint malt and hop flavor, light body but not watery, sort of flat and no finish. Heileman is now producing Heidelberg at Seattle.

National Brewing Co. National Bohemian, first brewed in 1885 in "the land of pleasant living," and National Premium have been continuously produced in Baltimore since repeal, and with expansion they were also made in National plants in Michigan, Arizona, and Florida, according to package labels. Today these two beers are produced only in Baltimore, the center of their market. Brands acquired in the National expansion usually continued to be produced "in place" for their established market, except for A-1 and Altes, which were made for a brief time in Baltimore, and Van Lauter, which was made earlier in Detroit and Phoenix. A Colt Beer and Colt .45 Stout Malt Liquor were in the National repertoire in recent years, but are no longer marketed.

A-1 LIGHT PILSNER BEER—medium gold, appetizing malt aroma, malty taste with some zest, medium body, somewhat filling. Originally this beer was known as Lancer's A-1.

NATIONAL BOHEMIAN LIGHT BEER—good clean malty aroma, sprightly clean taste, a touch of sweetness at first, then good hop and malt flavor, good finish, good balance throughout, crisp and clean aftertaste. Good beer at a reasonable price.

NATIONAL PREMIUM PALE DRY BEER—good malty aroma, pleasant taste with a slight hop flavor, good balance, pleasant aftertaste, a smooth brew, but it lacks zest.

NATIONAL BOHEMIAN GENUINE BOCK BEER—deep orange-brown, roasted malt aroma, very light body, very little flavor, no aftertaste. There is also a Stag Bock produced by Carling National "in season."

COLT .45 MALT LIQUOR—beautiful gold with small bubble carbonation, lovely malty aroma, alcohol somewhat noticeable, smooth and soft, very slightly sweet palate and aftertaste, all malt, no hops. Brand and recipe originated by Altes Brewing Co. of Detroit.

COLT .45 SILVER DELUXE MALT LIQUOR—pale greenish-yellow, dank aroma, malty palate, celerylike finish, long malty aftertaste with a sour nature.

DUTCH TREAT PREMIUM LAGER BEER (Dutch Treat Brewing Co.)—clear pale gold, almost no aroma at all, faint hops, fairly good body, very lightly flavored, touch of apple skin in the finish, pleasant aftertaste.

NINE O FIVE PREMIUM BEER (Carling National Div. of G. Heileman, Phoenix)—pale cloudy yellow, light sour malt aroma, sour malt flavor, thin body, brief slightly sour finish, very faint grainy aftertaste. Private label of 905 Liquor Stores, St. Louis, Missouri. There is also a 905 Light Beer produced by Heileman and also one brewed by Pittsburgh.

VAN LAUTER BAVARIAN LAGER BEER (Van Lauter Brewery)—pleasant malty nose, light-bodied, moderately pleasant flavor, not much character or zest.

ALTES GOLDEN LAGER BEER—supposedly reminiscent of the "Fassbier" (kegged lager beer) of Germany. Altes has a light clean malty aroma, a pleasant malty aroma, a pleasant malty slightly sweet taste, and an amiable lingering fresh tasting finish. Altes was originally a product of the Tivoli Brewing Co. and later, 1948, of the successor company, the Altes Brewing Co. It first appeared under the National label in 1955.

Tuborg Breweries, Ltd. Tuborg is produced by Carling National under license and authority of Tuborg Breweries, Ltd., of Copenhagen. Tuborg beer has been produced in Denmark since 1873 and marketed worldwide. It was the first European brand beer to be produced in the United States. Tuborg Beer was renamed Tuborg Gold in 1977 and widely marketed under the label. In the spring of 1982, new labels appeared, replacing the name with the original Tuborg Beer. At that time both labels were in use. Since 1979, the U.S.-brewed Tuborg utilizes the same recipe as Tuborg brewed in Denmark, 100 percent two-row malt and German hops, long secondary fermentation, low carbonation, and 4.4 percent alcohol by volume.

United Breweries, Ltd. of Copenhagen maintains close control of the U.S. production of the Tuborg brews. This control has resulted in development of the brewing industry's most detailed technical manual, a guide not only to the raw materials and procedures to be used in the brewing process, but one which adjusts itself for equipment and water demands at each brewery where Tuborg is produced. All materials and procedures have to be approved by United Breweries. Twice yearly each American facility producing Tuborg is examined by an inspection team and monthly reports are submitted by each brewing facility for review in Copenhagen. Further, samples of brews are sent regularly to Copenhagen for taste test and analysis.

TUBORG GOLD EXPORT QUALITY BEER—medium gold, small bubble carbonation, good well-hopped malty aroma, slightly sweet flavor, clean yet complex, lingering well-balanced pleasant aftertaste, excellent balance. Two-row barley from European strains, corn grits, and domestic and imported hops are used. Fine beer at an excellent price. Also available as Tuborg Beer.

TUBORG DELUXE DARK EXPORT QUALITY BEER—Red-brown copper color, nice malty molasses nose, light body, mild malty flavor that has some hops, lovely malty finish and aftertaste. Somewhat on the lines of a porter. Brewed with a black malt, caramel malt, and a regular malt.

Duncan Brewing Co. *(Auburndale, Fla.)* The Duncan Brewing Co. was founded in 1973 by L. N. Duncan, formerly of the Queen City Brewing Co. of Cumberland, Maryland. The product line included former Queen City brands, Fischer's Ale and Beer, which are made for the Wynn Dixie grocery chain, a newly introduced (1980) 90-calorie Fischer's Light Beer, Master's

Choice, made for the Albertson's grocery stores, Regal Premium Beer, a label owned by Carling National which Duncan made only for sale to distributors in the Miami area, Dunk's German Style Beer, Duncan's own label, and Dunk's Preferred Light, a low-calorie beer.

Duncan brewed and packaged the beer but neither delivered nor distributed. Local retailers had to pick up stock at the plant in Auburndale and many found it easier simply to sell Pabst, Schlitz, and Busch, which were brought to their door. In this environment, Duncan's fortunes ebbed and in May, 1980, G. Heileman acquired the brewery and gained access to the Florida market. Duncan is now a subsidiary of Carling National, owned and operated by G. Heileman. Since the Heileman purchase, Royal Brewing Co. (Dixie) has begun producing the Fischer labels, presumably with the Dixie recipe. This is in addition to Duncan-made Fischer, which is still being made for Florida.

FISCHER'S OLD GERMAN STYLE BEER—good malt aroma but on the faint side, heavily carbonated, metallic-malt flavor, flattens out rapidly after a very good start,

bitterness in the aftertaste. It is a shame that it sags so badly in the middle and ends poorly, for the first taste is extremely good.

FISCHER'S LIGHT BEER—90 calories, deep bright gold, lovely fresh and clean malty nose with a touch of yeast, thin body, slightly hoppy palate, sour finish, not much zest.

FISCHER'S OLD ENGLISH STYLE ALE—good fresh clean malty aroma, good hop flavor at the outset but it soon flattens out to a watery finish. It is not even remotely an English-style ale.

MASTER'S CHOICE BAVARIAN STYLE PREMIUM BEER—light color, slightly sour malty aroma, good hop-malt flavor with some character marred by a metallic background taste that became even stronger in the aftertaste.

DUNK'S GERMAN STYLE PREMIUM SELECT BEER—deep yellow color with a touch of brown, light hop-malt flavor with a metallic touch. Very similar to Master's Choice, but lighter.

REGAL PREMIUM BEER (Regal Brewery, Miami, Fla.)—slightly cloudy gold, toasted malt aroma, toasted malt and grain flavor, a little oxidized but still ok, interesting and zesty, grainy finish and aftertaste. Made by Duncan at Auburndale for distribution by Carling in the Miami area long before both became part of G. Heileman. It was originally made in Miami by the National Brewing Co. and bears the same statement on the label as Altes: "Tastes like Fassbier Draft Beer."

Other Heileman Products Heileman also

obtained other small breweries or brands in the Midwest, including the Fox-Head Waukesha Corp., of Waukesha, Wisconsin, and Heidel Brau from the Sioux City Brewing Co. These small firms and labels were gathered up in the Associated purchase. Fox de Luxe Beer was

produced by Heileman for a while, but has since been sold to the Cold Spring Brewing Co.

HEIDEL BRAU PILSNER BEER—faint malt aroma, light-flavored, very quaffable, pleasant but no zest, very little aftertaste.

SGA LIGHT BEER—pale color, clean malty aroma, slight hop character to the taste, some bite on the palate which eases toward the finish. A good beer at a low price. A little light, but good. SGA is a private label of Spirits Guild of America. An SGA Gold Label, made by Pittsburgh Brewing Co., appeared in 1980. This may mark the end of production of SGA by Heileman. Pittsburgh-made SGA is labelled as being made by the Magna Carta Brewing Co.

Jos. Huber Brewing Co.
(Monroe, Wisconsin)

Joseph Huber arrived in America from Bavaria in 1923 and was first employed by the Blatz Brewing Co. in Milwaukee. He later moved to Monroe and became brewmaster of the Blumer Brewing Corp. shortly thereafter. After having worked his way up to general manager, he took over the brewery in 1947 when Blumer went out of business. He remained in charge of the renamed Huber Brewery until his death in 1977 when his son, Fred, inherited the business. Fred Huber has since devoted his energies to producing the best possible brews and favors the heavy-bodied beers in the German style.

Augsburger Old World Bavarian Style Beer has become the lead entry in the Huber line to qualify for top honors among American brews. Already an excellent brew before 1977, it was improved in that year with the addition of specially selected and imported Spalt hops from northern Germany. Since that addition Augs-

burger has won wide acclaim as a result. It is available in Massachusetts, Pennsylvania, New Jersey, California, and Colorado in addition to Huber's regular markets. 1982 sales reached 275,000 barrels, mostly due to the Augsburger popularity.

The Huber brands include the following: Wisconsin Gold Label, Potosi Beer (formerly of the Potosi Brewing Co., Potosi, Wis.), Holiday Beer (Holiday Brewing Co. label, a Potosi Corporate name), Alpine Beer (another old Potosi label), Huber Premium, Huber Bock, Wisconsin Club, Bavarian Club, Rhinelander, Bohemian Club, Regal Brau, Hi-Brau, and the two Augsburgers. The Potosi Brewing Co. was a famous old brewing firm (of Potosi and Oshkosh) that originated in 1852 as the Gabriel Hail Brewery, became the Adam Schumacher Brewery in 1866, and then Potosi in 1906. It closed in 1972, at which time the brands were purchased by Huber.

REGAL BRAU BAVARIAN STYLE BEER—fresh clean malty aroma, good malt-hop balance in the taste, finish a bit too sweet, sour aftertaste. Introduced at Christmas 1965 as a special full-bodied holiday brew in the German tradition.

BAVARIAN CLUB PREMIUM BEER—faint bitter-sour aroma, slightly sour flavor with little zest.

WISCONSIN CLUB PREMIUM BEER—medium deep gold color, pleasant beery malt aroma, malt flavored, clean and light, good balance, slightly sweet malt finish.

RHEINLANDER GENUINE BOCK BEER—dark color, faint malt nose, pleasant slight hop flavor, good balance, good long finish. this is the *best* American-made bock beer that was found. It is hard to come by, but I cannot recommend it too highly. Super stuff!

STENGER BREWERY SESQUICENTENNIAL BEER—slightly cloudy gold, good sweet hop nose, sharp metallic taste up front, improves across palate, finish and aftertaste quite pleasant.

BOHEMIA CLUB OLD FASHIONED LAGER BEER—light sweet malty nose, taste on the yeasty side, flavor of grain and sweetness, finish a bit flabby. When this beer gets old, it gets better as it develops a roasted malt character. This brand was originated by the Bohemian Brewing Co. of Joliet and Chicago and was obtained by Huber with the Potosi labels.

HUBER PREMIUM BOCK BEER—deep red-orange brown, foamy, malty aroma, taste gradually becomes increasingly bitter across the palate until it is too bitter at the end.

HUBER CLASSIC BEER—tawny gold, beautiful complex malt-hop aroma, big hop flavor with the right amount of malt for good balance, a bit of sweetness in the finish. This is the beer that was specially prepared by Huber for the historic brewery series of cans.

AUGSBURGER OLD WORLD BAVARIAN STYLE BEER—golden color, hops dominate the nose, good character, plenty of zest in the flavor, extremely good balance, hops dominate throughout, bitter hop finish with a trace of the initial sweetness that reappears on the palate, a big flavorful beer and a very good one. Has to be ranked at the top of the list of all American beers. The Augsburger label, originally owned by the Monarch Brewing Co. of Chicago, was purchased from Potosi.

AUGSBURGER DARK OLD WORLD BAVARIAN STYLE BEER—red-brown color, sweet faint roasted malt aroma, carbonation mostly up front, faint touch of sweetness on the palate, malty finish and aftertaste. Another fine brew from this progressive small brewery.

WISCONSIN HOLIDAY BEER—sweet malty nose, low carbonation, natural with small bubbles, light hops in the flavor, slight cardboard flavor especially in the finish.

HUBER PREMIUM BEER—bright gold, good hop and malt nose, fresh clean slightly sweet hop and malt flavor, nicely balanced, good-tasting finish, long pleasant aftertaste, just a little on the light side.

RHINELANDER EXPORT PREMIUM BEER—bright gold, faint aroma, dry clean flavor, nice malty character and good tasting; not long on the palate, however, and the finish and aftertaste are brief. This brand originated with the Rhinelander Brewing Co., Rhinelander, Wisconsin.

AUGSBURGER OLD WORLD BAVARIAN STYLE BOCK BEER—deep copper-brown, faint malt aroma, smooth, dry malt flavor; there are mild hops on the palate, but it is mostly malt, dry finish, long on the palate with a medium to good body. Introduced in 1981, Augsburger Bock uses only the finest German hops. The brewmaster informs me that Augsburger Bock uses the same recipe as Rheinlander Bock. I checked that out with the taste panel, serving them the two bocks with the Augsburger Dark as a trio. In that combination, the two bock beers were clearly the same and rated identically by the panel. Augsburger/Rheinlander Bock is one of the two best dark beer recipes produced by a major American brewer today.

WISCONSIN GOLD LABEL LIGHT LAGER BEER—faint malt aroma, very little flavor, flat dull finish and aftertaste.

OUR BEER—gold, fragrant sweet malty-hop aroma, high carbonation, sweet malt mouth but not flabby, good balance. Private label of Del Farm and National Stores.

Peter Hand Brewing Co. *(Chicago, Ill.)* In 1890 Peter Hand organized a brewing company in Chicago whose premises were used for brewery operation from 1891, when the first beer was released for sale, until 1980, when the plant shut down, probably for good. The most recent organization bearing the name Peter Hand was

formed in 1973 when the old bankrupt Meister Brau plant and offices were purchased by a group headed by Fred W. Regnery and Fred Huber, who was also owner of the Huber Brewing co. The Meister Brau name had been associated with these facilities from 1967-1972 when that operation failed. Before the Regnery and Huber purchase, Miller Brewing Co. had acquired the Meister Brau label including Meister Brau Lite, which would evolve into Miller Lite.

Peter Hand became a multibrand brewing company with markets extending to California and New Mexico and eastward to New Jersey, but with products that found most of their market in the Midwest and South.

Technical data offered by the company stated that Lake Michigan water was used in all Hand beers since it is free of mineral content. The hops used for all products except Van Merritt (imported hops used exclusively) were grown in Oregon and Washington. Corn was used as an adjunct for enhanced clarity of brew. The robust flavor of their Old Chicago Dark is due to the use of five separate malts.

In early 1980, Peter Hand closed its doors and the Hand collection of brands were sold to the Joseph Huber Brewing Co., which plans to continue many of the products and will institute a major promotion for Van Merritt.

PETER HAND EXTRA LIGHT BEER—pale color, little aroma, extremely light body and flavor, no zest. A low-calorie beer.

PETER HAND 1891 EXPORT LAGER BEER—faint malty aroma, delicate bittersweet flavor, light body, lightly hopped finish.

OLD CHICAGO LIGHT LAGER BEER—skunky aroma with motor oil overtones, flabby semi-sweet flavor with a bitter finish. Many tried, all with the same results. After tasting Old Chicago, I heard this story. When the present management took over the operation, a large batch of this beer was in stock, undistributed. It had exceeded the expected shelf-life limit and should have been destroyed. Brewers regularly remove old unsold stock from store shelves and replace it with new. For whatever reason, runs the story, Hand released the old beer with the predictable results. Old Chicago Light was found wanting by all who tried it during that period. The recipe, however, is a decent one, and new batches of the beer should be given a trial.

OLD CHICAGO DARK BEER—good dark color, medium brown with tawny hues, very light malty nose, mildly flavored and pleasant tasting, a little short on aftertaste. This is a good domestic dark beer, one of the best produced in the U.S.

OLD CROWN LIGHT DRY BEER—mild, malty aroma, sour taste, dull finish. Old Crown beer and ale are products formerly made by the Old Crown Brewing Corp. of Fort Wayne, Indiana.

OLD CROWN PREMIUM QUALITY ALE (lazy-aged)—very light malty aroma, faintly hopped flavor, mostly on the neutral side, little aftertaste. Better than Old Crown Beer for character of flavor.

BRAUMEISTER SPECIAL PILSENER BEER—pale color, light, pleasant malty nose, highly carbonated, light neutral flavor, tasty finish and aftertaste. This brand was previously a product of the Independent Milwaukee Brewing Co. of Milwaukee, and the Independent Milwaukee Div. of G. Heileman, Sheboygan, Wisconsin. In 1974 it was produced by both Heileman and Hand. It is widely marketed.

BRAUMEISTER BOCK BEER—pale red-brown (rust) color, aroma of sweet toffee, licorice, treacle, harsh bittersweet unbalanced flavor that is mercifully weak, brief finish, little aftertaste.

BURGEMEISTER BREWMASTER'S PREMIUM BEER—very malty aroma, light body, nondescript light flavor, little finish. This brand originated with the Warsaw Brewing Co. of Warsaw, Illinois.

OERTEL'S 92 LIGHT LAGER BEER—spicy aroma, highly carbonated, light and sweet at the front of the taste, sour and bitter in the finish. The brand originated with the Oertel Brewing Co. of Louisville and later was produced by the Oertel Brewing Co. Div. of G. Heileman in Newport, Kentucky. It is an old label and the 92 is believed not to refer to caloric content.

VAN MERRITT BEER—virtually no aroma; salty, malty taste; salty finish and aftertaste. According to the label, Van Merritt is "the world's most honored beer" with "imported flavor" and is made from an Old World recipe originated in 1433 and improved through the centuries. Van Merritt was a brand of the Van Merritt Brewing Co. of Chicago, Burlington, Wisconsin, and Joliet, Illinois, and later, of the Old Crown Brewing Corp.

ALPS BRAU BAVARIAN STYLE PREMIUM BEER—faint grainy malty aroma, very little flavor, even less aftertaste. This brand was obtained from Old Crown and originated with the Centliver Brewing Co. of Fort Wayne, Indiana.

OLD GERMAN STYLE BEER—no aroma detectable, pale color, neutral flavor, highly carbonated, sour aftertaste. This brand was obtained from the Renner Brewing Co. of Fort Wayne.

ZODIAC MALT LIQUOR—faint sweet aroma, deep yellow-brown color, sweet fruitlike taste with acidic follow-through.

Hudepohl Brewing Co.
(Burger Brewing Co.)
(Cincinnati, Ohio)

This company began in 1855 when a Cincinnati distiller, Louis Hudepohl, and partner, Fred Kotte, purchased the old (and once famous) Koehler Brewery. Hudepohl & Kotte marketed brands Buckeye (named for the brewery on Buckeye Street), Muenchener, Dortmunder, and Hudepohl. When Kotte died in 1899, the business incorporated as the Hudepohl Brewing Co.

During Prohibition the company survived by

85

producing near-beer and soft drinks. Following repeal, public acceptance of Hudepohl beer necessitated increased production and in 1934 the Lackman Brewing Co. was purchased for a second plant. Eventually, the Buckeye plant was closed and the operation was consolidated into an industrial complex on the fringe of Cincinnati's downtown area.

The product line includes Hofbrau Deutschlager Bier, an all-malt beer sold only in draft, Hudepohl, and Hudepohl Draft (which is packaged in bottles that must be refrigerated). Since April 1973, when Hudepohl acquired the principal assets of the Burger Brewing Co., the product line has included the Burger and Tap labels. It is worth noting that Burger purchased the old Windisch Muhlhauser Brewery in 1943 and operated it until 1973. The Windisch Muhlhauser Brewing Co., founded in Cincinnati in 1866, was the fifth largest brewery in the United States in 1871 and 1872. Hudy Delight, with 96 calories appeared in 1978 and Burger Light, a 110-calorie version of Burger, appeared in 1980. Christian Moerlein, a super premium named for a German who founded a brewery in Cincinnati in 1853, was introduced in September 1981. A new natural bock, Ludwig Hudepohl, appeared in the spring of 1982.

Hudepohl has about one-third of the Cincinnati area market. It also makes its products available in Ohio, Tennessee, West Virginia, Virginia, Indiana, Kentucky, Illinois, and Michigan. Its promotions include "Process 14-K," a company-developed process which yields a clearer and brighter beer, and local Cincinnati professional and amateur sporting events.

In late 1983, Hudepohl became the first to offer a reduced alcohol brew: Pace Pilsener Beer, with less than 2% alcohol, and 85 calories. Beer marketers are watching this new product with great interest.

TAP LAGER BEER—pale gold, cereal grain aroma, sort of like oatmeal, dull malty flavor, medium body, finish shows some hops and the aftertaste has some duration, but the overall effect is not very interesting.

HOFBRAU BIER—deep gold, clean malt and hop aroma, medium to light body, spicy hop flavor up front on the palate, good solid malt and hop flavor with a little sweetness showing in the finish, long delicious aftertaste, flavor is very

good and refreshing, and a lot like a toned-down version of Christian Moerlein.

CHRISTIAN MOERLEIN CINCINNATI SELECT BEER—deep tawny gold, clean malt and hop aroma with great complexity, full body, excellent spicy hop character, touch of sweetness in the finish, long aftertaste, an excellent brew, and one of America's best super-premiums. In 1983, it became the first American brew to pass the German Reinheitsgebot.

LUDWIG HUDEPOHL ORIGINAL BOCK BEER—deep copper color, lovely roasted malt nose, smooth dry roasted malt flavor, long malty aftertaste, not heavy, and very drinkable. Bottle bears a neck label denoting the "vintage."

HUDEPOHL PURE GRAIN BEER—interesting spicy aroma, flavor definitely on the salty side, good body, salty nature carries through to the finish and aftertaste.

LUDWIG HUDEPOHL SPECIAL OKTOBERFEST BEER—very pale orange, dry malt aroma, good dry malt flavor, well balanced, refreshing malt aftertaste, good brew!

BURGER BEER—very pale gold, pleasant malty aroma, light malty flavor and finish.

HUDY DELIGHT BEER—96 calories, very pale yellow gold, burnt malt and wood pulp aroma, burnt malt and straw flavor, dull and dry, unbalanced, woody finish. Likely a mishandled sample. Hudy Delight was introduced in 1978.

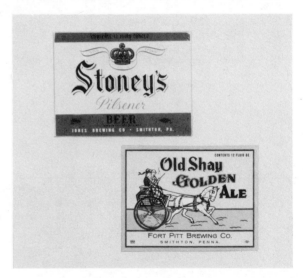

PACE PILSENER BEER—tawny gold, grainy beery nose, taste very light, low CO_2, clean, but very light, almost flat.

Independent Ale Brewing Co.
(Red Hook Brewery) (Seattle, Wash.)

This "microbrewery" produces only 100 percent barley malt Red Hook Ale on draught for Seattle's restaurants and bars. Red Hook is described by its fans as being similar to English pale ales such as Samuel Smith's. The brew is produced in 25-barrel runs using a new brew kettle purchased in Germany. The annual brewing capacity has recently expanded to exceed 3000 barrels.

Jones Brewing Co.
(Smithton, Pa.)

It would seem that fate was in a jolly mood when it arranged for a Jones to establish a brewery in a Smith town. This relatively young company (founded after Prohibition on the premises of the defunct Eureka Brewing Co.) caters to regional tastes in the area about twenty-five miles south of Pittsburgh.

STONEY'S PILSENER BEER—good malty aroma, salty flavor, salty-sour finish and aftertaste. This is a beer that performs well with food, but shows poorly when tasted by itself as at a tasting.

ESQUIRE PREMIUM BEER—faint austere aroma, sour metallic taste, sour metallic aftertaste. Needs to be very cold to overcome the tinny nature and the excessive sourness. I cared little for it; it did not perform well in the taste trials. A number of people did like it well enough to ask where they could find more.

OLD SHAY GOLDEN CREAM ALE—light gold, some particulate matter, albumin aroma, light and watery, touch of sweet malt flavor, metallic-soapy finish and aftertaste.

FORT PITT SPECIAL BEER—pale yellow, faint sweet malty nose, flat dry dull flavor, mostly malt with very faint hops, metallic aftertaste.

Fred Koch Brewery
(Dunkirk, N.Y.)

This brewery was founded by partners Fred Koch and Frank Werle in 1888, when they bought the Old Fink Brewery in Dunkirk. A few months later they, and their lone employee, moved to the present site of the brewery on Courtney Street. In 1896 a fire completely destroyed the plant. Koch bought out Werle's interest and rebuilt. The brewery was incorporated in 1911. Knowing that Prohibition was just around the corner, Koch purchased the Deer Run Water Co. and the Star Bottling Co. in 1919 and survived the period on spring water, soft drinks, a near-beer called Kobru, and liquid malty syrup.

Reopened as a brewery following repeal, the Koch Brewery expanded throughout the 1930s, 1940s, and 1950s to a capacity of over a hundred thousand barrels. Sales today are in the range of 80 thousand barrels per year with 40 percent of that as draft. The Koch Brewery was purchased from the Koch family in early 1982 by Vaux of Sunderland, England, which plans to continue the Koch brands and (eventually) market new brews. There are no current plans to produce Vaux Double Maxim at Dunkirk.

The Koch repertoire includes Koch's Light Lager Beer, Golden Anniversary Beer (introduced in 1938 to celebrate Koch's 50th), Deer Run Ale, Holiday Beer (every Christmas), and Simon Pure, a label acquired from the William Simon Brewing Co. of Buffalo in 1971.

Koch also produces the Iroquois brands, which were obtained from Iroquois Industries in

87

1972. This line of labels virtually doubles the number of Koch-produced labels on the western New York market. Included are Phoenix Cream Ale and Phoenix Premium Beer (formerly of the Phoenix Brewing Co. of Buffalo), Bavarian's Select Beer (from the Bavarian Brewing Co., Covington, Ky.), Iroquois Beer and Draft Brewed Beer (originally of the International Brewing Co. of Buffalo and later of the Iroquois Brewing Co., also of Buffalo), and Black Horse Ale. The Koch Black Horse used the same logo as the Black Horse produced by Champale, Inc., in New Jersey, where it is still listed as a subsidiary of Iroquois Brands Ltd., until 1980, when it changed to a very plain and attractive logo with a black label.

Koch products are marketed under various breweries of record, to include the Koch, Simon Pure, Black Horse, and Iroquois names, all identified as being of Dunkirk, New York. Many of the Koch brands were produced in cans until 1982, when this practice was discontinued.

KOCH'S GOLDEN ANNIVERSARY BEER—bright yellow gold, sour malt nose with hops in the background, good fresh flavor at the sart but finishes strange and sour, highly carbonated. Tastes very good until you begin to swallow it; something in it aggravates the taste buds on the back of the tongue.

KOCH'S LIGHT LAGER BEER—flowery yeasty nose, light body, malty yeasty flavor and a sour finish. Best part was the aroma.

PHOENIX PREMIUM BEER—medium gold, malty-grainy nose, highly carbonated, very hoppy flavor with a sharp component in the background that lingers, short aftertaste, starts better than it finishes.

IROQUOIS INDIAN HEAD BEER (Iroquois Brewing Co.)—malty aroma, dry lightly hopped and malted flavor, good balance, a reasonably pleasant brew in a very pretty can, a bit overcarbonated.

BAVARIAN'S SELECT BEER (Iroquois Brewing Co.)—clean yeasty aroma with good malt, taste of sour carbonation with a metallic finish, not too good. Not currently being produced.

SIMON PURE BEER (Simon Pure Brewery)—gold yeasty aroma, salty taste with high carbonation, faintly sour finish and aftertaste, CO_2 in the way all the way through.

KOCH'S HOLIDAY BEER—pale gold, sweet malt and hop nose; cereal grain, hop, and cardboard flavor; dull, brief finish, long aftertaste.

KOCH'S DEER RUN ALE—yellow, big creamy yeasty nose, foamy-creamy appearance, big sweet malt flavor but not flabby, lots of everything, good balance, good flavor, sweet caramel-like finish, good but would be better if drier.

BLACK HORSE PREMIUM ALE—bright gold, nice hoppy-malt aroma, rich flavor, good balance, a little sweet up front, clean in the mouth, lots of character, long aftertaste. Produced by both Koch and Champale, but are different in taste and style. Until 1980, both used the same logo, but Koch has since adopted a new attractive design.

FRED KOCH JUBILEE PORTER—deep copper brown, light toasted malt aroma, medium body, toasted malt flavor, sour in the middle, pleasant and complex, good finish and aftertaste, lacks balance.

The following brews are made for International Brewers Ltd. by the Simon Pure Brewery (Koch):

PIPING ROCK SUPER PREMIUM BEER—golden color, sweet malt nose with a sour hop background, sweet malt and hop palate, light body, a bit flat and a bit flabby, some sourness in the aftertaste, not balanced.

WINDJAMMER LUSTY LAGER—pale gold, light and good malt aroma, very dry malt palate, very brief but very drinkable.

PILGRIM'S PRIDE SPECIAL RESERVE BEER—pale copper, light toasted malt aroma, light toasted malt flavor, quite dry, very brief on palate, faint caramel aftertaste, light and refreshing, dry finish.

GOLDEN CREST ALE—medium gold, hop aroma, medium to good body, sharp hop palate, sour finish, lots of character, sort of Canadian-like but needs something to mitigate sharpness of the hops.

BLUE FOX CREAM ALE—pale gold, light malt and hop nose, flavor is pleasant malt up front with too much CO_2, fairly dry, little finish or aftertaste, just cuts off as you swallow it.

CHAMPION FULL BODIED BEER—brilliant copper red, lovely roasted malt aroma, pleasant roasted malt palate up front, good to the finish but then an overly sour aftertaste mars the effect.

SUMMIT AMBER BEER—pale copper, stinky cardboard nose, malty when swirled, faintly sweet palate, difficult to describe but not because it was complex, light-bodied, not in balance, not likable.

BULL'S EYE DARK BEER—deep copper, light roasted malt nose, palate to match, light body, watery at finish, aftertaste drier than palate.

Latrobe Brewing Co.
(Latrobe, Pa.)

In 1893 the Latrobe Brewing Company was founded in Pennsylvania and by 1899 had been absorbed by the Pittsburgh Brewing Company

Nips" and was the first beer seen in the new seven-ounce squat cans. It is also available in a variety of 12-ounce can and bottle packages.

ROLLING ROCK PREMIUM BEER—pale color, delicious light malt aroma with a trace of hops in the back; most of the flavor is up front where it is fairly zesty; there is some bitterness in the back, but it is not offensive. A very good value, worth trying and worth considering for regular use. Judged to be one of the best beer values in America and a pretty good little beer for drinking pleasure.

ROLLING ROCK "LIGHT" BEER—pale gold, faint malt aroma, light body, slightly sour malt flavor, light flavor, weak sour aftertaste. Introduced in 1982.

Jacob Leinenkugel Brewing Co.
(Chippewa Falls, Wis.)

In 1867 Jacob Leinenkugel and John Miller founded a brewery in Chippewa Falls. Leinenkugel bought out his partner in 1884 and became sole proprietor, and in 1889 the firm was incorporated in the name above. When Jacob died in 1899, the second generation, Matthias Leinenkugel and son-in-laws Henry Casper and John Mayer, took over the firm. Today the fourth generation, in the persons of William Leinenkugel and Paul Mayer, continues to own and manage this fine independent Wisconsin brewery.

The product line includes Leinenkugel's Beer, Bosch Premium Beer, and Gilt Edge Premium Beer (both former products of the Bosch Brewing Co. of Houghton, Mich.), Leinenkugel's Genuine Bock Beer, Leinie's Light, Chippewa Pride, and Tahoe Beer, packaged in old-fashioned cans and bottles for the Lake Tahoe area only. Leinenkugel products are mild beers using corn grits as an adjunct and Yakima Valley hops. Leinenkugel's was called second only to Coors by a recent magazine article and termed therein "the Coors of the East." The magazine had obviously not been written in Boston, where locals have pinned that appellation on Rolling Rock. Since it is doubtful that many Bostonians have tried Leinenkugel's, maybe a test between the principals is in order or Leinenkugel's could settle to be "the Coors of the Midwest," since it is marketed primarily in Michigan, Minnesota, and Wisconsin. Another national magazine named Leinenkugel's best of

syndicate. Today a small independent brewery by that name cranks out only two beers, but does it on a large scale and in many packages for its many devoted followers in the East.

Although very few profess Rolling Rock as their favorite, I've never found anyone who said that he out and out disliked it. It is widely sold along the Boston-Washington corridor at popular prices and has been seen as far north as Maine and as far south as Florida. In Massachusetts some refer to it as "the Coors of the East."

Rolling Rock has long been available in returnable seven-ounce bottles called "Little

89

the local (Chicago area) brands.

All Leinenkugel products are available in 12-ounce and 7-ounce returnable bottles, 12-ounce NR bottles, and in 12-ounce cans. Leinenkugel now has a new Hospitality Center and President William Leinenkugel extends a ready welcome to visitors. Guided tours, souvenir/gift shop, museum of breweriana, and a new Steinwirt for tasting privileges of Leinenkugel products are offered.

A note for can collectors: Leinenkugel cans are obtainable from the company at 1-3 Jefferson Avenue, Chippewa Falls, Wisconsin 54729, at a cost of $2 per pair, including postage and handling.

LEINENKUGEL'S BEER—made with Chippewa Falls water from the Big Eddy Spring; pale-colored, faint somewhat dull aroma, slightly grainy flavor with hints of a wood pulp or cardboard taste, surprisingly poor taste for the Coors of anywhere, and the samples came from a fresh source in Minnesota.

LEINIE'S LIGHT NATURAL LIGHT PREMIUM BEER—96 calories, tawny gold, appetizing malt and hop aroma, light body, light faintly malty flavor with some hops, grainy finish and aftertaste.

CHIPPEWA PRIDE LIGHT PREMIUM BEER—bright gold, very clean malty aroma with a hint of olives; more malt than hops, but good character, tart and salty at the start, smooths out to a good dry finish.

CHIPPEWA FALLS (1977 PURE WATER DAYS LIGHT PREMIUM BEER)—bright gold; similar to Chippewa Pride (and it may even be Chippewa Pride), but a little different, tart saltiness at the start, finish is sweet and brief, overall a very pleasant brew.

BOSCH PREMIUM BEER—pale gold, perfumy malt aroma; at first a bready taste, then a sour malty-cardboard flavor. "From the sportsman's paradise" says the label, formerly belonging to the Bosch Brewing Co. of Houghton, Michigan.

Lion, Inc.
(Wilkes-Barre, Pa.)

The Wyoming Valley of Pennsylvania once

could boast enough breweries to sate the combined thirst of all its residents. Today most of these local breweries have passed into history in the wake of the overwhelming advertising and production efficiency of the large national brewing companies. Only one, Lion, Inc., remains today, brewing its own Gibbons and acquired local brands, Stegmaier and Bartels.

Lion Brewery began in 1906 as the Luzerne Brewery, which went into receivership in 1908. Nine years later it was sold in a receiver's sale for $28,000 and named Lion Brewery. This inauspicious start did not portend the finish, however, for when Stegmaier closed down in 1974, Lion was the last surviving brewery in the Wyoming Valley. Lion produces a beer under the Gibbons name; an ale, a beer, a light beer, and a porter under the Stegmaier banner, Bartels Beer, Liebotschaner Ale and Bock, and a private label, Home Beer. Lion also recently obtained the Esslinger label from Schmidt's following the latter's purchase of Rheingold.

In 1979, when Star Markets of the greater Boston area made national news with its "No-Name" brands, many supermarket chains rushed to compete. Among the products included was No-Name or No-Frills beer. Most of such brews seen in the Middle Atlantic states are from Lion.

GIBBONS PREMIUM FAMOUS LIGHT BEER—pale color, very malty aroma, high carbonation, little flavor, neutral finish, a neutrally flavored beer with neither zest nor offense. Available in returnable bottles under $4 per case at Pennsylvania case outlets. Also available in cans and nonreturnable bottles.

GIBBONS FOUR STAR PREMIUM QUALITY ALE—medium tawny color, faint hop-malt aroma, light malty flavor, very light, inoffensive, slightly more character than Gibbons Beer, priced comparably, including the very inexpensive returnables. This product has recently been discontinued.

GIBBONS PETER PIPPIN PORTER—totally opaque brown, strong malty aroma, light body, light sickish-sweet flavor, faint sweet finish. Not good, but very inexpensive. This label was recently discontinued.

LIEBOTSCHANER CREAM ALE—pale color, very malty aroma, sour background to a sweet taste, pleasant-tasting finish and aftertaste. Not really an ale on the palate, more like a pilsener, but quite good, thirst quenching and slides down easily. Seen only in cans and nonreturnable bottles. The Liebotschaner name originated in upstate New York in the 1870s. Genesee made it in Rochester in 1878.

LIEBOTSCHANER BOCK BEER—copper-gold color,

light malty aroma, fair burnt malt taste, light-bodied austere finish, somewhat on the shallow side. Only seen in cans.

NO-FRILLS BEER (Pocono Brewing Co., distributed by Supermarkets General Corp., Woodbridge, N.J.)—yellow, small bubble carbonation, good malt slightly sour aroma, light clean flavor, short slightly malty finish. Tastes like Gibbons.

HOME PILSENER BEER (Pocono Brewing Co, Wilkes-Barre)—pale color, light malty aroma with some vegetal character, sweet light flavor, light sweet finish with some hops, dull and sort of strange. This brand is made for Astor Home/Home Liquors of New Jersey.

ESSLINGER PREMIUM BEER (Pocono Brewing Co.)—light yellow color, light malt aroma, light body, reasonably good flavor with good hop and malt balance. A very good beer at a very good price. This label originated with the Esslinger Brewing Co. of Philadelphia, founded in 1868 by George Esslinger. From 1937 to 1953 separate ale and lager plants were operated. In 1964 Esslinger closed and the brand was continued by Rheingold Breweries until late 1977, when it passed to C. Schmidt & Sons, Inc. and thence to Lion.

ECONOMY CORNER BEER—a no-name brand, gold color, sour malt aroma, highly carbonated, very light malt flavor, watery finish, weak sour aftertaste.

GIANT FOOD PREMIUM BEER—very pale, light malty nose, faint slightly sour malt flavor, sour finish, not very exciting. This brand is brewed for Giant Food, Inc., Washington, D.C., a grocery chain. It was produced earlier by Eastern Brewing Corp., Hammonton, New Jersey, and the Sunshine Brewing Co. of Reading, Pennsylvania.

SAVALOT BEER—very pale, virtually no aroma, flavor only of carbonation, slightly sour finish.

Stegmaier Brewing Co. *(Wilkes-Barre, Pa.)*

Stegmaier was the largest brewery in the Wyoming valley and once was one of the largest independent breweries in America. Charles Stegmaier's first venture into brewing took place in 1851, when he and John Reichard formed a short-lived partnership. By 1857 this effort had failed and Stegmaier had begun again with a new partner, George C. Baer. The Stegmaier & Baer Brewery lasted until 1873, when it went bankrupt. (John Reichard was more successful with his second try, establishing Reichard & Stauff, which lasted until 1939 under the names of Reichard & Son and the Pennsylvania Central Brewing Co.) Charles Stegmaier's third attempt, this time with his sons as partners, was a success. Begun in 1875, the firm was incorporated in 1897 as the Stegmaier Brewing Company and lasted ninety-nine years, closing in October 1974. In its heyday Stegmaier won gold medals at European fairs in 1909 and 1911 and had an annual production of a half-million barrels in 1940.

STEGMAIER GOLD MEDAL BEER—pale color, light malty aroma, light body, light malt flavor, almost no aftertaste, inoffensive.

STEGMAIER PORTER—brown and opaque, faint malty nose, light cloying flavor, mostly just carbonation, little finish, no aftertaste.

STEGMAIER LIGHT BEER—pale color, light malty aroma, very light body and flavor, mostly just carbonation, little finish, no aftertaste. Recently seen in a can marked Steg Light.

BASICS BEER—generic label or no-name brand of Grand Union grocery stores in New York, made by Stegmaier according to the package; pale, light malty aroma and taste,

little finish and aftertaste, light and inoffensive.

Bartels Brewing Co. *(Edwardsville, Pa.)* Bartels began in Syracuse in 1886 as the Germania Brewing Co. The founder, John Greenway, sold out in 1893 to Herman Bartels, who reorganized and expanded the company. He operated the Syracuse plant and was a partner in the Bartels Brewing Co. of Edwardsville and the Munroe Brewing Co. of Rochester, New York. The Edwardsville facility ceased operations in 1968, the Bartels label being acquired by Lion, Inc., in late 1967. Until recently, Bartels Beer was seen only in returnable bottles, but is now regularly packaged in cans as well.

BARTELS PURE BEER—pale to medium color, very faint malt aroma, neutral, rather dull taste, sour finish. Not much of a beer.

CRYSTAL PREMIUM BEER—bright pale gold, faint malt aroma, flavor of faint malt but mostly CO_2, refreshing.

F. X. Matt Brewing Co.
(Utica, N.Y.)

In 1856 Charles Bierbauer founded a brewery that became the Columbian Brewing Co. in 1885 and was to become the West End Brewing Co. under the supervision of F.X. Matt two years later. The brewery was so named because, of the twelve breweries then in Utica, it was the one that primarily serviced the west end of town. The present name was adopted in 1981.

The corporate name of F.X. Matt Brewing Co., long used on the widely marketed Maximus Super, is named for the company founder and grandfather of the present and third generation of company management. Matt's Premium Lager was also produced under the F.X. Matt corporate name. A Maximus Regular, introduced as a less alcoholic companion to Super, was not a market success and is no longer made. With the current interest in light beer (now reportedly accounting for 11 percent of beer sales in the country), it may yet make another appearance.

Only Utica Club Pilsener Lager and Cream Ale were marketed under the West End corporate name. An Old Enlgish Ale has been marketed in the Utica area, but only on draft and in limited quantities. It may no longer be available. In 1978 Matt introduced its "beer ball," a seamless polyethylene spherical three-gallon container with a reusable pump.

A Fort Schuyler brand was procured from the Utica Brewing Co. in 1959 and is now produced by Matt, attributed to the Fort Schuyler Brewing Co., to compete in the low-priced end of the market. Matt also began brewing and distributing its version of Billy Beer in early 1978 (see Falls City Brewing Co. for the story on Billy Beer). Billy Beer was discontinued in 1979. Utica Club Light also made its appearance in 1978 and has enjoyed great success.

The Matt products are found regularly in upstate New York and parts of New England only, although they are marketed in fifteen states. We have seen them in Connecticut, Maryland, Massachusetts, Pennsylvania, New York, and New Jersey. The excellent Max Super has been seen in many places outside the Matt marketing area; it has a scattered but very loyal following. It was seen as far south as North Carolina.

Correspondence from Mr. F.X. Matt, president and Chief Executive Officer of the F.X. Matt Brewing Co. and namesake of the founder, makes a point with regard to the term *lager,* a commonly misused word: "*Lager* comes from a German word meaning 'to age' and, historically, it was the Germans who added the refinement of aging to beer making. All modern beers are aged, even if *lager* does not appear on their label, although aging practices vary widely from brand to brand. The term *pilsener* refers to a type of pale-colored and milder-tasting beer which was first brewed in Pilsen, Czechoslovakia, and which represented quite a difference from the Munchener heavy, dark beers which were made in Munich, Germany. Today, practically all beers are of the pilsen variety and thus are known as pilseners." Notwithstanding its uselessness as a descriptive term, the word *lager* has become so popular among beer drinkers and label designers that nothing short of a cosmic catastrophe will diminish its popularity. You will note, from the first brand listed below, that even Mr. Matt has had to concede to popular usage.

It is worth noting that Matt packages carry a "pull date," at which time it is pulled from the shelf and replaced at company expense. The time allowed for Matt's Premium is 60 days and for the other Matt products it is 6 months.

UTICA CLUB PILSENER LAGER BEER—aroma of Concord grapes and corn, light malty vegetal flavor, light neutral finish, no aftertaste.

UTICA CLUB CREAM ALE—pale yellow, sour malt-hop nose, dry palate on the sour side, flattens out in the finish.

UTICA CLUB LIGHT BEER—96 calories, good golden color, malt aroma with some hops, taste reflects aroma, no finish.

MAXIMUS SUPER BEER—deep golden color, complex aroma of malt and hops, clean taste with an excellent balance of malt and hops, very Germanic in style, good flavor and good aftertaste. One of the best American beers.

MATT'S PREMIUM LAGER—light gold, nice fruitlike aroma; slight sweetness on front of palate, like apple peel, clean taste, not really beery, very drinkable, light body. Both rice and corn are used as adjuncts in this recipe.

FORT SCHUYLER LAGER BEER—grainy barley aroma that reflected the taste that followed, some hops underlying the grainy flavor, very dry, brief finish. A fairly good beer at its price. It is called "the beer drinker's beer," a claim that has got to be one of the more pretentious on a U.S. label; the prize, however, goes to "the expert beer drinker's beer" (Courage Draught of Australia).

BILLY BEER—bright yellow, sour malty well-hopped nose, faintly skunky in back, very dry, doubtful balance, short metallic finish. Totally different from Billy Beer of Falls City, this brew seems slightly similar to Fort Schuyler.

Miller Brewing Co.

(Milwaukee, Wis.; Azusa, Calif.; Irwindale, Calif.; Eden, N.C.; South Volney, N.Y.; Albany, Ga.; Fort Worth, Tex.; and additional plant in Trenton, Ohio was to open in 1983.)

The Miller Brewing Co. shares its beginnings with Pabst; both were founded by members of the Best family. When Jacob Best, Sr., retired from business in 1853, he was succeeded by his four sons. By 1860 Phillip Best (who was to be succeeded by his son-in-law, Frederick Pabst) had become sole proprietor of the Best Brewing Co. At that time two of the sons, Charles and Lorenz, left Best and formed a brewing partnership under the name of Best Brothers and founded the Menomonee Valley Brewery. Included in their accomplishments was the beginning of Milwaukee's "export" trade to New York. In 1855 Frederick Miller (who had entered the brewing business four years earlier in Rochester, N.Y.) purchased the firm and in 1888 a stock company was formed under the name of the Frederick Miller Brewing Co.

Today the Miller Brewing Co. ranks second only to Anheuser-Busch in beer sales. When Philip Morris, Inc., took over Miller in 1970 sales were under five million barrels. In 1982 sales reached thirty-nine million barrels, mostly at the expense of the other large brewers, many of whom actually experienced a drop in sales because of Miller's aggressive marketing. The product line is headed by popular and much advertised Miller High Life, "the champagne of beers", and Lite, introduced in 1975, the Miller low-calorie beer which evolved from Meister Brau Lite, formerly of the Meister Brau Brewing Co. of Chicago. Both are produced in all Miller plants. Meister Brau and Muenchener are produced only in Milwaukee for the Midwest market. Muenchener is sold only in kegs. Fort Worth has produced Players for test markets. Clipper Dark Light Beer, with a logo similar to Players', was introduced in 1980 on a limited basis. Miller Ale and Miller Malt Liquor have been discontinued. Magnum Malt Liquor and Miller Special Reserve appeared in late 1981. Miller introduced a pull date on cans and bottle crowns in 1979.

Import and distribution of Munich Lowenbrau had been handled by Miller for a number of years. In late 1977 the manufacture of Lowenbrau Light Special and Lowenbrau Dark Special began in all Miller plants. The Munich import was phased out with the domestic version as a replacement. The beers are very different and, although the domestic product is priced from one-fourth to one-third lower, the success of the maneuver remains to be seen because Munich Lowenbrau was very popular. Munich Lowenbrau is made from 100 percent barley malt without adjuncts and additives in accordance with strict Bavarian laws for brewing, and is krausened and fermented for over six weeks. Miller's Lowenbrau uses corn (about 28 percent, I have heard) and is fermented for a much shorter time. It is a good recipe but different and less expensive in ingredients and technique.

MILLER HIGH LIFE—bright gold, pleasant aromatic hop nose with touch of apple peel, clean, flavorful, refreshing, complex, tasty palate.

LITE PILSENER BEER—one of the original reduced calorie beer recipes, Lite remains one of the better ones and still the force to be reckoned with among nationally distributed low calorie brews. Pale gold, light-bodied, good malty aroma, pleasant and thirst quenching, no offensive features and usually available in fresh condition because of the high turnover. 97 calories.

LOWENBRAU LIGHT SPECIAL—light gold color, clean malty aroma, hops dominate the flavor, well-balanced, carbonation not overdone. A fine beer, an excellent effort; unfortunately, it is available to us only at the terrible price of losing the Munich Light Special that it replaces. Better to have them both.

LOWENBRAU DARK SPECIAL—deep reddish orange color, fine malty hop aroma, nose similar to Munich Dark Special, flavor highly hopped (relative to the Munich version, it is more highly hopped, but has much less malt), light body, almost watery at the end, very little aftertaste.

PLAYERS LAGER BEER—70 calories, gold, lightly flavored, pleasant aroma with a touch of sour malt, not as pleasant on the palate, almost no aftertaste. Better well-chilled.

MEISTER BRAU—bright gold, austere malt aroma, sharp and sweet up front like an ale, good hops in middle and finish, slightly sour aftertaste, fair amount of character. Meister Brau was obtained by Miller from Meister Brau, Inc., of Chicago in 1970. From 1940 to 1967 the brand was produced by Peter Hand. Miller reintroduced the brand in 1983.

MILLER MALT LIQUOR—medium pale, cloudy with particulate matter, sharp, sour, malty, apple nose, tangy apple taste, bit flat, wood pulp finish, dull, probably too old. No longer produced.

MAGNUM MALT LIQUOR—pale yellow, faint sweet and fruity nose, slightly sweet malty flavor, almost flabby, light-bodied, slightly sweet finish and aftertaste, small bubble carbonation.

MILLER SPECIAL RESERVE BEER—medium gold, faint malt and hop aroma, salty CO_2 flavor, smooth, good balance at the finish, although a bit sweet, pleasant aftertaste.

MILWAUKEE'S BEST BEER (A. GETTELMAN BREW-ING CO.)—pale gold, pleasant malt aroma, highly carbonated, light body, slightly sweet malt flavor, good finish, fairly long aftertaste. Introduced by Miller in 1984 as a low-price item.

New Albion Brewing Co.
(Sonoma, Calif.)

New Albion, in the heart of California's wine country, was incorporated in October 1976, with brewery construction completed in July 1977. Production of ale and stout began in August 1977 in one of America's smallest breweries with an annual production of 350 barrels. It entered the highly competitive industry marketing its brews in the San Francisco Bay area. New Albion gets its name from Sir Francis Drake, who named the Bay Area that on his visit there in 1597. The company labels depict Drake's ship, the Golden Hinde.

New Albion produces ale, porter, and stout in the British tradition, naturally conditioned in the bottle. Yeast is added at the time of bottling and two weeks' storage at 60 to 65° F. allows final fermentation to take place. It is neither pasteurized nor filtered. All beer is bottled, except for Red Dragon Ale, draught service only. John R. McAuliffe is president and master brewer and Suzanne D. Stern is vice president and secretary. The brewery is run entirely by McAuliffe and Stern with the exception of three additional people on bottling day, once each week.

NEW ALBION STOUT—brown, totally opaque, faint, slightly sweet malt aroma, very little hops, light body, dull, slightly sour malt flavor, fruity sour finish, very faint fruity sour aftertaste, more fruity than sour, but little of either.

NEW ALBION ALE—cloudy gold, very light but pleasant and interesting sweet hop alelike aroma, taste to match, delicious up front on the palate and good while it is in your mouth. As soon as you swallow it, the flavor disappears.

NEW ALBION PORTER—cloudy orange-brown, sweet ale aroma, citrus-like well-hopped ale taste, too much carbonation, sour and bitter finish, poor balance, light slightly sour aftertaste.

Wm. S. Newman Brewing Co.
(Albany, N.Y.)

The first and (as yet) only "boutique" brewery on the East Coast appeared on the brewing scene in late 1981 producing Newman's Pale Ale for draft service in Albany, Troy, and Schenectady, New York.

Its main product is an English style pale ale that is conditioned in the cask for ten days before release. It is a copper-colored brew with a rich creamy head, light malt and hop flavor, slightly bittersweet finish and aftertaste with a touch of grain in the background. It is a medium-density brew that some have described as being half way between an English pale ale and an American cream ale.

A recent innovation is the availability of Newman's Pale Ale in 1½ and 5-gallon containers at the brewery on Thursday, Friday, and Saturdays, a very American practice back in the 19th century, except today the brew is sold in plastic containers instead of being dispensed in buckets.

In 1982 Newman introduced Newman's Winter Warmer, a dark, sweet brown ale with high alcohol content, available in one-gallon packages.

William Newman, president and head brewer, studied brewing under Masterbrewer Peter Austin of the Ringwood Brewery in England and used the Ringwood recipe for the Newman brews. The brew is approximately 5 percent alcohol and is not filtered, pasteurized, or artificially carbonated.

The brewery's annual capacity for production is a hefty 5000 barrels.

Old New York Beer Co.
(New York, N.Y.)

Only a few years ago, Matthew Reich was an executive at Citibank and, later, at Hearst, but as a lover of good food and drink he was willing to put his life savings on the line and become one of the new breed of "microbrewers". After two years of study and research he developed his ideas for an all-malt heavily hopped British style New Amsterdam Amber Beer, and with the help of Dr. Joseph L. Owades, famed brewmaster and director of the Center for Brewing Studies in Boston, made the concepts become reality.

Using the brewing facilities of F. X. Matt in Utica, N.Y., New Amsterdam is handmade, using only two-row barley crystal and roasted malts with Cascade and Hallertau hops. It is filtered and flash pasteurized and kept refrigerated until delivery to outlets.

NEW AMSTERDAM AMBER BEER—light copper color, small bubble carbonation, toasted malt nose, flavor starts as bright and hoppy and smooths out as it crosses the palate. There is a sweetness in the nose that doesn't appear on the palate until the aftertaste. The flavor is a clean toasted malt with caramel undertones. Excellent balance. Deserves a try as it is one of America's best brews.

Pabst Brewing Co.
(Milwaukee, Wis.; Peoria Heights, Ill.; Newark, N.J.; Los Angeles, Calif.)

In 1844 Jacob Best, Sr., established a small brewing plant on Chestnut Street Hill in Milwaukee. Together with his four sons, Philip,

Jacob Jr., Charles, and Lorenz, he operated the successful Best Brewing Co. until he retired in 1853.

In the next few years three of the brothers withdrew from the business and in 1860 Philip Best became sole proprietor. By this time the Empire Brewery, as it was then known, had secured a high reputation, especially for the new chill-brewed beer.

In 1862 a Great Lakes steamer captain, Frederick Pabst, married Philip Best's daughter Maria, and two years later became a partner in the brewery. When Best retired in 1866, he left the operation of Philip Best & Co. to his sons-in-laws, Frederick Pabst and Emil Schandein.

Captain Pabst was a businessman of remarkable talent and under his leadership the firm grew rapidly. It was incorporated as the Philip Best Brewing Co. in 1873 with a capital of $300,000. A year later the capital exceeded $2 million and the company was well on its way to being a leader in the American brewing industry. When the output of the brewery passed the half-million-barrel mark in 1889, the stockholders voted to change the name to the Pabst Brewing Co. in recognition of Captain Pabst's forward leadership of twenty-five years.

When the brewery of Falk, Jung & Borchert was destroyed by fire in 1892, the business was absorbed by Pabst, increasing the capital stock to $10 million and the annual output to over one million barrels.

From the beginning the firm had attempted to maintain a forward posture in the industry. Philip Best had brewed the first lager in Milwaukee in 1851. Artificial refrigeration had been installed as early as 1878. In 1902 a Pabst brewery was constructed; the first plant in the country equipped with a pipeline system for conveying the beer direct from the brewery to the bottling house.

The pinnacle of these efforts came in 1893, when Pabst was named "America's best" at the Columbian Exposition in Chicago. Two years later the Blue Ribbon name was added to the Pabst label with an actual blue ribbon affixed to the neck of the bottle. This device, a blue silk ribbon tied by hand and bearing the word "Select," had been used by Pabst for a full thirteen years before achieving the award.

During Prohibition Pabst survived by manufacturing soft drinks, malt syrup, near-beer, and cheese. As Prohibition came to a close, Pabst completed a merger with the Premier Malt Products Co. of Peoria, Illinois, and in 1934 acquired a plant in Peoria Heights. Further expansion occurred in 1945, when a third plant was opened in Newark, New Jersey, and in 1948, Pabst added a fourth by purchasing the Los Angeles Brewing Co. in California. The Blatz Brewing Co. of Milwaukee was purchased in 1958, but the Justice Department obtained a court order requiring divestiture of this asset in 1969, so Blatz was sold to the G. Heileman Brewing Co. A new brewery was added in 1970 in

Pabst, Georgia (so named by a decree of the state). The Peoria Heights plant was closed in December 31, 1981.

Pabst began a new phase of expansion in 1979 when they took over Blitz-Weinhard and in mid-1982 reached agreement with the Olympia Brewing Co. on a merger. In late 1982, however, in what was described in *Advertising Age* as a bloody barroom brawl involving dissident stockholders and Falstaff/General/Pearl owner Paul Kalmanovitz, the G. Heileman Brewing Co. acquired control of Pabst and Olympia. Subject to U.S. Justice Department consent and the results of a number of lawsuits, Pabst and Olympia will complete their merger and be spun off by Heileman as an independent brewing entity. As part of the agreement, however, in return for Heileman's controlling interest in Pabst, ownership of the Pabst brewery in Georgia, the Blitz-Weinhard plant in Portland, Oregon, and the Olympia facility in San Antonio passed to Heileman as did the Blitz-Weinhard, Henry Weinhard, Red White &Blue, Burgermeister, Lone Star, and Buckhorn (Texas) brands.

The new Pabst will be independent but will be missing some of its choicest parts. The greatest losses are involved with the diminution of the lucrative beer market in the deep South and the loss of the southwestern market. Three million barrels' capacity reduction is the ledger total for Pabst, but its fourteen-million barrel output will still rank it fifth in sales in the nation. In addition, Heileman will have a five-year contract to brew Pabst brands in the Georgia and Texas breweries.

An interesting side note is that as the Pabst takeover struggle ended, August U. Pabst resigned as executive vice president and ended the Pabst family association with the brewery.

The Pabst Brewing Co. believes that its philosophy of naturally brewed products with no artificial ingredients is responsible for maintaining its large share of the American market. Pabst uses a high percentage of malt for its brewing process and employs only corn as an adjunct. The yeast used is a pure European strain that dates back to 1887. Real hops (a mix of European and domestic) are used. Fermentation carbon dioxide is liquefied and stored for reinjection into the beer before packaging as a method of natural carbonation.

Today Pabst markets Blue Ribbon, Andeker, Pabst Extra Light, Pabst Special Dark (a light-bodied dark beer available generally on tap, but introduced in cans in mid-1979), and Pabst Blue Ribbon Bock Beer. Eastside and Old Tap Lager are brewed only for the West Coast. Pabst Old Tankard Ale and Big Cat Malt Liquor have been discontinued. Following the lead of its major competitors, Pabst had reached agreement with Fürstenberg Breweries of Donauschingen, West Germany, to import and distribute that beer in the U.S.—but that agreement was terminated in early 1983.

Pabst is proudest of Blue Ribbon and Andeker and spares no effort to maintain the quality and reputation of these products. When Pabst became the first nationwide brewer to market in cans, in July 1935, the product offered was not the famed Blue Ribbon, but a Pabst Export, just in case the can really did taint the beer. Andeker is produced using two-row barley malt, long preferred by Bavarian brewers, and only imported hops. It is double-fermented and aged for over thirty days (not just one to two weeks, like most American-made malt products). The consideration and care show in the consistent quality of these Pabst products.

PABST BLUE RIBBON BEER—light-colored, lightly flavored, very clean taste, no mentionable flaws, dry, inoffensive, but lacking in body and character. It is brewed at all Pabst breweries and is available nationwide.

ANDEKER LAGER BEER—bright gold, sweet hop aroma, pleasant hop palate on the sweet side, nice balance.

JACOB BEST PREMIUM LIGHT—96 calories, pale gold, delicious malty-beery aroma, clean fresh malt flavor, crisp, good CO_2 level, pleasant finish and aftertaste, a little sweetness at the end. Highest rated low-calorie beer found.

PABST BLUE RIBBON LIGHT BEER—pale bright gold, pleasant malt aroma, light, dry and tasty, very drinkable, fairly long aftertaste. Good effort. 96 calories.

PABST BLUE RIBBON BOCK BEER—very dark color, slightly sour aroma, taste that borders on unpleasant, almost no aftertaste at all. Found with regularity only in the spring, and then everywhere.

BIG CAT MALT LIQUOR—fresh, fruitlike aroma, pleasant taste like the nose, pleasant sweetness soon becomes dull on the palate as it lacks complexity, lacks aftertaste. Big Cat has not been produced for several years

COURTESY OLYMPIA BREWING COMPANY

West Coast's largest brewery — Overlooking the rapids and waterfalls of the Deschutes River, Olympia Brewing Company's headquarters brewery ranks as one of the biggest tourist attractions in the Pacific Northwest. The company and its best-selling beer take their name from the City of Olympia, the state capital on the southern shores of Washington's Puget Sound.

and even though still seen occasionally, the contents of the packages available are very likely overaged.

EASTSIDE LAGER BEER—very pale yellow, dry straw nose, good depth, slight malt flavor with some hops in the background, dull finish. Eastside was a brand of the Los Angeles Brewing Co.

Olympia Brewing Co. *(Olympia, Wash.; St. Paul, Minn.)* Olympia was founded in 1896 by Leopold F. Schmidt. Twenty years earlier Schmidt had begun the Centennial Brewery of Butte, Montana. On a visit to Olympia in 1894, he found the artesian waters (and surrounding countryside) of nearby Tumwater so attractive that he sold his holdings in Centennial (then Montana's largest brewery) and formed the Capital Brewing Co. in Tumwater.

In 1902 the newly named Olympia Brewing Co. became a pioneer in the multiple-brewery concept. Four breweries were in operation by 1909, but none could produce a beer comparable to that of the home plant. To protect the quality of the name, Olympia was brewed only at Tumwater. When Prohibition closed the plant down in 1916, it was the largest in the state.

With repeal, the Schmidt family, which held the copyrights and trade names, built a new brewery. The publicly held company has since been continuously managed by the Schmidt family and today the president of the firm, Leopold F. Schmidt, is the great grandson and namesake of the founder. In mid-1982 Olympia reached agreement with Pabst on a merger.

99

Olympia—the standard bearer of the Olympia Brewery Company. "Oly" has a large following that is growing steadily.

Olympia was one of the first to recognize that consumer interest following World War II had shifted from draft to packaged beer. It decided that a small brewer could not survive the required capital investment and that it had to expand nationally. In 1970 Olympia was marketed in only eleven western states. With the purchase of the Theodore Hamm Brewing Co. of St. Paul in March 1975 and the merger with the Lone Star Brewing Co. of San Antonio in December 1976, Olympia products extended to twenty-six states. In 1976 Olympia was sixth in the nation in sales, but slipped to seventh behind Heileman in 1979 and dropped to eighth (behind Stroh) in 1980. The recent merger with Pabst involved Olympia in the 1982 Heileman

Olympia Gold, the Olympia entry in the low calorie market

takeover bid (see Pabst). When the dust settled, Olympia and Pabst had survived as an independent brewing entity, but the San Antonio brewery and the Lone Star and Buckhorn (Texas) labels had passed to Heileman. Heileman will continue to produce Pabst-Olympia brands at the San Antonio plant under special agreement for a period of five years.

The new Pabst Brewing Co. will be an independent brewing holding company, but more as a "super-regional" than a national brewer—with the loss of key assets in the south and southwestern markets.

Tumwater is open daily to visitors from 9 to 5, except Thanksgiving, Christmas, and New Year's. St. Paul is open weekdays, 11 to 4. Both operate brewery gift shops. Mail orders are

The Hamm's bear, who was a popular commercial personality in the '50s and '60s, made a comeback in the '80s as a TV personality in a new series of Hamm's advertisements.

available from Olympia Brewing Co. Merchandising Dept., P.O. Box 2008, Olympia, Washington 98507.

In 1982 Olympia introduced Grenzquell, a 100 percent barley malt import brewed by the Bavaria–St. Pauli Brauerei of Hamburg, West Germany, a member of the Reemstma group. It was discontinued in 1983, but some packages may still be around.

OLYMPIA BEER—a very pale beer with very light malt aroma, extremely clean light flavor with some hops noticeable in the finish. Oly has many followers who say it is better than Coors; together these two dominate the western beer scene. Samples we tried were much better when tasted fresh from the brewery; it may be our imagination, but Olympia from Washington tasted better than Olympia from St. Paul.

OLYMPIA GOLD LIGHT BEER—70 calories, pale gold, light fresh malty nose, very light flavor. Pleasant, but very light.

GRENZQUELL GERMAN PILSNER—brilliant gold, good well-hopped aroma, very German-like, lots of good barley malt character, big flavor; if you like a gutsy beer, this is a beauty.

GRENZQUELL GERMAN DARK PILSNER—deep copper, lovely roasted malt and hop aroma, nice roasted malt flavor with hops in balance, but unexpectedly thin, touch of molasses flavor in the long finish, short aftertaste.

MEDALLION SPECIAL BEER—deep yellow gold, rising hop and malt (slightly toasted) nose, medium body; thin, slightly toasted malt flavor that lacks much of the attractiveness of the aroma.

Theodore Hamm Brewing Co. The original Hamm brewery was built in 1884 by A.F. Keller and purchased by Theodore Hamm in 1895. It was incorporated as the Theodore Hamm Brewing Co. in 1896. "Born in the land of sky-blue waters," Hamm tried expansion to the West Coast in 1953 and 1957, but the move was not

successful. Hamm also obtained the Gunther Brewing Co. facility in Baltimore at this time but sold it to the F. & M. Schaefer Brewing Co. when expansion failed. Olympia purchased Hamm in 1975 and changed the Hamm formula shortly thereafter to bolster sagging sales.

HAMM'S BEER—bright gold, beautiful yeasty-malty nose, sweet pleasant malt flavor, short fruity-apple finish.

HAMM'S DRAFT BEER—pale color, sweet aroma with a touch of vegetable, overly carbonated, a too sweet taste, very brief flavor and aftertaste.

HAMM'S SPECIAL LIGHT—99 calories, medium deep gold, faint malty-hop aroma, watery, faint malty flavor, some hops, little finish and aftertaste, not well balanced.

BUCKHORN PREMIUM LAGER BEER—clean malty aroma, clean and pleasant taste, bitter finish, not very interesting. This label originated with the Buckhorn Brewing Co. of St. Paul and was acquired by Hamm in 1973. It is not the same Buckhorn that is produced by Lone Star.

PABST EXTRA LIGHT BEER—70 calories, pale color, very faint hoppy aroma, light mineral water flavor, slightly sweet, weak and watery, faintly mineral aftertaste. Pabst also markets a Pabst Light Beer (one hundred calories) in certain parts of the country; it is about the same as Pabst Extra Light.

PABST SPECIAL DARK BEER—clear copper-orange, light malty aroma, highly carbonated, light body, light malty flavor, no intensity of flavor, smooth, light and simple, nothing to offend. This brew is longer aged and a greater percentage of malt is used in this recipe than in most other Pabst brews.

Palo Alto Brewery
(Mountain View, Calif.)

Another in the string of micro-breweries that have popped up in California is Palo Alto, founded in 1983 by a father and son team, Kenneth and Jeffrey Kolance. Using British malt, British yeast, and the recipe for Brakspear Best Bitter (of the Henley Brewery Co. of England), they are producing ten to twelve barrels each week of their London Bitter. Sales are still limited to local pubs, where the brew is reportedly well received.

Joseph S. Pickett & Sons, Inc.
(Dubuque, Iowa)

Iowa's only commercial brewery is the Dubuque Star Brewing Co., according to the U.S. Treasury list of authorized breweries, but the owner, president, and master brewer, Joseph F. Pickett, Sr., assures me that the proper name is the one given above, which has been displayed on its labels since August 1971.

Joseph Pickett graduated from Duquesne University in 1931 with a B.A. in chemistry and bacteriology. After playing pro football with the Pittsburgh Steelers for two years, he took up the brewing trade, graduating from the Siebel Institute in 1934. For the next eight years he served many breweries, including Tube City, Storz, and Overland, finally becoming assistant brewmaster in Chicago for the Schoenhofen-Edelweiss Brewing Co. in 1942. He stayed with the firm through its merger with the Atlas Brewing Co. and its acquisition by Drewry's Ltd. U.S.A., Inc. (South Bend, Ind.), in 1951. When Drewry's merged with the Associated Brewing Co. of Detroit, Mr. Pickett became a vice president of Drewry's.

The Dubuque Star Brewing Co. began about 1898, and when Pickett assumed ownership in 1971, it was in sorry shape. Equipment was geared to the 1930s, with no can production facilities and with only a single bottle production line (returnables only). It was primarily a keg beer plant, an anachronism in the 1970s.

The two company brands, Dubuque Star and Vat 7, could command only a 5 percent share of the local market with sales of 11 thousand barrels annually.

Under the Pickett ownership, an extensive modernization program was begun, and by late 1977 was 95 percent complete.

In July, 1980, majority interest in the brewery was obtained by AGRI Industries of Des Moines, Iowa, a regional grain-marketing cooperative owned by local elevator cooperatives in six states. The Pickett family continues to oversee the brewing process and serve in management positions. AGRI plans to double Pickett brewing capacity of 150,000 barrels over the next five years.

The principal brand, Pickett's Premium, introduced in 1973, already accounts for 12 percent of the Dubuque County market and is now sold in Illinois and Wisconsin. The Edelweiss and Champagne Velvet labels were acquired in 1972, probably from G. Heileman, which had obtained them from Associated when it folded. Edelweiss should have a sentimental attachment to Joe Pickett, Sr., for he spent many years with the original brewer, Schoenhofen-Edelweiss.

Additional brands produced are Barbarossa Beer, for markets in southwestern Ohio, Weber Beer and E&B for Wisconsin, Regal Famous Premium, Vat 7, and Dubuque Star for distribution in eastern Iowa under the corporate name of the Dubuque Star Brewing Co. Pickett's Premium Light was introduced in late 1980. Two generics (Beer and Light Beer) appeared in early 1981. Pickett owns the rights to some thirty additional labels. Pickett also makes Eagle Rock Beer for Ken Lines of Idaho Falls, Idaho.

PICKETT'S PREMIUM BEER—light gold, faint malty aroma, light flavored with hops in the back, good balance, good-tasting brew, a touch of sweetness appears in the finish and carries into the aftertaste.

REGAL FAMOUS PREMIUM BEER—medium deep gold, foamy, very sweet yeasty aroma, medium body, sour and sweet flavor with an artificial component, sour finish, metallic aftertaste, an unbalanced brew.

EDELWEISS LIGHT BEER—pleasant malty aroma (maybe cheery beery, as the label once said), medium to light flavor with good balance, complex bitter finish and aftertaste, interesting. This brand originated with the Schoenhofen Brewing Co., which was founded in Chicago as the Peter Schoenhofen Brewing Co. in 1861 by Peter Schoenhofen and Matheus Gottfried. After Prohibition, it merged with the National Brewing Co. of Chicago to form Schoenhofen-Edelweiss, which came under the control of the Atlas Brewing Co. in 1940 and then Drewry's, Ltd. (branch of Associated Brewing Co.) in 1951. The plant was closed in 1972.

CHAMPAGNE VELVET—faint malty nose, sour salty taste, sour finish, likely an old bottle since I have been informed by Joseph F. Pickett, Sr., that the brand is not now being brewed by Pickett. It was once marketed all over the Midwest and through much of the east by the Terre Haute (Indiana) Brewing Co. This brand was also marketed by the Brewing Co. of Portland, Oregon, and the Atlantic Brewing Co. of Chicago in the 1950s.

DUBUQUE STAR BEER—pale gold, pleasant malt and hop aroma that is slightly sweet, very hoppy on the palate, but only lightly flavored, medium body, clean and refreshing, slightly sour malty aftertaste.

PICKETT'S PREMIUM LIGHT BEER—pale yellow, nice clean malty aroma with some hops, zesty on the front of the palate, but flavor drops off toward the finish and there is little aftertaste.

Pittsburgh Brewing Co.
(Pittsburgh, Pa.)

The Pittsburgh Brewing Co. syndicate was formed in 1899 when sixteen breweries were consolidated, each agreeing not to engage in an independent brewing business in the Pittsburgh area for a period of five years. The capacity of the combine was a huge 1.5 million barrels and the capital of the company a hefty $19.5 million. Included were the following Pittsburgh breweries: Iron City, Wainwright, Eberhardt & Ober, Keystone, Winter, Phoenix, Straub, Ober Bros., Bauerlein, Hauch, McKeesport, Connellsville, Uniontown, Mt. Pleasant, Latrobe, and Jeannette. Most of the smaller and older plants were closed after the merger. The first three listed above made up the greatest portion of the PBC operating segment.

Iron City roots go back to the year 1861, before the advent of steel, before Andrew Carnegie had even been heard of, and when Pittsburgh was, indeed, the Iron City. The first barrels of the brew were produced by two Germans, Edward Fraunheim and August Hoevler. They were soon joined by Leopold Vilsack, an experienced brewer. In 1866 the growing operation was moved to Liberty Avenue and 34th Street, the current address of the Pittsburgh Brewing Co. In 1890 the company name was changed from Fraunheim & Vilsack to the Iron City Brewery, after their popular product. When Iron City joined in forming PBC in 1899, it became part of what was then the third largest brewing company in America.

When Prohibition arrived two decades later,

PBC became Tech Food Products and survived by manufacturing ice cream, soft drinks, near-beer, and refrigeration equipment. It reopened as Pittsburgh Brewing Co. immediately upon repeal.

The early post-Prohibition years were not easy for PBC. The famous "beer wars" were touched off by the refusal of the local brewers union to join the Teamsters. Several years of beatings, firebombings, and truck vandalism followed until AFL-CIO affiliation ended the issue. In 1952 the Eberhardt & Ober plant was shut down and the Liberty Avenue facility became the sole PBC brewery. Thirteen years of million-dollar profits began with 1959, but real trouble was in the offing.

In 1971, black tavern owners organized a boycott of PBC products, charging that blacks were underrepresented in the brewery workforce. To assure black leaders that there was no intentional bias in hiring, PBC made a generous agreement with the NAACP on hiring policy. Pittsburgh's white middle class, already disturbed by government civil rights interference and feelings of uncertainty about the past decade of protest, felt that the terms of the agreement were too generous and reacted with the now famous white backlash boycott of Iron City beers. The boycott was effective; PBC profits began to sag and the workforce was commensurately reduced. Not only were few blacks hired, but few, in general, were hired. The 1975 operations were down to only 60 percent of capacity and the few remaining employees agreed to a wage freeze in lieu of further layoffs.

At that time (1975) PBC decided to attempt to counter the damage by becoming a multibrand brewer. A wide variety of labels were acquired, mostly from recently defunct firms that had competed in the PBC marketing area. This approach seems to have turned the fortunes of PBC; the first half of fiscal 1977 actually saw a small profit for the first time in several years. The company attributes some measure of the small success to the diversification. About two dozen labels are in the company repertoire, many enjoying considerable popularity and PBC is one of America's most prolific producers of beer brands. Two-thirds of its 90 thousand-barrel output is sold locally, but PBC brands are now well known in the fifteen states of its market. By 1979, PBC had reached one million barrels in sales (13th in the nation) and for the first time in seven years made a significant profit.

To the delight of collectors of beer cans and breweriana, PBC supplies a continual stream of juicy items, not the least of which is Olde Frothingslosh. This brand first appeared in 1954 when radio KDKA disc jockey Rege Cordic aired a series of zany commercials for the fictitious beer, Olde Frothingslosh, The Pale Stale Ale for the Pale Stale Male. Going along with the local gag, PBC put Olde Frothingslosh labels on 500 cases of Iron City Beer bottles for friends of the company for Christmas. The next year Olde Frothingslosh went "public," appearing at Christmas with a new set of labels. These bottles were quickly sold out as they were greatly appreciated gifts. Each year at Christmas new labels of Olde Frothingslosh appeared and by 1962 they were being marketed over a wide area, as far as Washington, D.C.

Olde Frothingslosh, "so light, the foam's on the bottom," "brewed from hippety-hops on the banks of the Upper Crudney in Lower Slobbovia," etc., made its appearance in cans in 1968 with the introduction of Fatima Yechburg, the 300-pound go-go dancer who became Miss Frothingslosh. A series of cans featuring the Frothingslosh lovely has since followed.

Among other collectibles are a series of cans depicting Pittsburgh history, sports, landmarks and local scenes. It is understood that all of the special cans are Iron City Beer. Several have been tasted and compared and there certainly is a family resemblance. The Oyster House and Seven Springs brands are admitted variations of the Iron City formula and are brewed especially for the Oyster House Tavern and the Seven Springs Resort.

Most of the current PBC labels originated with the Queen City Brewing Co. of Cumberland, Maryland, and the August Wagner Brewing Co. of Columbus, Ohio. Except for Old Frothingslosh, which might be found anywhere, PBC products are marketed in Pennsylvania, Maryland, Delaware, New Jersey, Ohio, Washington, D.C., and states adjacent to those named.

PBC beers, particularly Iron City, have a peculiar reputation among beer drinkers. They are deemed sour in the bottle and metallic-tasting in cans. Few will argue their merits served from a keg, however, and this "working-man's beer" has a loyal following among the beer-guzzling steelworkers. It is particularly well suited, I am told, as a whiskey chaser. Those who believe in washing away the heat and dirt of the day's work with a mug of "Arn," and then deadening the day's troubles with a shot, do so with regularity in Pittsburgh. Needless to say, it is quite unlike some of the smooth modern brews sought after by today's young "sophisticates."

PBC has never been able to capture much of the young (under 35) and female market. Its first try was Hop'n Gator, a pop mixture of beer and Gatorade, which reputedly got the alcohol quickly into your bloodstream. It was a poor attempt, especially disappointing for those who downed several cans and then sat around for hours waiting to "feel it." Robin Hood Ale and Mark V are aimed at this market, but the main hope is with a new all-natural and smooth light beer named Sierra. It was introduced early in 1978.

IRON CITY PREMIUM BEER—light malt aroma with very faint hops plus ordinary flavor with a slight prickly sensation on the tongue is the most offered. A typical average domestic brew.

IRON CITY DRAFT BEER—labeled "the beer drinker's beer," sweet malty aroma; too sweet a taste, but probably pleasant enough for most palates, good finish somewhat on the neutral side.

IRON CITY LIGHT—pale, sour aroma, weak cardboard taste, dry finish, 96 calories.

OLDE FROTHINGSLOSH PALE STALE ALE—faint grainy aroma, small bubble carbonation, little flavor, light body, watery; of course, the taste of this product is really secondary to the package.

AMERICAN BEER—skunky nose, small bubble carbonation, little flavor, less of an aftertaste, most of the palate sensation is CO_2. This is a former brand of the American Brewing Co., Cumberland, Maryland, probably a corporate name of Queen City. An American Beer was also previously produced by the Fuhrman & Schmidt Brewing Co. of Shamokin, Pennsylvania.

ROBIN HOOD CREAM ALE—light grain aroma; malty, salty, soapy flavor; medium to good body, pleasant. A very good effort. Formerly an August Wagner beer introduced by PBC in 1976.

HERITAGE HOUSE PREMIUM BEER—sweet malty aroma; very little flavor, but with a sweet aftertaste, very ordinary. Formerly a product of the Cumberland Brewing Co. (again, probably a corporate name of Queen City) and was produced on the West Coast under the Falstaff banner at San Francisco in 1974. Private label of Dominick's Finer Foods.

Eastern of New Jersey (1958), Storz of Omaha (1960), Maier of Los Angeles (1972), Walter Co. of Pueblo, Colorado (1973), Queen City (1973), and General, which still is producing the brand on the West Coast. Pittsburgh introduced it in 1975. It is a private label of Safeway Supermarkets in some states.

THE ORIGINAL OYSTER HOUSE BEER—slightly cloudy in appearance with a brown gold color, vegetal nose, very good slightly salty flavor up front, so-so middle, very dry finish. Really good with those oysters.

AUGUSTINER BEER—very light, pleasant, but ordinary aroma, badly balanced bittersweet taste, very foamy, finishes clean. Until 1975 this was an August Wagner product.

MUSTANG PREMIUM MALT LIQUOR—faint sweet malt aroma, big body, well-balanced, clean finish; smooth with a long-lasting, good-tasting aftertaste. One of the best domestic malt liquors tasted. Recently seen as Wild Mustang Super Premium Malt Liquor, a late-1980 name change.

2001 V.I.P. LIGHT BEER—clear yellow, clean malty aroma; clean malty flavor, but thin and watery, dull, faintly salty, no complexity, no character.

ULTRA LIGHT PREMIUM BEER (Dubois Brewing Co.)—96 calories, very pale, very light malty aroma, very little flavor, just carbonation, slightly sour finish.

MARK V LIGHT BEER—Pittsburgh's 96-calorie entry. Light pleasant aroma, weak start on the palate, poor in the middle, but finishes very well with good taste and some character. Not the best of type, but respectable. An August Wagner label.

POINT VIEW HOTEL—a special can, more than likely Iron City; medium-intensity malty aroma, very soft and light on the palate, watery finish.

WEIR BIG 14 RADIO PREMIUM BEER (brewed and packaged by Pittsburgh Brewing Co. for Pasco Distributing Co., New Cumberland, W. Va., and Iron City Dist. Co., Mingo Junction, Ohio)—mild malt aroma, light flavor with noticeable bitterness in the middle, very brief finish.

THE ORIGINAL OLD GERMAN BRAND PREMIUM LAGER BEER—labeled "the world knows no finer," it has a faint malty vegetal aroma like some foreign pilseners, a bitter taste, but most of the sensation is nothing more than carbonation. Previously a Queen City brand.

BURGUNDY BRAU BEER (Dubois Brewing Co., Dubois, Pa.)—deep red-brown color, salty-sweet aroma, sour-salt flavor backed by a tanninlike sensation as normally found in red wine, a very different sort of brew. The label says it contains a special (unspecified) ingredient. The Dubois Brewing Co., founded in 1897, was bought by PBC in 1967. The Dubois plant was closed in 1972, but the name is still used, at least on this product.

OLD DUTCH BRAND, THE GOOD BEER—a very clean malty nose, but very little flavor of any kind, only a faint sensation of malt with virtually no hops at all. This is another product that has for several decades been made by many brewers, including the Krantz Breweries and

SEVEN SPRINGS MOUNTAIN BEER—a better than average-tasting beer, clean grainy nose, good-tasting well-balanced flavor with a pleasing aftertaste. Comes in cans with the same logo in many different colors.

GAMBRINUS GOLD LABEL BEER—malty grainy aroma, light-bodied and light-flavored, a sweet style at first that tends toward sour in the back of the mouth and a short sour finish. This former product of August Wagner Breweries is named for St. Gambrinus or King Gambrinus, the patron saint of beer (or brewers). Background on Gambrinus is confused. He may have been Dutch or Belgian, or neither; he may have been a king; he may not have existed. The presumption is that he was at least a king and on this product he wears a crown. Gambrinus may be a corruption of the name of a Belgian nobleman and brewer, Jan Primus. There is also a brand called Gambrinus Gold, described below.

GAMBRINUS GOLD BEER—very similar to Gambrinus Gold Label, but much lighter in flavor, main impression is a taste like a light mineral spring water.

TECH LIGHT BEER—very pleasant grainy aroma as with most of the PBC beers, light body and flavor, metallic background to the taste with a dull salty finish. The product was marketed earlier by PBC as Tech Premium Beer.

OLD EXPORT PREMIUM BEER—strong vegetal nose, sharp salty bitter taste, astringent brackish finish. A very poor beer, tried again with the same results. Formerly a Cumberland Brewing Co. brand.

COY INTERNATIONAL PRIVATE RESERVE BEER—"Cask No. 34," deep gold, good malt aroma, very sugary sweet taste, long sweet finish.

BROWN DERBY LAGER BEER—faint typical PBC grainy aroma, little flavor, mostly just fresh light carbonation, ordinary and inoffensive. Over the past forty years, this beer has been made by a host of breweries, including Best of Chicago, Rainier in San Francisco (1939-41), the Los Angeles Brewing Co., Huber of Monroe, Wisconsin, Grace Bros. of Santa Rosa, California (1956),

International Brewing Co. of Findlay, Ohio, the Old Dutch Co. of Detroit, the Associated Brewing Co. and its successor, G. Heileman, and, most recently, Queen City.

STEEL VALLEY BEER—light color, light malty faintly hopped aroma, seems highly carbonated, slight sourness in the finish. This is probably a special package of Iron City.

WFBG RADIO'S KEYSTONE COUNTRY PREMIUM BEER (distributed by Reliable Beer Co.)—pale-colored, light, mostly malt, aroma, slight bitterness on the palate, but otherwise pretty light-flavored and light-bodied, slightly tinny finish, not much aftertaste.

ALT DEUTSCH BRAND DUNKEL BIER DARK BEER—deep copper color, very faint sour aroma, medicinal background to a generally sour flavor, flavor starts out as good roasted malt, but soon turns sour and the sourness stays in throughout the finish.

SGA GOLD LABEL PREMIUM BEER—pale gold, no aroma, light malt flavor with some hops, slightly metallic aftertaste. Made for Spirits Guild of America. (Also see G. Heileman.)

905 NINE O'FIVE LIGHT BEER—pale yellow, very foamy, pleasant fruity malty aroma, very little flavor beyond carbonation, watery. Private label of 905 Liquor Stores of St. Louis, Mo., also produced by G. Heileman.

BEER—pale colored, light malty aroma, highly carbonated, slightly tinny finish. This is the Pittsburgh generic, sold under the Dubois Brewing Co. corporate name. Seen in Vermont and New Hampshire.

MAGNA CARTA CREAM ALE (Magna Carta Brewing Co.)—pale gold, good hop-malt aroma, good hoppy taste with a creamy texture marred by a metallic background, highly carbonated. This beer is packaged in a 16-ounce can.

DUBOIS BOCK BEER (Dubois Brewing Co., Pittsburgh)—medium dark red-brown coloring, sharp and clear, strong roasted malt and hop aroma, sort of a pleasant burnt-sour aroma, light to medium body, dry flavor of roasted malt and hops with a slightly sour finish, a fairly decent bock and certainly one of the better American efforts.

BRICKSKELLER SALOON STYLE BEER—dusty cardboard aroma, sweet grainy "beer hall" flavor, almost cloying at the finish. Special brew for Brickskeller Saloon in Washington, D.C.

SIERRA NATURALLY BREWED PILSNER BEER—sour "off" aroma, a sort of "tin can" nose, sour malt flavor, metallic finish, recognizable as a Pittsburgh product.

ROSE ALE—rose colored with touch of orange, fruit punch aroma and flavor, very citruslike, no preservatives or artificial flavoring.

Real Ale Co., Inc.
(Chelsea, Mich.)

This new "microbrewery" produces ale, stout, and porter, all British-style brews using only imported Irish malt and hops. The ale is 4.8 percent alcohol with a bitter English style. The porter uses pale, crystal, and black malts and contains 5.4 percent alcohol. The stout is 6 percent. The brews were introduced in September 1982. The brewery is capable of producing some 600 barrels annually.

CHELSEA ALE—very slightly cloudy copper-gold, very small bubble carbonation, toasted malt and hop aroma with a nice ale tartness, creamy texture, light body, malt up front, hops in finish, slightly bitter long aftertaste. Could do with a little more body, but still very good.

REAL ALE CO. PORTER—medium to deep reddish-brown, very little carbonation, very faint roasted malt aroma, medium body, light malt up front on palate, rich sweetness in middle, slightly burnt taste on end, slightly bitter aftertaste. Good flavor but it really could use a bit more carbonation to balance off the middle sweetness.

REAL ALE CO. STOUT—opaque brown, light coffee-brown head, rich roasted malt aroma with a fresh ground coffee bean background, rich malt-hop flavor with a definite espresso background, beautifully balanced, very tasty, lingering aftertaste, a real "lip-smacker."

River City Brewing Co.
(Sacramento, Calif.)

This latest of the new breed of husband and wife brewing operations began in late 1980. The proprietors are James A. Schleuter (formerly with Schlitz) and Chris Schleuter. They started the brewery because it was hard to find a full-bodied all-malt American pilsener and they were appalled at the high failure rate of small American breweries. Being mavericks at heart and entrepreneurs in spirit, they decided to do something about it.

Since early 1981 they have been producing River City Gold, an all-malt pilsener, and the first release of River City Dark occurred in November 1981. In making their beer they use 100 percent two-row barley malt and Tettnanger leaf hops, boiled for one and one-half hours and fermented in shallow fermenters at 48-49° F. for seven to ten days. The beer is then krausened and stored for four to five weeks at 40° F. Only a light filtration is performed before bottling; no pasteurization or millipore filtration is done.

Initially, River City had a capacity to produce 1000 to 1500 gallons per week (about 1600 barrels per year). An expansion in capacity to 10,000 barrels was completed in 1983.

River City Gold sells for under $1 per bottle in fourpacks and kegs are available. The beer has a shelf life of one month if kept refrigerated.

RIVER CITY GOLD—brilliant gold with a tawny hue, lovely complex malt and hop aroma, bright hoppy flavor, medium body, good small bubble natural carbonation, a delicious brew with lots of character.

RIVER CITY DARK—medium deep bright rosy copper, very small bubble carbonation, sweet toasted malt aroma, smoky malt flavor, only medium body, but very smooth, pleasant and beautifully balanced, a sort of charcoal component in the aftertaste, but it is not obtrusive, an excellent brew.

RIVER CITY BOCK—bright copper, good tangy alelike aroma, complex zesty palate that is very big, hops somewhat sharp up front but soften in the middle as the malt comes through, very good balance, long on palate with slightly sour malt aftertaste.

August Schell Brewing Co.
(New Ulm, Minn.)

The New Ulm brewery of August Schell has had an extremely colorful history, at least in its early days. A young German immigrant, August Schell, began producing beer in the small brewery that also served as his home. The property was some distance from the main settlement and deep in the heart of Indian country. Curious Indians had always been welcomed at the Schell homestead and treated to food and traditional good German hospitality. When the famous Sioux uprising led by Chief Little Crow took place in 1862, the Schell family fled to New Ulm for safety. Over the next several weeks there was considerable loss of property and human life, but when the Schells returned to their home and brewery they found the buildings intact, even though there was much evidence of Indian presence during the period of absence. The Indians had not forgotten the kindness of the Schell family.

August Schell became in invalid in 1877 and was succeeded by his sons, Adolph and Otto. The brewery was incorporated in 1902 as the August Schell Brewing Co. and remains so to this day, operating as one of the remaining few small fine breweries in America. The beautiful Schell Gardens and Deer Park offer tourists and local citizens a peaceful and calm environment for tasting Schell beers.

The product line includes Schell's, a higher-priced Schell's Export, a bock, Fitger's Rex, low-priced Twin Lager, Steinhaus, generics labelled simply Beer (at least one of which bears a corporate identifier of Augie's Brewing Co.). Schell is very active in the production of special releases of beer for events and can collectors. Most are found only in Minnesota.

SCHELL'S ITS A GRAND OLD BEER—winelike aroma with some hop background taste, very much like a dry white wine, tends to flatten out toward the finish, a good beer, especially for a wine lover, excellent beer for meals, especially with seafood.

SCHELL DEER BRAND EXPORT II BEER—sour aroma, salty sour taste, sour finish, bitter-sour aftertaste, not a pleasant brew. This was one of two old Schell beer formulas recently found in excavating the property. The two were marketed to a limited extent and the public choice was to become Schell's Export, an import-type beer. Without having tasted the Export I, I was willing to lay odds on it after trying this one. At the end of 1977, Schell announced that Export I had been judged the best and will now be offered as Schell's Deer Brand Export Beer.

SCHELL'S DEER BRAND EXPORT BEER (formerly Export I)—gold color, lusty hop aroma, good character, nicely balanced, good hoppy flavor, malty finish.

SCHELL'S HUNTERS SPECIAL BEER—pale yellow, faint yeasty aroma, very faint yeasty flavor, inoffensive, a bit sweet, faint bready finish.

SCHELL'S EXPORT LIGHT BEER—pale color, "wet" aroma with some yeast, slightly musty, small bubble carbonation, light, semidry, little character, yeasty.

SCHELL'S 1978 XMAS BREW—very pale yellow, yeasty-bready aroma, obtrusive carbonation, weak flavor of yeast and malt, faint yeast and malt finish.

STEINHAUS NEW ULM BEER—pale yellow, bready-yeasty aroma, light flavor, mostly carbonation, sour finish.

FITGER'S BEER—medium gold, cloudy with particulate matter, yeasty nose with slight hops, tangy up front, sweet in back, only sweetness carries into the brief finish. Fitger was a Duluth, Minnesota, brewery founded by August Fitger and Percy Anneke. The trademark (and present logo) was a star enclosing the *S.S. Duluth.*

MACHO 1200 (A MAN'S BEER)—deep gold, malty aroma, lightly carbonated, light malt flavor with hops in back, tasty and pleasant, good balance.

CROSSROADS PILSNER BEER—pale gold, faint yeasty malt aroma, medium to light body, touch of apple and cardboard, slightly sweet finish, pleasant, slightly salty aftertaste.

FRIENDSHIP LOUNGE BEER—straw colored, light fruity cherry-pit aroma, medium body, unbalanced sweet-sour flavor, aftertaste not pleasant.

THE AVENUE FINE PILSNER BEER—brilliant gold, fine malty aroma, soapy-malty light flavor, thin, clean and refreshing, no finish or aftertaste, the only zest comes from the CO_2.

SCHELL'S (1979) BOCK BEER—bright and deep copper-orange, sweet and fruity malt aroma, light carbonation, sweet toasted malt flavor up front, good in the middle, brief finish, faint sour malt aftertaste, overall thin.

Christian Schmidt Brewing Co.
(Philadelphia, Pa. and Cleveland, Ohio)

Christian Schmidt, in 1859, founded a modest brewery on Edward Street in Philadelphia and put out about five hundred barrels of ale and porter each year. The brewery did not begin the manufacture of lager beer until 1880, quite late in the industry, but at that time remodeled the plant for that purpose and increased the annual output to 125,000 barrels.

In June 1892 the firm name was changed to C. Schmidt & Sons, the new members being Henry C., Edward A., and Frederick W. Incorporation was effected in 1902 as C. Schmidt & Sons Brewing Co. In 1980 the name was changed to the Christian Schmidt Brewing Co. and Philadelphia was removed from the brand names in an attempt at national marketing.

Edward Street in Philadelphia is still the home of Schmidt's, but the operation takes place on a much grander scale, the firm having acquired many famous eastern Pennsylvania brand names. A second brewery was added in 1963 when Schmidt acquired the old Standard

Brewing Co. plant in Cleveland from Schaefer Brewing Co. of Ohio (which purchased the plant in 1961 when Standard closed). Schmidt's closed the Standard plant down in 1972 when it moved its Cleveland brewing operations to a newly acquired plant obtained from the Carling Brewing Co., which had operated it from 1953 to 1971. This new Schmidt plant was originally operated by the Brewing Corporation of America.

Schmidt's had acquired the Adam Scheidt Brewing Co. properties in 1955, but large-scale expansion did not occur until the late 1970s. Duquesne was acquired in 1975, giving Schmidt's a western Pennsylvania market. In 1977, Reading and the famous Rheingold names were added with extensive markets reaching into New England. When Erie was acquired in 1979, western New York markets were added. Most recently, in 1981, major Philadelphia competitor Ortlieb sold out, leaving only Schmidt's to fill the glasses of those in the City of Brotherly Love.

The expansion through acquisition has been effective for in 1982 Schmidt's ranked tenth in sales in the nation. Schmidt's usually continues to market the brews of acquired companies, at least for several years. In addition to its line of alcoholic beverages for the domestic market, Schmidt's brews Tiger Beer for export to Nigeria and plans to reintroduce Birell, a nonalcoholic malt beverage, under license from Hurlimann of Switzerland.

In a recent advertising campaign, Schmidt's challenged the Coors mystique with its primary brand, Schmidt's of Philadelphia, which accounts for 90 percent of its sales. The firm has had considerable success with this ad campaign in calling attention to its product, a good one that apparently appeals more to regional tastes than does Coors. Schmidt's has since taken on Bud, Schlitz, and Miller on a one-on-one basis under the aegis of the independent Consumer Response Corp., of New York. In five major cities it claims victory. Our tests showed similar results repeatedly among different groups of tasters. Schmidt's is a good product.

SCHMIDT'S—deep gold color, good malty aroma with hops noticeable only in the background, a bright and crisp beer with lots of character, good hop-malt balance, clean and zesty, a good aftertaste. A good lively beer that should have widespread appeal.

SCHMIDT'S TIGER HEAD ALE—deep gold color with a tinge of brown, very little aroma, light taste, slightly on the bitter side, great bitterness in the finish. Not unpleasant and reasonably good for the type, but not very alelike. Available irregularly through most of the Northeast.

SCHMIDT'S BOCK BEER—very dark brown, sweet aroma, almost no flavor at all and very little aftertaste. Available only in season.

SCHMIDT'S OKTOBERFEST BEER—tawny, slightly roasted malt aroma, light, but very pleasant malt flavor, low in hops, very good for quaffing, light, almost watery finish. A pleasant brew that is worth a try.

SCHMIDT'S BAVARIAN BEER—very little aroma, slightly sour taste with a brief bitter finish. This is the replacement of Duquesne Bavarian. Although they taste quite different, the package has the same design only with Schmidt's replacing Duquesne. Duquesne was the only Bavarian seen up to early 1977, and since then it has been completely converted to Schmidt's with a short transition period when both were seen.

SCHMIDT'S LIGHT BEER—pale yellow, very faint malt aroma, faint malt taste, no character. 96 calories.

BREW 96 LIGHT BEER—a 96-calorie product with a pronounced yeasty aroma and a background of spruce boughs, a flavor briefly like the yeast and spruce of the nose, but it lasts for only a short time and then there is nothing to carry on to the finish. Marketed mostly in the Middle Atlantic states.

POC (PILSENER ON CALL) PILSENER BEER—faint grainy dank aroma, faint sour flavor, very austere and faintly sour finish. Available from Pennsylvania to Illinois. "POC" was a brand of the Pilsener Brewing Co. of Cleveland which closed in 1962. The letters stood for Price of Cleveland at that time.

CHRISTIAN SCHMIDT CLASSIC PREMIUM BEER—bright gold, highly carbonated, faint malt-hop nose, sweet malt flavor, a little too sweet, dull overall.

GOLDEN HAWK CLASSIC MALT LIQUOR—medium gold, candy nose, sweet malt flavor; a bit flabby, especially in finish where sweetness shows most; full bodied, medium duration.

BREAK SPECIAL LAGER—pretty bright gold; soapy malty, slightly sweet flavor; dry finish; slightly metallic aftertaste. A reduced alcohol brew with less than 2% alcohol, introduced in early 1984.

Adam Scheidt Brewing Co. *(Norristown, Pa.)*
This firm was founded in 1870 as Moeshlin Bros. Brewery. By 1879 it was known as C. & A. Scheidt & Co., with Adam Scheidt becoming the sole proprietor in 1884. In 1890 the firm was incorporated as the Adam Scheidt Brewing Co.

Following Prohibition, Scheidt reopened and brewed Valley Forge, Ram's Head Ale, and Scheidt's Prior. The story behind Prior is notable. There was a large market in eastern Pennsylvania for the true pilseners of Czechoslovakia. When these products became impossible to obtain following World War I, the Scheidt brewery tried to recreate them in Norristown, apparently with some success. The particular pilzen brew Scheidt copied was called Prior and the name survives today. In Czechoslovakia the cooperative that produced Prior has been absorbed and incorporated into the more famous Urquell. When Scheidt was purchased by Schmidt's in 1955, it is believed that there was some condition of purchase that required Schmidt's to continue to market the proud Prior products according to the original recipe. Following the Schmidt's purchase, the Scheidt brewery continued to operate under its own name until 1960, when it was renamed the Valley Forge Brewing Co. In 1965 this name was dropped in favor of the parent company on all of the former Scheidt products, except Prior, and the Norristown plant was closed. The brewery of record on Prior packages is still Prior Brewery.

VALLEY FORGE OLD TAVERN BEER—medium color, slightly malty aroma, very little sensation on the tongue other than carbonation.

PRIOR DOUBLE LIGHT BEER (liquid luxury preferred beer)—pale color, good malty nose, ferruginous background to the flavor (as you might get with spring water brought to you through a rusty pipe), smooth, malty, very low carbonation, long aftertaste with good hop balance, not a bad beer at all. Quite light if you are thinking of Urquell, but pleasant and low-priced. The Prior labels are available in the New York-New Jersey-Pennsylvania area and to some degree in other Middle Atlantic states and in New England.

PRIOR DOUBLE DARK BEER—very dark in color, light malty nose, malty flavor ever so slightly on the sour side, good clean finish, long pleasing aftertaste. The body is not as great as most foreign dark beers, but is ample. It is a product that is both satisfying and drinkable; you can enjoy one or several, depending on your mood. Novices and old hands alike have found it their number one domestic dark beer choice. Had there been no other "finds" in all the beers sampled in this lengthy examination of malt beverages, discovering Prior Double Dark would have been worth the effort. In 1969, Consumers Union rated this beer as America's best dark brew. In 1978, *The Great American Beer Book* confirmed this rating. Schmidt tried a Rochester test market in 1977 and got a positive response. The brew was repackaged for a 1980 appearance in a wide area, but unfortunately at a much higher price.

RAM'S HEAD ALE—skunky malty aroma, malt-hop taste with a slight sweetness in the back. An adequate brew, but with only light to medium body and little zest. Seen only in Pennsylvania, Maryland, and New England.

TUDOR PREMIUM—extremely light-bodied and light-flavored, very undistinguished. This is a private label of the A&P food stores. This brand has not been seen in fresh condition (or in an A&P) for some time now. Other firms have made Tudor for A&P over the years, among them Queen City and Cumberland of Cumberland, Maryland, Schwarzenbach of Hornell, New York, Best of Chicago, Metropolis of Trenton, New Jersey, Five Star of New York City, and Ruppert in Norfolk, Virginia.

TUDOR ALE—cloudy yellow, good malty aroma, very light body, watery, flavor disappears in the middle, poor and unbalanced aftertaste. Also an A&P private label.

Duquesne Brewing Co. *(Duquesne and Pittsburgh)* This company was founded in Pittsburgh in 1900. For many years it was a major Pittsburgh area brewer commanding a substantial share of that market, but began to falter in the 1960s. It was acquired by Schmidt's in late 1975 or early 1976.

DUKE BEER—bright gold, good malt aroma, yeasty palate, shallow and thin. The "prince of pilseners" is seen most regularly in the southeastern corner of the country. The brand, bearing Duquesne on its label, was seen as recently as early 1977. Earlier Duke was made in Pittsburgh as well as Duquesne. This leads to the suspicion that Schmidt's may have acquired the POC and Brew 96 labels in the Duquesne purchase.

DUQUESNE BAVARIAN BEER (made by Duquesne Brewing Co., Duquesne and Pittsburgh; then Duquesne alone; then Philadelphia; then Philadelphia and Cleveland)—soapy aroma, light body, light taste, minimal hops, not Bavarian style in any way, a very uninteresting beer.

Erie Brewing Co. *(Erie, Pa.)* Charles Koehler had been a grower of tulips in Holland for some years, then in 1840 he sold his land and sailed to America with his wife. In 1847 he decided that he would become a brewer and established a small plant at 25th and Holland in Erie. He had some success with the business and passed the brewing idea on to his sons. When he died in 1869, his oldest son, Frederick, together with brother Jackson and partner A. L. Curtze, continued the business as Fred Koehler & Co. Jackson left the firm in 1883 to buy the nearby Kalvage Brewery and both continued to operate independently until they decided to merge with the J. M. Conrad and Cascade Breweries to form the Erie Brewing Co. in 1899. The firm was managed by descendants of Jackson Koehler until 1979 when Erie was purchased by C. Schmidt & Sons, Inc.

The current product line includes two brews introduced in 1976: Imperial Cream Beer, a

OLDE PUB TAVERN BREW—aroma and taste of malty cardboard, inexpensive and just barely drinkable. Only seen in returnable bottles.

KOEHLER LAGER BEER—slightly pale color, light malty vegetal aroma, light to medium flavor, lightly hopped, light body, highly carbonated.

KOEHLER PILSENER BEER—medium to pale color, malty aroma, only slightly hopped, hops noticeable more in the flavor than in the aroma, good balance, some hops in the finish, very heavily carbonated.

OLD STYLE BREWER'S LAGER BEER (label says Forrest Brewing Co., Orange, N.J., but these are old labels; the beer is now made by Erie, as indicated by the bottle cap)—medium tawny gold color, austere malty nose, more a palate sensation of carbonated liquid than any real beer flavor, a little sour in the middle and finishes bitter. This product is made in returnable bottles only for the Brewer's Outlet chain of Pennsylvania. It is priced around $4 for a case of pints.

Reading Brewing Co. *(Reading, Pa.)* The Reading brands were obtained by Schmidt's in 1977, at which time the Old Reading Brewery

blend of choice barley, malt, rice and hops aged for a full three months for a hearty, robust old-country taste; and Light Lager Beer, a product low in carbohydrates and calories. The traditional Erie product line includes Koehler Beer, Ale, Pilsener, and Lager; Olde Pub (a "medium-light" brew), and Yacht Club (another "light"-brewed beer). The Erie market extends from New York to Chicago.

KOEHLER BEER (brewed with the Dutch touch)—pale color, good malty aroma, pleasant barley-malt flavor with some zest, a unique tangy finish and clean refreshing aftertaste. This is a fine product with a flavor quite different from those of the vast majority of American beers. If you like it, as I did, you may favor it for regular use.

ERIE LIGHT LAGER BEER (96 calories)—slight vegetal nose, a bit off in the aroma, a hint of that vegetable in the taste but a good taste, finish a bit thin with a fairly sweet aftertaste. Despite the weakness in the finish, it is a reasonably pleasant brew when viewed overall. It has more character than most of the low-calorie beers.

was closed and production transferred to Philadelphia. Reading was successor to an old firm established in 1886 with roots tracing to 1843.

READING LIGHT PREMIUM BEER—pale color, light malty aroma, pleasant malty taste with some hops, clean tasting, light-bodied, refreshing and with no offensive qualities. A good average beer that should be considered for regular home use, especially with its low price. Generally available in the Northeast.

BERGHEIM BEER—very faint and slightly sweet malt aroma, light, delicate flavor of malt and faint hops, almost no aftertaste. Inexpensive, but offers little. Found only in eastern Pennsylvania.

PRIZER EXTRA DRY PREMIUM BEER (Reading Brewing Co.)—cloudy gold, oxidized nose, tinny flavor, an old stale can.

Rheingold Breweries, Inc. *(Orange, N.J. and New Bedford, Mass.)*

The story of Rheingold is the story of much of the American brewing industry: the modest beginning, the sudden rush of success, constant growth, the struggle to survive Prohibition, recovery, postwar expansion, the economic agonies of the late 1960s and early 70s, and, last, the sale and closing of the brewery with the attendant scattering about of the brand names.

Rheingold's story begins in 1799, when Samuel Liebmann was born in Württemberg, Germany. After some forty years of farming, he bought a combination inn and brewery near Stuttgart. The business was successful until the outspoken Liebmann's views on personal freedom angered William I, the reigning monarch. Liebmann then sent his eldest son, Joseph, to America to choose a site for a brewery and in 1854 migrated to Brooklyn.

By 1855 Liebmann and his three sons had purchased a large site on Forrest Street and constructed a brewery. Success followed and S. Liebmann's Sons Brewing Co. was on its way. The father-to-son business, traditional in so many German-American brewing firms, seemed to work especially well at Liebmann. Small brewing firms in the neighborhood were gradually absorbed and the Liebmann facilities were constantly being modernized.

In 1902 Liebmann purchased the famous old Claus-Lipsius Brewing Co. of New York City. The last remaining neighbor, Obermeyer &

Liebmann, was absorbed during Prohibition (1924) and the corporate name was changed to Liebmann Breweries, Inc. Liebmann continued operating during Prohibition, producing near-beer and Teutonic (a terrible pun!), a concentrated liquid extract of malt and hops. Obermeyer & Liebmann had survived to 1924 by producing similar products, including Lion Tonic.

The Liebmann management did not decide to branch out immediately following repeal, as did many others. Instead, it waited until after the end of World War II. The next purchase, made in 1947, was the John Eichler Brewing Co. in the Bronx. Three years later it obtained the Trommer Brewery in Orange, New Jersey, home of the once famous Trommer's White Label. In 1954 two California breweries were bought, one in San Francisco and one in Los Angeles, both formerly owned by Acme Breweries. The San Francisco plant (renamed the California Brewing Co.) continued to brew the local brands, Acme Gold Label Beer and Acme Bull Dog Ale. Only Rheingold was brewed at the new Los Angeles Rheingold Brewing Co.

At this time Rheingold had more plants in operation than any other American brewer except Falstaff. All five of these plants operated

until 1957, when the Los Angeles plant was sold. Two years later the San Francisco plant was also sold. The Eichler plant in the Bronx was closed in 1961. Rheingold had shrunk to the plants in Brooklyn and Orange.

The Liebmann family sold out to Pepsi-Cola United Bottlers, Inc., in 1964 and the name of the firm was changed to Rheingold Breweries, Inc. Strangely, in 1965 Rheingold was the eighth largest brewer in the nation with sales of 4,236,000 barrels, but it was downhill from that time on. Even with the acquisitions of the Dawson plant in New Bedford, Massachusetts, in 1967 and the Esslinger (1964) and Jacob Ruppert (1965) labels, annual sales by 1973, when PepsiCo gained a controlling interest in Rheingold at a cost of $57 million, had dropped below 3 million barrels in the nation. The beer business had slipped so badly that the major interest in the 1973 purchase was the very profitable soft drink operations owned by Rheingold and not its beer.

Within a year, PepsiCo stopped production at the Brooklyn plant, site of 70 percent of the total Rheingold output, and in a grandstand move, designed to emphasize to New York City and Teamsters officials how serious the economics were, dumped 100,000 gallons of Rheingold into the East River, asserting it would be too costly to finish processing and packaging the beer. Rheingold's other plants (Orange and New Bedford) were said to be marginally profitable but insiders indicated otherwise.

With strikes, sit-ins, lockouts, lawsuits, and violence in the offing, a New York coffee company, Chock Full o'Nuts, came to the rescue and purchased Rheingold for the sum of $1 (it was more complicated than that, but $1 was the price tag). For almost two years Rheingold struggled on, with occasional months in the black, but mostly it was a losing business; the coffee profits supported the beer brewing. In 1976 the Brooklyn plant closed after 121 years of continuous operation.

The Orange and New Bedford plants continued to brew original Rheingold and acquired brands (McSorley's Gablinger, Esslinger, and Ruppert). The New Bedford plant was quietly closed in early 1977 and on 1 December 1977 the following cryptic note was received from Rheingold: "Effective 10/7/77 all Rheingold brands were sold to C. Schmidt & Sons of Philadelphia, Pennsylvania. The Orange, New Jersey, plant will close its doors tomorrow, December 2, 1977."

Rheingold left its mark on New York City life; what New Yorker of the 1940s and 1950s could ever forget Miss Rheingold? Even the name Rheingold has its legend. It is said that in 1885 David Liebmann, a true opera lover, paid tribute to Anton Seidel, head of the Metropolitan Opera Company, with a banquet. In honor of the occasion a special brew was prepared; because the last performance of the season happened to be *Das Rheingold,* the beer was named Rheingold. When introduced to the public, it was accepted enthusiastically.

Returning to Miss Rheingold, the first one in 1940 was radio and movie personality Jinx Falkenburg, who was selected by the brewery. For the next twenty-four years, however, Miss Rheingold was elected by ballot box stuffers (an old New York custom) and Rheingold-guzzling males fell in love with Rheingold winners and losers alike for over two decades. With candidates smiling at them from hundreds of billboards, posters, magazines, and newspapers, they could hardly resist. Rheingold appointed a final winner in 1965, stating that public interest in the contest had waned, but another theory has been regularly advanced. Rheingold had long been a favorite with the predominantly Jewish New York market. In the 1950s there had been a massive influx of blacks and Puerto Ricans, so much so that a black or Puerto Rican Miss Rheinghold became a definite possibility. The Rheingold management was afraid it would lose its white clientele if Rheingold became known as a black beer or a Puerto Rican beer. Yet it was equally concerned with keeping up its sales to blacks and Puerto Ricans, whom management felt it might lose should it keep Miss Rheingold in the traditional mold. Therefore, Miss Rheingold was quietly retired and we were never treated to a dark-eyed señorita or a Nubian princess. Interestingly, the racial aspects of a Miss Rheingold contest on beer sales might scarcely be worth a thought in the New York City of the mid-1980s.

In late 1977 Schmidt's purchased the Rheingold Brewery in Orange, New Jersey, the last surviving facility of the firm of Rheingold

Breweries, Inc. The Rheingold plant was closed by Schmidt's in December 1977. The transaction included the Rheingold, Forrest (Gablinger), Jacob Ruppert (Knickerbocker), and McSorley labels. By early 1978, Rheingold, Rheingold Extra Light, and Knickerbocker Natural were appearing under the Schmidt's banner and the Esslinger label had been sold to Lion, Inc. of Wilkes-Barre, Pennsylvania. The McSorley label was dealt to Henry F. Ortlieb in Philadelphia.

Schmidt's cans and bottles of Rheingold and Rheingold Extra Light are being produced by the Rheingold Breweries, Philadelphia and Cleveland. The Gablinger line is using the Ruppert name as the brewery of record (Ruppert Brewery, Philadelphia and Cleveland).

RHEINGOLD EXTRA DRY LAGER BEER—pale color, fresh malty aroma with faint hops in back, light-bodied, light-flavored, mostly malt but with some hop bitterness in back. Reasonably dry, as advertised; not bad, but doesn't have much zest or character, though more than most.

RHEINGOLD EXTRA LIGHT—pale color, light malty aroma, slightly sweet flavor with a sour aftertaste. Only 87 calories, this brand appeared in late 1977.

KOOL MULE FLAVORED MALT LIQUOR (Rheingold Brewery, Phila.)—pale gold, almond aroma, almond-flavored. America's first marzipan beer.

Forrest Brewing Co. Forrest was a corporate name of Rheingold used on Gablinger products and also found in use on one private label. Gablinger was the first widely marketed low-calorie, or so-called weight-control beer, which had its origin with Dawson's Calorie Controlled Ale and Lager Beer back in 1952. Gablinger was introduced in 1967 and there was a problem with the Food and Drug Administration over what could be claimed on the label. Since it was marketed for "special diet use," the label had to state the number of calories contained; however, the Federal Alcoholic Administration Act prohibited alcoholic beverage labeling that disclosed any information regarding calories. In this brewer's Catch 22, Gablinger was in and out of the courts for about two years until the ATF Div. of the IRS decided to allow the label to state, "Has only ninety-nine calories, 1/3 less than our regular beers."

GABLINGER'S EXTRA LIGHT BEER—deep gold color, good malty "soapy" aroma, very light in body and flavor, but very pleasant and very drinkable. Contains 95 calories, reduction claimed to be a result of a longer brewing process.

GABLINGER'S BEER—light color, slight malt aroma, almost no hops at all, light-bodied, light and ordinary flavor, little more than thirst quenching, but good for that. Contains 99 calories.

BREWER'S LAGER (private label of Brewer's Outlet chain of case-lot beer outlets of eastern Pennsylvania)—yellow-gold color, dull brackish aroma, slightly sweet taste, flat in the middle, slightly salty faint finish. Only available in returnable 16-ounce bottles at a very attractive price and of acceptable value because of that low price. Later this brand appeared with an Erie Brewing cap and a Forrest Brewing Co. label. The discussion became moot when Schmidt obtained both Erie and Forrest (Rheingold).

Dawson Brewing Co. *(New Bedford, Mass.)* Founded by Benjamin and Joseph Dawson in 1889, this firm specialized in ale and porter before Prohibition and converted to lager only after repeal, at that time building up a solid trade in New England. Everyone in New England during the 1940s and 50s was familiar with the Dawson jingle, a humorous fanciful note from history followed by:

> Our History might be askew, but one
> fact is very clear;
> When you want a better brew, call for
> Dawson's ale or beer—
> Time out for Dawson's.

Beer aficionadoes in Boston found the Dawson's Draft Light and Special Dark particularly attractive at Jacob Wirth & Co., a German restaurant on Stuart Street, although most of them never knew the brew by anything other than Jakie's Light or Special Dark. After Rheingold took over the Dawson plant, it continued to produce the Rheingold beers in New Bedford, but sold the Dawson label to the Eastern Brewing Corp., of Hammonton, New Jersey, which continues to produce Dawson Beer for a dwindling New England market. C. Schmidt brews Wirth's beer today, using the original formula.

Jacob Ruppert Brewing Co. *(New York City)* Franz Ruppert, who had been a grocer for ten years in New York, purchased the Aktien Brauerei in 1850. He renamed it the Turtle Bay Brewery and was joined in the business by his son Jacob. In 1867, two years before Franz was to

sell his share of the business, Jacob Ruppert struck out on his own, himself cutting the timber and clearing it from the site of his brewery.

In the first year he produced 5,000 barrels in the new brewery and by 1874 had erected an entire new plant. Huge ice houses were built in 1877 and 1880. Ruppert grew rich before Prohibition and easily survived it. He began an expansion program immediately following World War II, but expansion did not prove successful. The Baltimore plant was a short-lived venture and the Norfolk, Virginia, plant operated under the Ruppert name only from 1948 to 1953. Since 1954, it has been the southern home of Champale.

For years the Ruppert name had been a New York City fixture. Even those who did not enjoy an occasional beer could relate to the owner of the Yankees, which had been purchased by Jacob Ruppert, Jr. In 1965 Ruppert came to an end in New York City; the plant was closed and the

brand name sold to Rheingold, which continued to market beer under the once proud Ruppert name.

KNICKERBOCKER NATURAL—malty aroma, smooth, soft malty flavor with good hop balance, light body, good-tasting long aftertaste, very respectable brew, worth trying. This beer was previously called Ruppert Knickerbocker Beer. The Knickerbocker name was first used in 1892 by the Bartholomay Brewing Co. in upstate New York. This beer is very popular in New England, its major market.

JACOB RUPPERT BEER—pale color, light malty aroma, clean nose, quite yeasty and very light-bodied, sour flavor with a little bitterness. Not much of a beer, but very inexpensive. This beer appeared in late 1977, between the closing of the New Bedford plant and the closing of the Orange plant, which was listed on the label as its place of manufacture.

Henry F. Ortlieb Brewing Co. *(Philadelphia)*
The Ortlieb brewing firm had its start as a Weiss beer brewery founded in the early 1860s by August Kuehl. In 1869 Trupert Ortlieb bought the business, but sold it to Charles Blomer in 1885. Blomer's business failed and the plant closed in 1892. A year later the facility was bought by Henry F. Ortlieb and reopened. In recent years the chief executive and owner was the colorful Joseph W. Ortlieb, who would go on TV to urge Philadelphians to try "Joe's Beer." He also steadfastly refused to make a low-calorie beer, handing out bottles of carbonated water to mix with his beer. In the spring of 1981, after 111 years of family ownership and operation, Ortlieb's became part of the C. Schmidt Brewing Co., long its major competitor in the Philadelphia area.

Ortlieb products were seen mostly in Pennsylvania, New Jersey, and Delaware, and there was some limited marketing in New England. Schmidt's plans to continue the major Ortlieb product line in the same areas.

Many of the Ortlieb labels came with the purchase of the Fuhrman & Schmidt Brewery Co. of Shamokin, Pa., which Ortlieb acquired in 1966. F & S started as the Eagle Run Brewery in 1854. Messrs. Fuhrman and Schmidt came in as proprietors in the 1880s and soon bought the defunct Shamokin Brewing Co. and moved to that location in 1905 when Eagle Run burned down. The Fuhrman & Schmidt Brewing Co. continued to operate under Ortlieb ownership with the same management from 1966 to 1976, when the plant closed. Ortlieb intended to reopen the facility, but in 1977 the building was gutted by fire. Included in the labels obtained through the F&S purchase was Kaier, originally of the Charles D. Kaier Brewing Co. of Mahanoy City, Pennsylvania, which plant closed in 1968 after 108 years of operation; Neuweiler, originally from Louis F. Neuweiler's Sons of Allentown, Pennsylvania; Old German, Milwaukee, and Old Bohemian. The last three are now in the product list of the Eastern Brewing Corp.

The McSorley's Cream Ale brand came to Ortlieb in eary 1978 when it was sold to them by C. Schmidt, who had acquired it in the Rheingold purchase. Olde English 800 Malt Liquor was produced under license from Blitz-Weinhard for the East Coast until Pabst obtained control of Blitz and began producing the brew at its Newark, New Jersey, facility.

KAIER'S SPECIAL BEER (Charles D. Kaier Co., Philadelphia)—good malty hop aroma, balanced malt-hop flavor with good character and zest, quite good for a low-priced item. Available in cans and returnable bottles at a very low price. This beer has been widely marketed through the Ortlieb subsidiary in Shamokin, Furhman & Schmidt.

IVY LEAGUE BEER (Ivy League Brewing Co., Philadelphia)—the label touts "juniper berry flavor," but the beer's aroma seemed unusual (in addition to being slightly skunky); the taste was very strange, which I have to attribute to the Juniper berries (more commonly an ingredient of gin) and the beer had a short and strange aftertaste. If this is what is meant by a house flavor, I will pass. This is not a good beer, just strange. Over 100 years ago, brews with juniper berry flavor were very popular in Scandinavia and widely produced there. "Juniper Ale" is still widely brewed in Norway.

NEUWEILER CREAM ALE (Neuweiler Brewing Co., Philadelphia, since 1891)—a cloudy brew, carbonated with small bubbles indicating natural carbonation, sweet vegetal-metallic aroma, sweet malt taste with undertones of decayed vegetable material. I understand this beer is made with two-row and six-row choice barley malt with very little use of cereal grain adjuncts, a special Canadian top yeast, hand-skimmed to remove all possible astringent bitterness. It is also aged for two full months. It is surprising that it showed so poorly and additional tests were performed with similar results. Reintroduced by Ortlieb in 1974.

McSORLEY'S CREAM ALE—deep tawny brown color, tangy malty hop aroma, full-flavored, good balance, plenty of hops yet not overly bitter, a very fine ale at a reasonable price. Great with food. This brand was originally produced by the Fidelio Brewing Co. of New York City, founded in 1852, later by the Greater New York Brewing Co. (1939) for McSorley's Ale House, an East Side New York pub that permitted only male patrons for over one hundred years. In recent years, the brand was produced by Rheingold Breweries, Inc. until the acquisition of that firm by C. Schmidt & Sons, Inc., which sold the McSorley label to Ortlieb. In the post World War II period this brew was introduced as Rheingold Scotch Ale.

NEUWEILER IX CREAM ALE—gold, sweet well-hopped aroma, highly carbonated, foamy, strongly flavored, overly sweet, sweetness clashes with the hops.

ORTLIEB'S BOCK BEER—medium brown with rosy hues, strange grasslike aroma, sweet and strange, not good at all.

ORTLIEB'S PHILADELPHIA'S FAMOUS BEER—pale gold, light malty nose with some hops, sour malty flavor with a bitter hop finish and aftertaste, lacks balance.

OLDE ENGLISH 800 MALT LIQUOR (Blitz-Weinhard, Philadelphia)—one of the beers more like a "pop" wine, strong aromatic flavor that is overdone. Too sweet for a beer drinker, nor can I think of any food that would go with it.

COQUI 900 MALT LIQUOR—bright deep gold, slightly beerlike aroma, sweet and malty flavor, good clean finish. Coqui is being produced by Ortlieb to replace Olde English 800, which it no longer makes since Pabst obtained Blitz-Weinhard, the owner of the Olde English label.

OLD STYLE BREWER'S LAGER BEER (Brewer's Lager Brewing Co., Philadelphia)—pale color, sweet clean malty nose, tart "prickly" flavor, sweet in the back, sour in the front, unbalanced. Made by Ortlieb in cans only, a private label of the Brewer's Outlet chain of Pennsylvania.

BOARS HEAD SEAN O'SHAUGHNESSY STOUT (O'Shaughnessy Ltd., Philadelphia)—deep red brown, rich malty aroma with hops showing through, highly carbonated, thin, good flavor but weak, candy-like finish and aftertaste. The name O'Shaughnessy was selected more or less at random from the Philadelphia phone directory.

Schoenling Brewing Co.
(Cincinnati, Ohio)

The Queen City has been a haven for brewers for over a century. In the late 1800s it was the home of the fifth largest brewery in the nation and of over a dozen smaller firms. After Prohibition no fewer than ten brewers opened for business.

Only two of these remain in operation today and independents Schoenling and Hudepohl struggle to maintain their share of the area market with the onslaught of the other two Ohio brewers, Anheuser-Busch and Christian Schmidt. Schoenling commands the smallest share of the Cincinnati market, but its products are shipped outside the state and have been seen in Pennsylvania and in some southern states.

Schoenling products reported below have

117

been seen only in no-return bottles.

SCHOENLING CREAM ALE—deep yellow gold, clean burnt malt aroma, mellow with mildly tart flavor. A good tasting brew that is available in convenient seven-ounce bottles called "little kings."

SIR EDWARD STOUT XXX SPECIAL BREW—medium yellow-gold color, nice "beery" aroma, fresh and malty, very light flavor, slightly sour finish. It is a light pilsener-type, not a stout.

SCHOENLING DRAFT BEER BIG JUG—64 ounces, medium pale yellow, aroma like salty CO_2 and steel pickling solution, sweet flavor and high carbonation, label says not pasteurized, hop finish, uninteresting beer.

SCHOENLING DRAFT BEER—very pale, brackish aroma, unbalanced metallic bittersweet taste, flattens out at end. Label says not pasteurized.

BIG JUG BEER—pale gold, sour malty aroma, clean light sweet malt flavor, well-carbonated (too much so); very drinkable, but not much to it.

SCHOENLING OLD TIME BOCK BEER—deep red brown, highly carbonated, weak, wet sour nose, not much flavor, watery, finish faintly of roasted malt, most of the character comes from carbonation.

TOP HAT BEER (Top Hat Brewing Co.)—pale gold, lightly hopped aroma, hops greater than the malt and not in balance, bitter palate up front, smooths out in the middle, briefly sour at the finish.

Sierra Nevada Brewing Co.
(Chico, Calif.)

Sierra Nevada was established in 1980 by Paul Camusi and Ken Grossman. They brew handmade natural beer using only barley malt, whole hops, yeast, and water. They brew no more than ten barrels at a time to maintain tight control and avoid the use of additives and adjuncts. The brews are top-fermented and krausened in the bottle for natural carbonation. Sierra Nevada brews are neither pasteurized or filtered, so there will be sediment in the bottles.

The brewery is capable of producing 2500 barrels annually and extending to East Coast metropolitan markets.

SIERRA NEVADA BREWING CO. PALE ALE—deep rosy brown, complex tangy sweet hop and malt aroma, smooth rich malt flavor with hops coming in at the finish, delicious and long on the palate, slightly sour aftertaste. Three different kinds of malt are used in the brew.

SIERRA NEVADA BREWING CO. PORTER-deep rosy brown, complex tangy sweet hop and malt aroma, smooth rich malt flavor with hops coming in at the finish, delicious and long on the palate, slightly sour aftertaste. Three different kinds of malt are used in the brew.

SIERRA NEVADA BREWING CO. STOUT—opaque brown, big rich clean sweet nose, complex herbal flavor that is mostly up front, powerful and long lasting on the palate, sweet-smoked roasted malt finish, very long aftertaste of

sweet smoked malt, really wipes out anything else on your palate, and is a bit too intense for some tastes.

CELEBRATION ALE—cloudy orange, sharp and sweet aroma, big vinous hop flavor, huge body, long long aftertaste, an excellent brew.

CHICO PIONEER DAYS BEER SPECIAL ISSUE 1982— slightly clouded orange, perfumy candy-fruit nose, candy-fruit and sharp hop flavor, very long on the palate, but the bitterness hangs on a bit too strongly.

SIERRA NEVADA CELEBRATION ALE 1982—cloudy-orange, huge sharp malt and hop aroma with a fruity perfume, small bubble CO$_2$, sweet ale flavor of complex malt and hops, very long on the palate.

SIERRA NEVADA CELEBRATION ALE 1983—cloudy orange, powerful assertive sweet tangy citrus nose (grapefruit–mandarin orange–tangerine), small bubble carbonation, complex huge tangy sweet and sharp ale flavor, very long on the palate; a real sipping beer.

Spoetzl Brewery, Inc.
(Shiner, Tex.)

Founded and built in 1909 by the Shiner Brewing Association, a stock company of local citizens, the business faltered until 1914, when Kosmas Spoetzl, former brewmaster of the Pyramid Brewery in Cairo, Egypt, leased the brewery with option to buy. Early in 1915, after making several improvements to the brewery facilities, Spoetzl began producing a draft Bavarian-style beer made from pure malt and hops by his own recipe. The Shiner citizenry, mostly of Czech and German extraction,

acclaimed the new beer. Spoetzl purchased the brewery outright that year only to face Prohibition in 1918 (Texas was one of the first to go dry). He tried brewing near-beer, but the public never purchased enough of it to ensure survival of the firm, but the plant could make a living supplying ice to all of those Texans who were brewing their own alcoholic beer at home.

In 1933, 3.2 percent beer was legalized in Texas and Spoetzl fortunes began to turn. The new Texas Export Beer, later named Shiner Texas Special, was a success in south Texas. Throughout the 1940s, the popularity of Shiner Beer encouraged continual expansion and modernization of the brewery.

When Kosmas Spoetzl died in 1950, his daughter, Cecelie, became sole proprietress and the only proprietress of a brewery in the United States. For sixteen years Miss Celie, as she was known by friends and business associates, operated the firm, selling out in 1966 to former San Antonio brewmaster William Bigler. Bigler formed a stock company retaining the Spoetzl name. The brewery has since changed hands but the name remains.

Spoetzl products are marketed on a limited basis in major Texas cities, but most of them are sold close to home in Sublime, Sugar Land, and Sweet Home, Texas. Only one brand, Shiner Texas Special, is sold in package and on draft. Recently, Spoetzl has added private labels in cans, including a dark beer (Wurzfest 1979 Dark Beer, for example). Annual production is on the order of 40,000 barrels.

SHINER PREMIUM BEER—pale bright gold, beautiful big well-hopped malty aroma, highly carbonated, very well-balanced, slightly hoppy flavor, but the hops are more aromatic, aroma better than the flavor, hops reappear in the finish, a good pleasant-tasting and refreshing brew.

SHINER PREMIUM BOCK BEER—pale copper-orange, toasted malt nose with a faint sour fruit background, high carbonation that masks the otherwise pleasant malt flavor, little zest.

Stevens Point Beverage Co.
(Stevens Point, Wis.)

The Stevens Point Brewery was started in 1857 by two men named Ruder and Whale. It was bought in the early 1860s by Andrew Lutz and his brothers, who ran it until 1897, when it was sold to Gustav Kuenzel. Kuenzel ran the facility as the Gustav Kuenzel Brewing Co. until it was sold in 1901. It was incorporated as the Stevens Point Brewing Co. in 1902. During Prohibition the name was changed to the Stevens Point Beverage Co.

Only Point Special Beer and, in season, Point Bock Beer are produced for sale in a seventy-five-mile radius around Stevens Point, plus limited distribution in Milwaukee and Madison, Wisconsin.

Wisconsin's smallest brewer, with an annual production capacity of 50,000 barrels, is the pride of its home market. Point Special, described by the brewery as a European-style beer, has scored remarkably high in a number of independent taste tests run by newspaper columnists and beer book writers. It is described as light, clean, and smooth with a great beer aroma. Corn grits are used as an adjunct to the barley malt to afford much of these qualities. Tasters are warned, however, that packages found outside the Stevens Point area may be too old or mistreated since can collectors eagerly spread Point Special far beyond its marketing area.

The company remains strong despite considerable pushing by the local giants (Heileman, Pabst, Schlitz, et al.) and isn't worried because demand for their brew exceeds their capacity to produce it. Since there are no current plans for expansion, you have to go to Stevens Point to enjoy this fine brew. Like they say, "when you're out of Point, you're out of town." Point occasionally packages their beer in special cans, such as an annual item honoring the Appleton Foxes baseball team. Point also sells an interesting and amusing line of breweriana. Write to Grand Prix Products, Dept. PBC, Box 132, Stevens Point, Wis. 54481.

POINT SPECIAL BEER—pale gold, faint malt aroma, touch of hops, a bit of a burnt nature, light body, clean flavor, smooth and very drinkable.

POINT BOCK BEER—orange color, sweet creamy Sky-Bar bordeaux aroma, small bubble carbonation, watery, slightly smoky, a bit dull, and certainly brief.

Straub Brewery, Inc.
(St. Mary's, Pa.)

The nation's third smallest brewery, with an annual production of about fifteen thousand barrels, is an independent. In fact, it is one of the most independent breweries in America. There is no advertising; no public relations office exists; not even a salesman is heard.

Sixty-two-year-old brewmaster Gibby Straub was quoted in 1978 in a local newspaper: "We only make so much and that's it. All the Straubs like to hunt and fish too much; to hell with making all this money. Besides, we're selling all we make now."

All they make is for the north central Pennsylvania area around St. Mary's with its population of 7,500. Forty percent of Straub's output is on draught and the remainder is bottled. Sold only as far away as Emporium and Johnsonburg, Pennsylvania (a 100-mile sales region), the product line has been regularly turning a profit (since 1872). Straub has little fear of the industry behemoths.

The Straub product is not cheap, for the company never cheapened its formula. It believes that you can't make good beer with cheap ingredients and production shortcuts. It concentrates on making good beer, not in competing with cheap beer.

The Straub recipe calls for two tons of barley malt and one ton of untoasted cornflakes mixed into a 143-barrel batch with water in a mash tub. It is mashed, blended, and simmered in a giant copper kettle built in 1901. Dried hops from Washington, Oregon, and Idaho are added at three different times in the brewing (which takes twelve hours at Straub) and the wort is cooled for its long (six- to seven-week) fermentation. The Straub Brewery may be the only one in the U.S. still using a porous Lampson carbonating stone to carbonate the beer naturally.

Since the beer brews and ages longer, it is slightly higher than most domestic beers in alcohol and a slight bit lighter than many in carbohydrates and calories. Locals are often heard to order a Straub's beer by asking for "a bottle of high test."

Straub has no public relations staff, but does invite visitors to stop by any afternoon (except Wednesday) to enjoy its fine brew, as long as the guests are twenty-one and wash their own glasses.

The brewery was founded by Peter Straub, who came from Germany in 1869 at the age of 19. After working in several Pennsylvania breweries, he bought the old Volk Brewery (dating from 1872) in St. Mary's. The company has remained in Straub hands continuously since that time.

STRAUB BEER—pale gold with a well-developed firm head, light and clean grain taste, extremely dry at the start, eases a bit in the middle, then finishes dry as it started. This is the driest domestic beer I have ever tasted and there was not a single sour note. Straub is a really fine beer, and should be excellent with all food. The people of St. Mary's and environs are indeed lucky to have such a fine local brew.

Stroh Brewery Co.
(Detroit, Mich.)

Stroh, the oldest brewing firm in Michigan, was founded in 1850 by Bernard Stroh. It was called the Lion Brewery in 1870, when the lion crest of Kyrburg Castle in Kirn, Bohemia, was adopted as the Stroh emblem; the crest remains on the Stroh label to this day. In 1882 the name was changed to the B. Stroh Brewing Co. and finally to the Stroh Brewery Co. in 1909.

The major Stroh product is Stroh's Bohemian Style Beer, which is said to be "America's only fire-brewed beer," patterned after the practice of the Municipal Brewery of Pilsen, Bohemia. Brewing over direct fire (rather than by steam under pressure as is done by most brewers) was an innovation implemented by Stroh in 1912.

Stroh Light was introduced in 1978 to compete in the lo-cal market. Rounding out the product line is a bock brewed in the traditional manner, from an all-malt blend containing roasted malts.

National Prohibition did not begin until January 1920, but Michigan went dry in May 1918. The Stroh Products Co. survived the fifteen years by making ice, ice cream, soft drinks, near-beer, and malt extract. Stroh thrived in the post-Prohibition era, reaching annual sales of a million barrels for the first time in 1953. Growth from that time was even more rapid and by 1976, Stroh was seventh in the nation with sales in 5.75 million barrels and sixth nationally in single-brand sales. Sales in

An early example of Stroh print advertising

1977 passed the 6 million mark, but Stroh slipped to eighth place in sales (because both Olympia and Heileman purchased additional breweries, adding substantially to their production capacity and sales). In 1980, Stroh regained the seventh spot and the Schaefer acquisition ensured its grip on it for 1981. Schaefer's New York to Baltimore market exceeded 3 million barrels annually.

In April of 1982, following disapproval of a merger between G. Heileman and Schlitz, Stroh made a successful takeover of Schlitz. Schlitz remains as an operating subsidiary of Stroh, and the Stroh-Schlitz combine has become the No. 3 largest brewer in America, with 1982 sales at 23 million barrels.

The Goebel Brewing Co. of Detroit was acquired by Stroh in 1964 and since that time Stroh has produced the Goebel labels, brands well known in the Midwest.

Stroh plans to continue its fire-brewing tradition and has readied fire-kettles at the Allentown plant. To firm its grip on its No. 3 position, Stroh has implemented an improved formula and aging duration for Schlitz and more stringent quality control and shelf-life guidelines for Schaefer.

STROH'S BOHEMIAN STYLE BEER—bright gold, fresh

Stroh Brewery, Detroit, Michigan

malt aroma, bright hop and malt flavor, good "beery" finish and aftertaste, a good well-balanced brew with a strong following on eastern and midwestern campuses.

STROH'S OWN BOCK BEER—medium deep copper, good malt aroma with lots of character, excellent balance, very flavorful, good aftertaste, a smooth and very drinkable brew, made with real caramel malt. An authentic and good bock beer with excellent taste.

STROH LIGHT BEER—115 calories, clear, pale gold, light malty aroma, light malt and spring water flavor, touch of iron in the finish. Good character for a light beer.

GOEBEL GOLDEN LIGHT LAGER (Goebel Brewing Co.)—pale gold color, faint malty nose, lightly flavored, but a good balance between the malt and the hops, clean taste, good tasting throughout, a little too much carbonation, but overall a very fine brew worth trying.

STROH SIGNATURE—bright gold, lovely hoppy nose with complexity, small bubble CO_2, good dry well-balanced malt and hop flavor, long on palate, good finish, good-tasting aftertaste. An excellent super premium, using 100 percent European hops.

Joseph Schlitz Brewing Co. *(Van Nuys, Calif.; Tampa, Fla.; Winston-Salem, N.C.; Memphis, Tenn.; Longview, Tex.)* The firm of Joseph Schlitz began in 1849 when August Krug erected a small brewhouse on Chestnut Street in Milwaukee, just three years after the city was incorporated. When Krug died in 1856, Joseph Schlitz took charge of the business and in nine years doubled the brewery's capacity and sales. The stock company, Joseph Schlitz Brewing Co., was formed in 1874. The next year Joseph Schlitz died in a shipwreck off the coast of England while on a voyage to visit his native Germany. By order of Schlitz's will, August Uihlein and his three brothers, all nephews of August Krug, assumed control of the business with the stipulation that the company name remain unchanged. The company continued to grow under the leadership of the Uihlein family. By the turn of the century, the brewery's capacity had exceeded one million barrels annually.

Schlitz expanded from a one-plant company with the purchase of the George Ehret Brewery in Brooklyn in 1949 and three years later was the leading brewer in America with a record 6,347,000-barrel output. Although the Brooklyn plant was closed in 1973, Schlitz continued expanding, opening a plant in 1977 at Baldwinsville, New York, which has since been sold to Anheuser-Busch. The Hawaii Brewing Co. of Aiea, Oahu, was also a division of Schlitz,

producing Primo, the beer of Hawaii.

In the spring of 1980 Schlitz began marketing its first super premium, Erlanger Classic 1883 (so-called because Schlitz brewed an Erlanger back then), as its fifth nationally distributed brand following a favorable response in test markets. Tribute Light Beer appeared in test markets in late 1980 and Old Milwaukee Light was released. In 1980 Schlitz also began test-marketing a menthol-flavored beer named Kuhlbrau. After struggling for several years to hold its position as third in beer sales in America, Schlitz slipped to fourth in 1980, and lost that position to Heileman in 1981.

The original Milwaukee brewery was closed by Schlitz in 1981 and the beer that made Milwaukee famous continued its slide. With its position unimproved in 1981, Schlitz became a prime candidate for takeover, and G. Heileman

123

and Stroh made offers. In April, 1982, Schlitz agreed to its purchase by the smaller Stroh Brewery, and, under the terms of the merger, became a Stroh subsidiary.

SCHLITZ (The Beer that made Milwaukee Famous)—pale gold color, light malty nose with faint hops, light flavor, lightly hopped, inoffensive on all counts, very pleasant tasting but lacks zest, slightly sour aftertaste, overall quite dry.

SCHLITZ LIGHT BEER—pale color, vanilla nose, light malty vanillalike sweet taste, pleasant, but with little zest, some family resemblance to Schlitz above. This label was introduced in 1975; 96 calories.

OLD MILWAUKEE BEER—bright pale gold, faint hop aroma with some malt, good malt flavor, good tasting, pleasant finish and aftertaste.

SCHLITZ MALT LIQUOR—hearty malt aroma, good lusty malt flavor at the start, flattens out somewhat in the middle, but leaves a good malty aftertaste. Quite good for the type. Introduced in 1964. Seen labeled Schlitz Stout Malt Liquor in the Southwest.

ERLANGER CLASSIC 1883—beautiful golden color, good malt and light hop aroma, very smooth on the palate, a bit too much carbonation but not noticeable on the palate. It reminds me very much of Heineken Light and should compete well in the market. This sample was a fresh one brewed in Los Angeles. Freshly delivered samples taken in New Jersey did not fare so well. Erlanger is now available nationwide on draught.

OLD MILWAUKEE PREMIUM LIGHT BEER—pale yellow, faint clean beery-malty aroma, carbonation dominates the palate, little more than dull malt, slight malty finish, no aftertaste.

PRIMO HAWAIIAN BEER—According to the package "island brewed since 1897," but prior to 1974 the wort was shipped to Hawaii from the Schlitz plant in Los Angeles. That year a new brew house was opened and Primo was once again island-brewed. The beer itself is a sorry affair, greatly lacking in flavor. Primo is very pale in color, has a faint sweet aroma and its predominant feature of flavor is carbonation, yet the beer itself is not highly carbonated. Schlitz acquired the Hawaii Brewing Co. in 1964. Primo is now being made in Memphis, but it is not known where this production is being marketed.

F & M Schaefer Brewing Co. *(Lehigh Valley, Allentown, Pa.)* Frederick and Maximillian Schaefer founded this firm in 1842 when they purchased the Sebastian Sommers Brewery in New York City. In 1848 they became one of the pioneers in the manufacture of lager beer in

America. The stock company that began the present company name was organized in 1878.

Following Prohibition, Schaefer operated only from its plant in Brooklyn, which provided Schaefer products for the New York metropolitan area until 1977, when a transfer of operations to the new Lehigh Valley plant was completed. A second facility, the old Gunther plant in Baltimore, was purchased from the Theodore Hamm Brewing Co. in 1969, along with the Gunther label (it closed in 1978). Schaefer purchased the Beverwyck Brewing Co. plant in Albany shortly after World War II but gave it up in the late 1960s. Schaefer also operated the old Standard Brewing Co. plant in Cleveland as Schaefer of Ohio during the late 1950s and early 1960s. Newark, New Jersey, was listed on Schaefer products as late as 1976, but it is not known if Newark ever housed more than

corporate offices for the firm. In recent years, Schaefer has also produced the Piel Bros. brands.

Schaefer has been a staunch supporter of Metropolitan New York sporting events and the "Schaefer Circle of Sports" sponsors a wide variety of athletic endeavors through direct sponsorship or through radio and TV coverage. Some of the product's popularity is known to be the result of fan appreciation.

Schaefer is a big seller in the New York City area, upstate New York and Pennsylvania. It has been well-received in the Baltimore area and there is little else available on the Delmarva peninsula.

In 1980, the Stroh Brewing Co. of Detroit became the principal sharcholder of Schaefer stock and entered into an agreement which allowed each company the right to manufacture, package, and process each other's products.

SCHAEFER BEER—bright golden color, good malt and hop aroma, fine taste up front with plenty of zest and character, good body, good balanced flavor all the way through, well-hopped long aftertaste, good brew.

SCHAEFER BOCK BEER—brown with red-orange hues, malty aroma, a brief touch of strong hops in taste, then it flattens right out, poor balance, scratchy in the throat, slightly foamy.

SCHAEFER CREAM ALE—creamy, light gold, faint sour aroma with yeast background, yeast and malt flavor, medium body, reasonably dry for type.

SCHAEFER LIGHT LAGER BEER—bright gold, virtually no aroma, very faint malt only, small bubble CO_2, faint hops and sour malt on palate, very little flavor or finish.

Gunther Brewing Co. *(Baltimore, Md.)* This

firm dates back to 1900, when it was founded by George Guenther (Günther—the umlaut got lost in Americanization), who earlier had been a cofounder of the Bayview Brewery in Baltimore, which was absorbed by the Maryland Brewing Co. (see Carling National). Gunther Beer is now made at the Lehigh Valley plant and is being marketed over a much wider area than before, including upstate New York and New England.

GUNTHER LIGHT LAGER BEER—pale color, faint malty aroma, little character and no zest, not much of a beer, too light for real beer taste.

Piels Bros. *(Brooklyn, originally)* Brothers

William, Gottfried, and Michael Piel founded a large brewery in Brooklyn in 1883 and became successful as Piel Bros. After reopening in Brooklyn following Prohibition, Piels enjoyed many good years before suffering economic ills in the mid-1960s. Before being absorbed into Schaefer, Piels operated for a brief time in the Hampden-Harvard-Drewry's plant in Willimansett, Massachusetts. Piels will be long-remembered for a series of commercials featuring Bert and Harry Piel (voices of Bob Elliott and Ray Goulding) which were particularly entertaining. Curiously enough, there was a similar series of commercials using Bob and Ray as the voices of Godfrey Gunther, Sr., and Godfrey Gunther, Jr., in Washington in the late 1950s. Piels breweries of record during the 1948-74 period included New York City, Brooklyn, Staten Island, and Stapleton, New York, and Willimansett, Massachusetts.

PIELS LIGHT BEER—light gold color, light malty aroma, pleasant tasting but with little zest and personality, a long and pleasant aftertaste. A good beer, one of the better light domestic pilseners, no faults except a lack of character, a common trait in American beers. Inexpensive and worth trying. Thirst quenching and pleasantly so.

PIELS LIGHT PREFERRED BEER—pale gold, light hop nose, good hop flavor, lots of character, malt shows well in the aftertaste. Obviously the Stroh influence is beneficial.

PIELS REAL DRAFT PREMIUM BEER—bright gold, clean malty aroma, carbonation dominates the flavor.

Thousand Oaks Brewing Co.
(Berkeley, Calif.)

Thousand Oaks is a real home-style brewing operation using malt syrup and pelletized hops. The brew is fermented in a 55-gallon food drum.

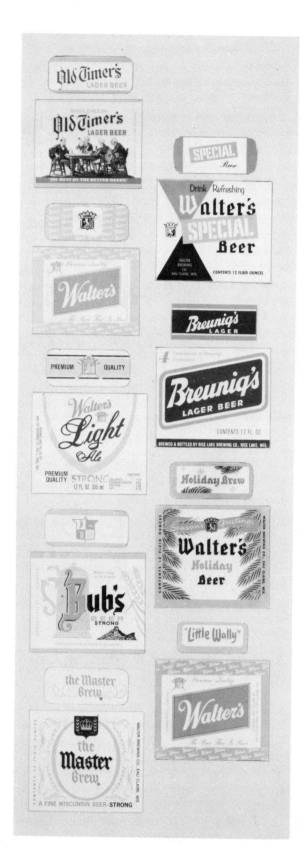

In 1982, sales totaled 40 barrels. It was founded in 1981.

THOUSAND OAKS PREMIUM LAGER—slightly cloudy, deep gold, fairly strong hoppy aroma, very unusual flavor much like some kind of a dark beer (like birch beer, but not birch), flavor intensifies to the finish and the aftertaste is very long. A very strange and unfamiliar flavor for a beer.

GOLDEN GATE MALT LIQUOR—cloudy yellow, faint sweet malt aroma, lightly carbonated, light fruity sweet flavor, good finish, long aftertaste, clean, tasty, but not dry, a bit like fruit pop.

GOLDEN BEAR DARK MALT LIQUOR—opaque red-brown, sweet malt nose with a trace of lactic acid, sweet malt flavor, low CO_2, medium body, clean finish, long aftertaste, decent brew of type.

Walter Brewing Co.
(Eau Claire, Wis.)

John Walter moved to Eau Claire in the early 1880s and founded the John Walter Brewing Co. Operation was continuous to 1916 and has been continuous since 1933, when the brewery reopened following repeal. The brewery remains healthy today, even in the face of increasing competition from the large national brewers; its sales approach 100,000 barrels annually.

Products include the traditional Walter's Beer; Breunig's Beer, originally brewed by the Rice Lake Brewing Co. of Rice Lake, Wisconsin; Old Timer's, originally brewed by the West Bend Lithia Co. of West Bend, Wisconsin; Bub's Beer, previously a product of the Peter Bub Brewing Co. of Winona, Minnesota; Master Brew, and several private brands including Otto and Elm Grove. Walter is also one of the most prolific producers of collector cans for special interest groups.

As far as can be ascertained, there was no connection between this firm and the the now defunct Walter Brewing Company of Pueblo, Colorado. An interesting note concerns the West Bend Lithia Co. This old firm, which dated back to 1849 and ended in 1972, was obtained by Martin F. Walter in 1911. It obtained its unusual name during Prohibition, when production changed from beer to a type of water, lithium carbonate. Prudence suggested deletion of "Brewing" from the corporate name in favor of "Lithia."

Most sales are within a radius of seventy-five

miles, with other concentrations in Minnesota, Chicago, and southeastern Wisconsin.

WALTER'S (design of can identical to that traditional to Walter Brewing Co. of Pueblo, Colorado, before its demise)—bright gold, austere slightly hopped nose, sweet malt taste without any hops noticeable, very drinkable with a long pleasant finish. Lacks character because of the lack of hops in the flavor, but still good tasting.

WALTER EXTRA LIGHT ALE—pale color, aroma of carbonation, malt, vegetation, light flavor, watery, CO_2 dominates palate, brief finish.

MASTER BREW—bright gold, very faint malt aroma, light and very sweet, no character, sour finish. A poor beer.

OLD TIMER'S LAGER BEER—same can logo as Master Brew, pale yellow, slightly "off" light malty aroma, light yeasty-grainy taste, highly carbonated.

WISCONSIN OLD TIMER'S LAGER BEER (The Best of the Better Beers)—pale gold, light malty aroma, light clean malty flavor, smooth, neutral finish with a tinge of sweetness. This can had the same logo as West Bend Old Timer's Lager Beer produced by the West Bend Lithia Co., West Bend, Wisconsin, as recently as the early 1970s.

BILOW GARDEN STATE BOCK BEER—copper orange color, nice hop and roasted malt aroma, high carbonation impairs flavor of good malt and light hops, brief finish, no aftertaste. Bilow is a central New Jersey liquor store chain. Lud Bilow is an avid can collector and delights in producing special can designs for his friends and associates—including one saluting *The Great American Beer Book*. Walter does all of the Bilow cans now. Previous Bilow labels were produced by Eastern and Fuhrman & Schmidt.

BREUNIG'S LAGER BEER—pale gold, big malty aroma, dry malty flavor, a good beer that is even-flavored all the way through, no real highs but no faults. Breunig's was a label of the Rice Lake Brewing Co. of Rice Lake, Wisconsin, until obtained by Walter.

BUB'S BEER—medium gold, very little nose at all, at first a brief taste of hops, then the flavor is a very light sour malt with a neutral ending. The motto of Bub's is "Makes It Fun to Be Thirsty." This label came from the Peter Bub Brewing Co. of Winona, Minnesota.

WALTER'S BEER—design of can common to Walter's of Eau Claire for the period 1967 to present, bright gold, nice malty nose, foamy, flavor starts out sweet, but soon turns to malty sour, salty and bitter aftertaste.

BILOW GARDEN STATE PREMIUM BEER—bright pale gold, clean brisk malt aroma with good hops, good body, good malty-hop flavor, metallic astringent finish, slightly sweet aftertaste.

BILOW GARDEN STATE LIGHT BEER—similar to the premium, but lighter, less complex, less flavorful and less interesting, similar, but cheaper brew. This brew is actually Walter's Light, and Bilow Premium above is actually Walter's Premium.

Yakima Brewing & Malting Co.
(Yakima, Wash.)

This firm opened in 1982 producing Grant's Scottish Ale, Grant's Christmas Ale, Light American Stout, Russian Imperial Stout, and Grant's India Pale Ale for draught service in Yakima, Seattle, and Portland.

The Scottish Ale is a deep red full-bodied ale, spicy and aromatic. The IPA is sharply bitter, long and dry. The Stout is black, rich, sweetish and alcoholic (over 7 percent). Current brewery capacity is 800 barrels annually.

D. G. Yuengling & Son, Inc.
(Pottsville, Pa.)

In 1903, stated *One Hundred Years of Brewing,* D. G. Yuengling & Son was "one of the oldest brewing establishments in the country in continuous existence." That claim is still true; Yuengling is the oldest brewery in the United States for continuous operation (even during Prohibition) and for continuous ownership by the same family (since 1829).

David G. Yuengling was born in Germany in 1806 and came to America in 1828. After residing in Reading and Lancaster for one year, he moved to Pottsville and established the brewery, becoming one of the first in the country to make the new "lager" beer.

In 1873 Frederick G. Yuengling was admitted to the partnership and the same year David G. Yuengling, Jr., established an ale brewery in New York City. The New York operation was extended to a second plant manufacturing lager beer, but neither of these ever became successful and each required continual financial support from Pottsville. They were finally closed down in 1897. A second abortive attempt at expansion was initiated about that time with a firm in Richmond, Virginia, under the name of Betz, Yuengling, & Beyer.

Members of the Yuengling family have maintained continuous control of the company; the current president is master brewer Richard L. Yuengling, a direct descendant of the founder.

Throughout the entire period, the firm of D. G. Yuengling & Son, Inc. (incorporated as such in 1914) has remained at the forefront of modern brewing technique and has maintained an extremely high-quality product line.

Yuengling products are marketed primarily in eastern Pennsylvania, but can be found in nearby New Jersey, Maryland, and Washington, D.C. The product line is headed by the very fine Yuengling Premium Beer. The firm also produces Old German Brand Beer, Lord Chesterfield Ale, Yuengling Porter, Yuengling Bock Beer, and a Bavarian Type Premium Beer, attributed by the label to the Mount Carbon Brewery of Pottsville, Pennsylvania. Recently, Yuengling Premium and Porter were selected for national distribution by Merchant du Vin, a wine and beer importer. Also, Yuengling recently entered the collector can business. Most of these are clearly marked Yuengling, but a few, like Pocono Beer and Haentjen's Ale take closer reading.

YUENGLING DARK BREW PORTER—deep copper-brown, rich malty coffee-like aroma, coffee flavor, finish a little bitter, lingering aftertaste. Brewed from 100 percent dark roasted Larker malt and is top-fermented. Usually seen in the East in returnable bottles.

YUENGLING PREMIUM BEER—light gold color, good malt aroma with a subtle hop background, excellent balance, fine malty finish and aftertaste. For flavor, few beers start off as well as this one. The first few mouthfuls are incredibly clean and fresh with plenty of good hop character and a bright zesty flavor. Then, inexplicably, the flavor sags and becomes quite ordinary after several more sips. That initial effect is very pleasant, however, and sufficient to ensure that this will be ranked high on the list of America's finest. Try it by all means; it has been seen from Washington to Boston, but not regularly at any one place. Now nationally marketed by Merchant du Vin. This beer is made without any artificial ingredients; only the finest barley malt, corn grits, hops and natural spring water are used; it is lagered three months. A package change in 1980 changed the name of the brew to D. G. Yuengling & Son Premium Beer.

OLD GERMAN BRAND BEER—darker color than the premium, deep yellow gold, aroma of burnt baked potato, sharp hop taste, bitter finish.

LORD CHESTERFIELD ALE—yellow gold, good sweet malty aroma that faded quickly, perfumy sweet and bitter ale taste, plenty of body, lingering aftertaste. Good value for its type, priced quite reasonably in returnable bottles, seen only in Pennsylvania.

BAVARIAN TYPE PREMIUM BEER—medium color, sweet malty aroma with hop background, most of the initial flavor is hops, then flavor flattens out in the middle and the finish is quite bitter. The Bavarian label was obtained from the Mt. Carbon (Pennsylvania) Brewery when it closed in 1965.

129

Australia

Australia ranks fourth in per capita consumption of beer (trailing Czechoslovakia, Germany, and Belgium), downing about twenty-five gallons per person each year, but the inhabitants of Darwin in Northern Australia are the world's record-holders with a staggering annual consumption of over sixty gallons per person.

Beer in Australia is more than a way of life; it is almost a religion. It is a symbol of manliness, the totem of the rugged individualist, the drink of the frontiersman. It is said that much of the beer drinking in Australia today may be caused by doubts concerning that rugged individualism, for Australians now cluster in cities, for the most part, involved in factory or office jobs, which can scarcely be deemed the milieu of the rugged individualist. So they drink enormous quantities of their fine beers, while watching bruising Australian athletic competition.

Brewing began in earnest in Australia in the middle of the nineteenth century and by the 1880s production was about thirty million imperial gallons, with consumption around thirty-two million. The Australian brewing industry has grown in leaps and bounds since then and today a substantial quantity of its beer is exported throughout the world. Several years ago, Foster's boasted that its lager was the third largest nationally distributed imported beer in the U.S. It was third immediately following saturation advertising to promote sales of the huge 740 milliliter cans (almost a U.S. quart), but it does make the point.

Australian beer is very much like English-style beer, even though the majority of it is light-colored lager. There usually are more hops in the recipe and a higher alcoholic content than in American-style brews.

Carlton & United Breweries, Ltd.
(Melbourne)

Carlton & United (CUB) is the largest brewer in the Southern Hemisphere and some say it is among the ten largest brewers in the world. Several roots of this conglomerate can be traced to the mid-nineteenth century and to the Foster Brewing Co., originator of Foster's Lager. CUB operates ten breweries in Australia and shares ownership of a brewery in Fiji. It is Australia's leading exporter of beer.

Foster's Lager is the primary export, being shipped to the U.S. in bottles and 25-ounce cans (those cans are 26-2/3 ounces in Australia). It is made from all-barley malt, hop extract, and untreated water.

FOSTER'S LAGER—light yellow, often slightly cloudy when served iced (as is the practice in Australia), fresh light malt and hop aroma, light body, fresh well-hopped flavor, pleasantly balanced, good finish, tasty, fizzy, but not offensively so. Being able to obtain the Foster's Lager for the Australian market, I compared the two. There were great similarities, but the nonexport version was much maltier, in fact, it was more intense on all counts. It would seem that the export Foster's has been "adjusted" to American tastes.

CARLTON LIGHT—deep gold, clean malty aroma, small bubble CO_2, slightly sweet, dull finish, very little aftertaste. The flavor is slightly hoppy and sweet with overriding carbonation.

VICTORIA BITTER ALE—yellow-gold, pungent hop-malt aroma, plenty of hops in the flavor, especially up front, big body, clean and refreshing. A big sharp beer for those who like beer powerful.

CARLTON DRAUGHT—slightly cloudy gold, lovely malt and hop aroma, flavor more hops than malt, creamy texture, nicely balanced finish, good aftertaste.

ABBOTS LAGER—yellow gold, very faint apple aroma, soft, very little flavor with a faint touch of fruit way down, slightly sour finish, short neutral aftertaste.

MELBOURNE BITTER—amber gold, malt aroma, light body, light bitter flavor that is most bitter in the finish and aftertaste.

Castlemaine Perkins, Ltd.
(Brisbane, Adelaide, et al.)

There have been a number of breweries in the history of Australia with the name Castlemaine, all stemming from a parent brewery established at the town of Castlemaine in 1857.

CASTLEMAINE XXXX BITTER ALE—faint aroma of grain and hops, big ale flavor much in the British style, very well-balanced, sour hop finish, a really good British-type ale.

CASTLEMAINE XXXX EXPORT LAGER—light gold, sweet arbor vitae aroma, big hop and spearmint flavor, good hops, but unbalanced with a sour finish.

CASTLEMAINE XXXX DRAUGHT—deep tawny gold, pleasant hop-malt nose, big hop flavor, bright and refreshing, tinge of sweetness in the finish; long, long aftertaste.

CARBINE STOUT—deep orange-brown, heavy malty aroma, dry roasted malt flavor, good balance, finishes well with a good complex roasted malt aftertaste.

Cooper & Sons, Ltd.
(Upper Kensington, Burnside, Leabrook)

Thomas Cooper established this firm in 1862. Since that time the company has prospered as successive members of the family assumed control of the business. Only stout and ale were

131

produced prior to 1957, when Gold Crown Beer was successfully introduced. Cooper introduced its newly released Real Ale to the U.S. in 1979. Real Ale is made by centuries-old methods and receives final fermentation in the bottle. Real Ale is labeled Sparkling Ale in Australia and was available in the U.S. in limited quantities under that label prior to 1979.

Cooper began packaging its brews in cans in 1962, but today canning is almost entirely for the export market due to local Australian can deposit legislation. The Cooper product line includes Sparkling Ale, Dinner Ale, Diet Beer (DB), and Extra Stout, in addition to those listed above.

The company also produces special editions to celebrate events. Labels of these special releases usually bear the date of the event. Cooper brews are imported by Boles & Company, Inc. of Menlo Park, California.

COOPER SPARKLING ALE—cloudy yellow with green cast, spritzy more than carbonated, flavor on the bitter side, very bitter aftertaste. Made at the Upper Kensington brewery.

BIG BARREL AUSTRALIAN LAGER—deep gold, no aroma, light hop flavor, slight metallic character, finishes well, dry aftertaste, overall dull.

THOS. COOPER & SONS STOUT—opaque brown, big

creamy head, sweet fruity apple-peel malt aroma, powerful, very complex coffee, licorice, caramel, and roasted malt flavor, a most interesting taste that really gets your attention, good finish, long clean aftertaste, well-balanced and very good.

THOS. COOPER & SONS FINEST PREMIUM LAGER— Copper gold, roasted malt aroma that was almost coffee-like, light watery body, good roast malt flavor but it is too light, short aftertaste.

*THOMAS COOPER & SONS REAL ALE—*slightly cloudy deep gold, big head, faint sweet grapefruit and cherry nose, slightly sweet up front but the middle palate is lacking, there is some zest and complexity, odd sour aftertaste.

*COOPER GOLD CROWN BEER—*deep yellow, fruitlike aroma (apple peel and hops), good malty flavor at start and at finish, vanished in the middle of the palate, creamy texture, sweet aftertaste. Made at the Burnside brewery.

*COOPER BEST EXTRA STOUT—*dark brown, faint aroma like the Chinese Hoi-Sin sauce, rich malty flavor, very good finish and aftertaste. A good stout of medium body and complexity. Made at the Upper Kensington brewery.

*TRAK—*brilliant yellow-gold color, creamy, faintly sweet malt aroma with good hops in back, carbonation interferes somewhat with otherwise good malt and hop flavor, slightly sour finish and aftertaste.

*COOPER'S REAL ALE—*cloudy gold, distinctive malt aroma, old English ale-style flavor, in some respects, almost like a dry cider, a bit pungent at first, touch of yeast, sharp hop finish and aftertaste. A good heavy-bodied brew with a great complex ale flavor. It is not pasteurized and must be tasted with care.

Courage Breweries, Ltd.
(Melbourne)

Courage is a subsidiary of Courage of England.

*COURAGE DRAUGHT ("The expert drinker's beer," says the label)—*cloudy yellow, faintly sour malt nose, light body, sweet and yeasty flavor, taste is brief, no finish to speak of.

*CREST LAGER EXPORT QUALITY (Courage Australia Pty, Ltd.)—*faint skunky aroma, a flavor that can only be described as being like antiseptic gauze (as like bandage). A very poor beer.

South Australia Brewing Co., Ltd.
(Adelaide)

The company was incorporated in 1888 for the purpose of acquiring the West End Brewery (established 1859) in Adelaide and the Kent Town Brewery (1876) in nearby Kent Town. In 1938 the Walkerville Brewery in Southwark was acquired and renamed the Southwark Brewery (in 1949).

Beginning in 1957, production of all draught beer was concentrated at West End and all packaged beer at Southwark. In 1962 the company acquired a 25 percent interest in Cooper & Sons, Ltd., by a share exchange. Since Cooper does not produce draught brews, South Australia Brewing Co. produces all draught beer in the state under the West End and Southwark brands.

Current products are West End, Southwark, and LA (low alcohol) beers supplied in casks, West End and Southwark in bottles and cans, West End Draught bottled beer, Southwark Premium Beer, Southwark Export Pilsener, and Southwark Special (low carbohydrate).

The company describes its brews as follows:

*SOUTHWARK BITTER BEER—*full-bodied, clean hop bitterness, pleasant finish.

*WEST END XXX BITTER BEER—*full-bodied, same hop character as Southwark, but with slightly higher residual sweetness.

*SOUTHWARK PREMIUM BEER—*greater body than Southwark Bitter, same clean hop bitterness, greater middle palate.

*SOUTHWARK EXPORT PILSENER—*light with high degree of sweetness and a delicate hop bitterness.

*WEST END DRAUGHT BEER—*dry with significant malty character, clean hop bitterness and aroma.

*SOUTHWARK SPECIAL—*pleasant, aromatic, moderate clean bitterness.

*LA DRAUGHT—*moderately full-bodied, clean bitterness, 25 percent less alcohol.

*WEST END EXPORT—*lager style, full-bodied, clean hop aroma and palate, uses Tasmanian hops. Only West End XXX Export Beer is currently exported to the United States.

In our tastings, the descriptions were:

*SOUTHWARK BITTER BEER—*cloudy gold, hop aroma with a touch of yeast, bitter flavor with herbal-coffee background, harsh at first, better when palate becomes inured.

*FESTIVAL PILSENER—*cloudy gold, cedar malt aroma, sweet and dull flavor with a sweet finish, almost no hops.

*SOUTHWARK EXPORT PILSENER—*cloudy yellow,

nice malt-hop nose, sweet and dull flavor with subdued hops, slightly sour finish, no aftertaste.

WEST END XXX BITTER BEER—yellow, mostly a hop aroma, salty-bitter taste, good balance, softens toward finish.

WEST END XXX BEER EXPORT—gold, strong hops in first puff of aroma, then softens, grainy malt-hop flavor, dry finish, long aftertaste, good brew with a touch of roast malt character.

Swan Brewery Co., Ltd.
(Perth)

Some eight years after the settlement of Perth in 1829, the first brewery was established in that colony of Western Australia. This brewery was the forerunner of the Swan Brewery Co., Ltd., which is the sole brewing company in the state.

The Swan Brewery, so named because it was situated on the bank of the Swan River about a mile from Perth, was established in 1889. It experienced early rapid growth when gold was discovered nearby at Coolgardie and Kalgoorlie.

Swan operates a large brewery at Canning Vale and a small brewery at Kalgoorlie. The product line consists of Swan Lager, Emu Export Lager, Swan Draught, Emu Bitter, Special Bond and reduced-calorie Swan Gold.

Swan has a high reputation among Australians and if offered a single choice, most would agree on Swan. During the Vietnam War, large quantities of beer were shipped from Australia to give Aussie troops a taste of home. The bulk of the beer selected for this purpose was Swan Lager, which was well-appreciated by the lads from "down under" sweating it out in Nam. Swan was one of the best-performing Australian beers in the tastings.

SWAN PREMIUM LAGER—yellow gold color, clean fresh apple winery aroma, good malty flavor with some pronounced hop bitterness up front, very British in style, comes right at you, long and good aftertaste.

SWAN LAGER EXPORT—pale yellow, clean malty aroma, light body, hefty hop flavor, weak finish and aftertaste.

Tasmanian Breweries Pty., Ltd.
(Hobart and Launceston; Cascade Brewery Co., Ltd.)

This firm dates back to 1824. It is not only

Australia's oldest brewery, it is Australia's oldest manufacturing concern. Two breweries are operated, one at Cascade (a suburb of Hobart) and in Launceston in Northern Tasmania. The product line includes Cascade and Boags Beers. The Cascade beer shipped to the U.S. no longer bears the title. To avoid a proprietary name use, the Cascade beer exported to the U.S. is called Tasmanian Lager Beer. Samples of "Cascade" that may be discovered now are likely much too old for enjoyment.

CASCADE SPARKLING PALE ALE—slightly cloudy yellow, highly hopped nose, bitter taste and finish, strongly hopped brew.

CASCADE SPARKLING BITTER ALE—yellow with some particulate matter, minty-hop aroma, taste dominated by hops, finishes a bit softer.

TASMANIAN LAGER BEER—pale yellow, slightly cloudy, hop aroma, big hop flavor, finish mostly hop bitterness, but malt begins to come through, ends with an excellent aftertaste of balanced hops and malt to give a spicy effect.

CASCADE DRAUGHT—deep yellow, well-hopped malt aroma, complex flavor, but hop bitterness dominates, bitter finish and aftertaste, too much hops for balance.

BOAGS XXX ALE—pale yellow, light malty nose, light and sweet palate, some bitterness in the finish, short aftertaste, not much to it.

Tooheys, Ltd.
(Lidcombe, Grafton, and Cardiff)

Tooheys Limited was incorporated as a public company in 1902 to acquire the brewing, hotel, wine, and spirit interests of J. T. and J. M. Toohey who had been operating from the Standard Brewery of Sydney for more than twenty-five years, on the site of the Albion Brewery, established in 1827.

Toohey, operates breweries in Lidcombe

(Sydney suburb), Grafton, and Cardiff. The major market of Tooheys is New South Wales. Tooheys is affiliated with Allied Breweries of the U.K.

The product line includes Tooheys Export Lager, Draught, Old, Flag Ale, Stay Lite, and Miller's High-Lo (a brand obtained from the

purchase of the Miller brewery of Newcastle, not Miller of the United States). Only the Export Lager and Lite are exported to the U.S. Tooheys brews Guinness and Lowenbrau under license for its home market.

TOOHEYS LITE LAGER BEER—beautiful tawny gold, faint malty aroma, grainy Postum soda pop flavor, very light, a hint of oxidation in the finish, very light grainy aftertaste.

TOOHEYS DRAUGHT—bright deep gold, malty aroma, light body, slightly sour malt flavor, finish and aftertaste, a bit watery overall.

TOOHEYS LAGER BEER—deep gold, grainy sour malt aroma with good hops, good body, complex flavor that develops well on the palate, quite dry, pleasant sour malt finish, long very pleasant aftertaste, satisfying, you know you've had a good beer. Ages well.

Tooth & Co.
(Sydney)

The first ale in Australia was made in New South Wales in 1795 by James Squire at Kissing Point on the Paramatta River. Fifty years later Tooth & Co. was founded, then known as the Kent Brewery. At the turn of the century, Tooth was Australia's largest brewer.

RESCHS SPECIAL EXPORT PILSENER—pale color, light, fresh aroma, lightly malted and lightly hopped, good, slightly sweet flavor (yet reasonably dry), finish is clean but brief.

TOOTHS KB LAGER—very pale color, almost no nose at all, light body, extremely light flavor somewhat on the metallic side of sour. Seen everywhere in the East in the "quart" cans. Not worth its price.

TOOTHS SHEAF STOUT—deep dark brown color, almost opaque, toffee-coffee nose, big smoky coffee flavor, medium body, long-pleasing coffee finish. A very good stout of the type.

Austria

Brewing began early in the territories of the Austro-Hungarian Empire. As mentioned, Pilsen (Bohemia) beer stretches back to 1292. In 1378 a brewery of substantial size was built at Dobrau, near Pilsen. Beer was drunk in Vienna as early as 1340. Until late in the sixteenth century only officers of the crown were allowed to brew and they were not permitted to sell their

product. At that time these regulations and privileges were abolished and the middle class was free to engage in the business.

The Dreher family had been brewers from 1632. Two hundred years later we find Anton Dreher extending the Dreher brewing business from Vienna to Bohemia, Hungary, and Trieste. At the turn of the twentieth century, the Dreher breweries represented the largest brewing business on the Continent under one management. Anton Dreher is credited with introducing many of the innovations still a part of modern brewing operations. Included among his accomplishments are leading the development of the bottom-fermentation process and the application of artificial refrigeration (following the lead of Sedlmayr in Munich). He is also credited with placing Vienna on equal footing with Munich in the quality of its lager beers.

Bruder Reininghaus Bräuerei A.G.
(Graz)

Steinfeld Graz lay in that part of Austro-Hungary called Styria and had a brewery as early as 1697. These facilities were purchased by Peter and Julius Reininghaus in 1853. By 1900 the firm was the second largest brewing firm in Austria outside of Vienna and fifth largest in the empire. The Reininghaus and Puntigam labels produced today are both highly respected. Only Puntigam appears to be available at present in the U.S.

PUNTIGAM EXPORT BEER—faint sweet aroma, sour vegetal taste with lots of hops, celery juice taste, dull finish. The Puntigam name is believed to have been derived from a merger involving the Erste Grazer Brauerei of F. Schreiner & Sons of Puntigam, Styria.

Bräuerei Fritz Egger
(Unterradlberg)

EGGER BEER PILS—yellow-gold color, first a puff of oxidation, then good roasted malt, roast malt flavor, it is a bit off in the finish which shows the brew's lack of balance (overall aftertaste is good, however).

Harmer K.G.
(Vienna; Ottakringer Bräuerei)

The firm producing the very fine Otta-kringer Fassl Gold is believed to be the

descendant of the brewing firm of J. & J. Kuffner of Vienna, although there may be any number of other breweries involved through mergers over the years. In any event, the beer now appears regularly in both cans and bottles and it is a real winner!

OTTAKRINGER FASSL GOLD EXPORT LAGER BEER—brilliant gold color, lovely hoppy nose, finely balanced hop-malt flavor of good intensity, clean-tasting medium body, pleasantly finished, long appetizing aftertaste, a very drinkable beer. Highly recommended.

OTTAKRINGER GOLD FASSL PILS—pale bright gold, faint hop and malt aroma, bitter without much character, bitter aftertaste.

OTTAKRINGER BOCK MALT LIQUOR—tawny gold, beautiful complex hop and malt nose, malty flavor with good hop background, has texture, lots of rich flavor, big body, high alcohol, lingering aftertaste, 5.8 percent alcohol.

Gosser Bräuerei A.G.
(Loeben-Goss)

Gosser Bräuerei A.G. is another well-respected firm with roots going back to the Austro-Hungarian Empire and, like Reininghaus, is located in the area that was known as Styria. The beers are commonly found in restaurants in Austria and two export brands are also now readily available in America.

GOSSER GOLDEN ROCK FAMOUS AUSTRIAN BEER—light malt-hop aroma with a background sweetness that can be best described as deodorantlike, oily metallic malt taste, not at all exciting.

GOSSER BEER—pale and cloudy, malt aroma, unbalanced burnt malt flavor with some hops in back, a strange beer

that tasted differently with each sip. Neither of these brands has the quality of Gosser brews tasted in Austria. May be mishandled.

GOSSER EXPORT BEER—deep bright gold, beautiful big hop nose with lots of hops, smooth good hop flavor, sour malt aftertaste, lacks depth, 5 percent alcohol.

Österrichische Bräu A.G.
(Linz)

AUSTRIAN GOLD LAGER BEER—rising hop nose with a sweet background; some sour, metallic unpleasantness in the beginning of each mouthful, otherwise a medium hop taste and a dull finish. This beer is not currently being imported, but odd samples may still be around.

ADLER BRÄU EXPORT—cloudy amber with particulate matter in solution, light toasted malt aroma, fairly hoppy flavor, sour in back, sharp finish.

Bräuerei Schwechat A.G.
(Vienna)

Schwechat is the original paternal plant of the Dreher brewing empire of Austro-Hungary. It is the plant established by the Dreher family in 1632 and it was once the property of Anton Dreher, who built much of what stands today. The label of its major export, reported below, bears notice that his was the first Vienna lager beer.

STEFFL EXPORT—strong pineapple aroma, sweet malt flavor with a decidedly pineapple taste, sweet-sour finish. Very disappointing.

Vereinigte Kärtner Bräuereien A.G.
(Villach)

This firm was founded in 1858.

VILLACHER GOLD EXPORT BEER—gold, slightly cloudy, good malt aroma with light hops, light body, good hop flavor up front, flattens out across palate and finished very faintly.

Bräuerei Zipf Vorm Wm Schaup
(Zipf; Österreichische Bräu A.G.)

This firm was established in 1858 as Bierbrauerei in Zipf, Upper Austria.

ZIPFER URTYP LAGER BEER—pale gold color, bright hoppy nose, very hoppy taste, unbalanced and overdone, unlikable bitter-sour finish.

Belgium

The manufacturing of beer in Belgium is of ancient origin, having been manufactured in Brussels in the twelfth century. In the fifteenth century, the popular beers were white beers made of wheat and oats called *walgbaert* and *hoppe*. There also were *roetbier* (red) and *zwartzbier* (black). In time, these varieties were replaced by *lambic* (strong beer), *mais* (small beer), and *faro,* a mixture of the two.

Belgian beers are similar to the beers of France and are rather vinous in nature. In modern times, certain local types have become popular, particularly the white sparkling summer beers of Louvain, the *bières brunes* of Malines, *saison* from Liège, the *uitzet* of Flanders, *fortes-saisons* of the Walloon provinces, and *arge* from Antwerp.

Beer consumption in Belgium has always been high, with per capita consumption of over thirty gallons, ranking it third in the world. Since 1919 the Belgian government has pursued a policy of encouraging beer drinking in order to cut down on the use of stronger alcoholic beverages.

In 1920 there were 3,349 breweries operating in the country. Today the number is under two hundred. The small independents are yielding to the onslaught of giant brewers from within and without, with their more efficient production and distribution. Two hundred is still a large number when one considers the size of the country and the population. Some loss of breweries can be traced to a decrease in beer consumption, down 40 percent since 1925. To spur sales, home delivery is offered by most local brewers.

Standard categories for labeling beer in the Benelux countries have been adopted. "Cat III" is for household beers at 3° (Belgian degrees, which can be roughly equated to percent alcohol by volume). "Cat II" is for 3.0° to 4.0° "export" beer. "Cafe" beers at 4.6° to 4.8° are "Cat I." Stronger beers are "Cat S" (*superieure*). The last category includes the Belgian versions of English-type ales (5° to 7°), abbey beers, and "Scotch" ales, which are 7° to 10°.

Brasserie D'Orval
(Villers-Devant-Orvan)

ORVAL ABBEY'S ALE BIÈRE LUXE—dark orange foamy appearance, soapy-sweet malt aroma, intense resinous aromatic flavor that fills the senses, sharp and sweet. This reminds me of a highly alcoholic spruce beer, which is definitely an acquired taste. Years ago an Englishman named Charlie Grimes used to make this in the little French seaside village of River Bourgeoise in Nova Scotia. It was very popular and reputed to have once put the local parish priest back on his feet when he was near death from the flu. I like it, but as I said, it is very much an acquired taste. This beer is made by the Cistercian monks of the order of St. Bernard and is considered to be one of Belgium's classics. Merchant du Vin began introduction of Orval to the U.S. in 1981. The monks say that the brew is best at age nine months; labels will indicate the bottling date with Roman numerals.

ORVAL TRAPPISTE ALE (Cat I)—pale orange, sharp hop nose, huge intense hop flavor, pungent sweet hop finish, powerful, but good taste, long aftertaste, excellent with sharp cheese. Belgian connoisseurs argue that this brew is best when matured one to three years in the bottle.

Arcense Bierbrouwerijen
(Arcen)

MAGNUS—cloudy brown, light malt aroma, heavy body, winy, alcoholic (about 7 percent), creamy, tasty sipping beer, all-malt flavor, long on the palate and very good.

P.H. Vandenstock, S.A., Brasserie Belle-Vue
(Brussels)

The firm was founded in 1913 by Mr. Philemon Vanden Stock. At first there was no brewery and lambics from diverse origins were obtained and mixed to produce gueuze. In 1927, Vanden Stock took over the Cafe Belle-Vue in Anderlecht which eventually (1949) gave its name to the brewery. In 1943 the brewing company was formed by Mr. Vanden Stock, his son, Constant, and his son-in-law, Octave Collin. At that time the Lambic Brewery in Molenbeek-St. Jean was acquired.

In 1944 Philemon Vanden Stock was arrested and placed in a concentration camp and never seen again. Young Constant found himself head of a firm badly weakened by the war. In the 1950s two lambic breweries were added through acquisition and in 1969 there were three more added, bringing Belle-Vue, by 1973, to a production level ranking it as the fifth largest in Belgium. Since then two more breweries have been added and the exporting of gueuze abroad has been initiated.

GUEUZE BELLE-VUE (Cat I)—pale cloudy brown, sour malty summer sausage aroma, terribly intense sweet flavor (almost nauseating in its intensity). Gueuze is a fruity beer that is a blend of "lambic," a wheat beer (30-35 percent wheat and the remainder barley) made using "wild" yeast of a type only found in the vicinity of Brussels. Gueuze consists of one-third old beer (two or more years of barrel fermentation) and two-thirds young, with the melange further fermented for a year in the bottle. Solids may or may not be filtered out, but unfiltered bottles are in danger of exploding. A good gueuze will have a strength of 5.2 percent or more and the brew is named "Sudden Death" by its followers. Belle-Vue is a mass market gueuze-type beer. Its production has been controlled by law since 1965.

BELLE-VUE CREAM BEER (Gueuze Lambic)—deep gold, good lambic aroma (fruity-wheaty, grainy, and very slightly lactic acid), good fruity citruslike flavor very long on the palate.

BELLE-VUE KRIEK BEER—cherry red, very foamy, cherry-lambic nose with good candy cherry up front, clean but very sweet candy cherry syrup palate, and very long on the palate; a bit like Cherry Heering.

Brewery Riva
(Dentergen)

Brewery established in 1896.

RIVA 2000 LAGER BEER—brilliant gold, well-carbonated, small bubbles, sweet malt aroma with hops and toast in back, very complex flavor, slightly bitter finish, very tasty aftertaste, very satisfying brew.

VONDEL TRIPLE (Cats)—Copper color, huge head, picquant candy-citrus nose, intense sweet tangy palate of long duration.

Brasserie Rodenbach
(Roeselare)

RODENBACH BELGIUM BEER—deep copper-red, sour roasted malt aroma, strong sweet tongue curling flavor, intense. Smells and tastes like Branston pickle. Rodenbach is the famous red beer of West Flanders and is known simply by its maker's name. A top-fermented brew is blended with a beer which has been aged at least eighteen months in oak. Before bottling, one part aged beer is added to three parts young beer. Barley, corn grits, semi-dark Vienna malts and caramel go into the brew and the formation of lactic acid in the brewing process imparts a flavor that is sharp and acid-sour. It is not pasteurized. It is an acquired taste, something that most Americans probably would prefer to do without. The Belgians enjoy it with fish or served as an apéritif with grenadine added.

Brie Dubusson Freres
(Pipaix)

BUSH BEER STRONG ALE (Cat S)—foamy orange brown, foamiest thing I ever poured, strong repugnant aroma, sour to the point of being nauseating, taste of gall or sweet bile (think about that for a moment), indescribably awful. This is the worst concoction I have ever experienced. It is so bad that I can't imagine it suiting even a local Belgian taste. There must be some trick to it or something that has to be mixed in. Unbelievable. Maybe it was spoiled. It is alcohol rated at 10°.

Brewery Van Hougaerde
(Leuven)

Established in 1679.

LEOPOLD PILS THREE STARS—pale gold, good malt-hop aroma with a fruitlike background, fruity up front, sour metallic at finish.

S.A. Bass N.V.
(Michelen)

LAMOT PILSOR BEER (Cat I)—yellow color, more hops than malt in the nose, strong hop flavor with sour background, not well-balanced, bitter overall, sour finish.

Brasserie de Abbaye de Leffe
(Dinant)

ABBEY de LEFFE BIÈRE LUXE (Cat S, 6.5 percent)—deep reddish-orange-brown, pure barley malt aroma, very sweet taste, but very clean and not cloying; persisting, however, is an aromatic ketonelike background to the flavor that evolves to sourness in the aftertaste. The beer is highly reputed.

Brasserie St. Guibert, S.A.
(Mont St. Guibert)

ABBAYE de LEFFE BLONDE ALE—deep gold, highly carbonated, light hop aroma with some off odors in back, good hoppy alelike flavor, long on palate.

141

LEFFE RADIEUSE BELGIAN ALE—deep copper, hop aroma, complex palate, sweet and bitter up front, slightly salty mineral finish, very long aftertaste.

LEFFE BELGIAN DARK ALE—dark copper, good malt and hop aroma, fine malt flavor with hops in back, well balanced, long aftertaste, pleasant to drink.

Brouwerijen Artois Brasseries
(Leuven/Louvain)

In a document of 1366, there is a mention of a tiny beer making plant in a house in Louvain named Den Horen or the Horn. This little brewery was destined to grow into the Artois Breweries.

In 1717 Sebastian Artois bought the Horn and bestowed his name on it. Later, grandson Leonard enlarged the business by adding two other small breweries to it—the Frase Kroon in 1787 and the Prince Charles in 1793. These three became known as the Artois Breweries.

Belgium did not begin to experiment with lagers until quite late in the nineteenth century and Stella Artois Lager first appeared in 1892. The current recipe dates to 1926. In 1979 the Artois group produced 6.5 million barrels in its ten breweries in Europe, most of it Stella and Loburg. Artois also makes a bock, double bock, export artois, special table beer, Gersten-Orge, and Double Gersten-Orge for the home markets. Only Stella Artois Light Lager is exported to the United States, where it is now available only in 12-ounce bottles.

STELLA ARTOIS (Cat I)—gold color, sour malt aroma with good hops, big hop flavor, nice hoppy finish, a complex clean-tasting brew with a sharp hop character.

LOBURG BIÈRE LUXE (Cat I)—yellow gold, well-hopped pungent malty aroma, hops dominate the flavor, but balance is good until the finish, slight bitterness in the aftertaste. Difficult to find in the U.S.

Brasserie des Trappistes
(Chimay)

BIÈRE des TRAPPISTES (Cat. S)—foamy brown appearance, sweet apple bubble gum aroma, strong herbal flavor like homemade root beer, carbonation only apparent in the finish, good aftertaste. My Aunt Beenie used to make a root beer that tasted very much like this and it was great stuff when the bottle didn't explode. Tough to find in the U.S., but possible. All trappist beers are top-fermented with yeast added during bottling for secondary fermentation (red-cap bottle; about 6°).

CHIMAY PÈRES TRAPPISTES—cloudy copper, foamy, faint cherry herbal-malt aroma, pleasant complex flavor with a touch of acid, very complex, has its pleasant aspects but it is still a matter of taste, i.e., if you like it, you'll love it. 7 percent alcohol with secondary fermentation in the bottle.

Brasserie Centrale S.A.
(Marbaix-la-Tour)

SAISON REGAL BIÈRE LUXE (Cat I)—pale orange-brown, foamy appearance, aroma initially sweet, but builds to a sweetness that actually becomes unpleasant with the hops clashing against the other aroma components, the flavor is an intense sweet cough medicine with a tenacious acetonelike character. This has to be some sort of regional Belgian taste. It is too much for me. This is the best known example of a *saison* and is top-fermented in the bottle.

Brewery de Kluis
(Hoegaarden)

HOEGAARDEN TRIPLE GRAND CRU (Cat. S)—cloudy pale orange, lovely apple-fruit aroma, complex grainy flavor that is fruitlike up front, slightly acidic in middle, grainy finish, long fairly dry aftertaste, very good and very interesting.

DIESTER'S BIER (Cat. S, 8 percent)—medium to deep copper-red, creamy head, light touch of fruity malt in nose, sweet lightly toasted malt palate, creamy texture, a bit winelike, long on palate, sweet throughout.

Lindemans Farm Brewery
(Viezenbeck)

The Lindemans family had been home-brewing during the winter months (when farming activities are at a low) for many years when, in 1861, they decided to commercially produce the traditional lambic beer. In 1930, the farming activity ceased completely and the facility was totally devoted to producing Gueuze and Kriek Lambic.

Lindemans uses a blend of 70 percent malted barley and 30 percent wheat which is mashed and placed in an open-topped copper fermenting vessel. No yeast is added and in three to eight days fermentation begins as a result of the natural introduction of airborne "wild" yeasts. Dried hops are soaked in water at length to reduce bitterness and are added to the ferment primarily as a preservative (rather than as a bittering agent as in most other brews). The new lambic is then aged in small oak casks.

Lindemans Gueuze is a blend of old lambic (approximately three years old) and young lambic (aged one summer), lightly filtered and bottled in heavy champagne-style bottles. Like champagne, fermentable extract causes a secondary fermentation in the bottle, which is sealed with a cork and a cap.

Lindemans Kriek (or cherry beer) is the result of adding black cherries to the aging lambic in the oak casks after one and one-half years of aging. This cherry lambic is aged another six months and is then blended with young lambic. It is then filtered and bottled, and when bottle-aged about one year, it is ready for consumption.

Gueuze and Kriek are best served at 60° to 70° F. Do not shake the bottle and when pouring, try to avoid serving the yeast precipitate. Lindemans and its importer, Merchant du Vin, state that the beers have remarkable lasting power and may be kept three to four years. These beers are in some respects, more like an apéritif wine than a beer. Liking them or not liking them is a matter of personal taste, but they should be tried for the experience.

LINDEMANS GUEUZE LAMBIC BEER—slightly cloudy peach color, intense lemony citric acid aroma, taste of Vitamin C, cloves in vinegar, horrible honey wine, stomach acid (all comments by various tasters to give you an idea of the complexity of the palate sensation), complex and intense, long finish and aftertaste—like the flavor.

LINDEMANS KRIEK LAMBIC BEER—beautiful pale pink, nose like faint cherry laid on gueuze, cherry-cinnamon and citrus flavor, the cherry seems to mitigate the intensity of the lambic, light body, fairly dry finish and aftertaste.

FARO LAMBIC BELGIAN ALE—medium pale copper brown, lactic acid aroma, intense sweet lactic flavor, thin body, long and tenacious sweet finish. Faro is a lambic sweetened with candy sugar.

GUEUZE LAMBIC BELGIAN ALE—cloudy orange, fruity lactic aroma, big head, dry tangy acidic flavor, quite dry overall.

Moorgat Breweries
(Breendonk)

DUVEL ALE—8 percent alcohol, pale cloudy orange; sweet tangy candy-fruit nose; creamy, complex candy, smoky, toasted malt flavor that tapers gently to aftertaste; interesting and unusual sipping beer.

St. Bernardus Bry
(Wajou)

ST. SIXTUS ABDY BIER (Cat S)—deep copper, sweet apple aroma, very sweet and very complex palate, finishes better than it starts, lots of character, extremely pleasant aftertaste, rolls off your tongue (as if your tongue doesn't feel wet after you swallow); if you like sweet beer, this is fabulous. St. Sixtus is actually an ale and like champagne, a "dosage" of candy sugar is added at bottling. This causes the ale to ferment additionally in the bottle yielding a final alcohol of 10.7 percent by volume. In its youth the brew is on the sweet side, but it will improve with 5-10 years of aging, during which time it will become drier and more alcoholic. This is a cellaring beer, made from a recipe of the St. Sixtus Trappist Abbey founded in 1850.

Brasserie Union S.A.
(Jumet)

CUVEE de l'HERMITAGE (Cat S)—tawny-orange color, rich malt aroma, sweet and bitter toasted-malt flavor, a strong flavor tending toward bitter in the finish, but not overly bitter in the aftertaste. This is real sipping beer, best Belgian beer ever tasted. Technically, this is a strong ale with a sweet palate, at about 8° alcohol.

Brasserie Wieze
(Van Roy)

WIEZE LAGER BEER (Cat I Belgium, Cat Luxe France)—brilliant gold, medium hop aroma with good malt, clean malt-hop flavor with well water background, slightly metallic finish, good balance, very drinkable.

Brasserie Bios
(Ertvelde)

Founded in 1789 and still owned by the Van Steenberge family in Flanders. Bios was introduced in 1890. It is made from wheat and barley.

BIOS COPPER ALE—medium deep cloudy red-brown, sharp yeasty sweet spicy aroma, sweet and sour lactic acid palate, very long, tenacious. Similar to Rodenbach; an acquired taste.

Westmalle Abbey
(Westmalle)

WESTMALLE "TRIPLE" ABBEY TRAPPISTE BEER (Cat S)—bright gold, fine bitter hop aroma and bright hop flavor, full-bodied, finely balanced with pleasing dry hop and malt finish, 8 percent alcohol. Westmalle is a Cistercian Trappist Abbey which has been producing beer commercially for over 100 years to keep up the monastery and its philanthropic works.

WESTMALLE TRAPPISTE BEER "DUBBEL" (Cat S)—medium deep cloudy orange-brown, delicious complex sweet malt aroma, rich and full, big roasted malt flavor, changes constantly across palate, complex right through to the long long aftertaste; a great beer.

Canada

While Canada never suffered a national prohibition, sectional prohibition began as early as 1878. Ontario had prohibition from 1916 to 1927 with beverage rooms not reopening until 1934. Saskatchewan closed the public bars in 1915 and had prohibition from 1917 to 1923. Quebec prohibited the sale of liquor for a time

Page of Canadian Churchman issue of March 31, 1903 with Labatt's India Pale Ale Advertisement.

but allowed the sale of beer and wine.

Today, laws governing the sale of alcoholic beverages in Canada are a strange lot and beer, wine, and liquor can be purchased in most provinces in stores operated by provincial liquor control boards, whose main purpose is to minimize consumption. Prices are inordinately high and there is an odd collection of blue laws still on the books governing the consumption of alcoholic beverages. Slowly, these laws have been changing, particularly in the more progressive provinces like Ontario, and beer drinking in public is not only legal in most places, but socially acceptable.

Canada produces some excellent beer. Although most of the beer sales today are lager beers, there is still a considerable market for ales, in part because of the long years of association with Britain and the large numbers of Scots, Irish, and English in the population. The beers of Canada usually have a slightly higher alcoholic content than U.S. brews, nominally 5 percent by volume.

Canadian beer has many loyal followers in the United States. The ales of the Molson and Labatt breweries are especially popular in the U.S. since there is really nothing in the repertoire of American brewers quite in their style. A poll taken of some East Coast U.S. retail outlets finds that sales of Canadian beers regularly exceed those of German beers. Part of this may be because of the lower price of the Canadian imports, but it does indicate that many Americans favor the style of Canadian brews.

Although there are about forty-six breweries still operating in Canada, most of the small independents have disappeared into the large conglomerates and only eight separately identifiable brewing companies remain, some of which are in grave financial trouble. These produce 117 labels, of which twelve can be called national brands.

The list of Canadian brewing companies, according to the Brewers Association of Canada, is as follows:

NEWFOUNDLAND
Carling O'Keefe Breweries of Canada, Ltd.,
St. John's Labatt Breweries of Newfoundland, Ltd.,
  St. John's, Stephenville
Molson Newfoundland Brewery, Ltd., St. John's

NOVA SCOTIA
Moosehead Breweries, Ltd., Dartmouth
Oland's Breweries (1971), Ltd., Halifax

NEW BRUNSWICK
Moosehead Breweries, Ltd., St. John
Oland's Breweries (1971), Ltd., St. John

QUEBEC
La Brasserie Labatt, Ltd., Montreal
La Brasserie Molson du Quebec, Ltd., Montreal
Molson Breweries of Canada, Ltd., Montreal
O'Keefe Brewing Company, Ltd., Montreal

ONTARIO
Carling O'Keefe Breweries of Canada, Ltd.,
  Toronto, Waterloo
Doran's Northern Ontario Breweries, Ltd.,
  Timmins, Thunder Bay, Sault Ste. Marie, Sudbury
Amstel Brewery of Canada, Ltd., London
Labatt's Ontario Breweries, a Division of
  Labatt's Ltd., London, Toronto
Molson's Brewery (Ontario), Ltd., Barrie,
  Toronto

MANITOBA
Carling O'Keefe Breweries of Canada, Ltd.,
  Winnipeg

Kiewel-Pelissier Breweries, Ltd.,
St. Boniface (Labatt's)
Labatt's Manitoba Brewery, a Division of
Labatt's, Ltd., Winnipeg
Molson Brewery Manitoba, Ltd., Winnipeg
Uncle Ben's Breweries (Manitoba), Ltd.
Transcona (presently inoperative, company head-
quarters are at Richmond, B.C.)

SASKATCHEWAN
Carling O'Keefe Breweries of Canada, Ltd.,
Regina, Saskatoon
Labatt's Saskatchewan Brewery, a Division of Labatt's,
Ltd., Saskatoon
Molson, Saskatchewan Brewery, Ltd., Prince
Albert, Regina

ALBERTA
Carling O'Keefe Breweries of Canada, Ltd.,
Calgary
Labatt's Alberta Brewery, a Division of
Labatt's, Ltd., Edmonton
Molson Alberta Brewery, Ltd., Edmonton
Molson's Western Breweries (1976), Ltd., Calgary
Sicks' Lethbridge Brewery, Ltd., Lethbridge (Molson)
Pinch Penny Investment, Ltd., Red Deer

BRITISH COLUMBIA
Carling O'Keefe Breweries of Canada, Ltd.,
Vancouver
Columbia Brewing Company, Ltd., Creston,
(Labatt's)
Labatt Breweries of B.C., Ltd., New
Westminster, Victoria
Molson Brewery B.C., Ltd., Vancouver
Old Fort Brewing Co., Ltd., Prince George

In liberal-minded British Columbia, a host of new breweries are in process of formation. The first of these include the Bay Brewery and Troller Pub of West Vancouver, Mountain Ales Corp. of Surrey, and Granville Island Brewing Co. of Vancouver.

Amstel Brewery of Canada, Ltd.
(E. Hamilton, Ontario)

This brewery began operation in June 1973 as the Henninger Brewery (Ontario), Ltd., with its plant being the refurbished Peller's Brewery in Hamilton, Ontario. Henninger was formed by E. M. "Ted" Dunal, who had previously been consultant to a holder of a brewery franchise from Henninger Brau of Frankfurt, West Germany.

Henninger, with a production capacity of 150,000 barrels, was Canada's smallest brewer, with sales accounting for only about one percent of its marketing area. Dunal believed that the

Canadian beer drinker was becoming increasingly sophisticated and that these more cosmopolitan consumers would be willing to pay a few cents more for German-style beer with more body and hop character.

The product line consisted of German-type beers (Henninger Export Bier and Henninger Meister Pils). Under a separate franchise with Brauerei A. Hürlimann, A.G., Zurich, Switzerland, the firm produced nonalcoholic (less than one-half of one percent) Birell, an internationally-known delicatessen beer. It also handled a Henninger import, a five-liter-draught can sold only in Quebec. The Henninger beers are all malt beers, using only German hops, are doubly fermented and naturally carbonated. A 70-calorie Brew Light was introduced in 1978 and Henninger offered a beer ball much like that introduced in the U.S. by F. X. Matt Brewing Co.

Amstel, a Heineken affiliate from Holland, bought out Henninger in August 1981 for $4.3 million and in November 1981 its new Hamilton Mountain Beer appeared in local Hamilton markets. As yet, the brew is not available outside of Hamilton. Amstel continues to produce the Henninger brands and also Amstel Beer and Amstel Light, previously produced only in Holland for the Canadian market. Market analysts expect that Heineken will use the new Amstel facility for additional ventures in the North American beer market.

HENNINGER EXPORT BEER--bright gold, beautiful hoppy aroma, small bubble carbonation, pleasant bright bitter hop flavor, good balanced hop-malt finish and aftertaste, a really good brew and very Germanic in style, as advertised.

HENNINGER MEISTER PILS PREMIUM PILSENER— pale gold color, malty aroma (a little stinky at first, but it quickly cleared), small bubble carbonation, well-balanced hop and malt flavor, palate is hoppy, but not as complex as might be expected for the style, sour finish and aftertaste. Another decent brew.

BREW LIGHT LIGHT BEER—2.5 percent alcohol by volume, 75 calories, pale yellow-gold, good hoppy aroma, lightly carbonated, very little flavor, brief finish, no aftertaste.

AMSTEL BEER—medium pale gold, light hop and malt nose, light hop and malt flavor, good body, finishes slightly hoppy, brief aftertaste. Fairly ordinary beer.

GRIZZLY BEER CANADIAN LAGER (Hamilton Breweries)—bright gold, lovely hop nose, good zesty hop flavor; has character without being sharp; a touch of

145

sweetness obtains throughout and all stays in harmony; good lager.

Bay Brewery and Troller Pub
(West Vancouver, B.C.)

Established in 1981, this brewery produces an English bitter-styled Bay Ale and Christmas Ale for the Troller Pub.

Carling O'Keefe, Ltd.

The business of the Carling end of this Canadian brewing giant began in 1840 when Thomas Carling opened a brewery in London, Ontario. He was succeeded by his sons, Sir John and William, who continued the business in their names until 1876, when the firm was named Carling & Company. In 1879 a fire destroyed most of the plant, including buildings only recently erected. The plant was rebuilt and in 1883 a stock company, Carling Brewing and Malting Company, Ltd., was formed. The head of the company at that time was Sir John Carling, who represented London, Ontario, in the Canadian Parliament and was one of the best known public figures in the Dominion.

At the same time that Thomas Carling was beginning that side of the house, Charles Hanneth formed Hanneth & Hard, a brewing firm in Toronto. In 1862 Eugene O'Keefe took over this business in partnership with George M. Hawke. O'Keefe was one of the first in Canada to recognize the potential for the new lager beer and in 1879 erected a plant devoted entirely to its manufacture. Sales of the new beer immediately justified the soundness of the idea and by 1892 O'Keefe's ale plant had been torn down to double the capacity for producing lager. In 1891 a stock company was formed, known as the O'Keefe Brewery Company of Toronto, Ltd.

Today Carling O'Keefe is one of the three giants of the Canadian brewing industry, with nine plants and coast-to-coast coverage (like the motto of Canada, *Ad Mare Usque ad Mare*, "from sea to sea"). Some thirty brands are produced, mostly in the province in which they are marketed. Until recently (April, 1979), Carling O'Keefe had an American subsidiary, the Carling National Brewing Co. In 1983, Carling O'Keefe entered into an agreement with the Miller Brewing Co. to produce Miller High Life for the domestic Canadian market. In return, Miller will test-market Calgary beer in the U.S. Included in the list of Canadian products is Carlsberg Lager Beer, brewed by Carling O'Keefe under the supervision of Carlsberg of Copenhagen. It also owns the Quebec Nordiques of the National Hockey League and the Canadian Football League's Toronto Argonauts.

The Carling O'Keefe brands by province and plant are (including alcohol percentage by volume if other than 5 percent):

BRITISH COLUMBIA, VANCOUVER
Black Label Beer★
Carlsberg Beer★
Carlsberg Light Beer★
Colt .45 Beer
Extra Old Stock Malt Liquor (5.6%)
4X Cream Stout (4.8%)
Heidelberg Beer★
Kronenbrau 1308 Beer
Old Vienna Beer
Pilsener Beer★
Toby Beer
Old Country Malt Liquor (6%)
★Also distributed in the Yukon Territory

ALBERTA, CALGARY
Alta 3.9 Beer (3.9%)
Black Label Beer★
Calgary Export Lager Beer★
Carlsberg Beer★
Carlsberg Light Beer★
Extra Old Stock Malt Liquor (5.6%)
Heidelberg Beer★
Old Vienna Beer★
★Also distributed in the Northwest Territory

SASKATCHEWAN, REGINA
Calgary Export Lager Beer
Carlsberg Beer
Carlsberg Light Beer
Heidelberg Beer
Black Label Beer

SASKATCHEWAN, SASKATOON
Black Label Beer
Calgary Export Lager Beer
Cascade Beer
O'Keefe Ale
Old Vienna Beer
Pilsener Beer
Red Cap Ale

MANITOBA, WINNIPEG
Black Label Beer
Calgary Export Lager Beer
Carlsberg Beer
Carlsberg Light Beer
Cascade Pilsener Beer (3.9%)
Extra Old Stock Malt Liquor (5.6%)
Heidelberg Beer
Old Vienna Beer

Pilsener Beer
Standard Lager Beer

ONTARIO, TORONTO
Black Horse Ale★
Black Label Beer#
Blended Ale#
Brading Ale#
Buckeye Beer
Calgary Export Ale
Carlsberg Beer★
Carlsberg Light Beer★
Carlsberg Gold Malt Liquor
Canadian Red Cap Cream Ale★★
Dow Ale#
Dow Porter (4.9%)
Golden Light★★
Heidelberg Ale (termed beer on label)#
Trilite Beer (60 Cal., 2.5%, introduced as Highlite)
Holiday Beer#
Kingsbeer Beer#
Magnum Ale
O'Keefe Ale★#
Red Cap Ale#
Calgary Export Lager Beer★★
Cinci Beer#★★
★Also exported to the U.S.
#Also produced at Waterloo, Ont.
★★Produced at Toronto only for export to the U.S.

QUEBEC, MONTREAL
Black Label Beer★
Champlain Porter (4.8%)
Dow Ale
Heidelberg Ale (termed beer on label)★
Kronenbrau 1308 Beer
O'Keefe Ale★
Red Cap Ale
Old Vienna Beer★★
★Also distributed in the Maritimes
★★Only distributed in the Maritimes

NEWFOUNDLAND, ST. JOHN'S
Black Horse Beer
Dominion Ale
Extra Old Stock Malt Liquor (5.6%)
Haig Light Beer (2.2%)
Black Label Beer

BENNETT'S DOMINION ALE—bright gold, big creamy head, hop aroma and flavor, touch of sour malt in finish, long long aftertaste, very much a regional taste and definitely in the style preferred by English people, who make up the vast majority of Newfoundland's population. Made by Carling O'Keefe for the Bennett Brewing Co., Ltd. The first brewery in Newfoundland was founded in St. John's by C. F. Bennett about 1850.

CARLING BLACK LABEL BEER—medium to pale gold, slightly sharp hop and malt aroma, high carbonation which, together with the hops, gives a bit too much bite, good dry flavor that would be fine except for the excess carbonation, pleasant dry aftertaste. Toronto bottling for the Canadian market.

O'KEEFE CANADIAN BEER GOLDEN LIGHT—medium yellow, slightly cloudy, sour malt aroma with some hops, complex flavor, sour up front, hoppy in middle and finish. For U.S. market.

MAGNUM ALE—deep gold, hoppy ale aroma with sour malt background, not well-balanced, sours and bitters clash in the finish. Originally called Magnum 5.5 (5.5 percent alcohol), the name had to be changed to satisfy a violation of Ontario law.

RALLYE ALE—Malty aroma and taste, pleasant, but lacking in character, light malt finish, little aftertaste.

BLACK HORSE BEER PREMIUM STOCK—yellow gold color, hop aroma, bitter hop flavor, fairly full-bodied, good aftertaste but on the bitter side. Made for Bennett Brewing Co., Ltd.

O'KEEFE'S OLD VIENNA LAGER BEER—cloudy with particulate matter in solution, taste was pleasant enough, but not very interesting. This is the export version made in Toronto.

BLENDED OLD STOCK ALE—gold, good well-hopped ale nose, too highly carbonated, good hop-malt flavor marred by the excess CO_2; except for the carbonation, the brew is well-balanced, smooth and tasty with a good dry finish and aftertaste. Give it a shake, then enjoy.

BRADING ALE—gold color with particulate matter in solution, faint hop aroma, creamy up front, soft and smooth, finish is overly bitter, dry aftertaste.

KRONENBRAU 1308 GOLDEN MELLOW BEER (brewed for the Drei Kronen Brauerei by Carling-O'Keefe, Vancouver)—5 percent, yellow-gold, sour hop aroma, mostly carbonation on the palate at first, then a sharp-sour hop taste.

BLACK HORSE ALE—gold, nice well-hopped nose with perfumy soap powder and talcum background, very pleasant sweet ale flavor, good hop balance, creamy texture, soft finish, no harshness, balanced all the way through. Made in Toronto for domestic Canadian market.

CARLING PILSENER BEER (brewed in Vancouver)—medium pale gold, light sour hop aroma, high carbonation gives it a generally gassy effect and interferes with the flavor, slightly sour malt aftertaste.

O'KEEFE ALE—gold color, slightly clouded, clean malty nose, malty flavor that trails off toward the finish. Made by La Brasserie O'Keefe, Montreal. This is the Canadian domestic version for the Maritimes.

O'KEEFE ALE—gold color, lovely well-hopped nose, good malt-hop balance, not alelike at all, high carbonation which mars the finish and aftertaste. Toronto version for the Ontario market.

O'KEEFE ALE—gold color, clean, complex, faint malty-hop aroma, light slightly sweet malty ale taste, highly carbonated, good finish, although the flavor is mostly up front, lingering pleasant aftertaste. Version exported to the U.S.-made in Toronto.

ALTA 3.9 BEER—gold color, pleasant malty-yeasty aroma, creamy small bubble carbonation, CO_2 dominates flavor,

light body, brief finish. The 3.9 means 3.9 percent, a labeling practice forbidden in some provinces. This beer is made with wheat and barley malt.

O'KEEFE'S EXTRA OLD STOCK MALT LIQUOR— brilliant deep gold, beautiful clean sweet malt aroma, good sweet hop flavor, excellent balance, long on the palate, pleasant malty finish and aftertaste.

*BUCKEYE ONTARIO SPECIAL ALE—*medium deep yellow-gold color, vegetal hop-malt aroma, watery body, dull flavor that flattens out to nothing at the end, long dull aftertaste. Beautiful logo of a buck's head and trillium, the Ontario provincial flower.

*CHAMPLAIN PORTER—*deep red brown, faint slightly smoky and roasted malt aroma, touch of sweetness, mellow and smooth, slightly too sweet flavor, lacks balance. Aroma excellent, tastes as if it has been enhanced with sugar.

*CALGARY EXPORT LAGER BEER (brewed for Calgary Brewing Co. by Carling O'Keefe, Calgary)—*pale yellow, sour malt-apple tart aroma, quite gassy with high CO_2 which dominates the flavor. This is the brew for the domestic market.

*CALGARY EXPORT LAGER BEER—*spring-water aroma, dully soapy taste. "Brewed from the heart of Alberta's world-famous Conquest barley, malt, and other grains. Have a good old barley sandwich." This can was made in Toronto for export to the U.S.

*CALGARY EXPORT ALE—*bright gold, creamy head, virtually no aroma, dry grainy taste with a faint herbal sweetness, unpleasant flavors in the finish, "off" aftertaste. Toronto bottling for Canadian market.

*COLT .45 BEER—*medium bright gold, light malty aroma with faint hops, creamy texture, inoffensive light malty flavor, little finish and aftertaste, just some slight grainy sourness. Made in British Columbia for the Canadian market. Same logo as Colt .45 Malt Liquor in the U.S.

*TRILIGHT LITE BEER—*originally Highlite, then Trilite, now Trilight, 2.5 percent alcohol, bright gold, malty beery aroma that is quite pleasant, thin body, highly carbonated, flavor is mostly sour malt, but there is some hop bitterness, sour malt finish and aftertaste.

*CALGARY STAMPEDE BRAND BEER—*gold color with a hint of brown, slightly skunky aroma at first but that fades, creamy, foamy, hoppy flavor but dull overall. Made for American market; imported by Miller; introduced in 1984.

*KINGSBEER LAGER BEER—*gold, fairly rich malty-hop aroma, sort of a classic ale character, too much carbonation on the palate, a little grainy malt and hop flavor, nothing offensive, masked by CO_2, clean finish and aftertaste.

*DOW CREAM PORTER—*4.9 percent alcohol, deep red brown, creamy, very faint malty aroma, slightly sweet pleasant taste, finely balanced, smooth, good carbonation level, dry light finish and aftertaste. Very drinkable and very tasty.

149

CINCI LAGER BEER—domestic Canadian version introduced in 1882; brewed in Toronto, gold, well-hopped malty appetizing aroma, dry balanced malt-hop flavor, dry finish, high CO_2, dry slightly malty aftertaste.

CINCI LAGER BEER—export version for the U.S., slightly off, hoppy nose, bitter hop flavor, bitterness continues through the finish into the aftertaste, not a Canadian-style beer at all.

STANDARD LAGER BEER—amber gold color, mild malty nose, good hops up front on the palate, mild hops turning to sour malt in the middle, sour malty finish. Decent brew, well worth consideration for regular use. Label says it was brewed especially for Manitoba according to an original process dating back to 1877.

TOBY ALE—no aroma, sweet ale flavor, unpleasant unbalanced finish. This is the export version made in Toronto brewed under license from Bass Charrington, Ltd., of England.

CHARRINGTON TOBY ALE—tawny orange-gold, slightly sweet hoppy-malt aroma, excellent flavor up front with a fine balance of hop and malt, flattens out in the middle, finishes slightly sour and bitter, poor unbalanced aftertaste. Toronto bottling for the domestic Canadian market.

HEIDELBERG FINE QUALITY BEER—faint touch of hydrogen sulfide in the nose, sour unappetizing taste. This was obviously a bad sample obtained freshly from a Nova Scotia Liquor Commission store which provides no temperature control. Made by La Brasserie O'Keefe, Montreal, for the Maritimes.

HEIDELBERG FINE QUALITY BEER—medium gold, faint hoppy nose, weak body, light malt flavor, touch of wood pulp indicating oxidation, very dull, faint finish, no aftertaste. Made in Toronto for Ontario.

DOW BLACK HORSE ALE—spring water aroma, spring water flavor, unpleasant metal background to the taste, as if it came from the spring in a very rusty pipe, very unusual finish, like dried apricots. Not greatly different in early impressions from the Calgary Export Lager Beer above. The Dow label goes way back in the history of Montreal brewing, to the firm of William Dow & Co. starting in 1809. This sample was made in Montreal for the local domestic market.

CANADIAN RED CAP CREAM ALE—clear deep yellow, light hoppy aroma with fruity background, highly carbonated, strong classic sweet ale flavor, CO_2 sharp on palate, dry in middle and finish, metallic CO_2 finish. Decent brew, recognizable as Canadian. For U.S. market.

CARLSBERG BEER—bright pale gold, sweet malty aroma, good flavor of finely balanced hops and malt, too highly carbonated, touch of sour malt in the finish and aftertaste.

CARSLBERG LIGHT BEER—4 percent alcohol by volume (compared to Carlsberg 5 percent)—tawny gold, very faint sweet malt aroma, high carbonation that completely overwhelms the flavor—like drinking high-powered seltzer—faint saltiness is all that comes through the CO_2 in the finish and aftertaste.

CARLSBERG GOLD MALT LIQUOR—6.5 percent alcohol by volume, bright gold, clean malty aroma with good hop character behind, a really lovely nose, a beautifully complex malt and hop flavor, excellent balance, a sweetness in the finish, long and pleasant malty aftertaste, marvelous brew. Note: Carlsberg brews are krausened and secondary fermentation runs 42 days.

CARLSBERG BOCK BEER—bright copper, light malt aroma, pleasant slightly sweet malt flavor, good finish and aftertaste, very drinkable.

Granville Island Brewing Co.
(Victoria, B.C.)

Established in 1984, this brewery produces a Bavarian-type unpasteurized lager for local pubs.

The Old Fort Brewing Co., Ltd.
(Prince George, B.C.)
(formerly Canadian Gold Breweries, Ltd.)

Operating from the old Prince George brewery (formerly Uncle Ben's), this relative newcomer to the Canadian brewing scene exports some of its brews to the U.S. Most of its products, however, are for the rough and tumble Prince George miners and lumberjacks.

PACIFIC GOLD BEER (Prince George Breweries, Ltd.)—medium deep tawny gold, pleasant fresh malty aroma with good balance of hops, hoppy brew with good balance, clean sweetness up front, small bubble carbonation, good-tasting hop finish and aftertaste.

BEER (Produced for Blacksmith Beverages Ltd., Richmond B.C.)—slightly cloudy yellow, faint hop aroma, good hop flavor, a bit thin and short on the palate, but pleasant.

YUKON GOLD PREMIUM PILSNER (Prince George Breweries, Ltd.)—tawny gold, beery fragrant malty hop aroma, small bubble carbonation, full-bodied, complex malt-hop flavor, good character like a malt liquor without the higher alcohol content. Export version for U.S.

YUKON GOLD CANADIAN LAGER BEER—pale yellow, slightly skunky at first, then sweet malt aroma; carbonation visible but flat on the tongue; flat dull brief flavor. This is probably a relabeling of the above brew.

CANADIAN GOLD PREMIUM CANADIAN PILS-NER—tawny yellow-gold, some particulate matter, sharp aroma and taste, probably an old spoiled sample.

ROYAL CANADIAN PREMIUM BEER (Prince George Breweries, Ltd.)—tawny gold with particles in solution, big malt and hop aroma, good hoppy flavor, but with little depth, medium body, some sweetness in and duration to aftertaste.

YUKON GOLD PREMIUM PILSNER BEER—faintly cloudy yellow, delicious appetizing sweet hoppy aroma, sweet malt and hop flavor, highly carbonated, very drinkable, not very beerlike, but very, very tasty. A domestic bottling using the corporate name of The Old Fort Brewing Co., Ltd., Prince George, British Columbia.

PACIFIC GOLD LAGER BEER (The Old Fort Brewing Co.)—bright gold, beautiful hoppy nose, faint trace of oxidation, overcarbonation masks the best of the flavor, creamy head, a little sourness in the finish, but the aftertaste is long and pleasant. This is the domestic version of Pacific Gold.

IRON HORSE MALT LIQUOR (Export)—bright gold, slight vegetal-malt nose, creamy, slightly sweet palate, medium body, pleasant light malt character, overall quite pleasant.

IRON HORSE MALT LIQUOR—bright gold, good malt and hop aroma, slightly sweet well-balanced palate, pleasant-tasting brew.

BULLDOG CANADIAN LAGER BEER—slightly tawny gold, pleasant hop aroma, good hop flavor, light body, good finish, no aftertaste.

OLD FORT LAGER BEER—pale gold, big head, malt and hop aroma with some sweetness and spice, spicy slightly acidic palate, may have been old, but was good.

COY INTERNATIONAL CANADIAN LAGER BEER (Cask 64)—pale gold, slightly skunky at first, then good malt and hops, more hops than malt; sweetness in back, medium body, grainy finish, dull aftertaste.

Id Foods Corp.
(Laval, P.Q.)

EUROPA 60 MALT BREW—bready aroma, long sweet lychee nut flavor. Would it go with Chinese food?

Labatt Brewing Co., Ltd.

The original Simcoe Street brewery of Labatt's was built in London, Canada West (now Ontario), by George Balkwill in 1828. It was burned and rebuilt and sold in 1847 to John K. Labatt and Samuel Eccles, an experienced brewer. Eccles retired in 1853 and Labatt operated the brewery as sole owner until 1866 when he died. He was succeeded by his son, also named John. Once more, the brewery burned down and was rebuilt (in 1874). Another fresh start was needed in 1899 when, you guessed it, the brewery again burned to the ground.

With the fire problem apparently under control, Labatt's Brewery was incorporated in 1911 and the name changed to John Labatt, Ltd. That year Labatt first began to brew lager beer.

Labatt's began "exporting" beer as early as 1853 with shipments to Hamilton, Toronto, and Montreal. In 1878 Labatt's set up a distribution agency in Montreal. For the next fifty years, gold medals were accumulated by the dozens at international competitions.

Prohibition came to Ontario in 1916 and lasted for eleven years. During that stretch of time, all but fifteen of the province's sixty-four breweries were wiped out. Only Labatt's opened

151

Harpo Marx Advertising Campaign 1958.

with the same management.

Labatt's went public in 1945 and, soon after, began one of the most remarkable growth sequences in Canadian industry. First Labatt's bought the Copland Brewing Co. of Toronto, a firm dating to 1830. In 1953, it bought Shea's Winnipeg Brewery, Ltd., and a controlling interest in Kiewel's and Pelissier's breweries. The corporate structure was decentralized in 1956 with the head office maintained in London and operating divisions in Quebec, Ontario, and Manitoba; the new Montreal brewery opened in June of that year. The Labatt labels were introduced in Manitoba marking the beginning of a national label in Canada. In 1958 Labatt's acquired Lucky Lager Breweries, Ltd., in British Columbia and an interest in the Lucky Lager Brewing Co. in the U.S. At that time Labatt's also formed a research alliance with Ind Coope, Ltd., of England and Lucky Lager.

Saskatchewan joined the fold in 1960 with the acquisition of the Saskatoon Brewing Co. (founded in 1906) and Labatt labels were immediately marketed in that province. In 1961 Labatt's diversified, established a special products division, and soon was deeply involved in international pharmaceuticals and chemicals.

Newfoundland was reached in 1962 with the purchase of Bavarian Brewing, Ltd., in St. John's. In 1964 an offer was made by the Joseph Schlitz Brewing Co. of Milwaukee to purchase 39 percent of Labatt stock. The offer was accepted by the Labatt family, but the U.S. Justice Dept. ordered Schlitz to divest itself of the Labatt

holdings and Schlitz sold the stock to three Canadian investment organizations in 1967. Meanwhile, the company had again reorganized with John Labatt, Ltd., surrendering its brewing license to a new wholly owned subsidiary, Labatt Breweries of Canada, Ltd., and construction began on a new brew house for the London plant, the largest in the world.

Skol International, Ltd. was formed in 1964 by Labatt's, Allied Breweries of Great Britain, Pripps of Sweden, and Unibra of Belgium to brew and market Skol beer throughout the world. Later that year a brewery was opened in Edmonton; General Brewing Co. of San Francisco began to brew Labatt brands and Labatt's entered the Canadian food industry through Maple Leaf Mills, Ltd.

Wines were added in 1965 when control of Parkdale Wines, Ltd., of Toronto was gained. Grimsby Wines, Ltd., of Ontario, Normandie Wines, Ltd., of New Brunswick, and the well-known Chateau-Gai Wines, Ltd., were added subsequently. Another major development in 1965 was formation of Guinness Canada, Ltd., with Labatt licensed to produce Guinness Stout in Canada.

In 1968 Labatt's began construction of a new brewery in Toronto, acquired the Ogilvie Flour Mills Co. and obtained a controlling interest in the Oakland Seals of the National Hockey League (which it later sold when a transfer of the franchise to Vancouver could not be arranged). Expansion into nonbrewing activities continued

Labatt products of the 1950s. Bottles of this shape are no longer in use in the Canadian domestic market.

This composite of early Labatt photos was long displayed in the company's head office in London, Ontario.

at an increasing rate throughout the 1968 to 1977 period as Labatt's grew into a giant well-diversified corporation. It makes interesting reading, but I'll leave that to someone who wants to write the history of Labatt's. Labatt's even obtained a forty-five percent interest in the Toronto Blue Jays of the American (baseball) League.

Nova Scotia and New Brunswick joined Labatt's in 1971 when the Halifax and St. John Breweries of Oland and Son, Ltd., were obtained. These facilities were renamed Oland's Breweries, Ltd., and became the Maritimes Region of Labatt Breweries of Canada, Ltd. The Oland family remained as directors of the new company. Later, the Alexander Keith Nova Scotia Brewery was acquired and closed, the manufacture of the Keith label being resumed at Oland's.

The Stephenville, Newfoundland, brewery of the Bison Brewing Co. was acquired and reopened in 1974, giving Labatt's the western Newfoundland market, and the Columbia Brewing Co. of Creston, British Columbia, was obtained in 1976.

As you can see, Labatt's Breweries is now a giant chain of fourteen regional breweries in nine provinces stretching from coast to coast with annual production over 7 million hecto-litres. Three of the Labatt national labels (50 Ale, Blue, and Special Lite, a low-calorie beer) are available in the U.S. in bottles and, in selected areas, on draft. Labatt accounts for about 5 percent of the U.S. import market. Labatt's 50 Ale is now the largest selling ale in Canada and Labatt's Blue is the third largest selling beer. Labatt also produces India Pale Ale, Cervoise, John Labatt's Extra Stock Ale, Cool Spring, Gold

Labatt Streamliner—in use until 1950.

Keg, Crystal Lager, Velvet Cream Porter, and Velvet Cream Stout. In Newfoundland it produces Blue Star, Jockey Club, and Black Label. In Nova Scotia the brands made are Keith's IPA and the Oland line. In Manitoba the brands produced are Manitoba 200 Malt Liquor, Manitoba's Select, White Seal, Club, and Country Club Stout. The labels produced by Labatt's in British Columbia are Kokanee, Kootenay Ale, Columbia, Silver Spring, and, names familiar in the States, Rainier and Lucky Lager Beer. In late 1978 John Labatt's Extra Stock was introduced as a "Commemorative Brew" to celebrate the 150th anniversary of the company. With an alcohol content of 6.5 percent, it is labeled a malt liquor. In the spring of 1980, Labatt offered another 6.5 percent brew, Labatt's Super Bock Malt Liquor. Super Bock is offered only in the early part of each year on a limited basis, primarily in Ontario. In 1981, under license from Anheuser-Busch, Inc. of the United States, Labatts began producing Budweiser in a 5 percent alcohol version in Quebec and Ontario after a short introductory period as an import.

A Listing of Labatt Brands by plant is as follows:
New Westminster, B.C.
  Blue, 50, Lucky Lager, Guinness
Victoria, B.C.
  Blue, Silver Spring, Cool Spring
Columbia Brewing Co., Creston, B.C.
  Blue, Kokanee, Columbia, Kootenay, Special Lite
Edmonton, Alta.
  Blue, Cool Spring, Velvet Cream, Club, Special Lite
Saskatoon, Sask.
  Blue, Cool Spring, Velvet Cream, Club, 50, Special Lite
Winnipeg, Man.
  Blue, Cool Spring, Velvet Cream, Club, 50, Special Lite, Select, 200, Country Club, Crystal, White Seal

Weston, Ont.
  Blue, 50
London, Ont.
  Blue, 50, Crystal, Skol, Gold Keg, Guinness
Waterloo, Ont.
  Blue, 50, Special Lite, Extra Stock, IPA, Velvet Cream, Grand Prix
Quebec City, Que.
  Porter, Cervoise, Blue, 50
St. John, N.B.
  Keith's IPA, Old Scotia, Schooner, Extra Stout, Oland's Ale, Blue, 50, Special Lite
Halifax, N.S.
  Keith's IPA, Old Scotia, Schooner, Extra Stout, Oland's Ale, Blue, 50
Stephenville, Newf.
  Blue Star, Jockey Club, Blue, 50
St. John's, Newf.
  Blue Star, Jockey Club, Black Label, Special Lite, Blue, 50

LABATT'S 50 ALE—pale color, pleasant malty aroma and flavor with good hop balance, good brew. The 50 was introduced in 1950 to commemorate fifty years of service by John (the Third) and Hugh Labatt, grandsons of the founder.

LABATT'S PILSENER BLUE—pale gold color, slightly tawny, faint sour malt aroma, light bitter-sour taste, lightly carbonated. This brand was introduced in 1951.

LABATT'S PILSENER DRAFT—medium gold color, clear and bright, light-flavored good malt taste with the right touch of hops for a well-balanced brew, clean and refreshing, little aftertaste.

Labatt's Anniversary Bridge — Korea 1952 complete with bullet holes.

Labatt domestic bottles. Note the squat shape common to all Canadian domestic bottlings.

GOLD KEG BEER—deep tawny gold, big hop and malt aroma, highly carbonated, good hoppy flavor, very tasty, pleasant sour hop finish, long aftertaste, a very good brew.

COOL SPRING LIGHT BEER—3.9 percent alcohol by volume, brilliant bright gold, almost no aroma at all, low CO_2, light body, faint sweet malt flavor which slowly fades across the palate, pleasant, but dull, faint and short aftertaste.

LABATT'S CRYSTAL LAGER BEER—5 percent, bright pale gold, pleasant malty aroma, highly carbonated, but the good malt gets through, light body, effect of the CO_2 is to make the brew creamy rather than to give it a harsh bite, smooth, balanced, long pleasant aftertaste.

CERVOISE ALE—pale gold, good malt aroma, good-tasting malty flavor in the front of the palate, short on the palate, quickly fades out to a dull finish and aftertaste.

LABATT'S IPA (INDIA PALE ALE)—bright tawny gold, lots of foam; at first the aroma was quite stinky, but this cleared after a few minutes, leaving a very good balanced malt and hop nose, good ale flavor, sweet hop taste with plenty of character, sweet middle, weakens toward the finish, faintly sweet aftertaste with a bitter backtaste.

LABATT'S ROYAL BLUE (100 Years of Service, The Royal Canadian Regiment)—gold, soapy hop aroma, very dry; crisp, refreshing, and clean; dries out at the end.

GRAND PRIX ALE—medium deep yellow gold, high CO_2, complex malty aroma, watery light body, slightly malty flavor, nothing offensive, but also not much to it. Introduced in 1980 in Ontario.

BUDWEISER—pale gold, very light malt and hop aroma, small bubble carbonation, good hop and malt flavor—the same as American Bud, dry good tasting finish. A faithful reproduction. 5 percent alcohol.

LABATT'S VELVET CREAM PORTER—deep ruby-brown, faint sweet malty aroma, flavor is shallow, pleasant sort of sweetness, but thin and lacks character, faint finish on the neutral side, aftertaste sort of dry.

JOHN LABATT'S EXTRA STOCK MALT LIQUOR COMMEMORATIVE BREW—6.5 percent, fairly deep bright gold, very complex malt and hop aroma, big body, complex hop and malt flavor, lots of good flavors, good tasting all the way through to the lingering complex aftertaste, very satisfying.

LABATT'S SPECIAL LITE LIGHT BEER—4 percent alcohol by volume, 96 calories, brilliant pale gold, mild hop aroma, slight hop flavor, short finish, little aftertaste.

LABATT'S SUPER BOCK MALT LIQUOR—6.5 percent, bright copper color, malty aroma, high CO_2, malt up front on the palate, hops come on strong to dominate the finish, not well-balanced, rapidly fading hop aftertaste.

KOOTENAY PALE ALE—medium to deep gold, lovely zesty hop nose, clean and bright at start, flattens out a bit to a somewhat dull finish (but still clean and fresh), slightly sour aftertaste, a pleasant and very drinkable beer overall. A Columbia Brewing Co. brew.

KOKANEE PILSENER BEER—medium gold, slightly cloudy, light hoppy aroma, pleasant and smooth, but lacks zest, finishes better than it starts. Another beer attributed to Columbia Brewing Co.

An early example of Labatt print advertising

JOCKEY CLUB BEER—good deep gold, pleasant malt-hop nose, very tasty, long aftertaste. Label says 5 percent, original Bavarian style, uncomplicated brew. Made in and for Newfoundland.

BLUE-STAR—tawny gold color, starts out sweet, quickly turns bitter with bitterness increasing toward the finish. Brewed in and for Newfoundland, this beer is very popular with the English of eastern Newfoundland and there is some resemblance to the "bitter" of England. A very dry brew with a neutral finish.

GUINNESS EXTRA STOUT—brewed in Montreal, opaque, copper brown, rubbery background to a roasted malt aroma, heavy body, coffee-malt flavor, complex, but with a chemical backtaste. Overall considered a good stout, but not up to the quality of the Dublin brew.

LABATT'S BEER—export version for U.S. market, gold color, highly carbonated, creamy, good well-balanced smooth hop palate, a little too much carbonation, but good.

LABATT'S CANADIAN ALE—export version for U.S. market, deep gold, medium hop aroma, good Canadian-style sweet ale flavor, light body, flavor is more up front than in finish, clean and tasty. Renamed *LABATT'S 50 CANA-DIAN ALE* in late 1982.

JOHN LABATT CLASSIC BEER—medium deep bright gold, sweet hop aroma, acidic palate with a bitter aftertaste.

I have been told this is an all-malt brew, but there is a distinct hop aroma.

COLUMBIA EXPORT MALT LIQUOR—5.65 percent, bright gold, big head, good grainy hop aroma, complex flavor, some sweet malt up front, sour hop finish, doubtful balance, good overall. Made in Vancouver.

157

Oland's Breweries, Ltd. Oland's produces many of the Maritime (Atlantic) Provinces' favorite beers. All were found to be worthy efforts. Oland's was founded in 1867 by Susannah Culverwell Oland, great-grandmother of the present Oland family members serving on the board of directors. Oland's Breweries, Ltd., became part of Labatt's in 1971.

OLAND EXPORT ALE—pale color, pleasant malty aroma, good clean taste, medium to light body, good balance, a little zest, no offensive features, no apparent faults, good clean aftertaste.

OLAND'S OLD SCOTIA ALE—yellow gold with tawny-brown hues, pleasant malty aroma, medium body, good flavor, but little character, inoffensive, very brief finish. Another pleasant brew.

OLAND'S OLD SCOTIA ALE—new package and new 5.5 percent recipe to celebrate the 1979 Gathering of the Clans in Nova Scotia, medium gold, well-hopped aroma backed with good malt, frothy but CO_2 not obtrusive on the palate, good body, noticeable alcohol, sweet up front, hops strong in the middle, long malt and hop finish, clean refreshing aftertaste, well-balanced ale flavor and smooth, a really good brew.

OLAND LITE BEER—4 percent alcohol, 28 calories per 100 grams (less than 99 for 12 ounces), bright gold, lovely hoppy aroma, touch of pleasant soapiness, good complex lightly hopped flavor, sourness in aftertaste.

OLAND'S SCHOONER BEER—pale color, very clean, slightly malty and lightly hopped nose, light and pleasant with a slight sour hop character and, sometimes, too much carbonation, mostly hops at the finish. A big seller in eastern Canada today.

OLAND EXTRA STOUT—dark brown color, light molasses aroma, light body, medium sweetness, good balance, overall impression is very good for a stout of a light style.

Alexander Keith's Nova Scotia Brewery, Ltd. This brewery, founded in 1830 by Alexander Keith, was the oldest in existence in Nova Scotia when obtained by Labatt's. In continuous operation since, its one very fine product, Keith's India Pale Ale, is now produced in Halifax at the Oland's plant.

ALEXANDER KEITH'S INDIA PALE ALE—slightly tawny gold color, fine malty aroma with good hop character, pleasant malty flavor with some hop bitterness in background, dry reasonably well-balanced, a good brew. Has plenty of character without being overdone.

Mountain Ales Corp.
(Surrey, B.C.)

Established in 1983, this brewery produces malt ales for five nearby pubs.

Molson Breweries of Canada, Ltd.

Molson is the oldest brewery in continuous operation in Canada and in North America, having been founded in Montreal by John Molson in 1786. It is now one of Canada's big three, with ten plants operating from Vancouver, British Columbia, to St. John's, Newfoundland. In 1972 the then nine Molson plants produced over 2 million barrels of their fine beer. In 1977 the Formosa Spring Brewery of Barrie, Ontario, was added as the tenth Molson facility.

Molson beers are equally popular in the U.S. and Canada. In the U.S., they are handled by the Martlet Importing Co., Inc., of Great Neck, New York, a firm established by Molson in 1971. Martlet distributed 26 million imperial gallons in 37 states during 1983, making Molson the number two import of all the brands shipped to the United States from all the countries of the world. Molson plans to increase distribution of its three major exports to all contiguous 48 states by the end of 1985 and increase the distribution of Brador Malt Liquor to the New York area. It also plans to introduce Molson Light to U.S. markets in late 1984 and to expand the availability of draft service of Molson brews accounting for 18% of U.S. beer imports.

A listing of the Molson brands by plant is as follows (all brands are 5 percent alcohol, except for Brador Malt Liquor, 6.2 percent, and Crown Lager, 3.9 percent):

MOLSON NEWFOUNDLAND BREWERY, LTD.
(St. John's)
India Beer
Molson Canadian Lager
Molson Export Ale

MOLSON'S BREWERY QUEBEC, LTD.
(Montreal)
Molson Export Ale
Molson Golden Ale
Molson Canadian Lager
Molson Cream Porter

Brador Premium Ale (ML)
Laurentide Ale

MOLSON'S BREWERY (ONTARIO), LTD.
(Toronto)
Molson Canadian Lager
Molson Oktoberfest Lager
Molson Diamond Lager
Molson Golden Ale
Molson Stock Ale
Molson Export Ale
Molson Porter
Molson Club Ale
Molson Light

MOLSON'S BARRIE BREWERY, LTD.
Molson Canadian Lager
Molson Export Ale
Molson Golden Ale
Keg Ale
Molson Cream Porter
Molson Club Ale
Molson Stock Ale

MOLSON ALBERTA BREWERY, LTD.
(Edmonton)
Molson Export Ale
Edmonton Export Beer
Molson Canadian Lager
Molson Golden Lager
Lethbridge Pilsner
Crown Lager

SICKS LETHBRIDGE BREWERY, LTD.
(Lethbridge, Alta.)
Molson Canadian Lager
Lethbridge Beer
Lethbridge Pilsner
Lethbridge Royal Stout

MOLSON BREWERY B.C., LTD.
(Vancouver)
Old Style Lager
Molson Export Ale
Molson Canadian Lager
Ryder

MOLSON BREWERY MANITOBA, LTD.
(Winnipeg)
Frontier Beer
Frontier Stout
Molson Canadian Lager
Molson Export Ale
Crown Lager

MOLSON SASKATCHEWAN BREWERY, LTD.
(Prince Albert)
Bohemian Lager
Pilsner Beer
Molson Canadian Lager
Molson Golden Lager
Molson Imperial Stout
Crown Lager

MOLSON SASKATCHEWAN BREWERY, LTD.
(Regina)
Pilsner Beer
Bohemian Lager

Molson Export Ale
Molson Canadian Lager
Molson Golden Lager
Crown Lager

The combined capacity of the Molson plants is just under 8 million barrels, with the Montreal and Toronto breweries each contributing 2.5 million of that total.

MOLSON CANADIAN LAGER BEER—pale gold, big clean sweet malty aroma with some hops in support, good body, finely balanced, good yeasty malty flavor with just a touch of hops. A fine light creamy flavorful lager with no apparent faults. This particular sample was a canned domestic version made in Montreal. Exports to the U.S. are bottled.

MOLSON EXPORT ALE—deep brilliant gold with a tawny cast, foamy appearance, but carbonation not very noticeable on the palate, clean grainy nose with distinctive hop character, good malty flavor with hops finely balanced in (called by many as being typical of "Canadian sparkling ale"), good tasting throughout with a long and pleasant aftertaste. The ale shipped to the U.S. is called Molson Ale; in Canada it is called Molson Export.

MOLSON GOLDEN ALE—Golden is an ale similar to Export but is paler in color, lighter in aroma, lighter and sweeter in taste. It is not bad at all, but the Export is better. Molson Golden is the largest selling Canadian beer in the U.S.

Mural in the Moosehead Brewery in St. John, New Brunswick

OLD STYLE PILSENER BEER—very slightly cloudy, medium yellow color, faint toasted malt aroma, highly carbonated, light toasted malt flavor, medium body, light finish like the flavor, similar aftertaste. Unusual to find a brew that is the same all the way through from aroma to aftertaste. This sample was a can made in Vancouver for export to the U.S. Since Molson literature lists Old Style Lager as the product made by the Vancouver facility, it is presumed that Old Style Lager and Pilsener are the same brew.

OLD STYLE PILSNER BEER—yes, it is spelled differently from above, bright gold, very aromatic nose with lots of hops and malt, highly carbonated, big flavor, well-balanced hops and malt, good-tasting finish and lingering aftertaste.

Familiar sights in New Brunswick — Moosehead Ale and Alpine Beer trucks

A very good beer and you know that you have a mouthful when you taste this one. Domestic bottling from Molson Saskatchewan Brewery, Ltd.

OLD STYLE PILSNER BEER—bright gold, small bubble CO_2, hoppy aroma, dull uninteresting flavor, very foamy when poured but little carbonation on palate. From Sicks' Lethbridge Brewery.

MOLSON MALT LIQUOR—bright gold, malt aroma, sweet malt flavor, no complexity, only malt and CO_2, medium to good body, fairly long on palate.

LETHBRIDGE BEER—bright gold, well-hopped nose, palate is dull, being little more than carbonation.

MOLSON STOCK ALE—deep gold, good mild hops and malt in nose, good small bubble carbonation, sharp bitter flavor that carries into a sour-bitter aftertaste.

INDIA BEER—bright yellow gold, good sweet malty aroma with good hop background, pleasant mild hop flavor, very good balance, fairly dry, pleasant finish and aftertaste with a touch of hops at end.

MOLSON PORTER—deep copper-brown, lovely roasted malt aroma, flavor mostly roasted malt, but the balance is excellent, just a touch of hops, a really nice porter, smooth, good CO_2 level, pleasant slightly sweet finish, slightly dry aftertaste. A winner!

BOHEMIAN LAGER BEER—medium to pale yellow gold, foamy, lovely malt and hop aroma, dry and pleasant, too much carbonation, some sweetness in the finish.

LAURENTIDE ALE—bright amber gold, pleasant malt aroma with light hops, highly carbonated, good dry malt and hop flavor, well-balanced, zesty, slightly sour finish and aftertaste. Good-tasting brew.

MOLSON LIGHT—pale gold, pleasant well-hopped malty aroma, light-bodied, watery, faint malt-hop flavor, little finish, not much here.

MOLSON EXPORT LIGHT—medium gold, good malt and hop aroma, very good taste up front with good hop tang that carries into the finish, lacks body and malt.

MOLSON BRADOR MALT LIQUOR—6.2 percent alcohol, gold color, sour malt aroma, big sweet-hop flavor, heavy body, alcohol noticeable.

MOLSON DIAMOND LAGER BEER—bright pale gold, austere malty aroma, too much carbonation that interferes with the otherwise bright hoppy flavor, slightly sour malt finish, dull brief aftertaste.

MOLSON OKTOBERFEST BEER—medium deep bright gold, faint but pleasant vegetal malt and hop aroma, dry straightforward hop flavor, some lack of complexity, but still good, somewhat short on the palate.

Moosehead Breweries, Ltd.
(St. John, N.B.)

The president of Moosehead is Philip Oland, and if you feel that Oland might be a familiar name in Maritime brewing, you are correct. Susannah Culverwell Oland, who founded the Halifax, Nova Scotia, Oland Brewing firm in 1867, was great-grandmother to both the Olands of Halifax and the Olands of St. John, New Brunswick. A breach in the family occurred in the 1930s due to the competitiveness and property disputes between Philip Oland's father, George, and his uncle, Sidney, leader of the Halifax side of the family. Since then the two sides of the family have gone separate (although similar) ways. The rift widened in 1971 when the Halifax Olands sold out to Labatt's.

Philip Oland is determined to maintain the independence of Moosehead, and his two sons,

who share his dislike of the mid-Canada corporate mentality, intend to preserve this company and its regional brews. With sales close to a million barrels annually, they are doing well in the fight for preeminence in the Maritime market.

Most of its sales are still in its good-tasting zesty ales, but its lager is gaining popularity. Moosehead also makes an interesting stout. All Moosehead brands are made from western Canadian barley and U.S.-grown, Canadian-milled corn, and U.S., Yugoslavian, and domestic hops. All are rated at 5 percent alcohol.

MOOSEHEAD CANADIAN LAGER BEER—for export to the U.S., light yellow, pleasant malty aroma, very good flavor of malt and hops, medium body, good balance of hops and malt, grainy finish, a fine brew.

MOOSEHEAD PALE ALE—pale gold color, malty yeasty light hop nose, sour well-hopped flavor and finish with a sour aftertaste, an average light or pale ale, not quite in the English style, but similar.

TEN-PENNY ALE—pale amber color, light hop aroma and flavor, good balance, dry sour hop finish and aftertaste. Similar to Moosehead Pale Ale, but has a lot of the zest that Moosehead lacks.

MOOSEHEAD SPECIAL ALE—pale amber gold, good sweet and bitter alelike aroma (sweet at first, bitter and sour behind), big "sweet" ale flavor and finish with plenty of hops, beautiful balance, very refreshing, good all the way through. Canadian domestic brew, 5 percent alcohol.

ALPINE LAGER BEER (Alpine Breweries, Ltd.)—pale, greenish-straw color, sweet vegetal aroma, malty grainy taste, nice flavor, pleasant, weak finish; for some reason, very filling even though the body doesn't seem to be great, perhaps it is the high carbonation.

MOOSEHEAD'S GOLDEN LIGHT BEER—pale gold, pleasant light sour malt aroma, a little watery, but pleasant, highly carbonated.

MOOSEHEAD LONDON STOUT—very deep brown, opaque, molasses malted milk shake, creamy texture. This one has to be called a dessert beer; it is unique in that respect.

MOOSEHEAD EXPORT ALE—same brew as *Moosehead Special Ale*, name change effected in mid-1981. Canadians have always been fond of the term "export", particularly on the brews for their domestic market.

Northern Ontario Breweries, Ltd.
(Sudbury, Sault Ste. Marie, Timmins, Thunder Bay)

Back in 1907 hotelkeeper and amateur boxer J.J. Doran got together with two partners and

bought the Sudbury Brewing and Malting Co. A few years later they bought out the Soo Falls Brewing Co. and the Kakabeka Brewing Co., both of Sault Ste. Marie. In 1928 J.J. built Doran's Brewing Ltd. in Timmins and by 1948 had added the Port Arthur Beverage Co., Ltd.

The five companies were merged in 1960 to form Doran's Northern Ontario Breweries. When J.J. Doran's son, William, retired in 1971, the business was purchased by Canadian Breweries, Ltd. (now Carling O'Keefe). Coulter was an accountant with Doran for years and served as president of the soft drink side of the firm and when the firm failed to make a profit for Canadian Breweries, he was concerned that, with its reputation for buying and closing, it might shut down the five plants and throw 225 Doran employees out of work. When Carling O'Keefe stopped making the traditional Doran labels, Coulter began to round up pledges from employees to purchase the company. With some support from the Bank of Montreal, Coulter and 170 Doran employees bought the company back for about $4 million in 1977.

Now president of Doran's, Coulter believes it can get along for a while on the profitable Doran soft drink franchised bottling business while the firm generates renewed interest in the traditional Doran brands that hadn't been produced since 1974. Northern Ontario beer drinkers can once again enjoy Doran's Lager, Northern Ale, 55 Lager, Edelbrau, Encore Ale, Silver Spray, Doran's Cream Porter and Kakabeka Cream being made at Thunder Bay, Timmins, Sault Ste. Marie and Sudbury. All four plants produce draught beer for their individual markets, but only Sudbury and Sault Ste. Marie have bottling lines. No Doran (or Northern Breweries, as it is now called) products are canned. The first exports reached the U.S. in mid-1980s. Export brews are produced at Sault Ste. Marie and Sudbury. Northern offers a 56-bottle "beer ball" similar to that of Henninger of Canada and F.X. Matt of the U.S.

CANADIAN 55 LAGER BEER—yellow-gold with some particulate matter, sour malt aroma, almost skunky but not quite, highly carbonated, very dry, fairly clean and straightforward malt-hop flavor, dry finish and aftertaste, no complexity. Export version for U.S.

CANADIAN NORTHERN LIGHT BEER—gold color, faint sour hop aroma, thin sour and bitter flavor, highly carbonated, faint sour CO_2 finish, dry aftertaste, shallow and not likable. Export version for U.S.

NORTHERN ALE—bright yellow, light hoppy aroma, sour hop flavor, medium to thin body, oily texture, touch of malt in the finish and aftertaste. Domestic Canadian version.

SUPERIOR LAGER BEER—bright pale yellow, light hoppy nose with a touch of malt, creamy, light sour hop flavor, medium to thin body, slight oiliness, some malt in the finish and aftertaste. Domestic version.

Rocky Mountain Breweries, Ltd.

(Red Deer, Alberta)
(Leisure Lake Breweries, Ltd.)

In 1971 Ben Ginter, a former bulldozer operator from Prince George, British Columbia, who was involved in pulp mills, logging, and newspaper publishing, formed Uncle Ben's Breweries, a collection of small breweries in British Columbia and Alberta. When Uncle Ben's Industries went bankrupt, the Red Deer plant continued to operate producing the Uncle Ben's brands. The Prince George plant of Uncle Ben's is operating again, but under the auspices of a new and separate corporate entity.

UNCLE BEN'S MALT LIQUOR—medium yellow, cloudy, foamy with a big head, sour malt aroma, some yeast present in the nose, cereal flavor, high carbonation gives most of the palate sensation.

STEEPLEJACK SPECIAL BEER—orange-copper, grainy aroma, slightly sweet cereal-grain flavor, light on palate, some sourness in back.

GOLD PEAK PREMIUM LAGER BEER—medium deep gold, pleasant slightly sweet nose, big flavor of hops, tails off rapidly, little aftertaste.

TRAPPER MALT LIQUOR—yellow-gold, some particulate matter, big sweet malt-hop nose and flavor, sweet finish and aftertaste, not cloying, heavy body and noticeable (5.65 percent) alcohol.

"OLD BLUE" CANADIAN PILSNER BEER (Uncle Ben's Breweries of Alberta, Red Deer)—bright tawny gold, hoppy nose with some toasted malt, thin body, flavor starts off very good, but becomes "elusive" and fades to a soapy aftertaste.

TRAPPER BEER—pale gold, faint perfumy aroma, light body, light slightly sweet flavor, watery aftertaste.

China, Hong Kong, Taiwan, Singapore

Since this book is on beer, I shall take the very apolitical course of lumping these four together.

The most familiar of the four products listed is Mon-Lei, which apparently is no longer imported. Beer brewing on Taiwan and the Chinese mainland has only recently developed to any great extent.

The products reported below have all been found in Chinese restaurants and occasionally elsewhere.

Feng Shon Brewery
(Peking, China)

PEKING BEER—pale gold, clean malt aroma, fruity-malty flavor, hoppy finish.

Shanghai Brewery
(Shanghai, China)
(China National Cereals, Oils, and Foodstuffs Import and Export Corp.)

SHANGHAI GOLDEN BEER—brilliant gold, light body, toasted malt aroma, creamy, toasted malt flavor, sweet-sour aftertaste that seems a bit tinny. Overall it is pretty good beer.

SHANGHAI BEER—deep bright gold, toasted malt nose and flavor, light body, sweet-sour malt aftertaste.

Tientsin Brewery
(Tientsin, China)

GREAT WALL BEER—deep gold, toasted malty caramel aroma, light body, very good hops and malt flavor up front on the palate, but doesn't finish so well, ending bitter and burnt. Decent beer with Chinese food, however. Comes in a 24-ounce bottle. Said to be the same brew as Tsing-Tao, but it doesn't seem to be, from my taste.

Yuchuan Brewery
(Peking, China)

YUCHUAN BEER—brilliant gold, pleasant smooth malt aroma with good hops, sour and bitter flavor with a sweet "off" finish, long metallic aftertaste.

Tsing-Tao Brewery
(Tsing-Tao, China)

TSING-TAO—murky yellow color, faint malty aroma, sour-salty taste, sour aftertaste. Not unpleasant, but nothing to attract a retry.

TSING-TAO PORTER—extremely deep brown, heavy grainy, soapy aroma, heavy roasted malt flavor with a marred sour-bitter finish, aftertaste not pleasant, like a stout with licorice added.

Hong Kong Brewery, Ltd.
(Hong Kong)

MON-LEI BEER—pale yellow, very bright appearance, sour malt aroma, slightly sour flavor, finishes poorly with sour metallic aftertaste. May have been a little elderly. I can recall others that performed similarly except that the ending was sour malt without the unpleasantness. The name *Mon-Lei* means 10,000 miles, infinity, or the Great Wall. The implication is that it is "the infinitely better beer."

SUN-LIK BEER—brilliant yellow, extremely faint aroma (so faint I cannot identify any component), small bubble carbonation, strange salt and hop flavor and finish, not much aftertaste.

Taiwan Tobacco & Wine Monopoly Bureau
(Taiwan)

TAIWAN BEER—very yeasty aroma with a background of cardboard and vegetable soup (really), malty cardboard taste.

DYNASTY TAIWAN BEER—cloudy deep yellow, rich appetizing malt aroma, clean malty flavor with toasted malt in back, long clean malty finish. Good brew!

Malayan Breweries Pte., Ltd.
(Singapore)

ANCHOR PILSENER BEER—deep gold, hoppy cardboard-malt aroma, slightly roasted malt flavor, finish is mostly malt but there are some hops too, fair balance. Label says Archipelago Brewery Co. (1947), Ltd.

TIGER GOLD MEDAL LAGER BEER—gold, a few particles, good malt and hop aroma with an apple-fruit background, no flavor up front, all in finish, then dull and hoppy.

ABC EXTRA STOUT (Archipelago Brewery Co.)—opaque brown, brown head, faint hop aroma, palate sweet and herbal at first, malty in middle, malt and celery finish with molasses and licorice in back, ends quite dry, long dry malt aftertaste, very interesting.

Cyprus

Cyprus, Keo, Ltd.

KEO PILSENER BEER—deep cloudy yellow, malty tart fruit and berry pulp aroma (similar to rhubarb pie), malty paper flavor, flat and little finish.

Fermenting vats at Urquell Brewery in Pilsen, Czechoslovakia

Czechoslovakia

No work on beer could ever be complete without paying homage to Bohemia and the role it has long played in the development and history of beer. It was the ancient center of brewing in Europe and noted for the brews of Wenzel II in Pilsen in 1292. Franciscan monks brewed their fine brews there for centuries. Pilsen has always been associated with only the

Popularity of Budweiser name found its way behind the Iron Curtain in Czechslovakia

highest quality beers. The Saaz hops of Bohemia have long been regarded as the finest in the world and demand for them has always exceeded their availability.

When bottom fermentation came along in the mid-1840s, the success of the method in Bohemia was such that the beer became known as pilsener, the model for all lager beers to follow.

Czechoslovakia still holds a position of high regard today; its Pilsner Urquell is famous and sought after the world over. It is probably the main reason that the Czechs are the most prodigious quaffers of brew in the world (forty-plus gallons of beer per person each year.) Urquell means "original."

The Urquell brewery of today is the result of an 1842 consolidation of small firms in that city, then called Burgerliches Brauhaus Urquell. The beer was sufficiently popular that it was exported in 1856 and seen in America by 1873. Urquell disappeared from the American market for almost forty years after World War I, but there was no loss of its popularity on world markets. Today it is still recognized as one of the

166

world's great beers.

Brewery Pilsner Urquell
(Pilsen)

PILSNER URQUELL—deep yellow color, huge malty hop aroma, heavy body, marvelous malt-hop flavor with an attractive sour dryness, excellent balance between hops and malt. A fine beer, worthy of its reputation.

Denmark

According to the early Norse writings, ale or oel was the chief national drink of ancient Scandinavians. At their three great winter festivals, it was an effective means of lightening the gloom that came with winter nights that lasted for the greater portion of each day.

The ale was drunk very young and each feast was preceded by a great brewing. A special brewer was often engaged for private entertainment. The feast usually lasted until the ale was gone and then the guests went home. Even in recent times it was a custom of Norwegian peasants to brew a strong ale for Christmas and entertain neighbors until it was consumed. Today, Denmark ranks eighth in per capita consumption. Eighty percent of all beer produced and consumed in Denmark is brewed by United Breweries (Tuborg and Carlsberg). Eighteen other small brewers share the remaining 20 percent.

The names Tuborg and Carlsberg are considered synonymous with Danish beer throughout most of the world. Imported Carlsberg is available in the U.S.; imported Tuborg is available in Canada.

Albani Breweries, Ltd.
(Odense)

One of Denmark's smaller breweries, Albani produces some fine brews, one of them excellent.

ALBANI BEER FOR EXPORT—yellow-gold color, slightly malty nose with some hops in back, very pleasant flavor with good balance of hops and malt; unfortunately, the finish is too sour in the throat and mars the aftertaste.

GIRAF MALT LIQUOR—medium deep gold, lovely malt and hop aroma, bitter hops up front, malt in the finish, long malt and hop aftertaste, good tasting, 5.4 percent alcohol.

ALBANI PILSNER—medium hoppy nose, good flavor characteristic of a European pils, good balance, pleasant, but not complex, short pleasant finish.

ALBANI PORTER—deep molasses-brown color, smooth light malty aroma, big rich sourlike taste, pineapple background, long rich finish, complex, balanced and smooth, an absolute delight. I have found this only in Boston at the bargain price of 45¢ per bottle. One of the most enjoyable dark brews I have ever tasted.

Examining kegs of aging beer at Urquell Brewery in Pilsen, Czechoslovakia

The United Breweries, Ltd. (Carlsberg)
(Copenhagen)

The Carlsberg history begins before 1835, for at that time a small brewery passed into the hands of Jacob C. Jacobsen from his father, Christian. Young Jacobsen paid several visits to the famous Sedlmayr (Zum Späten) Brewery in Munich where the practicality of the "Bavarian System" (bottom-fermentation beer making) was being demonstrated with great success. He secured two pots of yeast from Sedlmayr and carried them by coach from Munich to Copenhagen, stopping at every resting place on the route to throw water on the yeast to cool it and keep it alive. This was in 1845. Jacobsen built a new brewery in a Copenhagen suburb, which he named Carlsberg in honor of his infant son, Carl, and the first brew appeared on November 10, 1847. In the first year the production of beer at Carlsberg was just under 100,000 gallons, now the daily production figure at Carlsberg.

A second and third brewery followed and Carlsberg became world famous. At the turn of the twentieth century, Carlsberg was deemed a model brewing facility. In *One Hundred Years of Brewing,* the definitive work on the subject at the time, Carlsberg was selected for the chapter describing a modern brewing plant. Today the plant covers approximately eighty-five acres.

On October 1, 1969, the Carlsberg Breweries and the United Breweries Co., Ltd. (Tuborg and the Royal Breweries), were amalgamated, the merger being a natural conclusion to the close cooperation entered into by agreement between the breweries in 1903.

CARLSBERG ROYAL LAGER BEER—deep golden color, light, pleasant, clean malty aroma with some hops in back, light and dry with good hop flavor and good balance, creamy with small bubble carbonation, finishes on the light and sweet side.

CARLSBERG ELEPHANT MALT LIQUOR—deep gold, light fruitlike aroma, like apple peel with good hops, pungent big flavor with lots of character, almost a sense of menthol, excellent finish! Could use a bit more malt to

balance off the hops.

CARLSBERG SPECIAL DARK BEER—dark rose-orange color, light balanced malt and hop aroma, weak body, very light flavor, hops show stronger in the finish, brief aftertaste.

TUBORG BEER—made in Denmark, distributed in Canada, pale yellow, good malty aroma with slight hop character, big pungent taste, mostly sour malt up front, strong hops in finish and aftertaste.

CARLSBERG BEER—bright gold, big hoppy nose, lovely bright hop flavor, good duration and follow through, fairly complex.

Harboes Brewery
(Skaelskor)

HARBOE BEAR BEER MALT LIQUOR—pale bright gold, fresh hop aroma, very sweet palate up front; this drops off in middle and finishes hop bitter, which hangs on till aftertaste.

HARBOE GOLD EXPORT BEER—deep clear gold, light malt and hop aroma, light flavor dry up front but finishes slightly sweet, good dry and well-balanced aftertaste.

Lolland-Falsters Bryghus
(Nykobing, Falsters Island)

Lolland-Falsters is a family-owned brewery established in 1866. The firm is headed today by Knut Synnestvedts, a present-generation family member. Their products are distributed on the Danish islands of Lolland and Falster. A notable feature of the primary product is that it is produced using a series of labels depicting twelve different native costumes.

LOLLAND-FALSTERS EXPORT DANISH BEER—bright gold, clean vegetal malt aroma, slightly toasted malt flavor up front, complex sweet-sour bitter finish, long highly hopped and smoky aftertaste.

Danish Interbrew Ltd., A/S

SCANDIA GOLD—deep gold, slightly tawny, lovely roasted malt and hop nose, big body, rich full roasted malt and hop flavor, complex, long on the palate. Well-made brew with an "up" flavor and good balance.

Thor Breweries
(Randers)

Brewery established in 1856.

THOR BEER—light gold, faintly sweet nose, small bubble carbonation, sour malt and hop taste, long unbalanced aftertaste.

Wiibroes Brewery
(Elsinore) (United Breweries, Ltd.)

This brewery dates back to 1840.

IMPERIAL STOUT—almost opaque black, rich complex stout aroma hiding all kinds of good things, rich luxurious malty flavor and a long, long finish, fairly dry for the type and might well please many American palates, quite good.

Ceres Breweries, Ltd.
(Aarhus, Horsens)

CERES BEER—faint apple nose, light taste with slight sweetness, bitter and short finish.

RED ERIC MALT LIQUOR—cloudy yellow, nose of hops and toffee-sweet malt, bittersweet toffee flavor, an overage sample that still shows character. Red Eric is probably a decent brew given a fresh bottle for sampling.

Neptun Brewery
(Silkeborg) (United Breweries, Ltd.)

NEPTUN DANISH PILSNER—brilliant pale gold, malty aroma with a methane background, wet cardboard flavor, bad sample.

NEPTUN GOLDEN BROWN—brilliant gold, big earthy hoppy aroma, huge hop and sweet malt flavor, each flavor component distinct and out of balance, sweet malt and bitter finish, long harsh bitter aftertaste.

NEPTUN PAASKE BRYG (Best Bock Beer)—medium to pale gold, initially a light touch of skunky aroma, but this slowly disappeared leaving a light malt aroma, some malt in the flavor, but mostly hops and a bit too much bitterness overall. *Paaske Bryg* means Easter Beer, a festival beer for Easter.

NEPTUN PINSE BRYG (Pinse Mik)—bright lime green, malt and big hop nose, hoppy flavor with a touch of malt, too hoppy, almost identical to the Bock Beer described above. *Pinse Bryg* means Whitsuntide (Pentecost) Beer, a festival beer for the seventh Sunday after Easter.

GREEN ROOSTER MALT LIQUOR—labeled "Lean, Green, and Mean," beautiful bright lime green, delicious aromatic clover hop aroma, complex hop flavor, long on the palate, full-bodied, balanced, malt in the finish, excellent lingering aftertaste. A fantastic brew for those who like them hoppy. Don't let the color put you off.

England, Scotland, Ireland

England has long been a source of great beer for the world and aside from Germany, no other country has a greater reputation for the quality of its malt beverages. When it comes to ales there is absolutely no competitor worth naming, for the pale ales of Burton and the nut-brown ales of Scotland have known no peer since inception.

For the most part, the enjoyment of malt beverages in Britain takes place in the pub. Rather than being places of escape, as are the bars in America, they are social gathering places, friendly and warm. It is almost impossible to be alone in an English pub. They are places to meet the locals, learn their customs, and drink their favorite brews. Any foreign visitor should hie off to the nearest pub soon after arrival lest he miss an opportunity to take part in British life.

British pubs come in two styles: "tied," whose complete line is that of a single brewery or brewing conglomerate and those that are free to serve a selection of their choosing. It takes a lot of pub visits to sample all of England's beers and most locals never stray beyond their nearest favorites.

Home consumption of beer in England is still a small percentage of the total consumed and most beer in Britain is top-fermented. For a number of years, I have heard that lager is gaining a following in the United Kingdom, but even yet it accounts for no more than 25 percent of British production. There is a trend toward paler beers, but they are more alelike than lager, in the American sense.

Allied Breweries (U.K.), Ltd.
(Burton-on-Trent, England)

The name of Allsopp is inseparably linked to the brewing trade of Great Britain and to the famous ales of Burton-on-Trent. The area is first mentioned in history as being connected with

171

brewing in the year 1295. By the time of King Richard and the Crusades, the monks had discovered the fine qualities of Burton ales and were commencing to add to their fame. Hugh de Allsopp, who won his spurs with Richard in the Holy Land, was founder of the honorable Derbyshire family, which was to become prominent in the brewing trade and closely attached to royalty. According to Samuel Pepys' diary, an Allsopp was appointed as king's brewer

to Charles II. The Allsopps were not to become involved with Burton brewing until 1805.

Meanwhile, the Burton ales were becoming famous. They were known throughout England and Russia, where they were great favorites, particularly with Peter the Great and Empress Catherine.

One of the leading brewers of this (mid-eighteenth century) period was Benjamin Wilson. In 1805 his firm was headed by Samuel Allsopp, descendant of the ancient family of Derbyshire and eventually it became Samuel Allsopp & Sons, Ltd.

Samuel Allsopp is credited with being the force behind the development of what was to become India Pale Ale, the actual work having been done by Allsopp's maltster, Job Goodhead. This ale was the forerunner of the Double Diamond, Britain's top-selling ale.

Allsopp prospered throughout the years, finally merging in 1934 with another famous Burton brewery, Ind Coope, Ltd., a company with roots reaching to 1799 that had a high reputation in southern England. More firms, including Benskins and Taylor-Walker, were acquired in the 1950s and in 1961 Ind Coope merged with

Tetley Walker of Leeds and with Warrington & Ansells of Birmingham to form Allied Breweries, Ltd.

IND COOPE DOUBLE DIAMOND BURTON PALE ALE—tawny deep gold, aroma like dry coffee or coffee beans, bitter roast coffee flavor with sourness in the back, flavor actually quite light, finish dry and brief. Somewhat disappointing for Britain's top-selling ale. Probably an old and spoiled sample.

IND COOPE DOUBLE DIAMOND PILSENER BEER—cloudy amber, pungent sour hop aroma, big dry hop flavor, creamy beautiful head, small bubble carbonation, not tasty, could use more malt.

TETLEY SPECIAL PALE ALE—medium copper color, toasted malt aroma, flavor starts out very nice with toasted malt and hops in balance, then the hops build in intensity toward the finish where they become very sharp, giving a harsh aftertaste with the roasted malt sliding into the background, questionable balance.

Lorimer Breweries, Ltd. *(Edinburgh)* Originally known as Usher's Brewerys, Lorimer was purchased by the Vaux Brewery of Sunderland in 1976. It was sold to Allied Breweries (UK), Ltd., in early 1980. Lorimer's Ale is labeled barley wine in Scotland, but that term is not permitted in the U.S. Both Lorimer brews imported here are top-fermented and thus are really ales. The Scotch Ale reportedly reaches 8 percent alcohol by weight and the "Beer" is 3.2 percent according to the label. The latter is considered a mild ale in the U.K. (and labeled light ale there) and the former was rated one of the three "best bitters in Britain" by the *London Sunday Mirror* in 1978.

LORIMER'S TRADITIONAL SCOTCH ALE—golden amber, beautiful toasted malt aroma with good hops and a beneficial touch of sour malt that give balance, intense roasted malt flavor, lingering malty aftertaste (very long). A big and powerful brew. 7.2 percent alcohol by volume.

LORIMER'S SCOTTISH BEER—golden amber, big hoppy aroma, huge mouth-filling malt and hop flavor, good balance, slight excess sourness in finish.

Alpine Ayingerbrau (U.K.), Ltd.
(Tadcaster)

ALPINE AYINGERBRAU LAGER—sour aroma, sour taste, sour aftertaste. Can says it's brewed in the U.K. under license, but doesn't say whose.

Boddington's Breweries, Ltd.
(Manchester)

Established 1778.

BODDINGTONS' BITTER BEER—deep bright gold, intense roasted malt aroma, pleasant roasted malt flavor lacks body, faint hops show only in the throat.

Bass Charrington, Ltd.
(Burton-on-Trent, Runcorn, Tadcasrwe, Belfast, Sheffield, Birmingham, Glasgow, and Edinburgh)

William Bass erected the first Bass brewery in 1777. He was succeeded by his son, Michael, and his grandson, Michael Thomas, who built additional breweries in 1853 and 1864. When his great-grandson, Michael Arthur, took over in 1884, the brewery was entirely rebuilt. Michael Thomas Bass began the Bass political tradition, representing Derby in the British Parliament for 33 years, and Michael Arthur Bass, his eldest son, was made a peer, under title of Lord Burton.

The pale ales of Bass & Co., introduced in 1823, became famous the world over. By 1900 the Bass, Ratcliff & Gretton plant had expanded to over 750 acres. Despite the firm's efforts to brew the ales elsewhere, as in London, those ales were never the equal of the ales brewed at Burton. This interesting fact is discussed at length later in this book.

The brewery of William Worthington actually dates back to 1744 and Worthington & Co. of Burton-on-Trent quickly entered export trade to St. Petersburg, Russia, a trade of considerable magnitude at the time. Over the next century, Worthington & Co. was to absorb three neighboring Burton breweries. By 1900 it was, by reputation, the largest brewery in the U.K. in the hands of one family. Worthington & Co. merged with Bass, Ratcliff & Gretton in 1926.

In 1961 Bass Worthington merged with Mitchells and Butlers to form Bass, Mitchells & Butlers and in 1967, a further merger with Charrington United Breweries created the huge Bass Charrington Group. The Charrington name, popular in London and vicinity, is another old firm dating back to 1766 and John Charrington. Mitchells and Butlers was the result of an 1898 merger between two prominent Birmingham brewing families.

Bass Charrington operates twelve breweries in the United Kingdom and one in Belgium. Bass produces eight packaged lagers, twenty-one packaged ales, two packaged stouts, and eighteen draught ales. Many of the names are familiar to Americans and include Carling Black Label, Lamot Pilsor, Tuborg Gold, and the Tennent, Bass, Charrington, and Worthington brands. Draught Bass is now frequently found in the U.S. much to the delight of British ale fanciers.

Wine buyers will recognize the Bass Charrington name as readily as beer drinkers in the United States. In recent years some heavy Bass Charrrington investments in bad vintages have cost the firm dearly; consequently, it has dumped enormous quantities of its better wines on the market at a severe loss to stablize its cash position. Most of the Charrington wines carried the Alexis Lichine label.

BASS PALE ALE (Draught)—brilliant copper, big malt and hop aroma, full rich malty flavor, excellent balance, long finish, marvelous rich aftertaste. Very satisfying brew. I found it difficult to just drink one.

BASS PALE ALE I.P.A.—imported by Guinness-Harp Corporation, pleasant malty aroma, medium body, good malty flavor, not heavy-handed, excellent balance, long finish, a beautiful ale. (Note: The Bass symbol, a red triangle, is the oldest registered trademark in the world. It supposedly stands for a divinity of the pyramid builders called Tammuz or Bassareus the Fortifier, who was son of the goddess Ops. His symbol was a cross (X), and he was honored by the Egyptians with libations of wine and malt. Through the centuries, Tammunz became Thomas, Bassareus became Bass, X became XXX, and you can just guess what Ops became. Perhaps Tammuz father was the god Ogwash.) The IPA in very small letters on the label quietly announces that Bass is a classical India Pale Ale.

WORTHINGTON E BRITISH BEER—pale amber, toasted malt nose with little depth, smoky well-hopped toasted malt flavor, complex, long on the palate, good flavor, but short on depth.

WORTHINGTON'S ORIGINAL PALE ALE (WHITE SHIELD)—cloudy yellow, yeasty aroma, delicate and complex hop and malt palate, some yeast in the background, smooth and rich, long aftertaste.

Tennent Caledonian Breweries, Ltd. *(Glasgow and Edinburgh)* The history of J. and R. Tennent, Ltd., goes back to 1556. The Tennent name has been linked to many of the happenings in the Glasgow area since then. By the late eighteenth century the firm of Tennent, headed by John and Robert Tennent, was well established.

In 1963 Tennent joined the Charrington United Breweries Group with the original company of J. and R. Tennent, to become part of the Tennent Caledonian Breweries, Ltd., the Scottish unit of the Group. Since then Tennent has become part of Bass Charrington, the largest brewery organization with over 12,000 tied public houses.

TENNENT'S LAGER BEER—tawny golden color, creamy texture, clean malty aroma and flavor, taste very slightly soapy, clean fresh finish, a very pleasant and fresh-tasting brew that most beer drinkers should favor. An excellent import seen quite frequently in cans featuring Penny, a scantily clad voluptuous blonde.

PIPER EXPORT ALE—dark amber color, aroma of roasted mash, burnt toffee-apple flavor, sourness in the back of the palate, assertive at first with too much of the burnt flavor, mars the pleasant aspects.

Beamish & Crawford, Ltd.
(Cork, Ireland)

Established 1792, Beamish is Ireland's oldest brewery. It is now owned by Carling O'Keefe of Canada.

BEAMISH IRISH STOUT—deep ruby-brown, big thick head that really stands up, little aroma, light body, thin bitter coffee flavor, faint coffee finish and aftertaste, disappointing. I have heard that Carling O'Keefe has made Beamish Stout in Canada, but I have not seen it there.

Belhaven Brewery
(Dunbar, Scotland)

Firm established in 1719.

TRAQUAIR HOUSE ALE—bright copper, lovely roasted malt aroma, intense roasted malt and sweet ale flavor, real sipping beer, great finish, long aftertaste, a spectacular brew.

BELHAVEN SCOTTISH ALE—clear copper color, roasted malt and hop aroma, sour hop flavor up front, smoother toward finish but dies at the end. Not a bad taste but not well balanced. I have widely varying reports on the performance of this brew.

Caledonia Brewery
(Edinburgh, Scotland)

MACANDREW S SCOTCH ALE—bright copper, strong aromatic hop and toasted-malt nose with a spruce-pine resin background, very complex, smoky malt (like Scotch whisky), licorice, and peat flavor, big sipping brew.

Castle St. Brewery
(Sunderland)

HERITAGE ENGLISH ALE—a barley wine-style ale, bright copper-orange, delicious toasted malt, sharp palate with complexity and sweetness, sour aftertaste, extremely complex ale taste (licorice, orange peel, etc.), big bodied, well-balanced. Contains a hefty 7.2 percent alcohol by volume.

Edwin Cheshire Ltd.
(Stansted)

KINROSS SCOTCH ALE—bright copper, sweet cara-melized malt nose and flavor, not overly sweet, consistent across palate, good balance, long aftertaste, pleasant sipping beer.

Courage, Ltd.
(London, Reading, Plymouth, and Bristol)

The roots of this firm run deep in the London brewing trade, resting with Courage & Co. and the firm of Barclay, Perkins & Co. The Barclay side has a most interesting history; its original Anchor Brewery was erected on the site of the old Globe Theater in the Southwark district of London, made famous by Shakespeare's plays. Although the Anchor Brewery was not established until the seventeenth century, the ales of Southwark were remarked by Chaucer. In the latter half of the eighteenth century, the brewery was owned by the Thrales, who were fine, intellectual people and friends of Samuel Johnson, who was a constant visitor to the brewery. The Barclays purchased the brewery upon the death of Mr. Thrale.

The most famous product of Courage, Ltd., is Russian Imperial Stout, which came to the firm via Barclay, Perkins. This strong brew is so named because it was the choice of Catherine the Great in 1795. The highly reputed brew is aged for two months in cask and matured for at least one year in bottle. It is the only beer believed to be "vintaged," that is, labeled with the year of brewing. Like rare vintage port, vintages of Russian Stout are discussed and compared by aficionados; they are in fact corked and "laid down" like port. If you get the opportunity to sample the stout, please do.

Visitors to the London area can't miss the brews of this firm for they are found almost everywhere. Each bears the rooster trademark and the exhortation to "take courage."

175

COURAGE LAGER EXPORT BEER—cloudy yellow gold, heavily carbonated, hops dominate the nose and palate, sour aftertaste.

JOHN COURAGE EXPORT—tawny color, foamy, sweet malt aroma, unbalanced, bitterness dominates the flavor throughout, shallow, slightly sweet finish.

BULLDOG PALE ALE—pale yellow, hoppy aroma, dull hop flavor up front, slight hop finish, virtually no aftertaste.

BULLDOG LAGER BEER—bright pale gold, intense malty fruitlike aroma, big body, lots of hops in the taste all the way through. Good brew, seen rarely.

Cumbrian Brewery Co., Ltd.
(Warrington)

BEAVER EXPORT LAGER BEER—slightly cloudy tawny-yellow, faintly sweet malt aroma, sharp acidic taste, an overage or mishandled bottle.

Felinfoel Brewing Co., Ltd.
(Llanelli, Wales)

DOUBLE DRAGON ALE—tawny amber, grainy barnyard aroma, mild hop flavor not alelike, tasty with food.

JOHN BROWN ALE—copper brown, faint malt aroma, faint malt flavor.

FELINFOEL BITTER ALE—gold, hop aroma, palate of sharp hops at first, then softer, thin body, sour at finish, watery aftertaste.

Fuller Smith & Turner, Ltd.
(Griffen Brewery, Chiswick, Established 1845)

FULLERS PALE ALE—cloudy tawny, toasted malt aroma, toasted malt flavor up front, bitter in middle and finish, thin and watery.

FULLERS LONDON PRIDE—TRADITIONAL ENGLISH ALE—pale amber, lightly toasted malt in nose, hops dominate flavor, malt in back, some sourness in the finish and aftertaste.

Greenall Whitley & Co., Ltd.
(Warrington and Wem)

CHESHIRE ENGLISH PUB BEER—pale amber, brilliant, thick creamy head, very faint fruity malt aroma, good hops in the flavor with some sweetness, light body, fair balance, but not very interesting. Not at all like any English pub beer I've ever had.

George Gale & Co., Ltd.
(Horndean)

Firm established in 1843.

ANGEL STEAM BREWED BEER—bright copper color, sweet roasted malt aroma, a lot of carbonation, roasted malt and sharp hop flavor, the brew has a great deal of character, but has a little too much bite for some tastes; bitters and malt flavors clash on the palate, complex but not very attractive.

ANGEL STEAM BREWED ALE—copper-orange color, good roasted malt aroma, some hops in the background, fine hop and roasted malt flavor, light bodied, pleasant finish, very nicely balanced, long-pleasing aftertaste, very tasty and very good with food.

Greene King, Ltd.
(Bury St. Edmunds and Biggleswade)

Founded 1799.

GREENE KING ALE—bright amber, faint sour nose slightly bitter water with a sour aftertaste. 3.2 percent.

ABBOT ALE—pale amber, nose of artificial sweet apple, bitter up front, sour metallic finish, very long aftertaste that is not good. 5.4 percent alcohol by volume.

Hall and Woodhouse, Ltd.
(Blandford Forum)

Firm established in 1777.

BROCK LAGER—slightly cloudy yellow, wood pulp and malt aroma, watery, sour and faintly salty flavor, weak finish.

BADGER LIGHT ALE—pale sherry color, slightly cloudy, faint toffee aroma, light body, molasses-flavored water, off balance with metallic tones; flavor is good, but the body is too weak for satisfaction.

St. James's Gate Brewery, Arthur Guinness Son & Company, Ltd.
(Dublin)

Porter (so-called because of its popularity with the working classes, porters in particular) was introduced in 1722 and there were as many as thirty small breweries in Dublin making brown ales in 1735. But excellence was not achieved until 1759, when St. James's Gate Brewery came to the forefront of the industry.

Founded by Arthur Guinness in that year, the brewery began with a porter that was quickly recognized as being the best. By 1825 Guinness porter was famous abroad. In 1856, 62,000 barrels were exported and by 1881 the annual production of Guinness products had passed one

million barrels. In 1914, St. James's Gate Brewery was the largest in the world. It is still the largest brewery in Europe.

Today Guinness sells 85 percent of its output in Ireland and the United Kingdom, but its market includes 147 countries. The product line is extremely popular in Africa, and Guinness breweries stand in Nigeria, Ghana, and Cameroun. There are also plants in Malaysia and Jamaica. Guinness supervises the brewing of its beers in all its breweries worldwide.

Harp Lager Ltd., which brews and sells lager in Great Britain and Ireland, is a consortium of Guinness, Courage, Scottish and Newcastle Breweries. Lager now accounts for 26 percent of malt beverage sales in Great Britain.

In the United Kingdom a number of Guinness Stout "mixtures" are very popular. Guinness and bitter is "Black and Tan," a name which would seem to lack general popularity in much of Ireland. Guinness and cider are "Black Velvet," and among the higher-income that term is used for Guinness and champagne.

Guinness uses only barley grown in Ireland and England (even exporting it for beers brewed overseas) without any adjuncts or artificial ingredients. The flavor and color are entirely natural. Only the recipe is changed to suit the tastes of the various markets. Brews packaged for the Irish and English market are unpasteurized and not refrigerated. The bottled

export variety is pasteurized, a completely different brew with higher alcoholic content and added hops. The export version is also shipped unpasteurized in kegs. It is far superior to the bottled variety.

GUINNESS EXTRA STOUT—opaque red-brown color with a creamy, tawny head, very full-bodied, dense and thick, a complex spicy Worcestershire sauce aroma, dry coffee-toffee flavor with a chocolatelike finish (but still dry). Good stuff if you like it; may be a bit overpowering for the uninitiated. Try it and if it is too much for you to enjoy "neat," try it mixed with a lager.

GUINNESS EXTRA STOUT (draught)—almost black, certainly opaque unless you have a very powerful light source, creamy head, heavy-bodied, complex spicy aroma, less carbonated than the bottled version, smooth, mellow, extremely well-balanced, head lasts to the bottom of the glass.

GUINNESS CREAM STOUT—extremely deep brown, very little CO_2, strong burnt malt flavor, bitter and flat, very harsh.

HARP LAGER (Harp Lager Brewery)—deep gold color, pungent hop aroma, flavor very bitter, carries right through to the end. Bitterness may be a bit much for some American palates, but for those who prefer a well-hopped brew, try this one by all means. It is very satisfying. Harp Lager made its appearance in 1960. It is produced in Ireland, England, and Scotland.

HARP LAGER BEER (Brewed in Ireland, exported to Canada; 4.8 percent)—pale gold, lovely well-hopped aroma, small bubble carbonation, bright strong hop flavor, good balance, more hops than malt, a very good brew.

Jarvis Canning Co., Ltd.
(Bedford)

KELLERBRAU LAGER—pale gold, highly carbonated, chicken manure aroma, slightly salty-sour flavor, fades out to nothing, must have been an old sample. Probably made by Charles Wells Ltd.

177

James J. Murphy & Co., Ltd.
(Lady's Well Brewery, Cork)

Firm established in 1856.

MURPHY EXPORT STOUT—opaque black with red tone when held to strong light, faint sweetness in back of a generally sour and dry nose, flavor dry up front, sour at end, a bit out of balance.

The Old Brewery
(Tadcaster)

This brewery, established in 1758, is the oldest one in Yorkshire.

SAMUEL SMITH'S OLD BREWERY GOLDEN BROWN ALE—copperish color, burnt malt aroma of medium intensity with a touch of orange oil, sudsy texture, smooth fruity-toffee flavor, mellow on the tongue, well-balanced, pleasant appetizing finish. A good-tasting brew. It is labeled "strong brown ale" on the can with a "golden brown ale" sticker attached. Not presently available in U.S.

SAMUEL SMITH'S OLD BREWERY PALE ALE—pale copper-gold, copper-colored foam, lovely roasted malt and molasses aroma, big hop flavor well-supported with roasted malt, big body, tiny bubbles. A lovely brew. The importer, Merchant du Vin, designed an attractive clear Victorian-style bottle. In its taste description, it suggests an aftertaste of watermelon. The brew is krausened and lagered five weeks in wood casks. It is endorsed by CAMRA, the Campaign for Real Ale, a group in England that supports the brewing traditions of an earlier time. 4.7 percent alcohol by volume.

SAMUEL SMITH'S NUT BROWN ALE—red-brown, complex sweet toasted malt and apple-peel aroma, medium body, big complex ale flavor, slightly sweet finish, dry malt aftertaste.

SAMUEL SMITH'S OATMEAL STOUT—almost opaque red-brown, delicate sweet aroma, rich, full-bodied, well balanced, fairly dry up front, sweetest at finish, soft and smooth, no bite whatever; a delightful stout with a sweet aftertaste of medium duration; oatmeal and barley malt are used.

TADDY PORTER—brilliant deep red-brown, generous brown head, complex dry coffee bean aroma, dry and rich

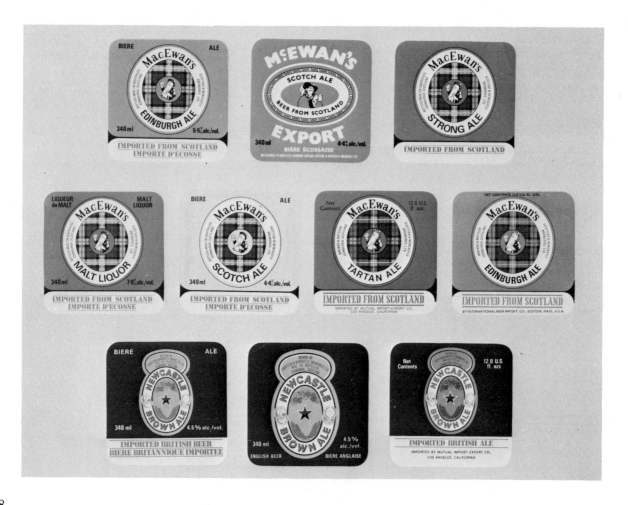

clean malt and hop flavor with a mochalike background, delicious and satisfying, clean dry finish and long, long aftertaste. The head stays on right down to the last drop. This is one of the best of the recent imports, an outstanding brew. It is top-fermented much in the same way as porter was 200 years ago.

James Paine Brewery Ltd.
(St. Noets)

PAINE'S PALE ALE—tawny gold, good hop aroma, light body, light watery flavor, bready and dull.

G. Ruddle & Co.
(Oakham, Rutland)

RUDDLE'S COUNTRY ALE—medium tawny brown color, pungent malty nose, sour taste with a bitter finish. Not one of the winners.

Scottish and Newcastle Breweries, Ltd.
(Edinburgh)

William MacEwan started this firm in Edinburgh in 1856. He was convinced that there was both a home and an export market for high quality Scottish ale. By 1900, MacEwan was producing nearly ninety percent of all the beer consumed in northeast England and had a rapidly growing export trade.

Today, MacEwan's Brewery, still located on the original site, produces over a million barrels annually. MacEwan's is now joined in the Scottish and Newcastle Breweries, Ltd., by Wm. Younger & Co., Ltd. (since 1931), and the Newcastle Breweries, Ltd. (since 1960). The product line includes some of the finest brown ales found in the world; fortunately, they are readily available in the U.S. and Canada.

Father MacEwan, mainstay of the MacEwan labels with his traditional Scot's garb and tartan background, is being replaced by a cavalier motif and less colorful label on the Scotch Ale and Strong Ale (formerly called Tartan Ale) packages. MacEwan's Extra Stout is no longer in production.

The MacEwan brews are presently imported only in 12-ounce bottles, but have been available in 12-ounce and 16-ounce (Newcastle Brown only) cans in the recent past.

MACEWAN'S SCOTCH ALE—deep-hued amber, creamy texture with a good foamy appearance without being highly carbonated, heavy malty aroma with some piquancy, big-bodied, distinctive mealy-malty taste with some bitterness for zest, a solid big-flavored beer with a good finish and lingering aftertaste. An excellent brew.

MACEWAN'S TARTAN ALE—dark brown with red hues; again creamy textured, but with less foam and head, some family resemblance to Scotch Ale except that the flavor has more sweetness and more intensity, yet not cloying. It finishes well with licorice and malt and has a very long-lasting aftertaste. The balance on some samples has been questionable, but it is another fine brew from MacEwan.

MACEWAN'S EDINBURGH ALE—deep brown color, creamy texture, only medium to light head, faint, but richly endowed malt aroma that is unusually complex, beautiful roast-bacon flavor with a smoky aftertaste, an absolute delight that I found to be the perfect balance between the two ales reported above.

MACEWAN'S STRONG ALE—deep copper and gold color, clean delicate malty nose, rich full-flavored taste on the sweet side, but not cloying, very heavy body. This is the same brew as Tartan, but with a different label for markets outside the U.S.

MACEWAN'S MALT LIQUOR—label says 7.8 percent alcohol; extremely dark brown color, almost opaque, light toffee aroma, heavy body, rich very sweet flavor like Tartan only more so, bitter finish, toffee aftertaste. Available only in Canada.

NEWCASTLE BROWN ALE—medium brown with tawny hues or dark amber, equipped with a good head, but not as creamy a texture as the MacEwan's, nutty aroma, smooth and mellow with a good malty taste, just a touch of bitter in the finish, a long-pleasing aftertaste. Wonderful beer in the can or bottle; extraordinary on draft, but you have to go to Scotland or England for that treat.

MACEWAN'S STRONG MALT LIQUOR—6 percent alcohol, deep dark real brown color, slightly sweet toasted malt aroma, sweet caramel and toasted malt flavor with a touch of licorice, big body, lingering aftertaste, balanced all the way. Found in Canada.

YOUNGER'S KESTREL LAGER—bright amber gold, good hop and malt aroma, strong bitter hop flavor up front, touch of sour in the middle, finish soft and fairly pleasant, very drinkable brew. Appeared in mid-1979 in a 9-ounce can.

Eldridge Pope & Co., Ltd.
(Dorchester)

THOMAS HARDY'S OLD ALE—bright reddish-persimmon color, intense hoppy nose, very heavy body, robust malty-herbal hop flavor that carries through to a long rich finish, a luxurious richly flavored brew. Label says if stored at 55°F it will last 25 years. This sample was bottled on January 1, 1979, and not supposed to be ready before 1989. Pope produces this brew every 2-3 years. It is vat-matured for 6 months or more.

179

POPE'S "1880" BEER—copper orange; complex roasted malt, orange-peel, sweet malt and hop aroma; creamy licorice, molasses, and toasted malt palate; extremely complex, very dry, very long, very big.

T. & R. Theakston
(Masham and Carlisle)

The Theakston brewery dates back to 1827. The Masham brewery was built in 1875 and is still in use today. In 1974 a second brewery, located in Carlisle, was added. This brewery has a history dating back to the mid-eighteenth century. The product line includes Old Peculier (a strong traditional robust Yorkshire ale), Theakston, Light Mild, Pale Ale, Special Brown Ale, Cider and Theakston Bitter. Theakston uses traditional methods and ingredients, including the old variety of hop known as the "fuggle." Only Old Peculier is exported. Old Peculier refers to the peculier (sic) powers of the local ecclesiastical court.

THEAKSTON OLD PECULIER YORKSHIRE ALE—brown color, aroma of canned brown bread, dry malty molasses taste, malty finish, light aftertaste. Canned in little seven-ounce tins and more rarely, bottles; this, we understand, is one of the "new-wave" beers made in the style of the traditional, old (rather ancient) English brews. Have tasted a number of these and found them quite variable. When fresh, it is excellent of type. It is endorsed by CAMRA, and was voted Britain's strongest ale. The recipe is unchanged from 1837.

THEAKSTON BEST BITTER ALE—tawny gold, fragrant hop aroma with a touch of apple cider, light carbonation, good malt and hop flavor, good balance, bitter finish, long aftertaste; comes in a big plastic screw-top bottle that may not hold the carbonation sufficiently.

Daniel Thwaites and Company, Ltd.
(Blackburn)

Firm established in 1807.

BIG BEN ENGLISH BEER—tawny gold, clean malt and hop aroma with toasted malt background, pleasant and clean tasting, but has little depth, flavor is lightly of toasted malt with a sort of "ashy" nature.

Tollemache and Cobbold Breweries Ltd.
(Ipswich)

Founded in 1723.

TOLLY ORIGINAL PREMIUM ALE—bright pale copper, toasted malt aroma, strong toasted malt flavor, medium body, intensity eases toward finish, sharp and sour aftertaste, a bit coarse.

Vaux Brewery
(Sunderland)

The Vaux Brewery was established in the late nineteenth century. The Double Maxim recipe was named and brewed to honor Sunderland's Maxim Gun Detachment, led by Major Ernest Vaux in 1899 during the Boer War.

VAUX DOUBLE MAXIM SUNDERLAND BROWN ALE—copper-orange, mild hop and strong malt nose, good hops on palate, a little sour tasting at first, but good in middle and finish, sour aftertaste, weak body for a brown ale. Vaux is the number-two-selling brown ale in England. It is top-fermented and produced from the dark Vienna malts.

S. H. Ward & Co., Ltd.
(Sheffield) (Subsidiary of Vaux)

WARD'S ENGLISH ALE—copper-orange, small bubble CO_2, mild sweet ale nose, lots of flavor but light body, pleasant taste, best in the finish, slightly sweet malt aftertaste, lacks depth. 4.9 percent alcohol by volume.

WARD'S GOLDEN ALE—bright copper-orange, faint hop nose with sweet ale background, good body, smooth, mild sweet ale flavor, small bubble CO_2, no offensive features, no raves, but very pleasant. 3.8 percent alcohol by volume.

Watney-Mann & Truman Brewers, Ltd.

(Norwich, Mortlake, London, Edinburgh, Manchester, Trowbridge, Halifax)

This brewer comprises nine regional companies: Watney Combe Reid, Truman, Ushers, Dryboroughs, Wilsons, Websters, Phoenix, Norwich, and Manns.

WATNEY'S BEER—pale copper, rich malt aroma, pungent smoky caramel flavor up front, softens in middle, hop finish, dry aftertaste.

WATNEY'S RED BARREL BEER (brewed and bottled for Watney's, Mortlake Brewery, London)—copper gold, toasted-malt aroma, flavor starts out strongly malty, but finishes sour, long aftertaste on the sour side. A much better product on draft.

WATNEY'S STINGO DARK ALE—opaque brown, treacle all-malt aroma with a sour component, taste of heavy molasses-malt that is a bit cloying, tenacious sweet malt aftertaste.

MANN'S, THE ORIGINAL BROWN ALE (brewed for Watney-Mann, Mortlake Brewery)—nut-brown color, good rich coffee aroma with burnt charcoal in back, lightly carbonated with very small bubbles, full-flavored with all-malt taste, no hops noticeable, smooth and mellow, good balance, slightly sweet finish. A delight, excellent of type, much like the "mild" of the British pubs.

Charles Wells, Ltd.

(Bedford)

GOLD EAGLE BITTER—tawny gold, beautiful big hop-malt aroma, good balance, bitter hop flavor with caramel aftertaste.

CHARLES WELLS LIGHT ALE—tawny gold, pine hops and barnyard aroma; hops in front, but background a distinctively unpleasant barnyard-chicken coop flavor.

CHARLES WELLS BOMBARDIER ALE—bright copper, big head, complex and elusive nose of flowers and hops, toasted malt flavor but with little depth, light body, slightly bitter aftertaste.

OLD BEDFORD ALE—deep brilliant copper, mild toasted malt aroma with a sour component, potent strong hop flavor with a good malt, alelike sweetness in middle, big body, intense finish, long aftertaste, perhaps a little too strongly flavored for most American palates.

Whitbread & Co., Ltd.

(Cheltenham, Durham, Faversham, Leeds, Liverpool, Luton, Marlow, Portsmouth, Romsey, Salford, Samlesbury, Sheffield, Tiverton, Wateringbury)

Whitbread & Co. was founded in 1742 and ranked second in London as early as 1760. Like the Bass family, the Whitbreads were active in politics. At the turn of the century, Whitbread was judged one of England's top half-dozen breweries and had a capitalization in excess of two million pounds sterling. Whitbread beers reached America as early as 1759, and have been, more or less, regularly available here since. All Whitbread products are made from pure British malt, without adjuncts, from British, German, Yugoslav, and Czech hops and from the firm's own strain of cultivated yeast.

WHITBREAD TANKARD LONDON ALE—tawny brown coloring, nose of caramel and yeast, fair to good balance, good malty flavor, short finish. A good, better than average ale that lets down only at the very end.

WHITBREAD ALE—deep tawny brown color, beautiful smooth rich caramel aroma, taste decidedly caramel, very pleasant and appetizing, finely balanced, long finish and aftertaste. Smooth and mellow.

WHITBREAD BREWMASTER—brown gold, highly carbonated, malty aroma and flavor, neutral finish, lacks balance.

MACKESON STOUT—extremely deep brown color, almost opaque, rich malty aroma, heavy body, syrupy, rich malty flavor like a coffee beer and a thick one at that. An excellent stout. Guinness's greatest rival and the preference of many. If you like stout, you must try this one.

GOLD LABEL NO. 1 SPARKLING BARLEY WINE—orange rose color, sweet candy-apple nose, assertive aroma and flavor, tastes like a powerful sweet cough medicine, "puckery" on sides and back of tongue, bitter aftertaste. This demands an acquired taste.

MACKESON TRIPLE STOUT—extremely deep opaque brown, roasted malt aroma, sweet malt flavor, rich tasting, big body, quite drinkable for its heaviness.

CAMPBELL'S CHRISTMAS—medium deep copper, big sweet rising malt nose, rich, complex, intensely flavored, delightful sipping beer made for the Belgian market, rated Cat S. A must for series beer drinkers. The Campbell name comes from a firm, Campbell, Hope and King of Edinburgh, bought by Whitbread in 1967 and shut down.

Fiji

Carlton Brewery (Fiji), Ltd.

FIJI BITTER BEER—cloudy tawny, no aroma to speak of (maybe the faintest suggestion of something apple-like), flavor starts out slightly malty with a faint fruit (cotton candy) background, weak wood pulp middle flavor, fades to a grainy finish. Imported by South Pacific Suds!

Finland

The climate of Finland, like that of Sweden, is not conducive to growing barley because of the severe night frosts. Nevertheless, a small brewing industry thrives producing some very fine products that are exported widely.

Osakeyhtio Mallasjuoma, Inc.
(Lahti, Heinola, Oulu)

Mallasjuoma claims its waters spring from inside gravel eskers formed during the glacial period. They say it is the finest filter known.

FINLANDIA GOLD FINEST FINNISH EXPORT BEER—lovely malty aroma, pleasant malty taste, excellent balance, plenty of hop character without being bitter, good, long aftertaste with only the slightest hint of bitterness. An excellent brew. A pleasure to sip for its complexity of flavor.

FINLANDIA LIGHT EXPORT QUALITY BEER—bright tawny gold, mild hop aroma, hoppy flavor, but shallow and unbalanced, sour finish. This was a sample freshly arrived in the U.S., but it must have been mishandled since the Finlandia Gold was so good.

ERIKOIS EXPORT OLUT IVA LAHDEN—cloudy and tawny, roasted malt toffee-molasses aroma, toasted grainy flavor, very pleasant despite some imbalance at the finish. Class IV is 4 to 4.5 percent alcohol by weight. Other classes are I, 2.25 percent; II, 2.25 to 3 percent; and III, 3 to 3.7 percent.

Hartwell Co., Inc.
(Kaarina, Turku, Vaasa, and Karelia)

KARJALA EXPORT BEER—deep tawny gold, fine hop aroma, sprightly hop flavor, big body, spicy finish, very satisfying and very filling.

Sinebrychoff Brewery
(Helsinki)

This brewery, the first founded in Finland, was established by the Sinebrychoff family in 1819 when Finland was part of the Tsarist Russian Empire. "Koff," as it is popularly known in Finland, survived a national prohibition from 1919 and 1933 and today, with the Porin Olut Brewery, commands 26 percent of the Finnish market.

KOFF FINNISH BEER—bright gold, bright hoppy nose, big hop flavor, good balance, a little edge to the finish, long, long hop aftertaste. Hops aplenty for those who dote on them.

KOFF IMPERIAL STOUT—top-fermented, 5.5 percent alcohol, very deep brown, almost opaque, caramel and hop aroma, dry rich flavor, lots of hops on the palate and also a lot of malt, bitter and dry finish with a touch of something like ginseng (medicinal-herbaceous), neutral aftertaste.

France

France commenced brewing malt beverages very early. In the days of Julius Caesar the ancient Gauls brewed a beverage similar to the white beers that afterward were made from wheat and oats. In the eighth and ninth centuries the subject of brewing received royal notice. Charlemagne and his son, Louis de Debonnaire, enforced regulations regarding the monastic beers, fixing, in some cases, the amount of grain to be used and encouraging the making of malt liquors in moderate quantities because of the high price of wine.

Hops were cultivated in France even in the time of Pepin the Short, father of Charles the Great; a certain paper referred to the transfer of a field of hops to the Abbey of St. Denis in 768. Hops, however, were not with certainty known to be in use in French malted liquors until the thirteenth or fourteenth century. At that time the brews were called *godale, goudale,* or *servoise.* The word *bière* does not appear until near the middle of the fifteenth century. The brewing industry is believed to have spread from the Low Countries to France via Normandy and thence to Paris about the eleventh or twelfth century. Despite their avowed preference for wine, the French rank seventh in world malt beverage production.

Alsace-Lorraine constitutes historic ground in French brewing with important breweries founded as early as 1259. Much of the beer exported from France to the U.S. today is brewed in that region.

Brasserie/Bräuerei Adelshoffen
(Strasbourg, Schiltigheim)

ADELSHOFFEN BIÈRE SPECIALE D'ALSACE—Cat I, deep yellow with some particulate matter, sweet fruity-malty aroma with a touch of hops, a very complex flavor of fruit and faint hops, not dry, somewhat wine-like, interesting, with a roasted malt finish.

ADELSHOFFEN TRADITION—medium deep gold, very pleasant fruity aroma, light body, pleasant slightly burnt fruit flavor, not much depth, pleasant finish and a short aftertaste.

ADELSCOTT SMOKED MALT LIQUOR—bright orange, butterscotch, and sweet smoky barbecue aroma; smoky sweet malt palate, light body, very pleasant and very drinkable. Made with 100 percent peat-smoked malt, the same kind of malt as used in making Scotch whisky.

Brasseries Kronenbourg, S.A.
(Strasbourg)

This firm dates back to 1664, founded by the Hatt family, which still manages the firm for BSN-Gervais Danone, a food and beverage conglomerate. Its brews are widely available in the U.S. and Canada, especially since 1980 when it decided to compete with Heineken for the lead in sales in the New York City area.

KRONENBOURG 1664 IMPORTED BEER—medium gold color, light malty aroma, almost fruity, vinous flavor, light hops in the finish.

KRONENBOURG 1664 DARK BEER—deep copper, extremely light malt aroma, dull malty flavor, watery, salty birch-beer finish, dull aftertaste.

L'Alsacienne de Brasseries, S.A.
(Schiltigheim)

This brewery is part of a merger of four breweries called Albra, which in 1972 was taken over by Heineken.

MÜTZIG EXPORT BEER—pale gold, odd intense perfumy pine aroma, flavor of hops and wood pulp, weak body, wood pulp finish and aftertaste.

Brasserie Meteor
(Hochfelden, Haag-Metzger & Cie., S.A.)

METEOR PILS BIÈR DE LUXE—cloudy pale yellow, faint pilsener nose, small bubble carbonation, hops dominate the crisp flavor, clean hop finish. Seen only in Cambridge, Massachusetts, at Cave Atlantique; may be a unique import by that firm.

Brasserie du Pêcheur
(Schiltigheim, Brasserie Mattiere du Pêcheur, S.A.)

FISCHER GOLD LA BIÈRE AMOUREUSE—sweet fruity aroma, fairly intense, sweet vinous malty flavor, long malt finish, a fairly good beer of the winy type.

FISCHER PILS FRENCH BEER—light vegetal aroma, pale color, rusty metal (ferruginous) and vegetable taste with excessive bitterness especially toward the finish.

FISCHER LA BELLE STRASBOURGEOISE—malty grainy aroma, flavor improved as it slid across the tongue, metallic finish. Very attractive package.

Brasseries Pelforth, S.A. (Brasseries Pelican)
(Lille)

PELFORTH PALE BEER—LA BIÈRE BLONDE DE FRANCE—deep gold, good malty nose, very nice malty hop flavor with excellent balance, sweet malt finish that is pleasant, but would be better if drier.

GEORGE KILLIAN'S BIÈRE ROUSSE (Red Ale)—color of deep cherry (orange brown), cloudy hoppy aroma with high malt content, molasses and caramel in there as well, good balance with hops starting off the flavor and roasted malt ending it, dry, big-bodied, good balance, small bubbles, clean dry aftertaste, a fantastic brew! This top-fermented brew is supposedly the same as that brewed by master brewer George Killian of Enniscorthy, Ireland in 1864.

Schutzenberger Brewery
(Schiltigheim, Alsace)

SCHUTZ PILS LUXE BIÈRE D'ALSACE—tawny gold, fair to good hop-malt aroma, bitter taste very good up front, good malt in the middle, first sip finishes sour and bitter, second sip is better, sips thereafter are fine, sour aftertaste that is unpleasant can be avoided by steady drinking. This eventually will catch up to you.

SCHUTZENBERGER JUBILATOR FRENCH BEER—pale yellow, good hop nose with a touch of sweetness, sharp palate that is sour at first, then slightly sweet at finish, complex, dry aftertaste.

Societe Européenne de Brasseries
(Sevres)

SKANSEN SPECIAL LAGER—cloudy yellow with a brown tinge, roasted malt aroma with a touch of skunk, sweet toasted malt flavor, a spicy hot taste at the finish.

GOLD de KANTERBRAU BIÈRE SPECIALE—yellow gold, malty aroma, sweet alelike up front, then palate turns to roasted malt with a sharp hop background, a little oxidized, long hop and roasted malt aftertaste, balance between the bitter and sweet components seems a bit off and it changes back and forth as to which is the more intense.

Union de Brasseries
(Paris)

Union, a subsidiary of Brasserie et Glaciers de L'Indochine, was founded in 1954 and is France's largest brewery, with five major brewing plants and two bottling centers. Their brews are filtered rather than pasteurized.

"33" EXPORT BEER—more than 4 percent alcohol, deep bright gold, medium carbonation, clean bright malty aroma with good hops and some yeast, big flavor with lots of hops and loaded with character, hops in front, malt in back, good body, sour malt finish, balanced, well-hopped aftertaste. Very good beer, wakes up your palate. Americans in Vietnam were familiar with this beer, locally made in Saigon.

SLAVIA EXTRA DRY—deep tawny gold, sweet fruitlike aroma with a touch of something spicy like woodruff, big toasted malt and hop flavor, long aftertaste.

ROEMER PILS—"an Alsace tradition since 1824," deep yellow with some particulate matter, touch of skunk in an otherwise hoppy aroma, sour tart flavor with a medicinal background, long aftertaste marred by the dominance of the more unpleasant flavors.

PORTER 39 (made at St. Amand-les-eaux)—deep red brown, clean sweet fruitlike aroma with a touch of banana oil (amyl acetate), sweet burnt banana, roasted malt and horehound flavor, long finish and lingering aftertaste mostly of roasted malt.

"33" EXTRA DRY BEER BLONDE SPECIALE—higher alcohol than "33" (near 5 percent), deep gold with a touch of amber, bright well-hopped aroma, big flavor, mouth filling, good hops and plenty of toasted malt, complex with a touch of sweetness, well-balanced, a beer you can sink your teeth into. For those who say the French can't make beer, try this one.

"33" RECORD BEER—cloudy deep yellow, clean sweet malty nose with some hops, big rich sweet malt flavor with good hops, pleasant, dry finish with a touch of hop bitterness, good aftertaste finish. Also a fine brew, much like the "33" above. Could be another label of "33" Export.

PANTHER MALT BEVERAGE—1 percent alcohol, bright amber color, nice malty-beery aroma, feels like soda pop in your mouth, but the flavor is cereal grain and there is a bit of sharpness in the finish.

PANACH' BEER—pale gold with a slight brownish tinge, tuna salad aroma, citron soda pop flavor, somewhat like a lemonade or citron presse found in France, but not much of a beer.

Brasserie St. Leonard
(St. Leonard/St. Martin, Boulogne)

BRASSIN de GARDE de SAINT LEONARD—bright

peach color, very faint slightly toasted malt aroma, light toasted malt flavor, medium carbonation, a touch of hops in the finish. Labeled French malt liquor, it is winelike without being winy. Available in a champagne bottle with a wired-down cork.

Brasserie Nouvelle de Lutèce
(Paris)

Lutèce is one of France's few independent breweries and the only remaining brewery in the city of Paris. It was founded on its present site in the year 1313. Its brew uses choice malts from Gatinais and Champagne and is bottom-fermented with hops from Alsace and Burgundy. It comes in a 75 cl bottle that looks like a Burgundy wine bottle. It is recommended for robust French cuisine, especially that with garlic.

LUTÈCE BIERE de PARIS—beautiful brilliant pale copper color, light fragrant toasted malt aroma, light body, delicate toasted malt flavor with a caramel background, balanced hoppy finish, long dry aftertaste. Reminds me of a barley wine, only with a great delicacy and finesse that an English barley wine lacks. A marvelous brew, beautifully balanced. Recent labels have dropped the "Lutèce."

Gambia

Banjul Breweries, Ltd.
(Banjul)

JULBREW LAGER—cloudy yellow, old caramel nose, flavor of malt, caramel, paper, and linseed oil; the sample was too old to be fairly judged. This brew was imported for a very short time by a Washington, D.C. area importer, one shipment that was not repeated.

Germany

The history and the art of beer making in Germany are the history and art of beer making in the world. Without question, Germany is the beer center of the world and has been for centuries. Even where competitors rose to challenge German leadership in the trade, it was usually transplanted Germans who did so. As a race, the Germans are hardworking perfectionists who preserve quality at all costs. This is evident in their beer and the strict laws regulating production which are continually enforced to ensure that the highest standards are maintained. The fact that a beer is German-made is a considerable guarantee that it is a quality product.

The German government's laws regulating beer making were laid down in 1516 by Duke William IV of Bavaria. The "Reinheitsgebot" forbade using any ingredient other than barley malt, hops, yeast, and water. These laws are regarded as the standard of excellence in brewing throughout most of the world, and in a great many countries they are observed by choice, if not by law. German brewers are not bound to the purity laws for export, but most hold to them out of pride.

Beer is a household word in Germany. Hundreds of songs hail that great traditional drink and one such song proclaims that there is no beer in heaven, so you had better get all you can while here. Frankly, if there is no beer in heaven, then it is a poor place to send a German when he dies. He might well consider the offerings of the other place.

The local beers of Germany are a delight to sample. Distinctive regional tastes vary from town to town, each town better than the preceding (you see, the best beer in Germany is the one in front of you). As towns are only about twenty kilometers apart and most of them have their own breweries (there are still over fifteen hundred breweries in Germany), one could devote a lifetime to tasting the local brews of Deutschland.

Beer is served at all restaurants and hotels, even at those establishments that are not permitted to serve (or choose not to serve) wine or hard liquors. Everyone drinks beer with lunch or dinner, usually straight from the keg. Nearly 30 percent of all German beer sold is draft beer. The main meal of the day is served at noon, when a two-hour lunch break takes place. Dining is leisurely and the period is devoted solely to that function. No one hurries about running lunchtime errands for none of the stores or businesses are open then. The owners and clerks are at lunch.

Supper is a light meal, usually some bread and wurst washed down casually with beer. This meal is even more casual than lunch for even more time is available to devote to it. In each establishment there is a large table traditionally reserved for the "regulars," who, in a small town with only one Gasthaus restaurant, probably include the mayor and the rest of the city fathers; they will hold a leisurely court over Krugs of the fine local beer and discuss matters of state.

This is not to say that there is no drunkenness in Germany, for when the Germans have their festivals, they eat, drink, and frolic with the same passion and energy that they apply to their industry.

Each September the rites of beer reach a peak with the annual Volkfests, the most famous of them being the Munich Oktoberfest. At a Volkfest, huge tents are erected by the local breweries and outfitted with long tables and benches; a bandstand is in the center. Beginning at about seven o'clock each evening, everybody gathers for a time of wurst, chicken, camaraderie, laughter, song, and enormous quantities of beer made especially for the occasion. For four hours (it rarely goes past 11 P.M. on a weekday) all the old songs are sung and the old toasts remembered and repeated, new toasts made, jokes and stories told and retold, and friendships made and remembered. Consequently, a little part of every non-German will forever be German.

The German attitude toward beer is best summed up by the beer code of Heidelberg University, beginning at paragraph 11: "Keep on drinking." The university's students had societies of drinkers and meted out punishment to offenders against the beer laws. More serious offenses were punished with beer excommunication, which deprived the offender of beer and the good fellowship that attended drinking. Such a disability could be relieved only by a drinking contest, where four tankards of beer must be emptied in succession (with five-minute intervals). Drinking alone was strictly forbidden. Even a solitary sip could bring beer punishment. Challenges of up to eight tankards of beer were not uncommon and drinking duels continued far into the night, every night.

The excessive use of alcohol as a social norm and form of entertainment was not greatly different from the practices of some groups in today's society, but for sheer quantity the German student of the nineteenth century (and well into the twentieth) is unparalleled. For all his excesses, he was at least civilized enough not to talk shop while drinking, a barbarian custom all too frequently encountered in our society.

Drinking in Germany, as in England and other parts of the world lacking the sorry effects of stigmatism, is done for enjoyment of the taste and the occasion and not to escape the troubles of life. The least desired state is to be drunk, for you will miss the fun.

For years Germany has been either first or a close second (to Czechoslovakia) in per capita consumption of beer. Only in the past decade has the rate slowed and although near the forty-gallon mark, the German beer industry is viewing the slowdown with alarm. For the first time ever, German brewers are using advertising to pick up slack in sales that has resulted in a 20 percent overcapacity in the industry.

The slump has been attributed to changes in taste, revised attitudes toward alcohol and the strict measures taken to curb drunken driving. One source even suggested that young Germans have abandoned beer drinking so that their tight-fitting American designer jeans (a big status symbol in Europe) will fit more comfortably. Whatever the reason, in the last ten years the number of breweries in Germany has shrunk from 1,815 to 1,400, which is still over half the breweries in the world.

Brauhaus Altenmünster-Weissenbrunn
(Altenmünster)

This brewery was founded in 1648 by Cistercian monks as part of their monastery.

ALTENMÜNSTER BRAUER BIER— deep gold, smooth complex hop aroma, small bubble CO_2, big hop flavor, creamy texture, slightly sour finish and aftertaste, could use more malt, but still very drinkable. Comes in 16-oz. bottles with a ceramic stopper (like Grolsch), 11.2-oz. "Michelob"-style bottles, 1-liter guild jugs, and 2-liter decanters.

Augustiner Brauerei, A.G.
(Munich)

The origins of this brewery go back to 1328 and to a cloister brew house of the Augustine monks. It passed out of their hands in 1803 and into the possession of the Wagner family in 1829.

According to a Connecticut distributor, the beer is not pasteurized and must be kept refrigerated. This has been confirmed by other sources with the added information that the beer is subjected to a filtering process to pass U.S. import requirements. It is an excellent beer when fresh. It is popular in German restaurants outside Bavaria that wish to add a prestigious Munich beer to their list.

AUGUSTINER BRÄU MUNICH EXPORT LIGHT BEER—a beautiful bright beer, very attractive in appearance, clean, but very light aroma, malty taste on the sweet side with only a delicate hop flavoring, clean and light finish. Considerably lighter in flavor than most quality German imports.

AUGUSTINER BRÄU MUNICH MAXIMATOR DARK EXPORT BEER—pale brown with copper tones, strong malty hop nose, rich complex malty flavor with plenty of zest and character, slightly bitter finish. A powerful full-flavored brew. Extremely good of type, one of Germany's best, but not one of the mellow Bavarian darks. This one has gusto.

Bavaria-St. Pauli Brauerei
(Hamburg)

GRENZQUELL GERMAN PILSNER—gold, good hoppy nose, very Germanic, lots of good barley-malt character, big well-hopped flavor, if you like your beer German and with gusto, try this one.

GRENZQUELL GERMAN DARK PILSNER—deep copper, good hop and roasted malt aroma, flavor like the aroma, but unexpectedly thin, touch of molasses, long good-tasting finish, no aftertaste.

JEVER PILSENER—bright gold with tawny hues, aroma is more malty than hoppy, fine small bubble carbonation, big-bodied, flavor starts out malty, but bitterness builds across the palate, bitter finish and lingering bitter aftertaste.

ASTRA ALE—pale amber, good malt aroma, pleasant malt flavor, but too sweet, even becomes cloying as you drink more of it.

ASTRA MEISTER BOCK—medium gold, good hop-malt aroma, but light, light body, light malt flavor, faint molasses aftertaste.

Brauerei Beck & Co.
(Bremen)

Beck & Co. produces a fine Bavarian-style light beer that has been widely available in the U.S. for several years. The light beers of Bremen are very similar to the light beers of Munich and several of them provide as much competition to Munich as does Dortmunder brew.

BECK'S BEER—pale gold color, mild malty nose, light-bodied, light-flavored, pleasant, finely balanced, lightly hopped, faint on finish and with little aftertaste.

BECK'S DARK BEER—medium, dark color, hoppy aroma, big flavor, but too harsh and the harshness follows through to a bitter aftertaste.

Brauerei Becker
(St. Ingbert)

BECKER'S EXPORT—medium brilliant gold, faint hops in the nose, highly carbonated, very bitter on the palate, softens a bit as you drink it and become used to the bitterness, strong hops in the finish and aftertaste.

BECKER'S PILS—pale yellow-gold with some particles, fairly big hoppy aroma, strong tart hop flavor, sour finish and aftertaste that is a bit too sour. Hops are good, but that sour ending is unfortunate.

Exportbierbrauerei Berliner Bürgerbräu
(Berlin, East Germany)

Established in 1869.

BERLINER PILS EXPORT—deep tawny gold, big hop nose, tart palate with tones of celery, medium body, long sour aftertaste, very tenacious and not likable.

TÜRMER GERMAN BEER—gold, fresh malt nose, medium to light body, fruity-malty flavor with a sour finish and aftertaste. Not bad but not likable.

Berliner Kindl Brauerei, A.G.
(Berlin)

BERLINER KINDL PILS GERMAN BEER—pale gold; hop and malt aroma, but more malt than hops; medium complexity, sour in middle, bitter in back; good with food, so-so by itself.

BERLINER KINDL WEISSE—yellow-gold, very foamy, interesting complex yeasty-wheaty-bready aroma, too sweet and aromatic up front, sour finish, long sour aftertaste.

Binding Brauerei, A.G.
(Frankfurt)

Established 1516.

STEINHAUSER BIER—bright gold, light hop nose with good malt in back, light body, smooth hop palate, good finish, fair balance, good and long aftertaste.

Bitburger Brauerei Th. Simon
(Bitburg, Eifel)

Firm established in 1817.

BITBURGER PILS—pale tawny gold, hop and good roasted malt nose with a slightly sour background, more hops than malt on the palate, good brew until the finish where the balance falls apart and the flavor becomes excessively bitter and sour. I have good reports on this brew, but several samples tried showed poorly.

Burger Bräu Bernkastel
(Bernkastel-Kues)

Firm founded in 1825.

BERNKASTELER PILS—pale gold, strong sweet hop aroma, malt up front on the palate but the hops dominate, balance between hops and malt not achieved.

Dinkelacker Wülle, A.G.
(Stuttgart)

The Dinkelacker family and beer go back to about 1600. The present house was established in Stuttgart in 1888 and is one of the largest breweries in Germany today. Each day almost fifty thousand cases leave the brewery for markets at home and abroad, including some five thousand restaurants and hotels.

Dinkelacker produces a light, a dark, and a bock for export and a pilsener, a lager, and a diet-pils (80 percent lower in calories). A Weiss beer (Weizenkrone) is produced for both markets.

DINKELACKER PRIVAT LIGHT—gold, complex malty hop aroma, great heft and plenty of zest, a beer with flavor, body, character, and reasonably good balance. Used to be labeled Light Extra C.D.

DINKELACKER BLACK FOREST LIGHT BEER— cloudy, blueberry pulp nose, sweet slightly off taste, dank finish. Only poor Dinkelacker found. Also, the only one found without the usual Dinkelacker label or brewery identification.

DINKELACKER BOCK C.D. EXTRA—dark and cloudy, big malty aroma and taste, heavy body, extremely rich and long aftertaste. A very, very good beer for those who like their Germans rich, full, heavy, and zesty.

DINKELACKER DARK IMPORT PRIVAT—the new label of Dark C.D. Extra, which was tasted just to check on the recipe; unfortunately, it was a bad bottle with a brown-orange color, slightly skunky aroma and a sour metallic taste and finish.

DINKELACKER DARK C.D. EXTRA—brown, big malty aroma, yeasty flavor, slightly sour finish with a medicinal nature, however, it was good, but the bock is better.

DINKELACKER WEIZENKRONE—slightly cloudy yellow color, huge head, pleasant light malt aroma, high CO_2 on palate, neutral sour taste with little duration.

DINKELACKER DARK BREW (MALT LIQUOR)—rosy brown, big roasted malt nose, pleasant roasted malt flavor, sour finish, good balance but lacks complexity.

Dortmunder Actien Brauerei/Dortmunder Hansa Brauerei
(Dortmund)

The older of these two firms was formed in 1860 and transformed into a stock company known as Dortmunder Aktien-Brauerei in 1872. The Hansa brewery was founded in 1901. In 1971 the two companies merged, but separate facilities have been maintained.

The Hansa beers reported below are made with very nearly identical recipes and from the same ingredients. Barley malt is obtained from German, Belgian, and French suppliers and the

hops are the German strains, Hallertau-Nordbrauer, Hallertau-Goldbrauer, and Tettnang. None of them showed very well.

DAB Meister Pils is available in cans, bottles, and four-litre cans of draught. It has been reviewed quite well at each appearance in taste trials.

In terms of sales, DAB products are the largest selling product line produced in Dortmund and the company can boast that, in Germany, DAB outsells Beck and Heineken combined.

DAB now also produces an Altbier, a top-fermented beer of golden brown color (from use of a darker malt).

DORTMUNDER HANSA IMPORTED GERMAN BEER—vegetable aroma, sour malt flavor, bitter finish. Not a good beer and not presently exported.

ALT SEIDELBRÄU (Dortmunder Hansa)—deep gold color, hoppy nose with sour malt in back, bitterness dominates throughout the taste, an unpleasant, unlikable harsh beer.

DAB MEISTER PILS (Dortmunder Actien)—clean and malty aroma, fresh hop and malt flavor with a lot of character and zest, a very good-tasting brew. It obviously has earned its reputation as the best-selling beer in Germany.

DAB EXPORT—medium deep gold, lightly hopped nose, heavy body, big flavor with both hops and malt, good balance, but not dry, sweet finish, bittersweet aftertaste.

DORTMUNDER HANSA EXPORT—deep gold, strongly hopped aroma, heavy body, big hop flavor that has long duration, hoppy finish, long hop aftertaste, good, but lacks balance.

DAB KRAFT-PERLE CEREAL BEVERAGE—dark red-brown, burnt sugar aroma, taste like fermented maple sugar with butter, a bit cloying. (Nonalcoholic.)

DORTMUNDER ACTIEN ALT—deep bright copper, sweet and sour malt aroma, watery light body, sour flavor, long sour and bitter aftertaste.

DAB ORIGINAL BEER—bright gold, lovely hoppy aroma, lively hop flavor, medium body, very tasty brew.

Dortmunder Union-Brauerei, A.G.
(Dortmund)

Combined with Schultheiss, Berlin, since 1972, Dortmunder Union-Schultheiss is Ger-many's largest brewery combine. Dortmunder Union itself was formed in 1873 as an amalgamation of several small breweries, the business being formerly conducted by W. Struck & Co. The Schultheiss Brauerei, A.G., of Berlin was the largest brewery in Germany at the turn of the century. Union is the largest selling brewer in Germany.

Dortmunder Union exports several of its excellent brews to America and Schultheiss provides its famous Berliner Weiss.

DORTMUNDER UNION SIEGEL PILS—pale yellow gold, clouds when too cold, good sour malt aroma with some hops in back, fine malt-hops flavors, very much like Urquell in style, a good European pilsener. Has plenty of character.

BERLINER WEISS SCHULTHEISS—pale cloudy white, foamy, typical yeasty aroma and taste, traditionally served with a syrup (preferably raspberry schnapps to my taste). This famous brew is strictly a matter of taste. With the Himbeergeist, other fruit syrup, or woodruff (as most Berliners like it), it is somewhat like a liqueur. Berliner Weiss is served in bowl-shaped stemware called a *molle*.

DORTMUNDER UNION PILSENER—fairly deep tawny gold, balanced toasted malt aroma, pleasant toasted malt flavor, low carbonation, light body, a little sourness in the back, but it doesn't mar the flavor, toasted malt carries into the finish and aftertaste, but the brew is light and not complex.

DORTMUNDER UNION BEER—deep bright gold, toasted malt aroma, toasted malt flavor, medium CO_2, medium body, good flavor, but not enough of it, very drinkable but lacks complexity and depth.

DORTMUNDER UNION MALT LIQUOR—bright tawny gold, lovely rich roasted malt aroma, big on the palate, especially good up front, sour hop finish; slight sour and metallic aftertaste at first, but as you drink it, the aftertaste and finish improve until, after a few sips, the metallic component is no longer there.

DORTMUNDER UNION SPECIAL—pale gold, intense complex malty aroma, good malt flavor strongly accented with hops, good balance, straightforward, good throughout, especially favored by those who like a hoppier brew. A highly rated light beer with strong flavor and a great deal of zest.

DORTMUNDER UNION LIGHT BEER (PILSENER TYPE)—bright gold, hops dominate aroma with a metallic background, light body, light flavor is mostly CO_2 with a touch of sour malt, palate is cleaner than the aroma, brief finish.

DORTMUNDER UNION DARK BEER—medium deep copper, outstanding malt and hop aroma, medium body, small bubble carbonation, pungent flavor is mostly malt, sharp hop finish, flat and dry aftertaste. Good brew especially with luncheon meats like salami.

Dortmunder Ritterbrauerei, A.G.
(Dortmund)

Since a letter forwarding labels from Dortmunder Union contained samples of labels from Ritterbrauerei, I learned that this brewery is now part of the massive firm of Dortmunder Union-Schultheiss.

DORTMUNDER RITTER BRÄU LIGHT BEER—deep yellow color, big hop-malt aroma, huge hop flavor, a hearty brew, pungent at the end. A good well-hopped beer, robust for those who like their beer extra zesty.

DORTMUNDER RITTER PILS—particulate matter in solution, sharp hop aroma, sour hop flavor, heavy vegetal malt background, finishes softly without bitterness. Reasonably good in a Czechoslovakian style.

DORTMUNDER RITTER BRÄU BOCK MALT LIQUOR—deep gold, beautiful toasted malt and hop aroma, very complex, delicious, rich toasted malt flavor, excellent balance, a blockbuster, long, long aftertaste.

DORTMUNDER WESTFÄLIA SPECIAL—faint malty hop aroma, metallic overtones, sour metallic taste, iodine finish.

DORTMUNDER WESTFÄLIA EXPORT BEER—bright pale gold, light nose with medium hops, sweet in the middle of the palate after a neutral start, bitter finish and aftertaste.

GASTHAUS SPECIAL—medium gold, creamy, nice mild hop aroma, big body, good hop flavor, but monolithic, no aftertaste to follow a brief finish.

DORTMUNDER RITTER DARK—medium deep brown, heavy malty aroma with complex vegetal components (like celery and sage), some hops noticeable in the flavor, but the sour malt taste dominates to the detriment of the overall effect. Not a bad beer, but there are plenty more that are better.

DORTMUNDER RITTER EXPORT—deep gold sauerkraut aroma, strange bitter sour-sweet vegetal palate. Bad sample.

Dortmunder Stifts Brewery
(Dortmund)

DORTMUNDER STIFTS PREMIUM GERMAN PILSNER—bright gold, light sour hop aroma, sour and hoppy palate with the sourness and bitterness clashing, highly carbonated, harsh brew, aftertaste dry and reasonably pleasant.

Dressler Brauerei G.m.b.H.
(Bremen)

DRESSLER EXPORT BIER—yellow gold, slightly clouded, skunky aroma, sour taste. This sample was so poor I sought out additional bottles. The best found was not too good, being bitter in front and salty sour in the back. Not likable even at its best. According to industry sources, Dressler is closely affiliated with the Holsten Brauerei.

Privat-Brauerei Eder
(Grossostheim)

Firm founded in 1872.

EDER PILS—cloudy yellow, light hop aroma, flavor is all hops up front and sour malt in back, but has a fair balance. Sample was a bit old for fair assessment.

Erste Kulmbacher Actienbrauerei, A.G.
(Kulmbach)

EKU BAVARIA SPECIAL RESERVE—bright gold, complex hop and malt nose, hops more than malt, medium body, what malt there is shows best in the finish, little aftertaste. An ordinary German brew. 4.6 percent alcohol by volume.

EKU KULMINATOR URTYP HELL 28 MALT LIQUOR—deep orange-brown, strong and complex malt aroma, incredibly intense flavor, a good flavor, but there is so much of it that it is overwhelming, high alcohol, long aftertaste, more winelike in nature, but it is a beer. This is the famed Kulminator which reputably has a 13.2 percent alcohol level (by volume). The 28 refers to the density. It is brewed with pale malts, but the enormous concentration of fermentable solids produces the deep color and intense malty palate. The high density is achieved by partially freezing the beer so that the water can be extracted. It certainly is interesting and should be tried (with care, of course).

EKU BAVARIA DARK RESERVE—deep copper-brown, faint vegetal aroma, dry and dull brief sour finish, little aftertaste.

HOFBRÄU LIGHT RESERVE—tawny gold, big malty-hop aroma and flavor, hops seem to be a bit overdone, whole effect comes off clumsily, too much of everything except the balance and finesse, which are lacking.

HOFBRÄU BAVARIA DARK RESERVE—deep brownish orange, light malty aroma, strong malty taste, finish better than the start. An average beer, not up to the expected standards of a German export.

EKU JUBILÄUMSBIER—a superb *festbier*, bright tawny gold, appetizing malt and hop aroma that fills a room, marvelous malt-hop flavor that is initially sweet and finishes hoppy, dry aftertaste with a hint of toasted malt, good balance all the way through, excellent brew. 5.4 percent alcohol by volume.

EKU KULMBACHER EXPORT—brilliant gold, big head with small bubbles, absolutely beautiful fruity apple aroma, faint sweet fruity flavor which is badly marred by excessive carbonation, complex finish and aftertaste, but the components do not come together to provide the needed balance. 5.3 percent alcohol by volume.

EKU ALT BAYERISCHES HEFE-WEIZEN DUNKEL—cloudy light brown, really foamed up when poured, huge head, aroma like fermented wheat, touch of sweetness on the palate, but otherwise grainy; despite the foam producing an overabundant head, the carbonation left for the palate is excessive and mars the flavor. A fairly pleasant *weissbier* and the first dark one ever encountered. 5.3 percent alcohol by volume.

EKU PILS—medium deep gold, pleasant malty fruit-like aroma, a bit on the light side, bitter palate, poor balance.

KULMBACHER MAIBOCK HELLER BOCK—bright deep gold, creamy head, sweet hop aroma, huge body, complex malt and hop flavor; dry, yet has sweetness in finish; excellent balance; excellent brew. 7.7 percent alcohol by volume.

Erzquell Brauerei
(Erzquell)

ERZQUELL EDELBRAU BEER—deep copper-brown, light malty aroma, good CO_2, pleasant sweet malt up front, flat in middle, flabby finish, lacks depth and character. Label says it is an all-natural blend of light and dark half and half brewed for Erzquell Brauerei.

Privatbrauerei Euler, Gebr.
(Wetzlar)

STRASBRÄU PILSENER SPEZIAL HESSENLAND BIER—pale gold, yeast and malt aroma, small bubble carbonation, flavor mostly hops, complex but not well-balanced, a burnt flavor that shows up in the finish, dominates the aftertaste.

EULER LANDPILS—pale gold, lovely balanced hoppy aroma, hops dominate the palate, good body, sour hoppy finish, aftertaste a bit too sharp.

KLOSTER ALTENBERG KLOSTER BIER—bright gold, smoky toasted sour malt nose, slightly sour malt flavor with lots of hops, medium body, short aftertaste.

MAXIMILIAN TYP MUNCHEN HELLER BOCK—medium deep tawny gold, beautiful complex apple nose, lip smacking malt flavor, complex, a little on the sweet side, strong flavored but well-balanced.

Brauerei Felsenkeller
(Herford)

HERFORDER PILSNER (Real Original Lager Beer)—deep tawny gold, bright hoppy aroma, big sour hop palate, a bit too harsh, sharp finish metallic aftertaste, overdone.

HERFORDER PILS PREMIUM BEER—pale gold, faint malt and hop aroma with a trace of skunk, very light on the palate, slightly bitter aftertaste, not interesting.

Fürstlich Fürstenbergische Brauerei, K.G.
(Donauschingen)

The Fürstenberg tradition dates back to 1283 when Rudolf Von Hapsburg granted the Fürstenberg family the privilege of brewing beer.

FÜRSTENBERG PILSENER—aroma mainly malt, but here are some hops in back, flavor almost entirely hops, but yet not overly bitter, not complex at all, hops ease off toward the finish and aftertaste.

FÜRSTENBERG IMPORTED GERMAN BEER—deep bright gold, small bubble CO_2, nice even hoppy aroma with a touch of roasted malt, the malt is out in front of the hops on the palate and is done very well, good balance, complex and interesting, good finish and lingering aftertaste.

Hacker-Pschorr, A.G.
(Munich)

Hackerbräu originated with a brewery established on the site of an old brewing operation that dated back to the fifteenth century. Simon Hacker bought the plant in 1783 and in 1793 the Hacker firm was bought by Joseph Pschorr, the same year that he married Maria Theresia Hacker, Simon's daughter. In 1865 a large brewery was built by Matthias Pschorr and this plant was remodeled in 1881 when the stock company was organized.

The same Joseph Pschorr established the nucleus of the Pschorr Brauerei in 1820 and was succeeded in this venture by his sons and grandsons. Throughout the nineteenth century, the widely exported Pschorrbräu was famous not only in Germany, but throughout the world. That fame continues today.

Joseph Pschorr was Germany's most famous brewer in his time. He received many honors and was the only brewer to be elected to the Bavarian Hall of Fame in Munich, where his bust presides over the site of the Munich Oktoberfest. Well ahead of his time in the brewing industry, he created huge underground storage facilities, popularly known as "The Beer Fortress," which made it possible for beer to be brewed year round. On his deathbed, he called upon his two sons to choose, by lottery, who would run either of the two breweries in order to divide the inheritance into equal shares. Matthias became owner of Hacker and Georg became owner of Pschorr and they shared "The Beer Fortress" equally.

In post-World War II Munich, Hacker and Pschorr were two of the less famous breweries, but their products were well appreciated locally. As a tourist visiting the Oktoberfest of the early 1960s, I was pleased to find that their offerings were as satisfying as those provided by the more famous (and more crowded) Lowenbrau *festhalle.* In opinion, Pschorrbräu was slightly better than Hackerbräu and was my frequent companion at mealtime. It is still a good friend, for the current line of Hacker-Pschorr brews available in America is excellent and worthy of consideration.

Given the common origin of the firms of Hacker and Pschorr, their 1972 merger came as no surprise. It is a fitting combination in many ways.

HACKER EDELHELL EXPORT—medium hop aroma, good hoppy flavor with a sweet malty background, excellent balance, good body, a fine brew with lots of character and a long aftertaste. Very satisfying. One of the best beers I have ever tasted from a can.

HACKER-PSCHORR ORIGINAL OKTOBERFEST BIER BRAÜROSL-MÄRZEN—deep amber color, big hop nose with plenty of malt, big flavor to match the aroma, chewy, a beer of substance, big in all its features from aroma to aftertaste, yet magnificently balanced, closest thing to a

real Oktoberfest beer found in a bottle outside Germany. Excellent in all respects for those who dote on German beer. Don't miss it. It can also be found on draft.

HACKER-PSCHORR OKTOBERFEST MÄRZEN—pale copper, light malt aroma, bright malt-hop flavor, well-balanced, tasty finish, long aftertaste, very complex. Found in a German-style half-litre bottle.

HACKER-PSCHORR LIGHT BEER—pale gold, beautiful clean malt-hop aroma, big malt-hop flavor, very good balance, clean finish with some hops added to, but not marring, the finish. Another excellent beer. One of the best light German beers ever tasted in this country.

PSCHORR MUNICH (Malt Liquor)—bright copper color, caramel nose, no carbonation, heavy-bodied, winelike malt flavor, has "legs" like a wine; seems to be some hops showing in the finish and aftertaste, but it really is hard to tell. Because of no carbonation and a strong winy character, this beverage is not beerlike at all. If it was intended to have CO_2, it could be quite interesting.

HACKER-PSCHORR DARK BEER—medium dark brown color, malt-hop aroma with molasses in the background; malt flavor, but not heavy, finish sweet and a bit dull. Good, but not up to the excellence of other Hacker-Pschorr brews.

HACKER-PSCHORR WEISS—foamy pale yellow gold, yeasty aroma, medium body, sweet yeasty grainy dry flavor with a spicy smoky pine resin background, very pleasant served with a twist of lemon peel, which seems to enhance the flavor.

HACKER-PSCHORR MAIBOCK—brilliant deep gold, big smooth hop and malt aroma, good flavor, slightly unpleasant harshness overrrides in the middle palate, slight sweetness in the aftertaste. Decent brew but harshness is troublesome.

Henninger Brauerei KGuA
(Frankfurt)

Frankfurt's first beer was brewed in 1291. Some 350 years later, (1650), a small brewery was operated by the Stein family. A descendant of this family, Johannes Stein, built a brewery in 1869, which upon his death, was taken over by Heinrich Christian Henninger of Nürnberg. In

1880 this brewery was formed into a stock company known as Heinrich Henninger & Sohne. Today the brewery is the largest in Germany with an annual production of over 2 million hectolitres. Henninger is available in light, dark, light bock, dark bock, and a nonalcoholic beverage named Karamalz.

HENNINGER INTERNATIONAL—faint sweet aroma, highly carbonated unlike most German imports, dull malty flavor, too much on the sweet side, insufficient hops. This sample could have been bad, but the faults seem unlike those of mishandling.

HENNINGER BIER—deep gold, clean hoppy aroma with a touch of roasted malt in the background, good dry hoppy flavor, not bitter, excellent finish, low CO_2, mouth-filling, fresh tasting, excellent.

HENNINGER DARK BIER—rosy orange color, dry roasted malt nose yields some hops when swirled, good malt-hop flavor, complex, good balance, lots of character.

HENNINGER KAISER PILSNER—deep gold, slightly cloudy, delicious hoppy nose, excellent malt and hop flavor, extremely dry, pleasant dry finish and aftertaste, fine balance. Another very good brew from Henninger.

HENNINGER DOPPELBOCK DUNKLER BOCK—red-orange brown, aroma of hops, licorice, molasses, roasted malt, big flavor mostly malt, short finish, light on carbonation, good balance, excellent brew.

Brauerei Herrenhausen
(Hannover)

HERRENHAUSEN EXPORT LAGER BEER—medium gold, sharp malty-hop nose, flavor is malty up front, but the hops come through strongly by the finish, long malty aftertaste, very well-balanced, good brew.

HORSY DEUTSCHES QUALITATSBIER—bright tawny gold, big hop aroma with a perfumy malt effect, good balance in the nose, complex on the palate with the malt dominating, very flavorful, hops show well in the finish, extremely long malty aftertaste, a beautifully balanced brew. Horsy is a special label of Herrenhausen Export for the Buy-Rite liquor chain of New York and New Jersey.

Hofbräuhaus Munich
(Munich)

HOFBRÄU OKTOBERFEST BEER—amber color, big hop nose with plenty of malt, big chewy taste, a beer with heft and substance. Not a bad effort, but the lowest rated of the Oktoberfest beers available.

Holsten Brauerei
(Hamburg)

SENATOR URBOCK MAIBOCK—pale orange, smoky caramel nose, flavor to match, heavy body, long roasted malt aftertaste. Sounds better than it is.

HOLSTEN LAGER—yellow gold, aroma mostly of hops with a little malt peeping through, flavor too dominated by hops, even for those whose tastes run to German beers.

HOLSTEN CERVEZA TIGRE—light gold color, malty aroma, sour-bitter taste, sour finish, badly balanced. Seen only in Hispanic neighborhoods; probably aimed at that market.

EXTRACTO de MALTA HAMBURG MALT BEVERAGE—deep brown with very small bubble carbonation, heavy, even viscous, malty cereal aroma, stoutlike, molasses flavor, sweet but not cloying, some bitterness seeps through in the finish. Interesting.

HOLSTEN EXPORT—bright gold, big toasted malt aroma, some hops in the back of the nose, lots of hops in the flavor, but they are not sharp or unpleasant in any way, good toasted malt shows up on the palate for the finish.

Brauerei Hümmer
(Dingolhausen)

HUMMER GERMAN EXPORT BEER—cloudy tawny gold with particles, nose of mild hops over malt, sweet barbecue flavor, smoky salami, you can actually taste the meat; some hops in the finish, but they are too late.

Privatbrauerei Franz Inselkammer
(Aying)

CELEBRATOR DOPPELBOCK—deep red-brown, good toasted malt aroma, sweetness in back of nose, big body, complex overly sweet toasted-malt flavor, quite long on the palate.

Isenbeck Brewery
(Hamm, Brauerei Isenbeck, A.G.)

This brewery claims its origin dates back to 1645.

ISENBECK EXPORT DELUXE—pleasant sweet aroma, sweet-bitter flavor, all-bitter aftertaste.

ISENBECK EXTRA DRY—very mild beautiful smoky hop aroma, hops dominate the taste with a pulpwood-cardboard background, metallic finish.

ISI 08 SPECIAL BEER—medium to pale gold with some tawny hues, very little aroma; slightly beery, but mostly carbonation and paper, cereal grain aftertaste, a very low alcohol beverage.

Privatbrauerei Kaiserbrau
(Bamberg)

BAMBERGER KRONEN PREMIUM PILSENER BEER—bright gold, beautiful hop nose, bitter palate.

Kaiser Bräu
(Neuhaus)

Firm originated in 1522.

KAISER BAVARIA LIGHT BEER—medium gold, light hop aroma, austere, dry and well-hopped all the way through; tastes similar to Isenbeck Extra Dry, but with a little more pizzazz. Excellent among well-hopped beers.

Karlsberg Bräuerei
(Homburg)

KARLSBRÄU GERMAN LAGER—deep golden amber, some particles, faint hop and malt aroma, flavor of yeast and malt, some mild hops, sour finish and aftertaste. Probably a stale can.

WALSHEIM BEER—gold, beautiful malt-hop aroma, flavor starts out with candy-like sweetness, finishes as sour and metallic.

Kiesel Brauerei
(Traunstein)

KIESEL HEFE-WEISSBIER EXPORT—cloudy tawny brown, pleasant chocolate-almond ice cream and roasted wheat aroma, sharp wheaty hop flavor, tenacious, long on palate, good of type.

KIESEL PILS—gold, beautiful sweet malt nose with good hops in balance, touch of apple skin, big complex hop flavor backed with malt, rich and full.

KIESEL MÄRZEN—medium deep dull gold, light CO_2, pleasant malty aroma, tight grainy flavor, little hop character, short on palate, rather unexciting.

KIESEL EXPORT HELL—pale yellow, pleasant hop and malt aroma, medium body, good-flavored malt and hops, well balanced, nice hop finish.

KIESEL FESTBIER— pale yellow, good hop aroma, medium body, good flavor slightly on hop side, good balance, good hop and malt finish, long aftertaste.

KIESEL PERL-BOCK MALT LIQUOR DOPPELBOCK—medium yellow, malt aroma, heavy body, all-malt flavor, complex, big, winy, alcoholic, good but could use a touch more hops.

Klosterbrauerei Andechs
(Erling-Andechs)

Established in 1455, this monastery produces one of the world's finest beers. After all, it has had plenty of time to perfect the recipe. This brew is sold only in the area of the monastery, near Munich.

ANDECHS DOPPELBOCK DUNKEL—deep copper-

brown, rich malty aroma, flavor starts out strong and smooths out toward the finish, rich complex caramel-malt flavor, high alcohol (probably on the order of 10 percent), big body, soft finish, long rich slightly sweet aftertaste, marvelous balance, excellent brew.

Kloster Brauerei Hamm Gmbh.
(Hamm)

KLOSTER PILSENER—tawny gold, slightly smoky hop aroma, hop and sour malt flavor, malt aftertaste on the sour side.

König Brauerei, K.G.
(Duisburg)

KÖNIG-PILSENER—brilliant gold, lots of hops in the nose, smoothly balanced with malt, big hoppy flavor, malty finish, fairly well-balanced, lingering hop aftertaste.

Königsbacher Brauerei, A.G.
(Koblenz)

This brewery uses interesting winelike labels on its products, for example, *feinste bierqualitat* and *originalabfullung.*

KÖNIGSBACHER PILS—big malty aroma with vegetal backtones, semisweet vegetal malt flavor, long pleasant aftertaste. A decent brew, but too common for import prices.

KÖNIGSBACHER ALT—deep copper heavy roasted malt aroma, big malt flavor with plenty of hops, medium body, lots of character, good malty finish, short aftertaste, very drinkable.

Krombacher Privatbrauerei
(Krombach)

KROMBACHER PILS—deep brilliant gold, toasted malt aroma and palate, creamy, lightly carbonated, fairly intense flavor, good hop finish, complex aftertaste, good balanced brew.

Kulmbacher Schweizerhofbrau
(Kulmbach)

KULMBACHER SCHWEIZERHOFBRAU—bright gold, magnificent hop aroma, bitter hop flavor up front, malt in middle, slightly sweet finish. Good balance, comes in a bottle with a ceramic stopper, as does the excellent bock below.

KULMBACHER SCHWEIZERHOFBRAU BOCK—brilliant gold, lush hop aroma, good body, rich malt and hop flavor, extremely complex, marvelous balance, long, well-hopped finish, delicious. 6.8 percent alcohol. Not available on the East Coast.

Kuppers Kölsch, A.G.
(Köln)

KUPPERS KÖBES KÖLSCH—deep gold, beautiful aromatic hop nose, sweet hop flavor, faint touch of perfume in finish, long delicious aftertaste a little on the bitter side, complex and good.

Brauerei Robert Leicht, A.G.
(Stuttgart)

SCHWABEN BRÄU GERMAN PILSNER BEER—yellow-gold, light malt nose with little hops, dull malt flavor, bitter aftertaste.

Lederer Bräu
(Nürnberg)

LEDERER EXPORT—amber, good hoppy aroma well-backed with yeast and malt (appetizing and pleasant), big body; flavor of molasses, hops, and salt (each flavor separate, distinct, and strong), aftertaste mostly hops, finish of hops with some malt and hops, lacks harmony.

LEDERBRAU EXPORT LIGHT—pale yellow gold, very lightly carbonated, thin and watery, light and dull palate, very little aftertaste.

Lindener Gilde-Bräu, A.G.
(Hannover)

This firm gives 1546 as its birthdate.

GILDE RATSKELLER PILS-BEER—bright gold color, well-hopped nose, hops dominate flavor throughout, sweet malt comes through in the finish, dry aftertaste, lacks balance.

GILDE EDEL EXPORT—deep gold, slightly cloudy with tiny particles, good hoppy aroma, big body, big hop flavor, high in CO_2, hops fade at the finish and are replaced by malt, beautiful balance, marvelous brew.

Löwenbrau
(Munich)

Löwenbrau goes back to the year 1383, to a little brewhouse in Munich, supposedly producing beer by that name. It is known, for certain, that there was a brewery on the site producing Löwenbrau in 1818. It became a stock company in 1872 after many ownership changes. By the turn of the century, Löwenbrau was one of Germany's largest breweries with an export business as large as its domestic sales.

Löwenbrau was the largest-selling German beer in the United States until it was replaced by a domestic beer bearing the Löwenbrau name.

Munich Löwenbrau is now being made in Canada by Molson.

LÖWENBRAU MUNICH LIGHT SPECIAL—golden color, lovely hoppy aroma, enormously chewy beer with tremendous body and marvelous flavor, extremely well-balanced, deserving of a fine reputation. 5.5 percent alcohol.

LÖWENBRAU MUNICH DARK SPECIAL—deep brown with reddish orange hues, very clean malt aroma with some hops, strongly flavored with the malt intense up front, bitter finish, sour aftertaste. Good start, poor finish.

MUNICH OKTOBERFEST BEER—tawny color, beautiful hoppy aroma with a touch of caramel, big body, little too heavy, big hop flavor with a touch of toasted malt, long malt aftertaste. Introduced in a Boston test market in early 1980.

Privatbrauerei Gebr. Maisel
(Bayreuth)

HERRENBRÄU GERMAN PILSNER—gold, nice malt aroma with a touch of hops, decent hop-malt balance, unbalanced sour and bitter finish. A lovely brew until the finish. 4.9 percent alcohol by volume.

HERRENBRÄU GERMAN WEIZEN—pale gold with a dense head, pleasant smoky wheat aroma a bit like a day-old wet fireplace, sweet and sour wheat beer flavor, perhaps starting to turn; clean aftertaste on the sweet side. Weizen is wheat beer. 5.3 percent alcohol by volume.

HERRENBRÄU GERMAN LIGHT—fairly deep bright gold, fine hop and roasted malt aroma, very appetizing, tastes sharp and hoppy with the malt in behind, hop finish, long bitter hop aftertaste. 5.7 percent alcohol by volume. Advertised as a low-calorie beer, but the calorie content is not published.

FEST BEER (Christmas Beer)—bright orange-gold, *beautiful* well-hopped aroma with substantial malt and excellent balance, a delicious smooth brew, clean and well-balanced, good body, excellent flavor, touch of roasted malt in the aftertaste, great finesse. Excellent brew, one of the best I have ever tasted. 4.7 percent alcohol by volume.

MAISEL BAYRISCH—deep bright gold, foamy, complex hop aroma, hoppy complex palate, malt shows well in the finish (but briefly), short aftertaste.

MAISEL PILSNER—pale gold, light hop aroma, bright hop flavor, good tasting, well-balanced brew.

MAISEL MALT LIQUOR EXPORT—medium pale gold, light hop aroma, bright hop flavor, slight touch of cardboard (oxidation), otherwise similar to Maisel Pilsner.

MAISEL'S KRISTALLKLAR WEIZEN—deep bright gold, big head, tart nose, some lactic acid up front but softens toward finish, pleasant aftertaste. 5.3 percent alcohol by volume.

MAISEL'S HEFE WEISSBIER—pale cloudy orange, light pleasant malty aroma, sour banana flavor, long on the palate. 5.3 percent alcohol by volume. This brew is different from the above in that the yeast has not been removed.

Mönchshof Brauerei G.m.b.H.
(Kulmbach)

For many years Kulmbach has had a great reputation for the quality of its export beers. As early as 1831 Kulmbach beer was well known outside Bavaria. Kulmbach beer also was famous for its very high alcohol content. (The beer reputed to have the greatest alcoholic content—over 13 percent—is EKU Kulminator Urtyp Hell from Kulmbach.) The brewery producing these beers was founded in 1349.

The Mönchshof Brauerei produces a Pilsener, Diät-pils (lo-cal), Klosten schwartz (dark), Märzen (March beer), Maingold Export Hell (light), Heller Bock (light bock), Kolster-Bock Dunkel (dark bock), Kulm-Quell, Urstoff Starkbier (extra strong) and festival beers for Christmas, Easter, Kulmbacher Beer Week and the October Folkfest.

Only six Mönchshof beers are exported. The

Amber light and Kloster Bock bear a malt liquor notation on labels exported to the U.S. probably because of alcoholic content.

KULMBACHER MONKSHOF KLOSTER SCHWARZ BIER—deep copper brown, light roasted malt aroma, mellow and smooth, lovely malt palate, beautiful balance, no harshness, long on palate, super brew.

KULMBACHER MONKSHOF AMBER LIGHT BEER—gold color, fragrant aroma of roasted malt and hops, big body, big roasted malt and hop flavor with excellent balance, a definite winner and highly recommended.

KULMBACHER MÖNCHSHOF FESTBIER—deep gold, particulate matter in suspension, beautiful hop aroma, big well-balanced hop flavor, heavy body, long and delicious, smooth finish, long aftertaste.

KULMBACHER MONKSHOF DRY LIGHT BEER—pale gold color, good malty nose with hops in back, a touch of roasted malt, medium body, good toasted malt flavor, long on palate; hops appear in the finish, but overall, effect is dry roasted malt. Very good brew.

KULMBACHER MONKSHOF KLOSTER BOCK—medium deep copper color, big fragrant roasted malt aroma with good hops, big body, big flavor dominated by malt; a bit sweet for some palates, perfect for others, pleasant aftertaste, excellent finish, leaves your mouth feeling good.

KULMBACHER MONKSHOF DARK BEER—tawny brown with red hues, rich toasted malt aroma with some hops, rich full roasted malt flavor, long malty-molasses in middle and finish, excellent balance, a great beer with lots of character and fairly dry overall.

KULMBACHER MÖNCHSHOF OKTOBER BIER—brilliant gold, big toasted malt aroma with hops in back, light-bodied, light-flavored, finely balanced, slightly shallow finish. One could drink a lot of this brew.

KULMBACHER MONKSHOF HELLER BOCK (light Monk Brand Bock Beer)—medium to deep yellow, rising toasted malt and hop aroma, big body, flavor exactly like a German dark beer, powerful complex hop taste and finish, strong flavor with excellent balance. Heavy enough to limit your intake, good enough to enjoy regularly.

Tucher Bräu A.G. Nürnberg
(Nürnberg)

Firm established in 1672.

TUCHER UBERSEE EXPORT BEER—tawny gold, malty aroma, medium body, toasted malt and hop palate, sour hop finish, lightly sour hop and toasted malt aftertaste.

BRAUHAUS ROTHENBURG GERMAN PILSENER—gold, light hop nose, harsh hop palate, excessively bitter, sour metallic finish.

TUCHER GERMAN PILSENER—bright gold, nice hop nose with a little malt, big hop flavor dominates, lacks

balance, long bitter aftertaste.

Paderborner Brauerei G.m.b.H.
(Paderborn)

PADERBORNER LIGHT BEER (PB)—although not clear from the label, the general impression is that this may be a low-calorie beer that is less filling. It has a light malty nose, small bubble carbonation, a poor sour metallic taste and finish.

PADERBORNER PB REGULAR BEER—very deep gold, aroma mostly of hops, yeasty cereal flavor, mostly a malt finish, brief malty aftertaste.

PADERBORNER GERMAN PILSENER—fairly deep bright gold, mild malt and hop aroma, high carbonation, very hoppy flavor, sour metallic finish, poorly balanced.

Patrizier-Bräu, A.G.
(Nürnberg)

PATRIZIER EXPORT—deep amber with some particulate matter, lightly hopped aroma, medium body, good malt flavor with mild hops, malt and salt finish with a long aftertaste; not very exciting, but could be an old can.

PATRIZIER EDELHELL EXPORT—bright gold, good complex hop aroma, big hop flavor up front, a little malt shows in the finish, good balance, good brew, very complex, softens and gets better as you drink it, pleasant malt aftertaste.

PATRIZIER PILS—bright deep gold, toasted malt aroma with good hops, flat on the palate, some malt, some hops, but little character, very little aftertaste. Sample may have been slightly oxidized.

Paulaner Salvator Thomasbräu, A.G.
(Munich)

Aktien-Gesellschaft Paulanerbrau Zum Salvatorkeller was founded about the year 1634 as a cloister brewery of the order of Franz von Paula. In 1806, when the property of the religious orders had passed to the state, the ancient brewhouse was leased. In 1849 it came into the hands of the Schmeder family, whose descendants have since operated it. It became a stock company in 1886.

In 1928, it merged with Thomasbräu, one of the fine old smaller Bavarian breweries whose products were previously marketed mostly in the area of Bavaria, south of Munich.

PAULANER SALVATOR—gold color, toasted malt aroma, bitter toffee taste, faintly bitter finish, very short aftertaste. 7.7 percent alcohol by volume, a double-bock beer (reportedly the world's first).

PAULANER HELL URTYP EXPORT—rich malty aroma, strong hop flavor, sour finish that clashes with the bitterness of the hops, but pretty good even with that defect. Presently labeled Urtyp 1634 (see below).

PAULANER ALTBAYERISCHES—HEFE WEISSBIER—bright gold, clean wheat nose with a touch of yeast; bright, perky spicy dry flavor, big body, fresh tasting. Lemon twist enhances the flavor. 5.1 percent alcohol by volume.

PAULANER OKTOBERFEST BIER MALT LIQUOR—bright deep gold, well-balanced hop aroma, touch of roasted malt, toasted malt flavor, complex and balanced, lots of good flavor, good-tasting finish, long-pleasing aftertaste. 4.7 percent alcohol by volume.

PAULANER URTYP 1634—deep gold, toasted malt aroma, medium body, flavor much more malt than hops, lacks depth and character, slightly sour finish, 4.7 percent alcohol by volume.

PAULANER MÜNCHENER MÄRZEN—copper color, toasted malt aroma, creamy texture, rich toasted malt flavor, nicely balanced; hops in behind the malt, but they are there, good-tasting well-balanced finish and aftertaste, very refreshing and feels good in the mouth.

PAULANER ALT MÜNCHENER DUNKEL—deep reddish brown, very faint malt aroma; full-bodied, but the flavor is very light, what is there is lovely and malty, there is just too little of it; very little aftertaste. This brew and the Märzen above were further labeled malt liquor to satisfy California law, where they are marketed. 4.7 percent alcohol by volume.

PAULANER FEST-BIER MALT LIQUOR—bright gold, pleasant hop nose with a touch of cardboard, pleasant hop flavor, sample was a bit old but the brew felt good in the mouth, good long aftertaste.

PAULANER WIES'N-MÄRZEN MALT LIQUOR—labeled the "Original Münchener Oktoberfestbier"; slightly cloudy tawny-copper, delicate roasted malt aroma, pleasant toasted malt flavor that lacks depth, too much CO_2, dry finish and aftertaste.

PAULANER GERMAN PILS—slightly cloudy yellow-gold, small bubble carbonation, beautiful hoppy nose, delicious big hop flavor, metallic finish and aftertaste.

PAULANER MÜNCHENER UR-BOCK HELL MALT LIQUOR—amber gold, small bubble carbonation, toasted malt and good hop aroma, medium body, very good-tasting toasted malt and hop flavor, bitter up front, complex, plenty of toasted malt in the finish, long toasted malt aftertaste. Found in California, which explains the "Malt Liquor" on the label; any brew sold there with more than 4 percent alcohol cannot be labeled beer.

Brauerei Pinkus Müller
(Münster)

In the seventeenth century in Germany, each restaurant had its own (adjacent) brewery. Pinkus Müller was established as such a restaurant-brewery over 150 years ago and has been in continuous operation ever since. The brewery exists primarily to supply the restaurant. The brews are all natural and use only two-row barley malt.

PINKUS WEIZEN (WHEAT BEER)—very little head; faint, but pleasant wheat nose, clean wheat flavor, good balance, brief citrus finish, very drinkable, one of the most pleasant wheat beers sampled. Brewed with 30 pecent wheat and 70 percent malted barley.

PINKUS PILS—bright gold, pleasant hop aroma, good malt, flavor mostly hops with malt and carbonation coming in behind, highly hopped finish.

PINKUS MALZ BIER (MALT BEER)—dark brown, roasted malt aroma; thin, watery, sweet roasted malt flavor, mostly sweet and very clean tasting, sweet brief finish, nonalcoholic.

PINKUS ALT (PALE ALE)—deep tawny gold, strong hop and toasted malt aroma, toasted malt flavor with an acidic component, medium body, slightly off balance. Pinkus Alt uses all dark malts and is aged six months. The brewery refers to it as a high-acid beer, best served with a dash of raspberry syrup.

Bierbrauerei Wilh. Remmer G.M.G.H.
(Bremen)

BREMER DOM BRAU—pale yellow, sour vegetal nose that quickly fades leaving very little aroma at all, small bubble carbonation, extremely bitter palate, too harsh, unpleasant salty finish.

Radeberger Exportbrauerei
(Berlin, German Democratic Republic)

The only East German brewery to export to the U.S. since 1941.

RADEBERGER PILSNER—bright gold, medium to light hop nose with some malt, hoppy palate, hop finish; lingering hop aftertaste with very little malt, no complexity.

Reichelbrauerei Kulmbach
(Kulmbach)

KULMBACHER REICHELBRÄU HELL EXPORT DE LUXE—bright slightly tawny gold, big hoppy aroma with good malt, big hop flavor; malt comes through very nicely in the finish and stays through the long aftertaste.

KULMBACHER REICHELBRÄU FRANKISCHES URBIER—brilliant medium deep copper, pleasant toasted malt and hop aroma, big body, big malty flavor with a coffee background, good balance, long and dry on the palate.

KULMBACHER REICHELBRÄU EDELHERB PILS—bright deep gold, lovely flowery hop nose, bright hop palate, good balance, complex, malt shows in the finish, medium body, long duration.

Sailerbräu
(Martoberdorf)

SAILER PILS—pale gold, toasted malt nose, light body, toasted malt flavor up front, bitter hop finish and aftertaste.

SAILER WEISSE (YEAST IN BOTTLE)—pale slightly cloudy orange, huge head, good grainy nose, almost smoky, palate similar to other Weisse but sharper and lighter-bodied. Lasts longer but lacks the balance of the other.

SAILER WEISSE (NO YEAST IN BOTTLE)—foamy, pale golden orange, lovely malty grainy slightly sweet and piquant aroma, complex smoky malty flavor, slightly sweet finish, good balance, good duration. An excellent wheat and barley brew.

Schäffbrauerei
(Treuchtlingen)

SCHÄFF FEUERFEST EDEL BIER—cloudy tawny port color, beautiful roasted malt aroma, extremely heavy body, intense flavor of roasted smoked malt, very sweet, real sipping beer. Extremely complex like a dark beer liqueur, no carbonation. Described on the label as an apéritif beer. Also it is quite expensive at around $5 for an 11.5 oz. bottle.

Spaten Franziskaner-Bräu KgaA
(Munich)

This firm dates back to 1397, but it did not come into the possession of the Spaeth families until the early seventeenth century. From then "Spaethbrau" became a famous name in German brewing. In 1807 the brewery was bought by Gabriel Sedlmayr and has continued in that family since; it has been called the Brauerei zum Spaten since 1874. Spaten beers are now the largest-selling original Munich beers in America. The site of the present brewery dates back only to 1851. Spaten exports four brews to the U.S.: Munich Light, Munich Dark, Urmärzen Oktoberfest Beer and Club Weisse. The first three are available only in 12-ounce bottles, the Weisse comes only in a 17-ounce bottle.

Other Spaten beers for the domestic market include a Special Light, Altbier, Pils, Light Lager, Near Beer, Light Bock, Special Dark and Vitamalt.

CLUB WEISSE—big head, tawny gold, fresh clean nose only faintly of the wheat malt from which it is made, very fresh slightly grainy flavor, even-balanced, and refreshing; not long on the palate, but very good.

SPATEN OPTIMATOR (Doppelspaten)—very dark orange brown color with reddish hues, dry toast and malt aroma, heavy medium dry molasses and roasted malt flavor, sour malty finish and aftertaste, excellent balance. Really good when you are in the mood for it. Be careful not to overchill it; it tastes best closer to 50°F than to 40°F.

SPATEN MUNICH LIGHT—deep golden appearance, malty toffee aroma, heavy body, big bitter and malty flavor; a hearty brew with a long, long finish. May be overdone for some tastes, but perfect for those who like a heavy-handed bright hop character. Some packages of this beer have been seen in the U.S. labeled Spaten Gold. This is the German label.

SPATEN URMÄRZEN OKTOBERFEST BEER—gold-copper, good hop and toasted malt aroma, smooth and very well balanced malt and hop flavor, long on the palate, flavorful, complex, satisfying brew.

St. Pauli Brewery
(Bremen)

In the middle of the twelfth century, the monks of the Paulikloster began to brew "liquid bread" just outside the city gates of Bremen. By the mid-1800s, the St. Pauli Brewery was operating on the grounds of that monastery. Today, the brewery is located across the Weser River facing Bremen. Acquired by Beck & Co. following World War I, St. Pauli operates as a separate brewery sharing packaging, ware-housing, and shipping facilities with Beck and Hacke-Beck, two other Beck & Co. brewing operations.

The name "St. Pauli" was changed to "St. Pauli Girl" in the late 19th century when the label showing the traditional Bremen barmaid was created. The beer is available in Bremen and in over 80 countries around the world.

ST. PAULI GIRL BEER—pale color, faint malty-hop aroma, mild pleasant flavor with good hop-malt balance, slightly hopped finish, much like other Bremen area brews but somewhat milder and smoother.

ST. PAULI GIRL DARK BEER—deep brown; hops dominate the malty aroma, but the taste is heavy with malt, which comes as a sort of surprise after the hoppy aroma; good balance and a very appetizing finish and aftertaste. One of the most appetizing dark beers tasted, a nice compromise between the mellow types and the zesty well-hopped versions.

Privatbrauerei Jacob Stauder
(Essen)

STAUDER BEER—bright tawny gold, faint roasted malt nose and taste, little duration, light body.

Stern Brewery
Carl Funke, A.G.
(Essen)

Firm established in 1872.

STERN PREMIUM LAGER—bright gold, nice light malt and hop aroma, slightly toasted malt flavor, good balance, palate more malt than hops, good body, good malt finish, fairly long aftertaste.

Brauerei Stumpf
(Lohr)

ORIGINAL 1878 LOHRER BIER—golden amber, pleasant hop aroma, light malt flavor, hops show well in finish, dry slightly bitter aftertaste.

The City of Würzburg, West Germany, where the ancient Würzburger Hofbräu brewery brews beer for importation to the U.S. The Würzburger name is one of the greatest in German brewing. Würzburger beers date back to 1643.

This ancient wall encloses the Würzburger Hofbräu brewery in Würzburg, West Germany. One Würzburger Hofbräu product is imported to the U.S. by Anheuser-Busch, Inc.

Privatbrauerei Thier
(Dortmund)

The Thier Brewery was established in Dortmund in 1854. Fifth-generation family members own and operate the brewery, the only privately owned brewery in Germany. The product line includes Dortmunder Imperial Bier, a classic Dortmunder lager; Dortmunder Imperial Oktoberfest Bier, a dark rich malty brew; and Dortmunder Imperial Alt Bier, a top-fermented highly hopped and rich malt beer with a complex aromatic nature. These brews are imported by Iroquois Brands, Ltd.

DORTMUNDER IMPERIAL IMPORTED BEER—deep gold, beautiful well-hopped aroma with a touch of roasted malt, nicely balanced, touch of malt on palate at start then good hops, toasted malt in finish with a slight sour background, lingering pleasant aftertaste, good dry and complex brew, very appetizing.

DORTMUNDER IMPERIAL OKTOBERFEST BIER—orange-brown color, very faint roasted malt aroma, toasted malt flavor with little or no hops, pleasant and malty without complexity.

DORTMUNDER IMPERIAL ALT (DARK) BEER—deep copper, soft toasted malt aroma, hoppy flavor, lacks depth and balance; a little toasted malt flavor appears in the finish, but it is too late, very little aftertaste.

Brauerei Wagner
(Kemmern)

WAGNER BRÄU MÄRZEN—deep tawny gold, very faint malty aroma; lots of hops up front in the flavor, but poor balance, sour finish.

WAGNER BRÄU BOCK—medium deep orange-brown,

aroma so faint that it was difficult to pick out any identifiable sensation, big creamy head that lasts to the end, smoked coffee flavor, unbalanced, excess bitterness stays on too long.

Warsteiner Brauerei GEBR
(Warstein, Cramer K.G.)

This firm dates back to 1753 and is owned by Cramer Brothers. The new Cramer Brewery was completed in 1975.

WARSTEINER PREMIUM VERUM—bright pale gold, malt and hops both contribute to the well-developed aroma, good-flavored brew, more malt than hops, excellent balance up front, big hop finish, long malty aftertaste.

Brauhaus Weissenbrunn
(Marktoberdorf)

ORIGINAL BAVARIAN OKTOBER BIER—tawny gold, good malt and hop nose with roasted malt in back, good flavor with some excess hops, monolithic but decent, long bitter aftertaste.

Heinrich Wenker Brauerei/Privatbrauerei Dortmunder Kronen
(Kronenberg, Dortmund)

Dortmund had been granted the privilege to brew beer in 1293, so when Johann Wenker acquired the Krone am Markt brewery in Dortmund together with all its brewing equipment and the brewing rights in 1729, the Krone had already been in existence for at least three hundred years. It was first mentioned in town chronicles in the year 1430. In the very beginning, it may have been a "wine tavern," but by the sixteenth century, it most certainly housed a brewery.

Today the Krone is the only piece of property in Dortmund to have preserved its name from the Middle Ages. With 550 years as a brewery (the oldest in Westphalia) and 250 years as a family-run business, Privatbrauerei Dortmunder Kronen has a strong belief in upholding tradition.

Up to the mid-19th century, Kronen brewed two top-fermented brews, one very much like the alt beer of today and the other a strong beer of wheat and barley which was stored up to two years before it could be drawn. It was extremely intoxicating. Bottom-fermented beer (which was to become known as Dortmunder beer) was introduced to Dortmund in 1843 and has continued to gain popularity to the present day.

DORTMUNDER KRONEN CLASSIC—medium deep gold, big hoppy aroma, good hops and malt grain flavor, a touch of sweetness in the finish, medium body, complex and well-balanced, delightful.

DORTMUNDER KRONEN PILSKRONE—cloudy amber, toasted malt aroma, palate is mostly toasted malt up front, hops in the back, aftertaste on the sour side; good while it is in your mouth, but the aftertaste is a spoiler.

Westfälische Pils Brauerei/C.H. Andreas
(Hagen)

Firm established in 1848.

ANDREAS PILS—cloudy tawny gold with some particulate matter, clean hop nose with a touch of sweetness, good hop flavor up front with sweet malt in support, a burnt malt backtaste increases toward the finish, a bit out of balance.

Burgerbräu Wörner OHG
(Bamberg)

Firm established in 1718.

KAISERDOM PILSENER—brilliant deep gold, roasted malt with good hops and a touch of caramel, good roasted malt flavor, hops show up in the middle for a beautiful balance, long roasted malt finish, slight malt aftertaste. A delicious brew.

KAISERDOM RAUCHBIER (Smoked Beer)—deep copper-brown, rich nose like smoked meat and cheese, pepperoni flavor, a very tasty brew, definitely has a place on the menu; brewed with smoked malt and the smoke overrides the malt and the hops, but they are clearly there. Interesting, unique, and good.

BURGERBRÄU BAMBERG PILS—medium gold, sweet malt and hop nose, big hop flavor with malt showing in the finish and aftertaste, appetizing aftertaste of medium duration.

Würzburger Hofbräu, A.G.
(Würzburg)

The origins of Würzburg lie with a seventh century settlement chosen by Irish monks (St. Kilian, et al. in 689) for the center of Bavarian missionary work. About 740 Würzburg was elevated to a bishopric by Boniface. Over the next nine hundred years, secular power increasingly came to repose with the bishops of Würzburg. One of them, Prince-Bishop Johann Philipp von Schonborn, erected a brewery in 1643 to supply his court and the local citizenry with beer. As late as 1736, a prince of this same Schonborn family was conducting the business. Under Napoleonic occupation, the breweries were secularized and subsequently attached by the royal Bavarian government when they assumed political power following Napoleon's removal. The brewery did not long remain the property of the Bavarian kings, for in 1863 it passed into private hands. In 1884 a private stock company was formed and the business merged with that of another (Bauch) brewery.

Like all German brews, Würzburger is made only from pure barley malt (no adjuncts) and fermentation proceeds for several months. The brews of this fine old firm have been exported to the U.S. since 1882 and have always enjoyed a well-deserved popularity here.

WÜRZBURGER HOFBRÄU LIGHT BEER—golden color, marvelous balanced malty hop aroma (better than the aroma of Munich Löwenbrau), very Germanic malty sour and hop taste with a lingering finish and a very satisfying lingering malt aftertaste. An excellent brew, finely balanced. Was not available in U.S. while item below was offered. It is now slowly returning to the market.

WÜRZBURGER HOFBRÄU (Brewed in Germany by Würzburger Hofbräu A.G., imported and bottled by Anheuser-Busch, Inc. of St. Louis, Missouri at Newark, New Jersey)—medium brilliant gold, carbonation evident to the eye, delicate aroma with faint hops, light malty flavor, carbonation interferes with the flavor, especially the finish. Discontinued in late 1983.

WÜRZBURGER DARK BEER—deep amber brown, heavy malty nose, hearty rich malty flavor, mellow more than zesty, sour malty finish, very much in character for a dark Bavarian brew. Good stuff in the bottle, fantastic on draft.

WÜRZBURGER OKTOBERFEST BEER—medium amber-brown color; faint hops in the aroma, but more hops than malt, a soft and mellow brew beautifully balanced with the proper amount of hops, rich and lingering aftertaste. An excellent brew that could please both German and American tastes by striking a fine balance between the differences.

WÜRZBURGER BOCK BEER—very deep dark color, subdued burnt malt nose, hops noticeable in the aroma, roasted malt flavor dominates, very distinctive; lots of character, but the roasted quality is overdone.

Greece

Beer is neither traditional nor popular to any

203

great degree in Greece. Greece produces mostly the traditional pine-flavored *retsina* (which accounts for over eighty percent of the alcoholic-beverage consumption in the country) and *ouzo*, the spiritous traditional liquor.

Atalanti Brewery
(Athens)

AEGEAN HELLAS BEER—gold, malt aroma with just a touch of hops, malty flavor without complexity, light body, sour aftertaste, best of the Greek beers.

SPARTAN LAGER EXPORT—bright yellow-gold, pleasant malty nose with good hop background, dull sweet malty taste, dry and bitter finish and aftertaste.

Hellenic Brewery and Winery, S.A.
(Athens)

This brewery was established in 1864. Its beers have since won thirty-six gold medals in international competition.

ATLAS GREEK BEER—medium to pale gold, faint malt and hop nose, dull malt flavor with cardboardlike background (oxidation) that carries into the aftertaste.

FIX BEER (Karolos Fix, S.A.)—aroma of bubble gum reflected in the taste; very poor on the tip of the tongue, but flavor improves in the middle, the finish is again poor and the aftertaste decidedly unpleasant.

ATHENIAN GREEK BEER (Athenian Brewery, S.A.)—cloudy yellow, creamy head, light pilsener nose, slightly bitter flavor, not really pleasant tasting, no aftertaste to speak of.

MARATHON GREEK BEER (Athenian Brewery, S.A.)—cloudy yellow, faint malt nose, slightly bitter flavor, all features quite light, virtually no aftertaste.

FIX 1864 SPEZIAL—bright gold, lovely malt and hop aroma, sweet and dull palate up front, sharp finish, lacks character.

Holland

Beer dates back to early times in Holland. In the thirteenth century, Dutch scholars Isaac and John Hollandus wrote learned dissertations on the subjects of fermenting and brewing. Delft became as famous for its beers as for its ceramics and for many years, beer was the great staple of that port. In the nineteenth century, Gouda was a brewing center and as well known for its beers as for its cheese.

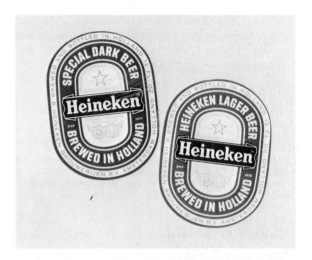

Beer has always been produced in great quantity in Holland to meet the high per capita consumption. But before the late 1800s, the major business interest in alcoholic beverages lay with distilled spirits, especially the world-famous Holland gin. In 1842 the Dutch Temperance League was formed to suppress strong drinks and to promote malt liquors instead. Success was achieved in 1881 when the Dutch government voted to regulate spirits, but not malt liquors, wine, and cider. At that time there were over 1000 breweries in Holland.

Temperance advocates then gave their encouragement to the manufacture of malt liquors, offering premiums and prizes for superior beers. Many of their number entered the brewing trade themselves. Indeed, the beer halls of the temperance societies at the 1886 Colonial Exposition in Amsterdam did the most thriving business. Since then, fine beer has been a Dutch tradition.

Heineken is the largest brewery in Holland today, accounting for nearly forty percent of all the beer consumed in the country. Heineken also exports to more than a hundred countries. Only thirteen breweries remain in operation in Holland today.

Heineken Brouwerjen
(Amsterdam, Rotterdam, Hertogenbosch)

Heineken operates three breweries today. The Amsterdam brewery is the oldest, dating back to 1433, and produces Heineken's dark beers and stouts. Hertogenbosch supplies the local market. Export lager is brewed at the Rotterdam brewery (built in 1874). The firm was founded in 1864 when twenty-two-year-old Gerard Adriann Heineken purchased the old De Hooiberg (Haystack) brewery in Amsterdam.

The company is still owned and operated by a Heineken, Freddy, who personally manages and directs the company's worldwide marketing and production.

It was Freddy's father who was so sufficiently impressed with the beer knowledge of Leo van Munching, bartender on the liner *Nieuw Amsterdam,* that he hired him to be Heineken's New York importer. This stroke of fortune played a major role in the Heineken success for it was Van Munching and his son who created the nationwide distribution system that is responsible for much of the sale of the beer in the U.S.

Heineken accounts for 40 percent of all imported beer sales in the U.S. and it can be purchased in 70 percent of all alcoholic beverage retail outlets. Impressive logistics keep fresh supplies at all points in the system and a recipe calling for a brewing process of eight days and a full six weeks of lagering affords a long shelf life. Together, these practices and a high regard for the product by Mr. Heineken, give a high probability that you will never encounter a stale or badly made bottle of the brew.

Worldwide sales in excess of $1.6 billion attest to the quality and popularity of the beer in the 140 countries where it is marketed.

The Heineken yeast culture dates from 1886 and was once widely sold to other brewers, but that practice ended with World War I. Heineken Lager is the leading imported beer in America. It is widely available and can be found on draft even in the most unlikely neighborhoods. It appeared in the U.S. first in 1933 when twenty-four quarter barrels and fifty cases of bottles were unloaded, the first shipment of beer from abroad following Repeal. Heineken Dark is an exceptional brew made from roasted caramelized malts and a high level of malt extract, resulting in a full rich flavor. Heineken also produces Amstel, a beer which in the past has been regularly available in the U.S.

HEINEKEN LAGER BEER—medium gold color, smooth bouquet of hops and malt, dry; well-hopped but not overpowering, finely balanced with a good dry and slightly salty finish. A good beer in bottle, excellent on draft. This is the first choice of a vast number of Americans who regularly drink beer.

HEINEKEN LAGER BEER (Draft)—medium gold, good head, medium strength hoppy nose, good hop flavor, big body, smooth finish with hops present only faintly in the aftertaste.

HEINEKEN SPECIAL DARK BEER—light copper gold, pleasant rich malty aroma and taste, fine balance, long-pleasing aftertaste. One of the best dark beers available in the world.

AMSTEL LIGHT—67 calories because it is packaged in an undersized bottle, pale yellow, faint malty aroma, dull dry flavor, not much of a beer.

Alfa Brewery
(Schinnen)

Alfa is a family owned brewery established in 1870 by Joseph Meens and is still owned by the Meens family. Alfa beer is 100 percent malt and lagered three months. Most of the firm's output is sold through the family's retail wine shops.

ALFA FRESH HOLLAND BEER—bright gold, sweet apple peel aroma, very sweet candy apple and caramel taste, light body, fairly shallow, short finish and faint sweet aftertaste.

Bavaria Breweries
(Lieshout)

This firm was founded in 1719.

BAVARIA LAGER—pale yellow color, slightly cloudy appearance, lettuce-leaf aroma, unbalanced with most of the flavor in the throat and on the far back of the tongue, lingering bitter aftertaste.

SWINKELS EXPORT BEER—medium gold, highly carbonated, pleasant beery malt and hop aroma, nice hop and malt flavor, very well-balanced dry finish, clean and refreshing. (Houba B.V. corporate identifier on label)

Bierbrowerij de Drie Hoefijzers
(Breda)

This "Three Horseshoes" brewery dates back to 1628. It is affiliated with Skol International and owned by Allied Breweries (U.K.), Ltd.

BREDA ROYAL HOLLAND BEER—strong hop nose, dull taste, neutral.

ROYAL DUTCH (N.V. de Posthoorn, Breda)—medium hop nose, dull taste consisting only of hops, very bitter finish and aftertaste.

ROYAL DUTCH KOSHER HOLLAND LAGER BEER *(Posthoorn, Breda)*—deep gold, skunky aroma, oxidized; bad sample.

Bierbrowerij de Leeuw
(Valkenburg)

LEEUW HOLLAND PILSENER—slightly cloudy gold, good malt and hop aroma (slightly toasted malt), malty palate that shows best in the finish, very tasty.

Grolsche Bierbrowerij
(Enschede)

GROLSCH NATURAL HOLLAND BEER—amber color, tart aroma, sour malty flavor with good hops, richly flavored.

GROLSCH LAGER BEER—bright gold, sour hop aroma; flavor is mostly hops with a dry sour component, hop finish, dry and slightly sour aftertaste.

International Beer Export, Ltd.
(Amsterdam)

THREE HORSES BRAND PILSENER LAGER BEER— sharp pilsener aroma, sour flavor with a bitter background, bitterness strong in the finish and aftertaste.

Oranjeboom Breweries
(Rotterdam)

ORANJEBOOM HOLLAND PILSENER DE LUXE— yellow-gold color, slightly cloudy, strong vegetal malt and wildflower hop aroma, tart flavor with slightly sour background, weak in the middle of the palate, but finishes well. Lots of character. Oranjeboom is also affiliated with Skol and owned by Allied Breweries (U.K.), Ltd.

Skol Associates in Holland
(under license from Skol Int'l., Ltd.)

SKOL LAGER BEER—tawny gold color, fairly brown for a light lager, small bubble carbonation, malty hop nose, taste little more than just hops.

B.V. Gulpener Bierbrowerij
(Gulpen)

X-PERT HOLLAND BEER—pale orange-gold, hop only aroma, thin body, watery light hop flavor with a bitter-sour finish, faintly bitter aftertaste.

United Dutch Breweries
(Rotterdam)

JAEGER BEER—strong aroma of apples and hops; complex flavor, but no harmony of tastes, hard bitter finish.

PETER'S BRAND HOLLAND PILSENER BEER—pale yellow, slightly cloudy; skunky aroma with light, malty, typically European pils flavor in back, the skunkiness stayed only for a short time, the skunky hop flavor soon developed into a good light hop flavor with some character. Once the skunk left, it wasn't bad at all; pretty good in fact. Seen only in San Francisco.

Royal Brand Brewery
(Wijlre)

This brewery, possessing documents dating from 1340, was bought by the Brand family in 1871. At its centennial, it was granted the title *Koninklijke* (Royal) by the Queen of The Netherlands.

BRAND HOLLAND BEER—pale gold, nicely balanced hop nose, good balance to the flavor, bright hop palate, and finish, clean, brisk, dry, and refreshing. Bottled in a white ceramic glass-lined bottle. Previously labeled Brand Lager Beer.

India and Pakistan

The British established breweries in India as early as 1834 to satisfy the demands of empire troops stationed there. Beer was not generally in use by the natives before or during that time. It is said that the British troops in India preferred the locally produced beer (by the British brewers, of course) to that imported from England, but economics may have colored that choice.

The Murree Brewery Company, Ltd., was established in 1861 at Gora Gully, near Murree in the Punjab. By 1900 it was the largest brewing establishment in India with its four breweries producing more than a million gallons of beer annually. Today the Murree plant is situated about ten miles from Islamabad, the capital of Pakistan. Murree produces an Export Lager for the international market, London Lager for the Indo-Pakistan market, and an Export Stout.

High Range Breweries, Ltd.
(Voranad, Kerala, India)

KINGFISHER LAGER BEER—brilliant pale gold, big aromatic hop nose with good malt, sprightly malt and hop taste, sour finish, slight lack of balance.

Murree Brewery Co., Ltd.
(Rawalpindi, Pakistan)

MURREE EXPORT LAGER—pale cloudy yellow, dry sour taste, quite astringent, awful. 4.5 percent alcohol. Bottles only.

Mohan Meakin Breweries, Ltd.
(Ghaziabad, India, Mohan Nagar Brewery)

GOLDEN EAGLE LAGER BEER—deep color, slightly cloudy, pleasant semisweet malty aroma (described by one taster as being like some brand of floor wax), unique smoky-salty flavor, fairly pleasant.

Khoday Brewing and Distilling Industries Private, Ltd.
(Bangalore, India)

SOVEREIGN LAGER BEER—tawny gold, aroma of ferruginous spring water and toasted malt, watery body, flavor like the aroma, good toasted malt finish, faint aftertaste. Rice is used as an adjunct and the brew is aged two months.

Mohan Rocky Springwater Breweries, Ltd.
(Khopoli, India)

EAGLE LAGER BEER—brilliant amber gold (very beautiful color), aroma of damp toasted malt, weak and watery, weak toasted malt flavor, brief finish.

Kalyani Breweries, Ltd.
(Calcutta, India)

TAJ MAHAL LAGER BEER—foamed up furiously on pouring, bright yellow-gold, long-lasting head, aroma of spruce balsam or pine needles, pine needle flavor obtains throughout, some malt appears in the finish, complex and interesting aftertaste.

Hindustan Breweries & Bottling, Ltd.
(Thana, India)

BOMBAY BEER—clear tawny gold, faint malt nose with a

touch of oxidation, light body, sweet background to a vegetal palate, slightly oxidized palate, low carbonation, neutral and dull finish and aftertaste.

Indonesia

P.T. San Miguel Brewery
(Tambun, Bekasi)

SAN MIGUEL BEER—deep gold, nice malty beery aroma with some hops, moderately pleasant malty palate, long sour and bitter aftertaste.

SAN MIGUEL DARK BEER—deep red brown, rich and sweet toasted malt aroma, good rich flavor of roasted malt and licorice, complex, lingering pleasant and balanced aftertaste. Compared to the Manila version, this is more subdued in flavor, but greater in body. An excellent dark beer.

Israel

The brewing industry of Israel is necessarily a young one. The first signs of an ongoing brewing trade appeared in the 1970s with the exportation of the two beers reported below. As with the Israeli wine exports, a good measure of loyalty to the ideals of the state of Israel is required for continued support of the beers.

Cabeer Breweries, Ltd.
United Dutch Breweries
(Bat Yam)

BEERSHEBA PREMIUM—slightly skunky aroma, astringently sour taste, highly carbonated, very lightly finished, almost no aftertaste.

National Breweries, Ltd.
(Tel Aviv)

MACCABEE PREMIUM BEER—pale color, creamy head, dull sweet apple aroma with a trace of wood pulp or cardboard; sweet candy-apple flavor, but not so sweet as to be cloying, sweet aftertaste mostly in the throat; not unpleasant for a sweet beer, but not dry enough for most beer palates.

Italy

With good inexpensive wine available in

207

profusion, a beer industry in Italy has never gained nationwide momentum, but the northern Italians have a taste for German and Swiss beers.

Up to the twentieth century, the thirst of the Italian beer drinker was satisfied largely by imports from Germany and Austria. Since then, production of beer in Italy has slowly risen nearly to match consumption.

The brewing industry in Italy had its beginnings when portions of Italy were included in the Austro-Hungarian Empire; the famous Austrian name of Dreher still appears on a fine Italian beer exported to America. In fact, the Italian beers exported to North America are of excellent quality.

Birra Dreher S.p.A.
(Pedavena and Massafra)

DREHER FORTE EXPORT LAGER BEER—dark yellow-brown color, dank sour aroma, sweet taste up front that is sour-bitter to the back of the palate, good balance, pleasantly finished, overall effect is very good.

DREHER EXPORT BEER—cloudy pale gold, faint malt aroma, weak body, malty flavor, dry, touch of sweetness in the finish.

Birra Forst S.p.A.
(Merano)

FORST EXPORT—bright gold, fine particulate matter, perfumy aroma, medium body, bitter flavor dominated by carbonation, bitter finish.

Peroni Breweries
(Naples, Rome, and Padova)

Firm established in 1846.

PERONI PREMIUM BEER—light brown, great zest and character, hops dominate nose and taste, strong-flavored.

NASTRO AZZURRO EXPORT LAGER—pale gold, slightly cloudy, aroma of faint hops, little malt, touch of yeast, big body, flavor dominated by hops with a sourness in back that becomes the aftertaste.

PERONI BIRRA—slightly cloudy gold, faint apple peel aroma, big body, big hop flavor that softens a bit at the finish.

ITALA PILSEN—pale gold with some particles in suspension, creamy, foamy, slightly skunky hop and malt aroma, highly carbonated, good hop-malt flavor, well-hopped, but not obtrusive, smooth, well-balanced, very drinkable.

ITALA PILSEN EXPORT BEER—deep amber gold, cloudy with particles; big head, but not creamy, light hop-malt aroma, big body, good complex malt flavor, noticeable alcohol, balanced until end when bitterness of the hops comes in strongly at the finish, otherwise quite smooth and a super good brew.

RAFFO BEER—brilliant pale gold with a touch of brown, toasted caramel aroma, bittersweet cardboard flavor (oxidation), slightly sour finish and aftertaste.

Birra Moretti S.p.A.
(Udine)

Firm established in 1859.

MORETTI PILSENER—foamed greatly upon pouring but little carbonation on the palate; deep gold, clean malt aroma and taste with good hop balance, light body; very tasty and very drinkable.

SCHLOSS-BIER EXPORT LAGER—gold, very cloudy and full of particles, creamy-foamy, nice hop and malt aroma, faint malty flavor, flat and dull, not much finish, little aftertaste, medium to light body.

MORETTI EXPORT BEER (BIRE FURLANE) RESERVA CASTELLO—brilliant gold, pleasant malty-hop aroma, sweet apple and wet cardboard light flavor, most of the flavor is up front on the palate.

MORETTI BIRRA FRIULANA—bright gold, big bubbles, grainy aroma, grainy flavor with good hop background, cardboard in finish, fairly long malt finish.

Birra Poretti S.p.A.
(Induno, Olona)

PORETTI ORO BEER—tawny gold, malty vegetal aroma with some hops, slightly oxidized; flavor has some hops, but it is mostly malt; decent brew, but the balance could be better, light finish, very little aftertaste.

SPLÜGEN ORO—deep gold, cloudy with particulate matter, creamy head, medium sour hop aroma, big body, sour flavor that intensifies toward the end, dull sour finish.

SPLÜGEN BOCK—creamy tawny gold, clean fruitlike aroma with hops in back, big body, hops nicely balanced with malt in the complex flavor with sweetness coming in very nicely at the end, well-balanced, all components can be identified, long good finish, almost perfect.

SPLÜGEN DRY—cloudy gold with particles, "old" hoppy nose, hint of strawberry, hops up front on palate, sour-sweet metallic finish.

Prinz Bräu Carisio S.p.A.
(Carisio)

PRINZ EXPORT—deep gold with some particulate matter, beautiful hoppy nose with a little smoke and a little skunk, medium hop flavor with little depth or complexity, dull slightly sour aftertaste.

Wünster S.p.A.
(Bergamo)

WÜNSTER EXPORT 14—gold, some particulate matter, beautiful hoppy aroma, big hop taste with malty sweetness underneath, malt comes in well at the finish, good balance. The 14 is a saccharometer rating (as is the 18 below) and is a measure of density.

WÜNSTER SUPER 18 DOPPIO MALTA SCURA (Double Malt Dark Bock)—red-brown, deep saturation, toasted malt aroma, big body, soft and smooth, beautiful tasty malt flavor, toffee aftertaste with a touch of licorice, long toffee finish, good balance.

Birra Wührer S.p.A.
(Brescia)

CRYSTALL WÜHRER BEER—medium yellow brown, nicely balanced malty hop aroma, bitter hop taste with a soapy background, relatively clean finish. Good-tasting brew.

SIMPLON BRÄU SPECIAL EXPORT—deep gold, cloudy, beautiful medium hop nose, harsh hop taste, no complexity, a bit softer in the finish and aftertaste.

Japan

It is said that sake has been in general use in Japan for over two thousand years. It is an alcoholic beverage brewed from rice and probably is still rightfully called Japan's national drink. If it is, however, it is not very far ahead of beer, for that beverage has been gaining steadily since its introduction shortly before the end of the nineteenth century.

Although a brewery had been built in Yokohama about 1870, the first event of national significance in the Japanese brewing trade took place in 1873, when a young man named Nakawara was sent by the Japanese government to Germany to learn the art of brewing and all of its branches. He remained in Germany for three years and then returned home to head a brewery built by the government in Tokyo.

Before 1887, however, domestic production was still quite small and most of the beer consumed in Japan was imported from Germany, but by 1899 production had risen so sharply that Japan began to export beer to Siberia, the Philippines, Hawaii, and Chinese ports.

With the Japanese inclination to Western ways, the consumption of beer increases each year and is approaching ten gallons per capita. The beer brewed is very pale, with rice used as an adjunct. The style of Japanese beer today, say some, is influenced more by Nordic beer (especially Finnish) than by German types.

Asahi Breweries
(Tokyo)

ASAHI LAGER BEER—very pale, almost water-colored; clean, fresh spring water aroma, interesting flavor like spring water with a ferruginous (iron) character, light and inoffensive, not very exciting for a real beer drinker.

ASAHI DRAFT—medium gold, light malty aroma, creamy texture; light malt and hop flavor, but not in balance (as if the malt and hops are separate), dull finish and aftertaste; drinkable, but not satisfying and not very beerlike.

Kirin Brewery Co., Ltd.
(Kyobashi, Tokyo)

It has been reported that the first brewery in Japan, the one which is mentioned above and which was founded by Americans Wiegand and Copeland in Yokohama about 1870, was the foundation upon which the Kirin Brewery originated. That may be partly so. The Japan Brewery Company, Ltd., is believed to have first marketed a brew called Kirin Beer in Yokohama about 1888. This firm was founded by an English corporation and may have been set up on the Wiegand business base. In any event, the Kirin (a mythical beast, combining a horse and a dragon) dominates the domestic Japanese brewing scene, commanding over sixty percent of domestic beer sales. In 1974 Kirin opened its twelfth brewery. It is the best of the Japanese beers tasted.

KIRIN BEER—pale cloudy yellow, complex aroma, good smoky malt flavor, very refreshing; some metallic taste in the background, but not obtrusive, soapy finish. Kirin is brewed from Japanese barley, rice, cornstarch, and corn grits. It is fermented eight days and stored two months before being filtered and pasteurized.

KIRIN LIGHT BEER—brilliant gold, faint sweet malt nose, high CO_2, otherwise little flavor; just some light malt, no finish or aftertaste. 106 calories.

Orion Breweries, Ltd.
(Nago, Okinawa)

ORION LAGER BEER—deep yellow with brown tinge,

209

malt aroma with a touch of the "grape," unappealing tart and sour taste.

Sapporo Breweries, Ltd.
(Tokyo)

The Sapporo brewery was founded in 1876 at Sapporo by the colonial government of Hokkaido to provide a market for barley grown in the vicinity. In 1886 the business passed into private hands and two years later was incorporated as the Sapporo Brewing Co., Ltd.

SAPPORO LAGER BEER—medium gold, mellow hoppy nose, pleasant flavor, but it flattens out toward the finish, same flavor all the way through, brief aftertaste, little complexity.

SAPPORO DRAFT BEER—slightly cloudy gold, fruity apple peel aroma, good malt support, palate is mostly carbonation, little character, slight bitterness in the finish.

SAPPORO BLACK BEER—opaque red-brown; heavy malty aroma with sharp, but faint sourness in the background, flavor is like the aroma, medium body, dull and neutral finish, creamy texture, faintly sour aftertaste.

Suntory, Ltd.
(Osaka and Tokyo)

SUNTORY BEER REAL DRAFT—gold, faint malt aroma, medium body, CO_2 dominates flavor, slight apple and wood-pulp background, dry finish, fairly bitter long aftertaste. In addition to the usual 12-oz. packages, this brew is available in a 2-liter plastic "minibarrel."

Korea

The beer of Korea has never developed any appreciable reputation. Soldiers returning from Korea were never heard to generate any enthusiasm for Korean brews; in fact, comments were usually quite to the contrary. Nevertheless, a Korean beer is exported to the U.S. regularly and somewhere there may be some beer drinkers who found the brew of their choice in a little pub in Seoul.

Oriental Brewery Co., Ltd.
(Seoul)

ORIENTAL OB LAGER BEER—pale color, some samples clouded, light apple-peel aroma, light sweet cardboard and apple taste.

Luxembourg

This tiny country has only six breweries, but produces some of Europe's finest brews. Diekirch is the largest of these breweries and Diekirch Pils is the largest selling foreign beer in Germany, which is quite a claim. As in Germany, the beers of Luxembourg can contain only barley, hops, yeast, and water. Luxembourg ranks sixth in the world in per capita beer consumption.

Brasserie Diekirch Brauerei
(Luxembourg)

The Diekrich Brewery was founded in 1871, but has origins dating to 1724. The firm produces its own malt, a relative rarity in brewing today. Locally grown barley is used and the beers are filtered rather than pasteurized. Lagering lasts three months. The Pils is 3.9 percent alcohol by weight and the malt liquor is 4.9 percent by volume.

DIEKIRCH PILS—good malty aroma, typical sour vegetable pils flavor, tart hop finish. A very good, well-balanced brew. No wonder it sells so well in Germany; it's one of Europe's finest beers.

DIEKIRCH MALT LIQUOR—deep gold, hoppy aroma with a trace of smoke and skunk (which quickly cleared), fairly intense flavor of hops and roasted malt, flavor gradually fades across the palate to a neutral finish and aftertaste.

DIEKIRCH MALT LIQUOR EXCLUSIVE—this label appeared briefly prior to 1979 in the U.S. I could not find a decent sample. It has since been discontinued and any samples found are too old and likely spoiled.

Mexico

Beer is a relative newcomer to Mexico. Until the last half of the nineteenth century, only the native drinks mescal, tequila, and pulque were in regular use. Even now, some hundred years later, these beverages are more popular than beer, probably because they are cheap and easy to make.

Pulque, the juice of the *maquey* or agave cactus, is fermented for twenty-four hours and then must be consumed immediately as it soon becomes unfit to drink. Tequila and mescal are liquors distilled from the same plant. Tequila

Cerveceria Cuauhtemoc

(Monterrey, Toluca, Guadalajara, Tecate, Mexico City, Nogales, Culiacan, Ciudad Juarez)

This firm was the third lager brewery founded in Mexico. It was established in 1891. Its Carta Blanca brand was once the most famous and largest selling beer of Mexico. It also makes Kloster, Monterrey, Colosal, and Cruz Bea. Cuauhtemoc was the last of the Aztec emperors, and died in 1521.

BOHEMIA ALE—deep gold, candy-apple and malt aroma, flavor like aroma but dry at finish, very malty with good hops, complex and interesting.

TECATE CERVEZA (Tecate Brewery, Toluca)—pale gold color, nice malty hop aroma, but very light, pleasant malty hop dry flavor, nicely balanced, but overall everything is just too lightly done. Tecate is popular in Mexico drunk straight from the can with salt crusted around the rim, softened with lemon or lime juice. It is at least an interesting taste.

CARTA BLANCA DARK SPECIAL—bright copper-rose, sour hop aroma, a little malt flavor up front, but thereafter the brew doesn't offer much to the palate, little or no finish and only a faint malt aftertaste.

CERVEZA CARTA BLANCA—pale color, dank offensive aroma, inoffensive flavor, almost nothing at all on the palate until the finish, which is faintly bitter. First Mexican beer to be imported into U.S.

INDIO CERVEZA OSCURA—reddish-orange-brown (copper) color, very faint malty aroma (caramel background), dull faintly sweet malt flavor, no complexity.

BRISA CERVEZA LIGERA—90 calories, very pale gold-yellow, faint sour aroma, watery, a slight malty character is all that is offered for flavor, little finish, no aftertaste. Introduced in 1979.

Cerveceria Moctezuma, S.A.

(Orizaba, Guadalajara, Mexico City, Monterrey)

This brewing firm was established in 1894 by a German brewmaster named Wilhelm Haase. Its Superior brand became Mexico's largest selling label as the national tastes tended to favor lighter beers. The recently introduced Tres Equis is even paler and doubtless aimed at satisfying a continuation of that trend. Dos Equis has its largest following in the United States, and is the largest selling Mexican beer in the U.S. Other brands include Sol Clara, Sol Especial, Moctezuma de Barril, and Bavaria. The firm also offers a line of consumer items, like point-of-sale T-shirts.

enjoys considerable popularity above the border as well, particularly among the under-forty group. It is sipped with salt, a practice that originated in the area of Mexico subject to high temperatures, which cause men to develop a salt hunger to replace body losses.

The earliest Mexican brewers made a brown beer from malt which, after having been spread on the roof of the brewery, was toasted by the sun. The first recorded brewing operation in Mexico was set up by Alonso de Herrera, a Spanish conquistador, in 1544.

Most brews at that time that gained popularity were like *sencilla*. It was brewed like a lager, but with less extract, and while some was cold-stored, much was consumed as soon as fermented.

Top-fermentation breweries existed in Mexico City as early as 1845. They used a malt of sun-dried Mexican barley mixed with a brown sugar, *pilancillo*. The beer so made was inferior, but these breweries survived until a good lager produced in Toluca appeared on the scene. In the 1860s the base of the present Mexican brewing industry was established with the arrival of the Swiss, Bavarian, and Alsatian immigrants. Lager beer made its appearance in Mexico about 1891.

Some 19 breweries operate in Mexico today, all owned either wholly or in part by the three major breweries: Cuauhtemoc, Moctezuma, and Modelo.

Cerveceria Cruz Blanca, S.A.

(Ciudad Juarez)

CRUZ BLANCA CERVEZA FINA—pale gold, pleasant malty aroma with a touch of hops, bitter and sour on the first sip; better on the second, but still dull and unbalanced, uninteresting aftertaste.

CHIHUAHUA MEXICAN BEER—pale gold, hop aroma, light hop flavor, brief finish, little aftertaste.

SUPERIOR LIGHT BEER—pale color, light malt aroma, light body, yeasty flavor with only a trace of hops. Although Moctezuma says only natural carbonation is used, the strong carbonations and foamy head indicate the use of injection and foaming agents. There was a problem in obtaining a good bottle of this beer in the eastern U.S. and then it was disappointing.

DOS EQUIS XX BEER—mahogany-brown with medium saturation, clean sweet malty nose, big malty flavor like molasses with a fine hop finish, reasonably dry, good balance, medium body. Recently renamed Amber Beer.

SOL ESPECIAL—bright gold, perfumy aroma, dry hop flavor, light body, pleasant finish and aftertaste.

TRES EQUIS XXX LIGHT BEER (Cerveza Clara)—very pale color, light malty aroma, fruity, sour, cardboard taste, wood pulp finish and aftertaste, too mild. This sample was obtained on the West Coast and is attributed specifically to the Orizaba brewery.

TRES EQUIS XXX CERVEZA OSCURA (dark)—deep copper red, slightly sour malt nose, strange bitter-herbal flavor, metallic herbal aftertaste.

DOS EQUIS XX LIGHT BEER—bright gold, very faint malt aroma, medium body, slightly woody flavor, clean malt finish, good malty aftertaste.

NOCHE BUENA CERVEZA ESPECIAL—brilliant pretty red-brown, soft malty aroma with light hops, flavor all hops up front, light roasted malt finish, good taste and good balance. Produced at Christmas with a holiday motif on the label, long dry aftertaste.

DOS EQUIS SPECIAL LAGER—bright gold, high CO_2, sweet floral malt aroma, sweet front and middle palate, slightly sour malt finish, malty aftertaste.

Cerveceria Modelo, S.A.
(Mexico City, Torreon, Guadalajara, Ciudad Obregon, Mazatlan)

MODELO ESPECIAL—clear tawny gold, faint aroma with hops deep down and an earthy quality, very little to offer the palate, flat, does have some rich malt flavor in the finish.

NEGRA MODELO DARK BEER—medium brown, nice malty aroma, roasted malt and hop flavor, excellent balance, dry clean finish, good duration, very drinkable.

CORONA EXTRA—bright gold, pleasant malt-hop nose, good hop flavor, dry finish, light aftertaste.

CORONA—brilliant pale gold, dry hoppy nose, dry even flavor, light dry and pleasant, very quaffable, good hot weather beer.

Cerveceria del Pacifico, S.A.
(Mazatlan)

CERVEZA PACIFICO CLARA—brilliant pale gold, interesting sweet hop aroma, very complex nose, surprising bone dry flavor without the complexity of the nose, brief finish, little aftertaste.

Cerveceria Yucateca, S.A.
(Merida)

MONTEJO PREMIUM BEER—slightly cloudy yellow, clean malt aroma with very slight hops, touch of soap, salty hop flavor, creamy texture, very light carbonation, salty finish, sour hop aftertaste. This brew is labelled Carta Clara for its domestic market.

MONTEJO DARK BEER—very deep copper with a tinge of rose, creamy, small bubbles, faint malt aroma, flavor is CO_2 and faint malt, not watery, just light. Carbonation is major palate feature.

New Guinea

The island of New Guinea has several breweries, including one that produces San Miguel, but the most famous of New Guinea beers is South Pacific, or simply, SP.

SP Brewery, Ltd.
(Papua)

SOUTH PACIFIC SP GOLD MEDAL DRAUGHT LAGER—medicinal aroma, flavor that lies somewhere in a mix of anise, cardboard, and the old Band-Aids you might recall from your youth.

SOUTH PACIFIC SPECIAL EXPORT LAGER—tawny color, flowery nose at first, faded to faint fruit, sour malt and apple, dull malt flavor, medium duration.

Papua New Guinea Pty, Ltd.
(San Miguel, Port Moresby)

SAN MIGUEL PILSNER BEER—medium gold, tuna fish in water aroma, sour wood pulp flavor, no zest, spoiled sample.

SAN MIGUEL NEGRA DARK BEER—pale reddish-brown, dry roasted malt aroma, very dry roasted malt flavor, slightly sour finish. Fairly dry all the way through.

New Zealand

The climate of New Zealand is materially different from that of its (distant) neighbor Australia and is more suitable to the making of beer. Brewing in New Zealand dates to 1773 and Captain James Cook, when he set up a brewery at Dusky Sound to make a beer from manuka and rimu tree branches with molasses and yeast. Brewing was unknown to the Maoris and they thought very little of Cook's brew, calling it *waipiro* or "stinking water."

By 1900, there were over one hundred breweries on New Zealand, most of them extremely small. In 1980, following years of consolidation (as in most countries), only eleven breweries controlled by three companies remain.

New Zealand brews its beverages very much in the English style, supposedly even more so than do the Australians. Heineken holds a significant interest in the New Zealand brewing industry.

Dominion Breweries, Ltd.
(Auckland)

DB EXPORT BEER—medium gold with some particulate matter, dry fruit aroma, winy on the palate, berry fruit (cherry) with a touch of oxidation for flavor, some hops in the finish.

DOUBLE BROWN BEER—slightly cloudy orange, faint apple-cardboard aroma, sweet and thin, wood pulp background characteristic of an oxidized sample, sweet finish, woody aftertaste.

Lion Breweries, Ltd.
(Auckland, formerly New Zealand Breweries, Ltd.)

In 1977 New Zealand Breweries changed its name to Lion Breweries, Ltd.; however, for export it retains the original name for continuity. Lion is the largest brewer in New Zealand and the second largest public company. Six plants and some three hundred hotels and taverns are operated. Only Steinlager is exported, but a wide variety of local brews are produced to slake the heavy thirst that ranks the country near fifth in per capita consumption.

STEINLAGER NEW ZEALAND LAGER BEER—pale gold, lovely aroma more of hops than malt; good hoppy flavor up front, but pleasant sweetness develops in the middle palate, well-balanced and good tasting, lots of character.

Leopard Brewing Co.
(Hastings)

LEOPARD LAGER—pineapple aroma with a gradual development of hops, sweet and fruitlike rather than malt, a finish of fizz and hops.

LEOPARD EXPORT LAGER BEER—very pale gold, pine needle and citrus sour malt aroma, light fruitlike flavor up front, sour finish, slight sour apple peel aftertaste.

LEOPARD STRONG BEER—tawny gold, sour fruit aroma

with a rubbery background, little flavor up front, at finish goes to apple seed or peel sweetness, light sour malt aftertaste.

Norway

Barley has been cultivated in Norway for hundreds of years, but a malt beverage industry could not develop until late in the nineteenth century because of a general preference for distilled spirits. In all of Scandinavia, however, the valleys of Norway offered the best climatic conditions for the cultivation of barley with some locations capable of yielding two crops each summer.

By 1900, forty-four Norwegian breweries were annually producing about four hundred thousand barrels, mostly for local consumption of draft. Today, fine Norwegian brews are exported around the world including the standard bearer of Frydenlund's, which had a fine reputation in the world over seventy-five years ago, the well-known and highly appreciated Ringnes line of beers, and the very excellent brews from the Hansa brewery in Bergen and the Aass brewery in Drammen.

Aass Brewery
(Drammen)

Aass is a family brewery established in 1834 and is currently in the hands of the sixth generation, Paul Lauritz Aass. It is the third largest brewery in Norway with an annual production of 175,000 barrels.

Aass brews are now being exported to English-speaking countries, which leads to some interesting advertising possibilities. Already I have seen point-of-sale ads exhorting beer drinkers to "Graab Aass" and a recipe describing a mixture of equal parts of Aass Export and Aass Bok as a "Half Aass." There is little doubt that these promotions will be noticed. The beers, at least, are in good taste.

AASS BOK BEER—very deep copper, complex yeasty malt aroma, big-bodied, full and rich roasted malt flavor, good long aftertaste. I couldn't drink much of it, it is so big, but it's absolutely delicious.

AASS NORWEGIAN BEER—light amber gold, light hop

213

aroma, medium hop flavor, high carbonation, slightly sour finish, unbalanced. After a brief trial, importing of this brew was discontinued in favor of the Export reported below.

AASS EXPORT NORWEGIAN BEER—amber gold, big hop nose, big hop and toasted malt flavor, slightly sour finish, finely balanced, a good brew worth trying. This beer has been seen labeled as listed here and as Aass Export. With Aass Norwegian being discontinued, Aass Export will be renamed Aass Norwegian in the U.S.

AASS JULE ØL (Yule Ale)—bright copper-caramel color, lovely light malt and hop aroma, almost no carbonation, delicious toasted malt flavor, sweet malt finish with a touch of hops, good appetizing aftertaste. Norway's Yule Ale is usually high in alcohol (as opposed to Denmark, where it is alcohol-free).

E.C. Dahl's Bryggeri A/S
(Trondheim)

DAHL'S PILS—pale gold with particulate matter, good hop-malt aroma, smooth, well-balanced hop and malt flavor, medium body, long aftertaste on sour and bitter side.

DAHL'S EXPORT—tawny gold with particles, beautiful hop-malt pilsener aroma, high carbonation, good hop flavor, good balance, hops not intrusive in finish, brief aftertaste.

Hansa Bryggeri
(Bergen)

Firm founded in 1891.

HANSA FJORD NORWEGIAN PILSENER BEER—pale cloudy yellow-green appearance, beautiful malty hop aroma, semisweet malty flavor with excellent hop balance, a luscious full-flavored and full-bodied brew with all kinds of character, complex yet refreshing. I have found nothing in the U.S. to compare with this brew. It is difficult to find, but if you happen to spot it, buy enough to last a drought. Most recently imported with a Hansa Beer from Norway label.

HANSA EXPORT (Exportøl)—bright pale tawny gold, salty malt cereal aroma, flavor to match, salty finish, very mild.

HANSA PILSNER (Pilsnerøl)—pale gold, hops back a faint apple aroma, taste all up front and all hops, not much finish, no aftertaste.

HANSA PILS—gold color, big hop aroma, sharp hop flavor, a beautiful well-hopped brew.

Frydenlund Bryggeri
(Oslo)

Established in 1859 in Christiania, Frydenlund's was the largest brewery in Norway at the turn of the century.

FRYDENLUND'S EXPORT III PILSENER BEER—hop aroma, bitter hop taste throughout with a sweet background at the beginning and a salty background at the finish.

FRYDENLUND'S NORWEGIAN PILSENER BEER—bright pale gold, skunky aroma, light body, salty-hop flavor, neutral finish and aftertaste.

NORSK BEER—medium yellow, initially a resinous skunky aroma that cleared within a few minutes to mild hops and malt, hoppy flavor up front, sour malt in back and finish, low carbonation, poor balance.

SKI BEER—medium gold, very light hop and malt aroma, nice well-hopped flavor but the body is thin, sour finish and aftertaste, highly carbonated and not well-balanced.

Ringnes Brewery
(Oslo)

In the 1860s brothers Amund and Ellef Ringnes moved to Christiania (now Oslo) and established a small brewery in partnership with Consul Heiberg. The name Ringnes & Co. was registered in 1877 with Amund brewing and Ellef selling their beer. In 1899 the business was incorporated. In 1981 the brewery produced 370,000 barrels.

Ringnes has a history of supporting cultural projects and humanitarian goals. The name Ringnes is especially connected with Norwegian polar expeditions and to Fridtjof Nansen, Roald Amundsen, and Otto Sverdrup and their famous polar ship *Fram*. It was the Ringnes support that made these explorations possible and islands in the polar regions of Canada still bear the names of the Ringnes brothers and Consul Heiberg.

RINGNES SPECIAL BEER—tawny gold, strong hoppy nose and big flavor, lots of hops and malt and plenty of character, good malt finish and aftertaste, big hop taste without being sharp, excellent beer.

RINGNES MALT LIQUOR—sweet malt nose, very sweet and very malty taste and aftertaste, sudden bitterness at the end.

RINGNES EXPORT—aroma of hops and caramel; starts out tasting very good, but sags in the middle, showing poor balance, a very poor finish of sour celery. Several of these were tried with similar results. I believe these were old or mishandled stock. Ringnes products have a very high reputation that these samples did not match.

RINGNES SPECIAL BOCK BEER—very dark red-brown color, strong roasted malt, a molasses and prune aroma, big body, heavy and thick, very light carbonation, good molasses-treacle flavor throughout with an excellent finish. A good brew, certainly the best from Ringnes.

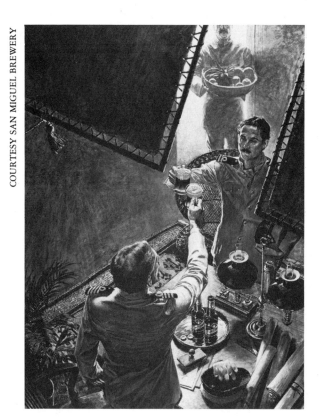

Early San Miguel Magazine Ad

RINGNES DARK—bright red brown, sweet malt aroma, light body, pleasant sweet malt flavor but could use a little more heft.

Schous Brewery
(Oslo)

SCHOUS NORWEGIAN PILSNER—gold, skunky aroma that hangs in there, smoked charcoal flavor without any of the skunkiness of the nose, some hops, little malt, unbalanced and watery, fairly dull brew.

Philippines

In 1889 Enrique Maria Barretto petitioned the Spanish crown for permission to establish a brewery in the colony. The grant was issued in the name of the four-year-old king, His Majesty King Alfonso XIII, by his mother, Queen Maria, and La Fabrica de Cerveza de San Miguel opened in Manila on October 4, 1890.

Since it was founded in 1890 as the first brewery in southeast Asia, the San Miguel brewery of Manila has been one of the most famous names across the Pacific. Rarely seen in the U.S. before World War II, San Miguel has long been a favorite with U.S. military personnel in the Pacific and Hawaii, even when Commodore Dewey did his thing in Manila Bay.

I have heard stories about how prime space aboard U.S. Navy vessels was reserved for San Miguel and have no doubt that priority was given to that great morale booster. Stories concerning San Miguel and World War II are popular in the South Pacific. One story allows how bombers on missions over Manila had specific instructions not to hit the brewery, reportedly a firm in which Douglas MacArthur held a substantial interest.

Regardless of the truth of any of the stories, no intelligent bombardier would try to hit what would eventually be the source of some really fine beers for the liberating forces. In the Pacific, it was always San Miguel, of course.

San Miguel operates three breweries in the

Philippines, three in Spain, and one each in Indonesia, Hong Kong, Guam, and Papua. The brews are tailored to their markets. For instance, the local Manila brew is more bitter than the export version because that's the way the Filipinos like it.

San Miguel was once produced in the U.S. (1952-1953) by the Muehlebach Brewing Co., Kansas City, Missouri. Muehlebach was sold by

San Miguel to Schlitz in 1956, which closed the brewery down in 1973.

San Miguel Brewery
(Manila)

SAN MIGUEL BEER (export for U.S.)—cloudy, pale yellow; strongly hopped and complex malt aroma; creamy, fresh tasting; excellent middle flavor and a very refreshing finish. One of the world's best beers.

SAN MIGUEL PALE PILSEN (domestic version)—pale straw yellow, grainy malt aroma, weak sour malt flavor and finish. I like the U.S. export version better.

SAN MIGUEL DARK BEER—extremely dark deep red-brown color; faint, but rich toasted malt aroma, a subtle complex, well-balanced rich toasted malt-hop blend with a toffee mint finish and a fine refreshing lingering aftertaste. A marvelous big-bodied brew. Of its style, none is better.

Poland

The history of Polish breweries can be traced in part to the time of the Austro-Hungarian Empire. For example, there was a brewing firm of substantial size in Okocim, Galicia, in 1900 by the name of J. Edler v. Goetz. Without visiting the brewery in person, one would be hard put to track down the pedigree of this or any other brewery in Poland because of the turbulent history of the area in the past seventy-five years. The Okocim Brewery says its origins reach to 1845; if so, it seems highly likely that the Edler firm formed at least the foundation of the present Okocim brewery.

Okocim Brewery

OKOCIM FULL LIGHT O.K. BEER—pungent soapy aroma, soapy metallic taste, metallic finish. Not as bad as it sounds, but nothing much to look forward to at the end of a hard day. It is said to be best served with seafood.

OKOCIM PORTER—dark brown color, malty burnt caramel taste, ponderous, sweet and heavy, overdone.

Zywiec Brewery

KRAKUS LIGHT BEER—faint sweet malt nose, creamy

Crew members of the Polish full-rigged ship "Dar Pomorzo" enjoy their native Krakus in New York at Op Sail '76.

texture, strong yeasty barley-malt flavor. Not bad for its type; best of the Polish imports.

ZYWIEC FULL LIGHT—dark color, malty soapy nose, sour-sweet mealy flavor.

ZYWIEC FULL LIGHT PIAST—very faint aroma, too faint to identify; sour malt taste; sour malt finish. Too sour to be interesting.

ZYWIEC BEER—5.2 percent alcohol, tawny gold, malty aroma with a sort of brackish background; flavor has good hops, but the salty nature prevails, fairly thin, brief finish, lacks balance.

Portugal

Commercial brewing began in Portugal in the early 1800s with the breweries mainly concentrated in Lisbon and Oporto. Up to that time there were no substantial brewing operations in the country and some of their brew was imported from England in exchange for port. Throughout the years many European countries influenced the style of Portuguese beers, but consumption has never been great because of the easy availability of good wine, which the Portuguese prefer.

Sociedade Central de Cervejas
(Lisbon, Vialonga, and Coimbra)

In 1881 one of the first Portuguese-owned breweries was established as the Leâo, or Lion, Brewery, named after an adjoining restaurant. By 1910 it was called the Germania Brewery, but during World War I, in 1916, it was patriotically renamed Portugalia. In 1934, during the depression, it joined with four other breweries to form S.C.C., which has about 70 percent of the Portuguese market.

CERVEJA SAGRES—pale yellow, slightly clouded, skunky vegetal aroma, wood pulp and cardboard flavor (oxidized), excessively bitter finish.

SAGRES DARK BEER—very dark brown, strong malt nose, very heavy and filling, bitter molasses taste with a sweet molasses finish and aftertaste.

Companhia União Fabril Portuense, Unicer-União Cervejeira
(Oporto, Leca do Balio)

This company is the result of the merger of

217

seven breweries in and around Oporto.

CRISTAL BEER—deep yellow-gold, faint malt aroma, very lightly hopped, medium body, clean dry flavor, small bubble carbonation, clean crisp finish, tasty aftertaste. Good thirst-quenching brew.

Samoa

Western Samoa Breweries, Ltd.
(Apia)

RAINMAKER IMPORTED PREMIUM BEER—slightly tawny gold color, slightly skunky aroma, complex interesting flavor, good hops up front, light sweet malt finish, long aftertaste, high carbonation, pretty good brew except for the skunk and excess CO_2.

South Africa

Brewing in South Africa began in the latter half of the nineteenth century and was greatly disturbed during the Boer War when many of the major breweries were being built or remodeled. At the turn of the century, South African Breweries, Ltd., was the leading South African brewer. It was a firm with its headquarters in London and a brewery of American design. In 1979 a reorganization of the alcoholic beverage industry took place in which South African Breweries effectively attained a monopoly of the beer market by acquiring its competitors. The consolidation was completed in mid-1980 when Carling O'Keefe, Ltd. (Canada) agreed to sell its Black Label and Red Cap beer trademarks in southern Africa to South African Breweries, Ltd., for $18.1 million (U.S.). All beers reported below are products of this company, the Castle brand going back almost one hundred years with the Castle Brewery of Johannesburg.

South African Breweries, Ltd.
(Johannesburg)

The brews listed here are not exported to the U.S. except for those packages brought in for can collectors. The beer in these cans is not likely to be in good condition, being either too old or mishandled.

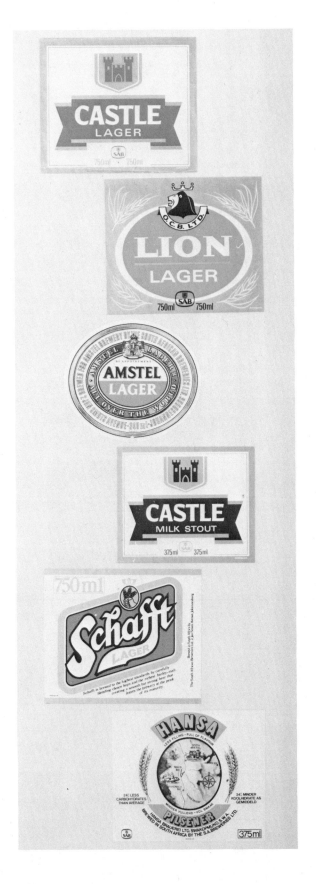

ROGUE LONG BREW BEER—faint applesauce nose, highly carbonated, very little flavor, slight bitterness in the finish.

CASTLE LAGER—deep gold, bright hoppy nose and pronounced hop flavor, small bubble carbonation, "neutral" hop flavor with no complexity, slightly bitter aftertaste. Originally a brew of Ohlsson's Cape Breweries, Ltd.

HANSA PILSENER (Hansa Brauerei Ltd., Swakopmund)—pale gold, lovely malt and hop aroma, highly carbonated, good balanced hop and malt flavor but this is marred by the excessive carbonation; good finish and a long clean aftertaste. An excellent brew except for the CO_2.

LION LAGER—pale tawny orange, pleasant lightly malted aroma, faint fruitlike flavor, slightly sweet with little complexity, very drinkable, pleasant but without zest. Another brew originally from Ohlsson's Cape Breweries.

AMSTEL LAGER—bright medium deep gold, light and balanced malt-hop aroma, highly carbonated, good malt flavor on the front of the palate, slightly sweet very pleasant finish, some bitter hops show in the finish, long good aftertaste. Would be a lot better without the excess carbonation. Brewed under license from Amstel/Heineken of Holland.

South America, Central America, and the Caribbean Islands

When the conquistadores arrived, the highly civilized Peruvians had developed agriculture to a high level, and were making the fermented beverage *chicha* from maize. Another fermented liquor, also made from corn, was *sora*. Sora was of such strength that the common people were forbidden to use it. The Incas, like the Aztecs of Mexico, also made *pulque,* and *chicha* was the national beverage. At the coronation of the last of the Incas, who received his crown from Pizarro, it is recorded that "the Inca pledged the Spanish commander in a golden goblet of the sparkling chicha."

As in Mexico, the beginnings of today's brewing trade in South America came with the arrival of European immigrants, among whom were experienced brewmasters, and may generally be dated 1860–1890. The first brewery in Colombia was established in 1889, Bieckert was Argentina's first in 1860, Brazil had one in 1870, Bolivia in 1882, and Ecuador got its first brewery in 1876.

Because of the high average temperatures, some of the early brews were pretty strange stuff. When the daily ambient temperature is over 85° F and there are no refrigeration facilities, the brew will likely be a desperate concoction. And so it was in South America. When modern refrigeration came along (about the turn of the twentieth century in Latin America), the beers became more like their counterparts in cooler North America, and in recent years the lighter-flavored and very pale pilseners have become the most favored.

Although every major city has a number of breweries, few Latin American beers ever find their way to North America. Most of them are rarely seen outside their city of manufacture.

Argentina

Compania Cerveceria Bieckert, S.A.
(Buenos Aires, Rio Segundo, Cochabamba)

Bieckert is the pioneer brewery of Argentina, having been founded by a man of that name in 1860. In 1889 the plant passed into the hands of an English syndicate, but is now believed to have been nationalized. Labels include Pilsen, Africana, Llavallol, Rio Segundo, Etiqueta Azul, Liviana, and Leon de Oro.

BIECKERT ETIQUETA AZUL PILSEN ESPECIAL CERVEZA BLANCA GENUINA—yellow-gold color with greenish cast, fruity malty (winelike) aroma, heavy body, complex sour malt flavor with a sense of licorice in the background. Interesting brew that can be extremely good.

BIECKERT ESPECIAL LIVIANA—deep apricot, toasted malt and prune aroma, burnt malt flavor with sour finish and aftertaste, complex, interesting, and strange.

LEON de ORO CERVEZA GENUINA—deep gold, delicate malt and hop aroma, big pleasant flavor, lots of hops, malt shows well at the finish, complex, good lingering aftertaste, a really fine brew.

Cerveceria Santa Fe, S.A.
(Santa Fe and Buenos Aires)

Brands include Rubia, Morena, and Especial.

SANTA FE PREMIUM LAGER BEER—deep yellow,

219

touch of brown; slightly skunky nose at first, but this went away, leaving an aroma of green hay, light sweet malt flavor up front, wood pulp finish.

Cerveceria Quilmes
(Buenos Aires)

QUILMES EXPORT—extremely pale yellow, high CO_2 which dominates the palate, what isn't carbonation reminds one of freshly cut alfalfa.

Barbados

Banks Barbados Breweries, Ltd.
(Bridgetown, St. Michael, and Wildey)

The Banks brewery was founded in 1961. Annual production now exceeds 2 million gallons and a product line of seven labels is headed by Banks Lager, Tiger Malt, Limelite, Cannon Stout, and Ebony. Although it advertises an all-malt brew, some cane sugar is added.

BANKS LAGER BEER—pale gold, heavily sedimented, delicate sweet aroma, delicate malt flavor that gradually fades across the palate. It is said that Banks does not travel well and this may account for considerable disparity in results of the tastings.

EBONY SUPER STRENGTH—deep brown, strong caramel, molasses, and roasted malt aroma, strong alcoholic flavor (two tasters reported that it sent a chill up their spine), portlike, long aftertaste. Powerful stuff.

Belize

Belize Brewing Co.
(Ladyville)

BELIKIN BEER—bright gold, large bubbles, good malt aroma with light hops, dry malt flavor, pleasant but lacks complexity.

BELIKIN STOUT—deep brown, sweet malt aroma, wine-like sweet complex palate, heavy body, faint bitterness in aftertaste.

Bolivia

Cerveceria Taquiña, S.A.
(Cochabamba and Santa Cruz)

TAQUIÑA CERVEZA EXPORT—pale yellow, slightly cloudy, nice sweet malt aroma with good hop balance, pleasant and malty up front, sour malt and hop finish, sour metallic aftertaste. Good brew when fresh.

Brazil

Companhia Cervejaria Brahma
(Rio de Janeiro, Sao Paulo, Porto Alegre, et al.)

The Brahma brewery was founded in the late nineteenth century by a German named George Maschke and was originally operated by George Maschke & Co. By 1900 it was one of South America's largest breweries. It now has an annual production capacity in excess of 10 million barrels and in 1980 purchased Skol Brazilian Breweries with its 13-million-barrel capacity. (See Skol-Caracu.)

BRAHMA CHOPP EXPORT BEER—cloudy greenish-yellow, vanilla malt cookie dough aroma and taste, not complex, sour malt finish, not really likeable at all. Chopp means draught.

BRAHMA BRAZILIAN PILSENER BEER—medium gold, fruity aroma with some cardboard background indicating oxidation, flavor the same as the aroma, highly carbonated, roasted malt background.

BRAHMA BEER—medium gold, pleasant malt and hop nose, medium body, hop flavor with a touch of apple peel, sweet in back, sweet finish, dry hop aftertaste. May be current label of the above (either or both).

Cervejaria Mogiana, Ltda.
(Mogi Mirim)

INGLESINHA STOUT—opaque brown, even the foam was deep brown, very faint roasted malt aroma, unbalanced, overly sweet soapy treacle finish and aftertaste.

Cervejarias Reunidas Skol Caracu, S.A.
(Rio Clara, Nova Lima, Guarulhos, Bonsucesso, et al.)

Skol is the largest selling international lager beer being brewed or sold in 55 countries throughout the world and is especially popular in England and several other European countries. I have never found it to be of much interest, being just a so-so German/Dutch-style beer. Reported below is the Brazilian version. Skol-Caracu was founded in 1904. A majority interest in the company was obtained by Brahma in 1980.

SKOL LAGER BEER—cloudy-yellow, small bubble carbonation, faint sweet malt aroma, clean grainy flavor, clean but austere finish, very little aftertaste. Quite different from European Skol.

CARACU CERVEJA FORTE STOUT—opaque brown, roasted malt aroma, low carbonation, a sweet stout with plenty of roasted malt, smoky character, big body; too sweet, however, almost cloying; good taste, but just simply too sweet, long clean aftertaste.

Colombia

Bavaria Brewery
(Bogota, Santa Marta, Bavaria S.A.)

This brewery was established in 1889 by a member of the house of Jacob Kopp & Sons of Frankfurt am Main, Germany. In 1897 it was sold to the German-Colombian Brewing Co. of Hamburg with the original owners retaining half the stock and the general management. The present company structure is not known.

CLUB COLOMBIA PILSENER-TYPE BEER—pale cloudy yellow with a greenish cast, malty pineapple aroma, malty taste that is too sweet at the start and too bitter in the finish, bitterness dominates the aftertaste, poorly balanced.

CERVEZA CLAUSEN EXPORT—medium yellow gold, interesting hop aroma, big hop flavor, reasonably well balanced except for some excess bitterness in finish and aftertaste. Good if you like lots of hops.

Dominican Republic

Cerveceria Nacional Dominicana
(Santo Domingo)

Although not found everywhere, this beer seems to sell quite well in Hispanic neighborhoods in major East Coast and southern U.S. cities. Major brands are Presidente and Malta Morena.

PRESIDENTE PILSENER TYPE BEER—deep yellow, very pleasant malty aroma with good intensity, disappointing metallic flavor that intensifies toward the finish, sour metal aftertaste.

Cerveceria Vegana S.A.

CERVEZA QUISQUEYA—bright gold, sweet buttery nose, sweet and fruity palate, good CO_2 level tones down the sweetness, buttery finish and aftertaste.

Ecuador

Cerveceria Club
(Quito)

CERVEZA CLUB PREMIUM—pale tawny gold, mushroom nose, hops at first, sweet middle, sour finish, palate completely screwed up. 3.9 percent alcohol.

Jamaica

Desnoes & Geddes, Ltd.
(Kingston)

This company produces Red Stripe, Red Stripe Light, Dragon Stout, and by license, Heineken and Mackeson Stout for the Caribbean market.

RED STRIPE LAGER BEER—slightly skunky aroma that fades with time, highly carbonated; slightly sweet spring water taste, but most of the palate sensation is the carbonation.

DRAGON STOUT—opaque, brown head, faintly sweet nose, medium body, lightly sweet coffeelike palate (not coffee flavor), and fairly long.

Peru

Cerveceria Backus y Johnston
(Lima)

CRISTAL—pale, slightly cloudy yellow; only the faintest of malt aroma, very faint sweet malt taste; clean, but weak and watery.

Compañia Nacional de Cerveza, S.A.
(Callao)

CALLAO PERUVIAN PILSEN BEER—pale yellow-gold, malty nose on the sweet side, good-tasting hop flavor, good balance, some zest, very drinkable, good brew. Label claims origins in 1863.

Puerto Rico

Cerveceria Corona
(San Juan and Santurce)

Cerveceria Corona was established in 1932 on the site of the Puerto Rico Brewing Co. (1912–1920), producer of a beer named Cerveza Palma Real. Prohibition had stopped the manufacture of Palma Real and the plant dedicated its facilities to soft drinks and ice. Upon repeal the company was reformed as the Corona Brewing Corporation. Steady growth and capital reinvestment in modern brewing equipment enabled Corona to reach an annual production of one million barrels of beer and malt. In 1979, Corona embarked upon a new modernization that will increase product quality and production.

CORONA BEER—pale golden yellow, slightly malty taste, nice hop nose, highly carbonated, flavor mostly CO_2, slight malt aftertaste. This beer was also made around 1960 in New York City by the Five Star Brewing Co. as Corona Cerveza Banda Blanca.

CORONA CERVEZA—"domestic" version, pale gold, sweet-sour celery nose, dull and flabby palate, no zest.

Cerveceria India, Inc.
(Mayaguez)

INDIA BEER—pale yellow, fresh malty aroma; clean taste, but unbalanced; dull, uninteresting finish and aftertaste.

INDIA LA CERVEZA DE PUERTO RICO—"domestic"

version, pale gold, pleasant malty nose, creamy texture, slightly sweet grainy-malty flavor, light but pleasant.

Brew Master's Corp.
(San Juan)

BREW MASTER'S LAGER BEER—medium deep gold, sweet malt aroma, sweet cardboard-fruit flavor, finish and aftertaste are more dry, but it doesn't pick up any more zest.

El Salvador

Cerveceria la Constancia, S.A.
(San Salvador)

PILSENER OF EL SALVADOR EXPORT BEER—pale tawny gold, light sweet hop aroma, light body, sweet palate up front, straightforward malt and hop flavor, dry hop-finish, little aftertaste but pleasant and thirst-quenching. An interesting label—the act of hearts.

Venezuela

Cerveceria Polar
(Caracas)

POLAR CERVEZA TIPO PILSEN—faint malt aroma, smooth, well balanced, a good-flavored blend of hops and malt. The best Latin American beer that was found in the U.S. over a long period of time.

Spain

Spain is not noted for its beers or its breweries mostly because inexpensive wine abounds. Spain's vineyards are copious and legendary, making it difficult to produce a beer competitive in price. Notwithstanding, reputable breweries do exist in Spain, several of which export their products to America.

Cervejeria San Martin
(Orense)

SAN MARTIN CERVEJA ESPECIAL—pale amber gold, faint malty aroma, salty sour taste, metallic aftertaste.

Sociedad Anonima Damm
(Barcelona)

Firm established in 1876.

ESTRELLA DORADA CERVEZA ESPECIAL PILSEN CLASE EXTRA—tawny gold winelike aroma with hops and toasted malt, good flavor up front, nutty-apple-malt, weak body, paper taste in the finish.

YOLL DAMM EXTRA CERVEZA ESPECIAL—tawny gold, pleasant malty aroma with just a touch of hops, creamy texture, strong sour hop flavor, harsh finish.

DAMM BEER—deep gold, faint grainy aroma, light grainy palate, slightly sweet up front, brief finish, slight dry aftertaste. Lacks character and zest. 5.6 percent alcohol by volume, 7-day fermentation, 6 weeks of aging.

San Miguel Fabrica De Cerveja y Malta, S.A.
(Lerida, Malaga, Burgos)

Firm established in 1876.

SAN MIGUEL LAGER BEER—cloudy yellow with some particulate matter in a recently imported batch, sour malty aroma, sour vegetal taste; same label as the Philippine product, but a very different brew.

El Aguila Breweries, S.A.

CERVEZA AGUILA DORADA—tawny gold, no aroma, unusual flavor with nougat foreground, almond and paper background.

AGUILA IMPERIAL—bright gold, good malty aroma, lightly toasted dry and crisp malt flavor, very long on palate, finely balanced, medium body.

Sweden

Until the nineteenth century, the production and consumption of distilled spirits were of such importance that malted liquors were hardly mentioned. Only in Sweden did the manufacture of malt beverages outside of homebrew exist. Late in that century, the Swedish people began to drink less spiritous liquors and more malt beverages. By 1901 there were 520 breweries in Sweden producing over two million barrels of beer annually.

The climate is not suited for growing barley; severe night frosts during much of the year are destructive to young crops.

The Swedish government continues to be concerned with excessive alcoholism. Since 1955 the tax structure on alcohol has been designed to encourage the consumption of beer rather than distilled spirits and wine.

Falcon Brewery
(Falkenberg)

The Falcon Brewery of Sweden dates back to 1896.

FALCON EXPORT III BEER—4.5 percent alcohol according to label, light malty aroma, bitter flavor, light cardboardlike finish and aftertaste. Found in a 16-ounce, very attractively designed can. A must for collectors.

Mariestads Bryggerie Aktiebolag
(Grängesberg)

MARIESTADS FESTIVAL BEER—deep yellow gold, a very faint aroma of malt and hops, watery, very little flavor, mostly CO_2, some residual bitterness.

Grängesbergs Breweries, Ltd.
(Grängesberg)

GRÄNGES BEER III—light gold, pleasant and balanced malt-hop aroma, flavor mostly hops, excessive malt extract results in scratchiness in throat, bitter finish and aftertaste.

GRÄNGES SWEDISH BLONDE BEER—tawny yellow, dry roasted malt aroma, good dry roasted malt flavor, light body, long on the palate, lingering aftertaste fades without losing its character.

Pripp Bryggerie
(Stockholm)

The Pripps Group consists of ten breweries and accounts for 70 percent of all the beer manufactured in Sweden. The product line includes light beer (2.25 percent): Lyckholms, Three Towns, Dart, Pripps Blå; "middle-strong" beer (3.5 percent): Pripps Blå; Three Towns, Pilsner, Medaljöl, Jubileum Special, Dart, Julöl, Carnegie Porter; strong beer (5.6 percent): Pripps Export, Three Towns, Jubileum Export, and Dart. Pripps also manufactures Tuborg and Carlsberg under license.

PRIPPS EXPORT III SWEDISH BEER—deep tawny gold color, hops dominate the nose and taste, malt shows well in the finish, malt and apple aftertaste character and full flavor. An excellent beer worth trying. It has all the gusto many others beers brag about, but lack.

THREE TOWNS—slightly cloudy tawny gold, beautiful sweet winelike fruity aroma, too highly carbonated, sharp hop flavor all the way through to the finish and aftertaste.

PRIPPS 150 JUBILEE EXPORT BEER—deep gold, fine classical European pils aroma of vegetal malt and hops, very clean big flavor with plenty of hops, good balance; fades too rapidly at the finish, but a good brew.

DART MÖRKT STARKÖL (Dark Beer)—copper red color, beautifully balanced hop and malt aroma, mild harmonious hop and malt flavor, lightly carbonated, good and you can drink a lot of it.

KALBACK LAGER—pale bright gold, very low carbonation; pungent hop aroma, but this nose is not reflected in the taste; instead the palate is soft, smooth and dry, but without any zest and there is virtually no finish, the flavor cutting off as soon as you swallow.

Switzerland

The beers of Switzerland are made according to the standards in Germany, that is, made with only water, malt, hops, and yeast. No additives are permitted. Brewing in Switzerland is recorded as early as 520 A.D., when a brewhouse was erected as part of the monastery at St. Gall. At the turn of the twentieth century, there were 367 breweries in Switzerland. Today there are 14.

Cardinal, S.A.: Feldschlossen, S.A.
(Fribourg, Sibra, Frankendorf, Rheinfelden, Waedenswil)

The beer industry in Fribourg commenced in 1788 when Francois Piller set up a brewery. In 1802 the brewery passed into the hands of Andre Keller, a master cooper. After several more changes of ownership, a watch manufacturer, Paul-Alcide Blancpain, obtained the brewery in 1877 and reorganized and modernized the company. In 1890 Cardinal's Beer was introduced in honor of the elevation of Monsignor Mermillod, bishop of Fribourg, to the cardinalate.

In 1901 Blancpain's sons, Achille, Paul, and Georges, took over the company and continued the firm's growth. Cardinal was joined by Feldschlossen in 1881 and both enhanced the firm's economic position in the highly competitive European beer market.

Cardinal Beer is an all-barley-malt beer made according to Bavarian beer laws and is aged a full eight weeks. The Cardinal line includes Pale Lager (a light beer), Pale Special (a bit stronger; this version of Cardinal is exported to the world as Cardinal Beer), Dark Special, Top (a rich malt beer), High Life (a light and sparkling luxury beer with a refined bitter taste), and Moussy, (a nonalcoholic beer exported to the U.S.).

CARDINAL LAGER BEER—tawny gold, smooth aroma with hops evident, finely balanced flavor with good hops and malt, great character and finesse. One of the finest beers tasted. Cardinal is produced at all five breweries; the export version is produced at Fribourg.

FELDSCHLOSSEN BIER SPECIAL (Spezial Hell)—dark tawny brown, but not a dark beer, malty Bavarian-style aroma; good malty, well-hopped flavor, excellent balance between malt and hops, long malt finish, fairly strong-flavored. Widely available in the U.S., relabeled Feldschlossen Hopenperle in 1980.

MOUSSY ALCOHOL-FREE LIGHT MALT BEVERAGE—50 calories, deep and clear bright gold, grainy malt aroma, grain and malt flavor, little zest, grainy aftertaste.

EX BIER—a 59-calorie near-beer, bright tawny gold, malty-molasses aroma, flat malt flavor, no zest, but flavor carries into a fairly long aftertaste.

Brauerei A. Hürlimann, A.G.
(Zurich)

This fine old firm was established in 1836 by Heinrich Hürlimann in Feldbach on Lake Zurich. The firm never did achieve notable success until son Albert set up the industrial enterprise that has grown to the large company we see today, which includes the former brewing firm of Uetliberg, Ltd.

HÜRLIMANN STERN BRÄU/SPEZIAL BIER—deep yellow-brown color, big sweet malt aroma with good hops, enormous malt and hop flavor, assertive, sour hop finish smooth and well-balanced. Available in cans and bottles. In cans, this brew is called Spezial Bier. The cans available are not regular exports to the U.S., but rather have been brought in for collectors. The brew in the cans may not be as fresh as that in the bottles. This Stern Bräu is the same brew as that sold in Switzerland. Some years back a Hürlimann Export Lager was made for the U.S. market. It was lighter than the Stern and had less aging time.

BIRELL MALT BEVERAGE—this famous international near-beer contains less than one percent alcohol; extremely pale colored, almost none at all; no noticeable body; a malty aroma, but weak and watery on the palate. Birell is available regularly in the U.S. only in bottles (330 ml). It exists in cans overseas, including an interesting can for the Arabian market.

Lowenbräu Brauerei
(Zurich)

This firm dates back to 1898 as the Aktienbrauerei Zurich. In the economic turmoils of the early twentieth century, it was involved in a series of amalgamations resulting, in 1925, in the present firm of Lowenbräu Zurich. Most of its export market today is in Italy and the United States. The primary product of this firm is reported below. Lowenbräu Zurich is one of the few unpasteurized bottled beers. Because of the special (and secret) filtration process, the beer is guaranteed to keep for a period of six months after bottling. It is lagered a full four months.

LOWENBRÄU SWISS BEER SPECIAL EXPORT LIGHT—very dark tawny brown color, creamy small bubbles, dark for a light beer, intense apple peel and malt aroma, strong malty flavor, bitter hop finish and aftertaste.

LOWENBRÄU ZURICH EXPORT LIGHT—pale gold, apple peel and malt aroma, creamy, good malt and hop flavor, good balance, good-tasting finish, a little unwanted sourness in the aftertaste.

LIBERO NON-ALCOHOLIC MALT BEVERAGE—pale gold, yeasty bready aroma with a touch of molasses, watery, dull malty flavor, brief finish, no aftertaste.

LOWENBRÄU ZURICH EXPORT DARK—deep copper-brown, faint vegetal nose, dry and dull, brief sour finish, little aftertaste.

Warteck Brewery
(Basel)

Firm established in 1856.

WARTECK NON-ALCOHOLIC MALT BEVERAGE—bright deep gold, malty skunky aroma, sour malt flavor with great duration.

Tahiti

Brasserie de Tahiti
(Papeete)

Founded 1914.

HINANO TAHITI LAGER BEER—pale gold, malty aroma with good hops, clean hoppy and faintly sweet taste, reasonably dry, slightly hopped finish and aftertaste. Hinano also brews Heineken for the local population.

Thailand

Amarit Brewery, Ltd.
(Bangkok)

AMARIT LAGER BEER—pale gold, some particulate matter, clean malty aroma with well-balanced hops; highly carbonated, taste like the aroma, but the carbonation interferes, bitter aftertaste.

Boon Rawd Brewery Co., Ltd.
(Bangkok)

SINGHA LAGER BEER—beautiful brilliant gold, nice malty aroma with good hop character, strong and bitter hop flavor, lingering harsh aftertaste.

SINGHA LAGER STOUT—the "stout" was labeled over "beer" and the label was overprinted "For export only," deep gold, sour grainy nose, sour malt flavor with noticeable hops that really hang in there, heavy-bodied.

Turkey

Turkey has two breweries, both in the European area of the country, that produce light and dark pilseners.

Efes Breweries
(Istanbul)

EPHESUS TURKISH PILSNER BEER—pale gold, sweet malty aroma with some hops in back, light body, lightly malted flavor, thin grainy finish and aftertaste.

Yugoslavia

The Balkan countries have slowly begun to establish a reputation for beer making, following the lead of the famous brews of nearby Czechoslovakia. Beer has been made in these countries for hundreds of years, but almost solely for local markets.

BI Pivovare (BIP)
Established 1850.

MARCUS BEER—slightly cloudy deep-yellow, pleasant light malt aroma, lightly carbonated, light malt flavor, slightly oxidized and a bit dull.

Niksicko Pivovare
(Niksic)

NIKSICKO PIVO—celery aroma, sour and bitter celery taste, salty molasses finish, malt aftertaste.

Union Pivovare
(Triglav, Ljubljana)

This firm dates back to 1864. It is the largest of Yugoslavia's thirty-one breweries.

UNION SVETLO PIVO—label says 12 percent alcohol, which may well be true since many of the local beers are long-brewed for a high alcohol content; vegetal, wood pulp, cardboard aroma; hops dominate taste. German in style, not bad, but not great. Domestic version. Union beers are brewed from all-barley malts.

UNION EXPORT BEER—medium gold, apple cider aroma with a malt background, heavily hopped flavor with a good malt-hop balance in the middle of the palate, high carbonation which shows in the finish a bit too strenuously, brief sour aftertaste. Good overall. Version exported to the U.S.

UNION EXPORT STOUT—extremely deep brown, austere pine needle and celery seed malt aroma, light-bodied, good roasted smoky malt flavor, short finish, slightly sour aftertaste. Very pleasant.

Zagrebacke Pivovare
(Karlovac)

This firm was established in 1854.

ZAGREBACKE KARLOVACKO SVIJETLO PIVO LIGHT BEER—pale yellow color, particulate matter in suspension, sour pilsener, vegetal aroma, sour-bitter flavor and aftertaste.

KARLOVACKO SPECIAL BEER—brilliant orange-yellow, faint winy aroma, slightly sweet and fruity, watery, low carbonation, faint papery-sweet flavor, dull, a little roasted malt character to the aftertaste.

KARLOVACKO LIGHT BEER—orange-yellow with particulate matter, malty-fruity aroma, fruity sour malt palate, very long aftertaste with a sweet-sour nature.

Jadranska Pivovare
(Split)

JADRAN BEER—slightly cloudy yellow, faint fruity and woody aroma, highly carbonated; flavor is mostly malt, but there are some hops, medium body, hops show a little better in the finish, aftertaste is mostly malt, not much character or zest.

6. HONOR ROLL OF BEER

In *The Great American Beer Book* there were only 570 beers to consider. Because most of them were available, a selection of the best eighty was made based on a simple and arbitrary number score criterion and the beers were submitted to a taste panel for a series of one on one comparisons. Pairings were done at random and if a brew was "defeated" twice, it was eliminated from the competition. Eventually a winner in each of 13 categories was selected by this double elimination method. Almost 200 comparisons were required to reduce the 80 brews to the 13.

This time there were over 1,000 brews to report and close to 200 brews would qualify for such a taste-off. The number of trials would probably exceed 500, one tasting each week for one year. Aside from that, the logistics of obtaining enough samples for this greatly

extended trial might well have become impossible to deal with. Many of the brews reported in this book were marketed in so small an area I was lucky to obtain two samples for the taste panel. With considerable regret, I decided not to take on the task.

After having tasted over 1,000 beers, however, I felt obliged to offer at least a listing of those that the tasters found to be the best. I considered a great variety of ways to do it, and none of them seemed to be fully adequate. Realizing that one man's meat is another man's poison does help to settle, if not solve the problem. Admittedly, it is sort of a cop-out to just list all the really good beers rather than pick and sort according to type and style, but there are so many good ones I wouldn't know where to begin to cut. So what I present here is the total list of all beers performing well in the trials, those that the tasters liked almost unanimously and that scored above 50 (for domestic) and 60 (imports) as described earlier. Two lists are offered: a list of beers made in North America and a list of beers made elsewhere. They are presented alphabetically. For scores, please consult Appendix I.

North American Beer Honor Roll

Anchor Porter (Anchor)
Anchor Steam (Anchor)
Andeker (Pabst)
Augsburger (Huber)
Augsburger Bock (Huber)
Augsburger Dark (Huber)
Ballantine India Pale Ale (Falstaff)
Black Horse Ale (Carling-Canada)
Black Horse Ale (Champale)
Black Horse Ale (Koch)
Bohemia Club (Huber)
Bohemia Pils (Molson-Canada)
Bohemian Pilsener (General)
Boulder Bitter (Boulder)
Brown Derby Light (General)
Budweiser (Anheuser-Busch)
Carling Black Label (Heileman)
Carling Red Cap (Heileman)
Carlsberg Gold (Carling-Canada)
Celebration Ale (Sierra Nevada)
Celebration Ale 1982 (Sierra Nevada)
Celebration Ale 1983 (Sierra Nevada)
Chelsea Ale (Real Ale)
Christian Moerlein (Hudepohl)
Colt .45 (Heileman)
Coors Banquet (Coors)
Corona (Modelo-Mexico)
Crystal Lager (Labatt-Canada)
Deer Run Ale (Koch)
Dos Equis (Moctezuma-Mexico)
Dow Cream Porter (Carling-Canada)
Genesee Bock (Genesee)
Genesee Twelve Horse Ale (Genesee)
Gold Keg (Labatt-Canada)
Golden Bear (Thousand Oaks)
Guinness Stout (Labatt-Canada)
Hanley Lager (Falstaff)
Heileman Light (Heileman)
Heileman Old Style (Heileman)
Heileman Special Export (Heileman)
Herman Joseph 1868 (Coors)
Huber Classic (Huber)
Iroquois (Koch)
Jacob Best (Pabst)
John Labatt's Extra Stock Malt Liquor (Labatts-Canada)
Kegle Brau (Cold Spring)
Keith India Pale Ale (Labatt-Canada)
Krueger (Falstaff)
Krueger Pilsener (Falstaff)
Labatt's Blue (Labatt-Canada)
Labatt's 50 (Labatt-Canada)
Liberty Ale (Anchor)
Löwenbrau Light (Miller)

Ludwig Hudepohl Bock (Hudepohl)
Maximus Super (F.X. Matt)
McSorley's (Schmidt)
Michelob (Anheuser-Busch)
Mickey (Heileman)
Miller High Life (Miller)
Molson Ale (Molson-Canada)
Molson Canadian (Molson-Canada)
Molson Porter (Molson-Canada)
Moosehead Lager (Moosehead)
Moosehead Special Ale (Moosehead)
Mustang (Pittsburgh)
National Bohemian (Heileman)
Negra Modelo (Mexico)
New Amsterdam (Old New York)
Noche Buena (Moctezuma-Mexico)
O'Keefe Extra Old Stock (Carling-Canada)
Oland Export (Labatt-Canada)
Oland Stout (Labatt-Canada)
Old Chicago Dark (Huber)
Old Foghorn (Anchor)
Old Milwaukee (Schlitz)
Old Scotia Ale (Labatt-Canada)
Old Style Pils (Molson-Canada)
Old Vienna (Carling-Canada)
Our Special Ale 1981 (Anchor)
Our Special Ale 1980 (Anchor)
Our Special Ale 1982 (Anchor)
Our Special Ale 1983 (Anchor)
Pearl (General)
Pearl Cream Ale (General)
Prior Double Dark (Schmidt)
Prior Light (Schmidt)
Reading (Schmidt)
Real Ale Stout (Real Ale)
Rhinelander Bock (Huber)
River City Bock (River City)
River City Dark (River City)
River City Gold (River City)
Rolling Rock (Latrobe)
Royal Amber (Heileman)
Schell's Deer Brand (Schell)
Schmidt's (Schmidt)
Sierra Nevada Pale Ale (Sierra Nevada)
Signature (Stroh)
Stag (Heileman)
Straub (Straub)
Stroh Bock (Stroh)
Tamalpais (Franklin)
Tecate (Cuauhtemoc-Mexico)
Time Saver (Falstaff)
Tuborg Dark (Heileman)
Tuborg Gold (Heileman)
Wiedeman (Heileman)
Yuengling (Yuengling)

Imported Beer Honor Roll

Aass Export (Norway)
Aass Jule Øl (Norway)
Aguila Imperial (Spain)
Albani Porter (Denmark)
Andechs Dunkel (Germany)
Augustiner Dark (Germany)
Augustiner Light (Germany)

Bass Ale (England)
Beck's Light (Germany)
Bieckert Pilsen Especial (Argentina)
Brassin de Garde (France)
Bulldog (England)
Callao (Peru)
Campbell's Christmas (England)
Cardinal (Switzerland)
Carlsberg (Denmark)
Cascade Spa (Australia)
Castlemaine Ale (Australia)
Club Weisse (Germany)
Cooper Stout (Australia)
Crystall Wührer (Italy)
Cuvee de l'Ermitage (Belgium)
Dahl's Export (Norway)
Dart Mörkt (Sweden)
Diekirch (Luxembourg)
Dinkelacker Bock (Germany)
Dinkelacker Dark (Germany)
Dinkelacker Light (Germany)
Doppelspaten Optimator (Germany)
Dortmunder Actien (Germany)
Dortmunder Imperial (Germany)
Dortmunder Imperial Oktoberfest (Germany)
Dortmunder Kronen Classic (Germany)
Dortmunder Ritter Bock (Germany)
Dortmunder Ritter Light (Germany)
Dortmunder Ritter Pils (Germany)
Dortmunder Siegel Pils (Germany)
Dortmunder Union Special (Germany)
Dreher Forte (Italy)
Dynasty (Taiwan)
EKU Jubiläumsbier (Germany)
EKU Maibock (Germany)
Erikois (Finland)
Estrella Dorada (Spain)
Fassl Gold (Austria)
Feldschlossen (Switzerland)
Fest Bier (Germany)
Finlandia Gold (Finland)
Foster's (Australia)
Fürstenberg Imported (Germany)
Gilde Edel-Export (Germany)
Gold Eagle (England)
Gränges (Sweden)
Green Rooster (Denmark)
Guinness (Ireland)
Hacker Edelhell (Germany)
Hacker Light (Germany)
Hacker Oktoberfest Märzen (Germany)
Hacker Oktoberfest (Germany)
Hacker Weiss (Germany)
Hansa Fjord/Hansa Beer (Norway)
Heineken Dark (Holland)
Heineken Light (Holland)
Henninger (Germany)
Henninger Dark (Germany)
Henninger Doppelbock (Germany)
Heritage Ale (England)
Holsten Export (Germany)
Horsy (Germany)
Imperial Stout (Denmark)
Isenbeck Extra Dry (Germany)
Itala Pils (Italy)
Itala Pils Gold (Italy)
Kaiser Bavaria (Germany)
Kaiserdom Pils (Germany)

Kaiserdom Rauchbier (Germany)
Karjala (Finland)
Kiesel Festbier (Germany)
Kiesel Pils (Germany)
Killian Bière Rousse (France)
Kirin (Japan)
Kulmbacher Amber Light (Germany)
Kulmbacher Dark (Germany)
Kulmbacher Dry Light (Germany)
Kulmbacher Festbier (Germany)
Kulmbacher Heller Bock (Germany)
Kulmbacher Kloster Bock (Germany)
Kulmbacher Kloster Schwarz (Germany)
Kulmbacher Oktoberfest (Germany)
Kulmbacher Reichelbräu Edelherb (Germany)
Kulmbacher Reichelbräu Frankisches (Germany)
Kulmbacher Schweitzerhofbrau Bock (Germany)
Leon de Oro (Argentina)
Lowenbrau Munich Light (Germany)
Lutèce (France)
Leffe Dark (Belgium)
MacAndrew's (Scotland)
MacEwan Edinburgh (Scotland)
MacEwan Scotch (Scotland)
MacEwan Tartan (Scotland)
MacEwan Strong Malt Liquor (Scotland)
Mackeson (England)
Magnus (Belgium)
Mann's (England)
Neptun Paske (Denmark)
Neptun Pinse (Denmark)
Newcastle Brown (Scotland)
Old Bedford Ale (England)
Ottakringer Bock (Austria)
Patrizier (Germany)
Paulaner (Germany)
Paulaner Fest-Bier (Germany)
Paulaner Münchener Märzen (Germany)
Paulaner Salvador (Germany)
Paulaner Ur Bock (Germany)
Paulaner Weiss (Germany)
Pelforth (France)
Peroni (Italy)
Peter's Brand (Holland)
Pinkus Weizen (Germany)
Pope's "1880" (England)
Pripps (Sweden)
Pripps Export (Sweden)
Pripps Jubilee (Sweden)
Ringnes Bock (Norway)
Ringnes Special (Norway)
St. Pauli Girl (Germany)
St. Pauli Girl Dark (Germany)
Samuel Smith Brown (England)
Samuel Smith Pale (England)
San Miguel (Philippines)
San Miguel Dark (Indonesia)
San Miguel Dark (Philippines)
Scandia Gold (Denmark)
Spaten Märzen Oktoberfest (Germany)
Splügen Bock (Italy)
Steinlager (New Zealand)
Stern (Germany)
Swan (Australia)
Taddy Porter (England)
Tennent's (England)
"33" Export (France)
"33" Extra Dry (France)

"33" Record (France)
Thomas Hardy Ale (England)
Toohey's Lager (Australia)
Tooth Stout (Australia)
Traquair House Ale (England)
Urquell (Czechoslovakia)

An early example of Stroh print advertising.

Warsteiner (Germany)
Westmalle (Belgium)
Westmalle "Dubbel" (Belgium)
Whitbread Pale (England)
Whitbread Tankard (England)
Wieze (Belgium)
Worthington Pale Ale (England)
Wunster 14 (Italy)
Wunster 18 (Italy)
Würzburger (Germany)
Würzburger (U.S.A. and Germany)
Würzburger Bock (Germany)
Würzburger Dark (Germany)
Würzburger Oktoberfest (Germany)

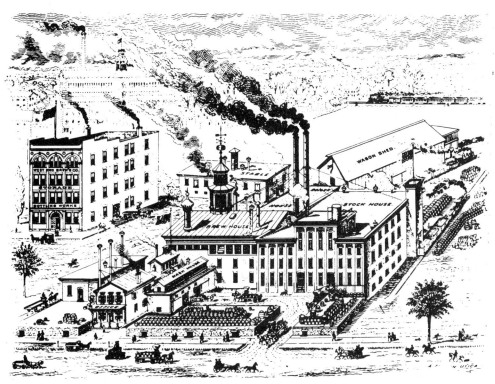

Premises of the West End Brewing Company, Utica, New York (1887)

7. THE BOTTOM OF THE BARREL

After all the suds had blown away, all the data gathered and analyzed, all the glasses washed, all the bottles thrown away and all the cans handed over to grateful collectors, it was time to review what had been learned (besides finding out what were the best beers). Some of the information that follows was learned directly by intentional investigation and experimentation. Some of it was discovered by accident, in passing, or by examining the results.

Labels

Beer labels the world over have one feature in common. With few exceptions, they guarantee nothing more than that there is some form of alcoholic malt beverage within. About the only label information required for beer in any country is alcoholic percentage and the U.S. is not one of those requiring such data. Nowhere do the legal requirements for labeling beer measure those regarding the identification of wine.

In the United States labeling practices are particularly atrocious. Terms like *ale* and *premium* are regularly misused. That a label identifies its product as an ale is no guarantee that it is a top-fermented brew and just about everything is called premium, export quality, or special. In most cases they are just buzz words. Even import labels are deficient in usable information.

One of the few times the U.S. government got involved in beer labeling was in the case of Gablinger (see Rheingold), in which the brewer was actually prohibited from including consumer information on the label. There is now a growing practice of including nutritional data on beer packages, especially when the product is aimed at the calorie-conscious market.

Age

Wine has often been described as a living thing. In its youth it is sharp and vigorous. With time it matures and becomes mellow and rich. With more time age takes its toll and the features fade; the wine becomes more fragile and eventually passes into the past tense.

Without the poetry, beer too is a living thing. It is rough and unbalanced in its brief "green" stage, at its best when mature, takes on some unpleasant characteristics with advanced age, and eventually will become too old and will die. Age and handling (as a function of style) are perhaps the two greatest factors bearing on the pleasure that can be derived from a beer.

The important question concerns the beer's being too old for its style. Can you judge if a beer is likely to be stale with age without actually having to buy and try it to find out if it is? A number of experiments were conducted to determine how old a beer can become before losing quality. Beers were held for varying amounts of time at a cool constant temperature (to minimize any handling damage) and in refrigeration. These were injected into the taste trials at random intervals and subjected to the criticism of the taster panel. The following results indicated no simple or single answer (just as with so many other facets of life):

a. Pasteurized beer has a greater life expectancy than unpasteurized beer.

b. Dark beer has a greater life expectancy than light beer.

c. Among light beers, life expectancy decreases with lightness. The paler the beer, the more fragile the constitution.

d. Beers with a high alcoholic content live longer than low alcohol beer. Low-calorie beers are at their best for a very short time. Only rare high alcohol beers improve with age after bottling.

e. Heavily hopped beers are longer-lived than lightly hopped beers. They are, however, subject to a flaw that results in skunkiness.

f. Beers with a high percentage of barley malt live longer than beers with a lesser amount. In its simplest form, that could be construed as a restatement of "c" above, but here I intend it to refer to heavier light beers and to dark beers. Some very dark, 100 percent roasted-barley malt

ales have an extremely long life expectancy, like a wine.

g. A beer constantly (and consistently) refrigerated is more likely to survive a given time perod than one kept at room temperature.

Note: The rules that apply to life expectancy directly apply to the fragility of a malt beverage, its susceptibility to harm from mishandling. Some examples of these rules: Perfection, the highly hopped richly malted beer from Horlacher, known to have been produced before Christmas, 1976, showed no signs of wear in mid-1980. However, a five-month-old sample of Coors showed considerable loss of character. India Pale Ale, highly hopped and with a relatively high level of malt and alcohol, was devised to be a viable beverage after months of ocean transport in conditions that would severely test any beer.

Translating the findings into practice yields the following guidelines:

a. Before purchasing an unpasteurized beer check for a pull date. If it is more than three months old, you run the risk of getting something less than what you paid for. Since there is no real reason to fear getting a beer that is too young, where there is a choice, get the youngest available. If unpasteurized beer is stored in a refrigerated facility (as it should be), you have only the concern that it is too old or that it might have spent some time out of refrigeration when you weren't looking. If unpasteurized beer is stored in an unrefrigerated area, even for a matter of hours, buy it elsewhere. So-called canned or bottled draft beer usually is pasteurized, to my knowledge (see note on filtered beers, below). Supposedly it is "draft" style, but that may mean little more than it is highly carbonated.

b. In dealing with pasteurized beer, you usually have nothing to go on beyond observable conditions at the retail outlet. Some have massive walk-in refrigerators and all beer is stored in and sold from that facility. This affords you the best chance of purchasing fresh beer. Most have some form of refrigeration, but unless turnover is high, the back stock is subject to the effects of aging from exposure to temperature extremes. This could be called premature aging. With separate facilities for beer "up front" and "in back," there is always the risk of improper stock rotation. Where there is no refrigeration, you are advised to buy only popular items. In these last two cases the object is simply to try to get the youngest, freshest package possible. Unless there is personal knowledge of a new supply, trust in the retailer, or other clues (like a change in package design), choice is by guess and by golly. If your store seems frequently to have stale beer in stock, buy it elsewhere.

It is worth noting at this point that several companies (mostly foreign) are using filtering techniques in lieu of pasteurization. Knowing that pasteurization is harmful to the taste of their product, but that U.S. food and import standards still have to be met, special "millipore" filtration processes have been introduced. A brew so filtered will supposedly stay fresh for up to six months after bottling without refrigeration and meet the same purity standards achieved through pasteurization. An increasing number of imports use this technique, first tried on exports to the U.S. by Lowenbrau Zurich and Augustiner of Munich. It is also now being used for some domestic brews, such as "draft-style" beers.

Foreign vs. Domestic

Most beer drinkers will freely admit that (in general) foreign beers are better than domestic beers. It is true of many commodities that the imports are equal to or better than the best comparable domestic product. Mostly, this is because a country normally exports only its best efforts. Foreign beers may be better for the additional reason that their manufacture is strictly regulated by law as to ingredients and purity of process. There is no comparable domestic regulation.

The scores resulting from the tastings indicate that the best imports are better than the best domestic brews. The best domestic brews, however, fared much better than the average import. This is mostly because there was a large percentage of imported beers that ranked very low.

The distribution of scores for domestic beers was much as would be expected for the quality of any commercially produced item. Most beers scored in a cluster near to the center of the possible scoring range with a scattering of values at the high and low ends. The distribution of scores for the imported beers differed. The distribution lacked the clustering effect expected for the center of the distribution. No area of the distribution resembled the expected bell shape. Most natural distributions follow some predictable shape that is or can be associated with normal or classical mathematical distributions. In general, the shape of the curve of distribution of values resembles a bell, with a great many values lumped somewhere on the curve (usually somewhere near the midrange point) and the rest scattered throughout the range, decreasing in quantity toward the extremes. The curve may be skewed toward one end or the other, but the bell shape generally obtains. When it does not, there usually is the effect of some outside agent.

There is no certain way to explain the departure of the import distribution curve from that expected, but it may be the result of getting a relatively large number of samples from abroad that were in an overage or mishandled condition. If it is assumed that the import beers would have had a distribution much like the domestic brews and that a significant number of samples tried had been so damaged, the distribution of scores would have turned out to be like that experienced in the tastings. The good products, with a larger following and a high turnover rate, would be obtained fresh and would perform as well as they could under ideal conditions. Average, middle-grade, or unfamilar (new) imports with little or no following, might have sat on a shelf for some time and could have been too old to perform up to their potential.

Accepting this explanation, which appears to be reasonable, one concludes that obscure or less popular imported beers should be bought with care. Newly marketed brews may be fresh on first appearance, but if they don't sell at a high rate, it may take a long time to deplete that initial shipment and the stock on shelves and in warehouses may become stale.

Shelf life is the single most significant factor to an importer. His success or failure will depend largely on the condition of the beer as it sits on store shelves. The brew must have a shelf life sufficiently long so that after transport to foreign port, loading on ship, transoceanic voyage, unloading at U.S. port, transport to distributor, and delivery to retailer, it is still fresh enough that customers will come back for more, repeatedly and regularly.

Each beer has a different shelf life potential based on its recipe, the ingredients used, processes of manufacture, duration of brewing, lagering, and storage. Some of the factors have been described earlier in this section under "Age." Complicating the determination is that brewers usually cannot obtain a sufficient quantity of the most desired hops and malt (or barley, if they make their own malt) to last for an entire production year. Most will have to use barley from a number of crops maturing at different times in different parts of the world to keep up their supply for production and even more chasing about is required as brewers vie for the limited availability of choice hops.

If a beer has been found wanting in performance in these pages, it is likely so because it was obtained too old. In other words, it was past its shelf-life expectancy. The brewer may complain that his beer is better than that described and he may be right. It is just that we did not find it so when we went out and bought, and if we found it in poor condition, there is some reason to believe you could find it that way as well.

Where brewers provided their beer to the taste panel in fresh condition, they were generally rated more highly than samples purchased in local stores.

Effects of Beer on the Palate

The effects of food on palate sensitivity were discovered early in the taste trials and have been discussed at length in chapter four, "The Great Experiment" (see under "Foods at Tastings"). But what about the effect of the beer itself on the palate? Surely, the ability of a human being to make valid judgments on the characteristics and value of a given beer will be reduced with an increasing number of samples, if for no reason other than the alcohol in his bloodstream. The limitations of tasters were tested by requiring them to taste different quantities of beers at each tasting and retrying the items tasted at later times of the experiment.

It was found that people have greatly varying tolerance and palate ability with regard to beer.

Some were able to judge relatively fine points of difference among brews after tasting over thirty samples. Others had judgment problems after a dozen or so. Since the portions of each sample were small and the time taken for tasting was on the order of three hours, it is believed that innate palate sensitivity was more of a factor than the effects of alcohol. Those oriented to tasting (anything) could discriminate between more beers in an evening than those who were not. One taster who does not normally drink beer, but who is highly experienced in wine and food tasting, was able to perform like the most experienced beer connoisseur on the panel, once he had been thoroughly briefed on the criteria.

Another effect noted was that the tasting ability of an individual varies. On a given night, a person's taste buds might be off right from the start or after only a few samples. At those times his reaction to a brand might be at odds with the reactions of other tasters.

Since all the beers were being tasted in pairs, there was some concern about the effects of the pairings. Would a beer be unfairly rated because it had the misfortune to be sampled along with something very good or very bad? To see if there was any cause for worry, several dozen beers that had already been sampled by the panel were included in tastings again but paired differently. The second set of scores was virtually the same, well within the variance that would be expected from a subjective examination (within 10 percent).

An American Taste

Is it possible to identify and describe a typical American taste for beer? Could it be done with any other national group?

The large beer companies seem to think so. They have computer programs that have taste preference worked in as a parameter, but at the same time new beers are subjected to trial marketing, so they aren't certain. There is certainly such a thing in America as regional taste. But like the chicken and the egg, which came first? Did the beer satisfy the market for that regional taste or did the taste become inured to the beer available? Belgium is a classic example of regional taste, yet sales of the Artois and Loburg beers, both very different from any of the unique regional types, indicate that they are at least candidates for a Belgian national palate preference.

In the taste trials and experiments there was no method for quantifying an American national taste preference, but there were data on the opinions of a random sampling of American beer drinkers from widely diverse backgrounds over a wide geographical area. With over three dozen tasters and over one thousand beers, some observations can be made.

Collectively they preferred beer that was zesty, but not very highly hopped, beer that was naturally and lightly carbonated, beer that was richly flavored with a high percentage of barley malt, and, above all, beer that was balanced. Perhaps it is more revealing to identify what they didn't favor: very pale, very light, or low-calorie beers; soda pop, winy, and highly carbonated beer; highly hopped beer and ale like those so popular in Great Britain (Harp, Double Diamond, etc.); and so-called house flavors. Although their collective preference takes a middle-of-the-road taste, it was surprisingly cosmopolitan. They liked well-made beers from all over the world. They did not approve of the vast majority of American beers that have arrived on the market in the past half decade, which may indicate a difference in opinion with the computer. Miller's domestic Lowenbrau Light is one of the few recent additions that met with the approval of the taste panel.

Individual Preference

"Before we could go out to the cabin we'd pick up a case of Genesee. It's my favorite. I can pick it out of a crowd anytime."

"Budweiser is my brew. They tested me in a bar once. Three times I picked my Bud out of a group of four beers.

"That Blatz is real horse—."

"I had my brother-in-law haul in a case of Coors from Boulder last summer. It's the one thing I really miss since I moved east."

The Genesee fan couldn't tell his beer without being shown the label in his "day in court." The Bud lover couldn't successfully pick his beer out of a pair. The Blatz hater gave it the highest score of the evening. The Coors "importer" picked Schmidt's when he didn't know which was which and in a second try selected Old Frothingslosh.

In dozens of tests, long-time beer drinkers failed to recognize their beer in blind trials. Not only could they not pick their long-time preference from a group of two, *most* of the time they failed to select their avowed favorite as their choice. Only once did a taster recognize his favorite, the distinctive Maximus Super. Another time he failed to recognize it, but did give it the higher score.

In its advertising campaign during the 1980 professional football playoffs, Schlitz tried to capitalize on this knowledge in competing live against major national brands. That almost half of the avowed Budweiser, Michelob, or Miller drinkers selected Schlitz comes as no surprise.

In short, beer drinkers are hard pressed to identify their favorite brew unless they know it is being served to them. Random guessing would have produced better results for picking out a favorite than the results obtained in the tastings.

On the other hand, tasters could reliably predict their preference as to style or type of beer. If a taster stated that he preferred German beer, he invariably scored German or German-type beer higher. If ales were the avowed preference, the taster could be depended upon to score ales higher than lagers.

The effect of advertising on preference should not be underestimated. Tasters' descriptions of beers served "open" closely matched the qualities promised by advertisements. This effect has long been noted in the wine trade, where the reputed qualities of a famous wine are likely to be observed by tasters more when they can see the label than when they cannot. Descriptions from "blind" trials are usually different and much more critical of the product.

No wonder that many of the top brewers in the country spend more money on advertising than on the product.

I suppose everyone should have his collection of mystique items, including a beer that he knows is better than any other. Our testing indicates that the need could be served equally well by a beer that is inexpensive and readily available if you wish to go by taste alone. If your beer must be hard to come by and expensive as well, you will find brews costlier and rarer than Coors.

Cans vs. Bottles

It is commonly believed that beer tastes

better in bottles than in cans. This belief was common long before the glass industry began promoting the thought on TV. Cans are lighter to carry around, have a reputation for being faster to chill and don't present the hazard of broken glass. Bottles are usually a few cents cheaper and are easier to drink from. Those features can be traded off easily enough, if only one knows what truth there is in the taste belief.

After 379 beers had been sampled, the record for bottled products was compared with that for canned beers. An arbitrary score of 60 (two-thirds of the maximum possible points) was selected for imported beers and an arbitrary cutoff value of 50 was selected for domestic beers. The number of canned and bottled beers that equaled or bettered the arbitrary values would be compared to see if there was a difference in quality between bottled and canned beer.

Of the 379 beers involved, 229 were in bottles and 150 in cans. The results were:

Total Cans—150
  Canned beer scoring above cut-off—18 (12%)
Total Bottles—229
  Bottled beer scoring above cut-off—58 (25%)

CAN BREAKDOWN:
Foreign—26
  Foreign cans above cutoff score—5 (19%)
Domestic—124
  Domestic cans above cutoff score—13 (10%)

BOTTLE BREAKDOWN:
Foreign—167
  Foreign bottled above cutoff score—42 (25%)
Domestic—62
  Domestic bottled above cutoff score—16 (25%)

These results show a clear advantage for bottled over canned beer by a two to one margin. Bottled beer products showed equally well for foreign and domestic brands. Foreign cans also appear to have shown well, but the sample size is too small for a conclusion.

The explanation may be related to environment. Aluminum conducts heat much better than glass. According to the *Handbook of Chemistry and Physics,* the conductivity* of aluminum is 0.504, whereas glass is 0.002.

This means that a canned beer is able to recieve heat from the environment at a rate over 250 times greater than would bottled beer in the same circumstances. Actually, since the conductivity is specified for a given thickness of the material, the conductivity of a can would be 250 times greater than that of a bottle having the same thickness as the can. Since bottles are much thicker than cans, the actual difference in conductivity rate is probably more on the order of 1,000 than 250. You can test this for yourself by placing a chilled bottle and can in a room, pouring them into glasses after fifteen to thirty minutes, and measuring their temperature with a thermometer. The fluid from the can will have risen closer to room temperature than the fluid from the bottle.

It would seem that beer packaged in cans faces a higher possibility of damage from exposure to extremes of temperature simply because damaging exposure can occur in a shorter period of time. Of course, mistreatment over a long period of time will be equal in cans and bottles. After several hours, the heat transfer will be complete and the contents of can or bottle will rest at the ambient temperature. It is only in short-term exposure that the difference in conductivity between glass and aluminum is notable. A sixpack of bottles left on the hood of a car on a hot day may not be significantly affected in a half-hour, but the same treatment could materially affect a sixpack of cans.

Discussions with various brewers indicate that many of the problems encountered with canned beer are caused by oxidation. There is an air space in any package be it can or bottle. The significant factor in dealing with oxygen and its effect on a malt beverage is the surface area of exposure. In a narrow necked bottle with a good fill, the surface of exposure is very small. In a can, the surface is the full cross-sectional area of the package.

A number of additional experiments were conducted with tastings of pairs of the same beer, tried in can and bottle together. The sample was a bit too small for profound conclusions, but the results indicated a slight edge for the product in the bottles. The taste of fresh samples was so close as to indicate no advantage for can or bottle. In thirty-nine comparisons of fresh samples, the taste panels preferred the bottled version twenty times and the canned version nineteen times. With more aged samples, a three to two preference for bottled beer over canned resulted, supporting the thesis offered above.

---

*Number of Calories per second transmitted through a plate 1 sq. cm. when the temperature difference is 1°C.

From all the data, analysis, and experiments, one can conclude that with fresh stock, it makes little difference whether you buy your beer in cans or bottles. If, however, there has been exposure to potentially harmful conditions or if you intend to keep the beer a long time before using it, bottled beer is the sounder choice.

Beers of Mystique

When I was twenty-five years younger, the mystique belonged to Michelob. "Everybody" knew it was the best beer he could get. It was rarely found in those days in the East and was available only on draft. That last part guaranteed that it was great stuff. We would thumb down to Framingham, to the only place for miles that had it, and sip the nectar in a dingy smelly bar. When Michelob was packaged and readily available, the mystique left and we drank it less than when it was hard to get.

At another time, cases of San Miguel made their way all over the Pacific in U.S. Navy ships to ensure that the best was available to swabbies wherever they served. Knowing the premium at which space on board ship is regarded, you can well imagine how esteemed those goods were. During World War II bomber pilots striking at Manila had strict orders not to damage the holy of holies, the San Miguel brewery. Of course, Douglas MacArthur's supposed financial interest in the brewery had little to do with it.

In our time the Coors mystique is the big item in beer. Long before I arrived in Colorado, I had been told what I had best drink while there. Dutifully, on arrival, I hied over to the Antlers (Colorado Springs' great and, alas, late hot spot) and took a long draft of Coors. It was heavenly, like everything else about Colorado. Thereafter I joined the long list of those who smuggled Coors east. The bloom began to fade from the rose one evening in Cody, Wyoming, when my wife, in her ignorance of the subject, noted that the Olympia she was drinking tasted better than my Coors. To prove her wrong, we did a miniblind tasting of the two. Coors lost. I passed it off as a bad sample and nothing more was thought of it until Schmidt's ran its Coors-Schmidt's test ad campaign. Much to my surprise, we preferred the Schmidt's. But a mystique dies hard and there had to be an acid test. I rounded up a dozen Coors lovers and had them compare the two. Schmidt's trounced Coors eleven to one to the amazement of the twelve confirmed believers. A little later in the evening, I suggested we repeat the experiment. This time nine tasters voted seven to two against Coors, only the opponent was Old Frothingslosh, a frequently derided beer from Pittsburgh which is actually the Christmas package of Iron City Beer.

In all fairness to Coors, the supplies of the beer that are available on the East Coast are usually too old and the beer is particularly sensitive to the effects of age. Also, since Coors is not pasteurized, there is a good chance that supplies on the East Coast have been mishandled. Coors should be regarded for what it is, a very good, well-made, lightly flavored beer that can be enjoyed with food or with friends and that is at its best only when young and properly treated. It can be an extraordinary experience when fresh, especially when you are very thirsty. But it doesn't measure up to the demands of "mystique."

The Sensory Perception of Beer

Modern brewing is a complicated demanding industry. As in winemaking, there are literally hundreds of faults that can disrupt the quality of a brewed malt beverage. The understanding of what occurs chemically in brewing has increased 100-fold in the past fifty years and that is a great help to the brewer, but competition is keen and modern brewing techniques have introduced new problems.

For example, the use of extracts and adjuncts (hop extracts in place of hops and corn and rice as partial replacement of barley) has created problems for the brewer in separating the wort from the trub. This problem is eased by the addition of coagulants to rid the wort of undesired constituents and to facilitate separation of clear wort. Such additives, however, may induce still other problems.

Beer making is a chemical process. Only two reactions in brewing are not produced by enzymes (the formation of calcium oxalate and the transformation of humulones in hops into the isohumulones in beer). All other reactions are produced by enzymes and yeasts (which are tiny sacks of enzymes). So, we must look to chemistry for a better understanding of what it is that we like (or dislike) in a brew.

Since aroma constitutes a major portion of the apparent quality of all foods, chemical gas detection and analysis equipment has been used to develop *gas chromatographic data* for beer. For those who like numbers, some 54 major beer flavors have been identified and computer analysis of quantitative data on these indicates eleven peaks (mainly esters and alcohols) which varied significantly with temperature of storage and other factors. Categorizing the flavor constitutents of beer according to their intensity results in the following table:

Table I. Flavor Constituents of Beer

PRIMARY FLAVOR CONSTITUENTS

(intensity above 2.0 Flavor Units)

> Ethanol
> Hop bitter compounds (e.g. isohumulones)
> Carbon dioxide

> *Specialty beer components:*
> Hop aroma compounds (e.g., humuladienone)
> Caramel-flavored compounds
> Esters and alcohols (high-gravity beers)
> Short-chain acids

> *Defects:*
> 2-trans-nonenal (oxidized, stale)
> Diacetyl 2-2, 3-pentanedione (fermentation)
> Hydrogen sulfide, dimenthyl sulfide, etc. (fermentation)
> 3-Methylbutyle-2 Enylthiol (light struck hops)
> Other (microbial infection)

SECONDARY FLAVOR CONSTITUENTS

(intensity 0.5-2.0 Flavor Units)

> *Volatile:*
> Banana esters (e.g. isoamyl acetate)
> Apple esters (e.g. ethyl hexanoate)
> Fusel oil (e.g. isoamyl alcohol)
> Aliphatic acids
> Ethyl acetate
> Butyric and isovaleric acids
> Phenylacetic acid

> *Non-volatile:*
> Polyphenols
> Various acids, sugars, and hop compounds

TERTIARY FLAVOR CONSTITUENTS

(0.1-1.5 Flavor Units)

> 2-phenethyl acetate
> Isovaleraldehyde
> Acetoin
> Methional
> Valerolactone

OTHER (less than 0.1 Flavor Units)

> All remaining

Now that the flavor constituents have been identified, it is time to discuss many of the more familiar ones. The aroma and flavor of the malt are readily recognized, especially if it has been roasted (as in many fine English ales) or smoked (Kaiserdom Rauchbier). The distinctive aroma and taste of hops used for bittering are also well familiar to beer drinkers. Less familiar are the complex odors and flavors resulting from the use of aromatic hops. Most of the pleasant herbaceous, complex, and fragrant components come from these hops. Unpleasantness in beer often has a complex or obscure origin and can be traced to raw materials, the brewing process, contamination, improper handling in shipment and storage (as exposure to temperature extremes, vibration, or light), or excessive elapsed time from brewing to consumption.

The more commonly encountered odors and flavors are described below, together with clues to their origin.

Table II. Common Odors and Flavors in Beer

PLEASANT HERBAL ODORS—aromatic hops which may give sensations of clover, verbena, sage, parsley, orange, orange peel.

VINOUSNESS (WINELIKE QUALITY)—presence of esters, an organic compound formed by the reaction of an acid and an alcohol. While it is considered an advantage in an ale, it is not attractive in a pilsener.

LEATHER, PAPER, CARDBOARD, WOODINESS—oxidation, exposure of the brew to oxygen.

SOAPINESS—octanoic acid (or caprylic acid), a fatty acid which may take on animal tones or a rancid character.

CHEESE—isovaleric acid resulting from the oxidation of isopentyl alcohol (isopentyl alcohol is also called isoamyl alcohol or simply amyl alcohol).

BANANA—isoamyl acetate, an acetic ester of amyl alcohol from fusel oil, called also amyl acetate, banana oil, or pear oil.

MILK—lactic acid resulting from bacterial fermentation of starch, molasses or sugar.

GREEN APPLE—acetylaldehyde or dehydrogenated alcohol, reactive organic compound intermediate in the state of oxidation. Undergoes self-esterification when heated.

MEDICINAL—phenolic, soluble acidic compound derived from actions of a phenol with an aldehyde.

CORN—dimethyl sulfide, a compound containing two methyl groups in the molecule.

BUTTERSCOTCH, BUTTER—diacetyl (or biacetyl), a diketone with a buttery flavor; it is the flavor in butter, a contributing flavor in coffee and tobacco, and is used to synthetically flavor margarine.

RUBBER, BOOT, SKUNK—presence of mercaptans, a compound analagous to alcohols and phenols, but containing sulfur in place of oxygen.

NAIL POLISH REMOVER—acetone (or dimethyl ketone); in beer it is probably caused by bacterial fermentation of corn mash.

RANCID BUTTER—butyric acid resulting from oxidation of normal butyl alcohol or butyl aldehyde or by fermentation of molasses. May also be caused by the action of anerobic bacteria on lactic acid.

WET BASEMENT—butyric fermentation or oxidation.

The range of odors and tastes listed in Table II covers most of those that the average person can expect to encounter in a lifetime, but it must be remembered that some of these can occur in combination. For example, a common combination in an old sample is the presence of a phenolic in an oxidized brew which smells like antiseptic gauze or an old Band-Aid from the 1940s.

Knowing about what problems may be faced by brewers is fine for understanding what is wrong with your brew, but it is obviously more meaningful to know what can be done to avoid such problems. Brewers try to maintain scrupulously clean conditions, for once a microbial infection gets into a brewing plant, it may be nearly impossible to get rid of it. Strict quality control and continuing inspection and analysis is done. Most brews are filtered or pasteurized. Otherwise they must be refrigerated "end-to-end." Intricate distribution arrangements (sometimes even using competitors' facilities) are set up to speed delivery, since all brews have a finite and limited shelf life, beyond which time latent defects or weaknesses (very much present in the pale, low malt, low alcohol brews popular today) can make their appearance.

High temperatures will accelerate unwanted reactions, particularly oxidation. It is virtually impossible to package a brew without leaving some oxygen in the air space. Vibration will cause bubbles to form and the shaking will then break those fragile bubbleskin structures and the proteinaceous flakes will be sedimented or, more likely, suspended in solution. Extended severe chilling also can cause clouding and may alter the character of the brew. Freezing tends to take the zest out of beer.

The chemical effect of light on beer, particularly sunlight, has long been known. Until about forty years ago, it was not well understood, except that if the beer was not bottled in dark green or brown bottles it became skunky. Chemists knew that light could bring about a reaction in a system where no reaction was taking place, catalyze a reaction already taking place in the dark, or change the course of a reaction already ongoing in the dark by the formation of new products. One of the things that puzzled them all was that beer seemed to be very susceptible and soft drinks were not. Experimentation showed that the tiniest trace of ethyl mercaptans and other low molecular weight sulfhydryl compounds would produce the skunky smell in beer. Beer contains proteinlike bodies derived from malt of which sulfur is a characteristic element and sulfur compounds which contain the sulfhydryl group are known to be present in yeast. Both the metabolism of yeast and the exposure of malt protein to sunlight can form traces of simpler sulfhydryl bodies. Subsequently it was found that also hops can react with sunlight to form these skunky compounds.

There is little the consumer can do to avoid the defects implanted in a brew by the brewer, distributor, or retailer beyond shopping elsewhere. If your store obviously mistreats beer or the beer that he sells you is frequently defective, go elsewhere for your brew. Patronize those who have proper storage facilities and who have high turnover. Don't allow your beer to become overheated, overchilled (for extended periods of time), or excessively exposed to light or vibration. These are the elements within your control that contribute the most to the defects in your beer. In these respects, treat your beer as you would treat fine wine. Lastly, and most importantly, consume your beer while it is still fresh. The longer it sits, the more likely it is to have developed faults. There are virtually no beers available in the United States that improve with aging.

Beer on the Dinner Table

A goodly part of the world's population enjoys malt beverage with meals. Without a question beer goes well with Oriental, Mexican, Indonesian, and Indian food. These foods are either highly spiced or exotically sauced and it is difficult, if not downright impossible, to enjoy their character with either wine or soft drinks. Only the dryness of beer and tea seems to be suitable.

As an experiment, more than anything else, beer lovers have been trying their hand at something much more complex than enjoying their favorite brews. They have been attempting to orchestrate multi-course dinners of fine French cuisine with beer. They feel that if this area of culinary endeavor, unquestionably the province of the fine wines, can be satisfactorily enhanced by clever matching of brew to course, then beer drinking shall have been elevated in the eyes of gourmets and thrust nearer to its rightful station.

In the July-August, 1980 issue of *The Friends of Wine,* Bob Abel's article "Beer Is Not a Proletarian Drink" outlines a French dinner with beer. Mr. Abel's choices were excellent examples of how beer can be used to augment fine dining on a course by course basis every bit as effectively as can wine. His choices are given below in the hope that you may be inspired to try your hand at it.

An appetizer of mussels steamed with white wine (flavoring of parsley, onions, bay leaf, and thyme) was matched with Pilsner Urquell. Molson Ale was served with a watercress soup. The fish course, poached filet of sole with mushrooms, merited a Kronenbourg. The meat entrée, a roast duckling in orange-flavored brown sauce, French fries, and Brussels sprouts braised in butter needed a full-bodied Carlsberg Elephant Malt Liquor. Beck's Light was served with the salad, a course of delicate Bibb lettuce with oil and vinegar, and the chocolate mousse dessert was served with Würzburger Dark. An after-meal platter of fruit and cheese was enhanced with Black Velvet, Guinness Stout and Champagne. It all sounds delicious.

I have tried beer with French menus and have to rate them quite successful. This is not to say that beer is better than wine (or worse than wine) for fine dining. It is only different and for those that love beer, another pleasant and interesting experience.

It should be noted here that the amenities of serving wine should not be ignored when serving beer with fine food, although those amenities may be different to some degree.

The glass should be clean and dry. No trace of soap and (especially) detergent should remain. Rinsing and air drying is recommended. Some even go so far as to wash their beer glassware with baking soda.

Pour down the side of the glass until almost full. If the last ounce or two is then poured down the center of the glass, a nice head will be achieved. This method yields the desired head without overly sacrificing the carbonation needed to keep the brew lively if you intend to drink it slowly.

Alcoholic Beverage Control

There are about as many variations of alcoholic beverage control as there are political subdivisions. It is not enough that it is different from state to state or province to province, but stepping across a county or town line will put you under the restrictions of different laws in most of North America.

The simplest way to discuss these controls is to examine them one by one.

PERCENTAGE ALCOHOL

In Canada most brews are 5 percent (by volume), but the laws are lenient and brews of 6-8 percent are available in most areas. In the U.S. the percentage is lower. In Utah and West Virginia, beer must not exceed 3.2 percent. Other states allow the sale of beers stronger than 3.2 percent only in liquor stores (Iowa, Kansas, Minnesota, and Montana) and those beers stronger than 3.2 percent may be specially marked (as "Strong" in Minnesota, for instance). In some states only 3.2 percent beer can be sold on Sunday. In California any beer with more than 5 percent alcohol must be labeled as something other than beer (e.g., malt liquor, ale, stout, etc.). Other areas have similar laws so that consumers won't get loaded unexpectedly.

TIME OF SALES

Sales times will vary by county and town in most of the United States and by province in Canada, but in general the major division is with regard to Sunday sales. Some states do allow Sunday sales of beer, but mostly it is afternoon only. I have found no Canadian Sunday sales.

WHERE TO BUY

Most states allow grocery stores to sell beer, some by local approval only. Some dozen states allow off-licensing for taverns, others for drug stores, and some even permit gas stations to dispense beer. With the exception of Alabama (which has no liquor stores) states have either privately owned or state-owned liquor stores. Beer is available in all of these except for New York and Pennsylvania. In New York beer is available just about everywhere except for liquor stores and in Pennsylvania beer is sold only in taverns or in special case beer outlets. In Canada beer is usually sold in provincial liquor or beer outlets.

AGE

Allowed age for purchasing alcoholic beverages varies from 18 to 21. In several states with a 21-year minimum requirement, sales of 3.2 percent beer are allowed for younger drinkers.

PACKAGE SIZE

I have always found it curious that governments regulate the package size for beer sales in their area. I don't think there is any regulatory agency that really cares what size package are used, but it is a holdover from stricter times and no one yields power easily. Beer sizes range from 7 to 128 ounces with 12-ounces being considered the universal size.

The "Intellectual" Pursuit of Malt Beverages

The more affluent segment of mankind has long pursued wine intellectually as a class hobby for centuries. Many in North America, during the affluent 1960s and 1970s, took up the pleasant pursuit. It is only natural that this intellectual interest should eventually extend to malt beverages, particularly with the pinch of inflation as encouragement.

Even though their budget has shrunk, the intellectual interest started by the wine and fine food remains. These people still had the taste for exotic foods and beverages. It was thus no surprise that they should discover malt beverages and turn to an examination of that subject with much of the same zeal that they had earlier applied to wine.

It didn't take industry analysts long to recognize that sales of imported beer had increased substantially and numbers of foreign beers on the market increased rapidly to meet this new demand. The initial flood of brews was not too satisfactory from a beer drinkers' viewpoint for the demand had been confused with the can-collecting interests. Quite a number of these canned imports were old and stale. The good ones, however, sold like hotcakes.

Shortly, the wine importers got into the act and the quality improved. Wine importers had supplied this interest group for years and were more attuned to the demand. Further, they were wine people and not beer people, so they could take a fresh look at the subject, not prejudiced by previous (and now outmoded) experience.

Perhaps the best example of such a firm is Merchant du Vin of Seattle headed by wine and beer afficionados Charles Finkel and Elizabeth Purser. Using the experience of Bon-Vin, a company formed by Finkel to distribute good quality wines from little-known wineries across the United States and a deep interest and affection for malt beverages, Merchant du Vin has set out to bring the world's great beers to the Americas.

Such an importer tries to span the full width and breadth of beers made worldwide and such diverse brews as Samuel Smith's Pale Ale, Lutèce Bière of Paris, Lindeman's Gueuze and Kriek Lambic, Kaiserdom Rauchbier, Rodenbach, Aas Jule Øl, and Pinkus Weizen are available to beer drinkers in North America for the first time.

It is clear that such firms as Merchant du Vin are going to enrich the palates of American beer lovers. They deserve our support. Note: For those who would like to know more of Merchant du Vin and their product line, they publish a parody of *Barron's* called *Beeron's* which contains background information on all their imports. Write to them at 214 University St. Seattle, Washington 98101. In mid-1981 they issued a second informative "newspaper" named *Alephenalia*, highlighting their most recent imports.

Small-Brewery Resurgence

Once America was dotted with small independent family-run breweries. Nearly every community had a brewery it could call its own. Gradually they disappeared, either as a result of Prohibition or because they could no longer compete with the industry giants. By the late 1970s even some of the large brewing companies were succumbing to the same maladies that had befallen their smaller brethren in the recent past.

That there is a resurgence of small breweries today is not completely unexpected. With rising beer prices and a decided lack of zesty regional beers, many beer lovers tried homebrewing, a hobby which allows the homebrewer the opportunity to cater to his individual taste. When this love of beer was coupled with a high level of brewing competency, it was only natural that they should wish to try their hand at commercial enterprise. Additionally, many of them have sufficient means from either their profession or retirement that they are not entirely dependent on the income from brewing. This is valuable protection from some of the business reversals that are possible.

The qualifications of these brewers are quite varied, but all share a common love for finely made all-natural malt beverages. In addition to those included in this book, a large, number of others are in process of setting up their business. Watch for Berkeley, Mendocino, Stanislaus, and Humboldt Bay in California; Britannia in Florida, Mariner and Nashawannuck in Massachusetts; Legendary in Arkansas; Chesapeake in Virginia; and Eagle Rock in Idaho. Also, watch for a similar phenomenon on Canada's west coast, where significant numbers of small-brewery applications are being considered by the British Columbia Liquor Board.

For those of us who consume, it can only bode well. A greater variety of tastes will become available and any one of them could hit that happy combination that suits us just right. At the moment these brews tend to be expensive (around $1-$1.25), but this could ease a bit given some of the improvement in efficiency that time and experience usually provide.

Should you find some of these new brews, you should remember that they are not pasteurized and require end-to-end refrigeration and some time before drinking to allow the sediment to settle. It is suggested that they be decanted so that none of the bitter dregs find their way into your glass and thence to your palate. If you take these precautions, you may experience a real treat of the brewer's art.

Summary

The most important fact learned about beer in this entire exercise is that it is a fragile commodity, just like wine. Handled with care and thought, beer drinking can be a rewarding experience.

The consumer of beer has little protection from mishandled or overage beer beyond his personal limited knowledge and experience. Labels tell almost nothing. With the current popularity of "natural" products and the brewers' need to exploit that trend, the number of brews on the market today containing additives represents only a small percentage of the total and those additives must be approved by the U.S. Food & Drug Administration.

Foreign beers are better from the standpoint of ingredients, since they are strictly regulated in that regard. But there is a greater likelihood that imported beer has been mishandled or is overage.

Taste sensitivity is affected by foods, the number of beers consumed and the conditioning effects of advertising. Beer tastes as good from cans as from bottles, when both are fresh. But with age or exposure to extremes of temperature, the bottle is more reliable.

Beer should be enjoyed without stigma. In most of the world it is regarded as a food. It certainly has a long record of success as a means of promoting temperance. In short, make an effort to learn which beers you find most enjoyable and then enjoy them with food and friends. Thereby you will add a measure of satisfaction to your life.

Here's looking at you, friend!

APPENDIX I

Alphabetical Listing of Beers Tasted with Ratings by Taste Panel

This alphabetical list gives a shortened form of the of the brand name, the type of beverage (B-beer, A-ale, P-porter, RA-reduced alcohol, S-stout, IPA-India pale ale, ML-malt liquor, W-Weiss, ST-steam, BK-bock, LO-low-calerie, NB-near-beer,, MB-malt beverage. European equivalent of near-beer, L-lambic), the manufacturer for U.S., Canadian, and Mexican beers, country of origin for others, and a taste panel rating on a scale of 0-90 according to chapter four, "The Great Experiment," under "Rating the Beers." The list is divided into separate sections for the United States, Canada, and Mexico, Central America and the Caribbean, South America, Africa, Asia, Australasia, and Europe.

The reader is advised to view the numerical scores with some caution. They are the upper figures of scores given by a panel of tasters and must simply be regarded as quantitative measures of a very subjective subject, personal taste and preference. The same set of tasters examining the same set of beers conceivably could come up with different results at any time. That they did not ever come up with substantially different scores in retrials of a brew does not mean that the numbers applied are hard and fast. Where two brews achieved greatly different scores the reader may safely assume that the higher scoring item is the better of the pair. Where the scores differ only by a small amount, like within 10-15 percent, no such assumption should be made.

United States

BRAND	TYPE	COMPANY	RATING
ABC	B	Eastern	41
ABC ALE	A	Eastern	32
ACME	B	Heileman	21
ALPS BRAU	B	Huber (Peter Hand)	21
ALTA	LO	Heileman	30
ALT DEUTSCH	B	Pittsburgh	37
ALTES	B	Heileman	30
AMERICAN	B	Pittsburgh	28
ANCHOR PORTER	ST/P	Anchor	83
ANCHOR STEAM	ST	Anchor	50
ANDEKER	B	Pabst	54
ANHEUSER NATURAL LIGHT	LO	Anheuser-Busch	40
A-1	B	Heileman	36
ARROWHEAD	B	Cold Spring	36
AUGSBURGER	B	Huber	72
AUGSBURGER BOCK	BK	Huber	58
AUGSBURGER DARK	B	Huber	50
AUGUSTINER	B	Pittsburgh	36
AVENUE	B	Schell	46
BALLANTINE	B	Falstaff	48
BALLANTINE ALE	A	Falstaff	23
BALLANTINE BOCK	BK	Falstaff	25
BALLANTINE DRAFT	B	Falstaff	34
BALLANTINE INDIA PALE ALE	IPA	Falstaff	70
BALLANTINE LIGHT LAGER	LO	Falstaff	20
BARTEL'S	B	Lion	34
BASICS	B	Lion	32
BAVARIAN CLUB	B	Huber	37
BAVARIAN DARK	B	Heileman	26
BAVARIAN'S SELECT	B	Koch	24
BAVARIAN TYPE	B	Yuengling	25
BEER	B	Falstaff	26
BEER	B	General	20
BEER	B	Pittsburgh	28
BERGHEIM	B	C. Schmidt	33
BILLY	B	Cold Spring	24
BILLY	B	Heileman	26
BILLY	B	F.X. Matt	28
BILOW BOCK	BK	Walter	28
BILOW GARDEN STATE LIGHT	B	Eastern	22
BILOW LIGHT	B	Walter	29
BILOW PREMIUM	B	Walter	45

BIG CAT	ML	Pabst	34
BIG JUG	B	Schoenling	30
BLACK HORSE ALE	A	Champale	65
BLACK HORSE ALE	A	Koch	54
BLANCHARD'S	B	Eastern	39
BLANCHARD'S	B	Falstaff	24
BLATZ	B	Heileman	43
BLATZ LIGHT	LO	Heileman	33
BLATZ LIGHT CREAM ALE	A	Heileman	26
BLITZ-WEINHARD	B	Heileman	36
BLUE FOX	A	Koch	36
BLUE RIBBON	B	Pabst	45
BLUE RIBBON BOCK	BK	Pabst	37
BLUE RIBBON LIGHT	LO	Pabst	45
BOAR HEAD STOUT	S	C. Schmidt	45
BOH BOHEMIAN	B	Falstaff	24
BOHEMIAN CLUB	B	Huber	56
BOHEMIAN PILSNER	B	General	62
BOSCH	B	Leinenkugel	24
BOULDER BITTER	B	Boulder	55
BOULDER PORTER	P	Boulder	38
BOULDER STOUT	S	Boulder	39
BRAUMEISTER	B	Huber	17
BRAUMEISTER BOCK	BK	Huber	32
BREAK	RA	C. Schmidt	23
BREWER'S GOLD	A	Falstaff	39
BREWER'S LAGER	B	C. Schmidt	37
BREW 96	LO	C. Schmidt	9
BREW 102	B	Falstaff	41
BREW 102	B	General	38
BRICKSKELLER	B	Pittsburgh	20
BROWN DERBY	B	General	27
BROWN DERBY	B	General (Pearl)	20
BROWN DERBY	B	Pittsburgh	24
BROWN DERBY LIGHT	LO	General	54
BRUENIG'S	B	Walter	36
BUB'S	B	Walter	31
BUCKHORN	B	Olympia	38
BUCKHORN	B	Heileman	37
BUDWEISER	B	Anheuser-Busch	51
BUDWEISER LIGHT	LO	Anheuser-Busch	32
BUFFALO	B	Heileman	14
BULL'S EYE	B	Koch	40
BURGEMEISTER	B	Huber	31
BURGER	B	Hudepohl	20
BURGERMEISTER	B	Pabst	18
BURGIE LIGHT GOLDEN	LO	Pabst	20
BURGUNDY BRAU	ML	Pittsburgh	26
BUSCH BAVARIAN	B	Anheuser-Busch	34
BUSCH PREMIUM	B	Anheuser-Busch	32
CANADIAN ACE	B	Eastern	40
CANADIAN ACE DRAFT	B	Eastern	31
CAPE COD	B	Eastern	16
CAPRUS	NB	Eastern	20
CARLING BLACK LABEL	B	Heileman	59
CARLING BLACK LABEL LIGHT	LO	Heileman	49
CARLING RED CAP	A	Heileman	53
CARLING 71	LO	Heileman	20
CELEBRATION ALE	A	Sierra Nevada	63
CELEBRATION ALE 1982	A	Sierra Nevada	60
CELEBRATION ALE 1983	A	Sierra Nevada	63
CHAMPAGNE VELVET	B	Pickett	12
CHAMPALE	ML	Champale	40
CHAMPION	B	Koch	28
CHELSEA ALE	A	Real Ale	50
CHERRY HILL	B	Champale	28
CHICO PIONEER DAYS	B	Sierra Nevada	22
CHIPPEWA FALLS	B	Leinenkugel	38
CHIPPEWA PRIDE	B	Leinenkugel	29

CHRISTIAN MOERLEIN	B	Hudepohl	60
COLD BRAU	B	Cold Spring	40
COLD SPRING	B	Cold Spring	38
COLD SPRING EXPORT	B	Cold Spring	42
COLT .45	ML	Heileman	51
COLT .45 SILVER	ML	Heileman	18
COLUMBIA	B	Heileman	33
COOK'S GOLDBLUME	B	Heileman	33
COOR'S BANQUET	B	Coors	59
COORS LIGHT	LO	Coors	26
COQUI 900	ML	C. Schmidt	24
COUNTRY CLUB	ML	General (Pearl)	20
COY	B	Heileman	38
COY	B	Pittsburgh	30
CROFT ALE	A	Falstaff	33
CROSSROADS	B	Schell	29
CRYSTAL	B	Lion	33
DAITCH SHOPWELL	B	Eastern	17
DAWSON	B	Eastern	35
DAWSON SPARKLING ALE	A	Eastern	23
DEER RUN ALE	A	Koch	52
DE LIGHT BREW	NB	General	9
DIXIE	B	Dixie	33
DIXIE LAGER	B	Dixie	47
DIXIE LIGHT	LO	Dixie	48
DIXIE LIGHT LIGHT LIGHT	LO	Dixie	42
DOUBLE K	B	Falstaff	32
DREWRY'S	B	Heileman	30
DREWRY'S DRAFT	B	Heileman	33
DRUMMOND BROS	B	Heileman	39
DUBOIS BOCK	BK	Pittsburgh	46
DUBUQUE STAR	B	Pickett	34
DUKE	B	C. Schmidt	29
DUNK'S	B	Heileman	38
DUQUESNE BAVARIAN	B	C. Schmidt	44
DUTCH TREAT	B	Heileman	33
EASTSIDE	B	Pabst	35
ECONO BUY	B	General	26
ECONOMY CORNER	B	Lion	21
EDELWEISS	B	Pickett	29
ERIE LIGHT	LO	C. Schmidt	23
ERLANGER	B	Schlitz	44
ESQUIRE	B	Jones	30
ESSLINGER	B	Lion	41
FALLS CITY	B	Heileman	38
FALSTAFF	B	Falstaff	45
FALSTAFF FINE LIGHT	B	Falstaff	27
FALSTAFF LITE	LO	Falstaff	27
FALSTAFF 96 EXTRA LIGHT	LO	Falstaff	36
FINAST	B	Eastern	25
FISCHER'S	B	Heileman	39
FISCHER'S ALE	A	Heileman	38
FISCHER'S LIGHT	LO	Heileman	21
FISHER	B	General	20
FITGER'S	B	Schell	18
FORT PITT	B	Jones	20
FORT SCHUYLER	B	F.X. Matt	42
4077TH MASH	B	Falstaff	36
FOX DE LUXE	B	Cold Spring	26
FOXHEAD 400	B	Eastern	47
FOXHEAD 400 DRAFT	B	Eastern	22
FRANKENMUTH DARK	B	Geyer	30
FRANKENMUTH LIGHT	B	Geyer	48
FRIENDSHIP LOUNGE	B	Schell	24
FYFE & DRUM	LO	Genesee	40
GABLINGER	LO	C. Schmidt	41
GABLINGER EXTRA LIGHT	LO	C. Schmidt	49
GAMBRINUS GOLD	B	Pittsburgh	10
GAMBRINUS GOLD LABEL	B	Pittsburgh	28

GEMEINDE BRAU	B	Cold Spring	29
GENESEE	B	Genesee	47
GENESEE BOCK	BK	Genesee	50
GENESEE CREAM ALE	A	Genesee	49
GENESEE CREAM LIGHT	A	Genesee	42
GENESEE LIGHT	LO	Genesee	26
GEORGE KILLIAN IRISH RED	A	Coors	38
GIANT FOOD	B	Lion	34
GIBBONS	B	Lion	34
GIBBONS ALE	A	Lion	26
GIBBONS PORTER	P	Lion	18
GLUEK PILSENER	B	Cold Spring	26
GOEBEL	B	Stroh	44
GOETZ	B	General	44
GOETZ PALE	NB	General	23
GOLDEN ANNIVERSARY	B	Koch	20
GOLDEN BEAR	ML	Thousand Oaks	51
GOLDEN CHAMPALE	ML	Champale	16
GOLDEN CREST	A	Koch	41
GOLDEN CROWN	B	General (Pearl)	32
GOLDEN GATE	ML	Thousand Oaks	35
GOLDEN HAWK	ML	C. Schmidt	35
GOLDEN LAGER	B	Coors	25
GRAIN BELT	B	Heileman	34
GRAIN BELT PREMIUM	B	Heileman	26
GRAND UNION	B	Eastern	25
GRIESEDIECK BROS. GB LIGHT	B	Falstaff	30
GUNTHER	B	Stroh	39
HAFFENREFFER	B	Falstaff	47
HAFFENREFFER	ML	Falstaff	35
HAMM'S	B	Olympia	48
HAMM'S DRAFT	B	Olympia	29
HAMM'S SPECIAL LIGHT	LO	Olympia	32
HANLEY	B	Falstaff	54
HARRY'S WHITE LABEL	NB	Eastern	9
HAUENSTEIN	B	Heileman	45
HEDRICK	B	Eastern	26
HEIDELBERG	B	Heileman	35
HEIDEL BRAU	B	Heileman	20
HEILEMAN'S LIGHT	LO	Heileman	50
HEILEMAN'S OLD STYLE	B	Heileman	50
HEILEMAN'S SPECIAL EXPORT	B	Heileman	64
HENRY WEINHARD DARK	B	Heileman	27
HENRY WEINHARD S PRIVATE RESERVE	B	Heileman	45
HERITAGE HOUSE	B	Pittsburgh	39
HERMAN JOSEPH 1868	B	Coors	68
HI-BRAU	B	Huber	24
HOFBRAU	B	Hudepohl	49
HOF-BRAU	B	Falstaff	30
HOF-BRAU	B	Pearl	24
HOME PILSENER	B	Lion	35
HUBER BOCK	BK	Huber	42
HUBER CLASSIC	B	Huber	54
HUBER PREMIUM	B	Huber	45
HUDEPOHL	B	Hudepohl	18
HUDY DE LIGHT	LO	Hudepohl	14
IRON CITY	B	Pittsburgh	41
IRON CITY DRAFT	B	Pittsburgh	41
IRON CITY LIGHT	LO	Pittsburgh	11
IROQUOIS	B	Koch	50
IVY LEAGUE	B	C. Schmidt	16
JACOB BEST	LO	Pabst	57
JACOB RUPPERT	B	C. Schmidt	32
JAX	B	General	42
J.R. EWING	B	General	46
KAIER'S	B	C. Schmidt	49
K&B PILSENLAGER	B	Dixie	20
KAPPY'S	B	Falstaff	35

KARLSBRAU	B	Cold Spring	20
KASSEL	B	General	38
KATZ	B	Falstaff	44
KEG BRAND	B	General	25
KEGLE BRAU	B	Cold Spring	54
KINGSBURY	B	Heileman	17
KINGSBURY BREW	NB	Heileman	15
KNICKERBOCKER	B	C. Schmidt	32
KOCH HOLIDAY	B	Koch	17
KOCH JUBILEE	P	Koch	44
KOCH'S LIGHT	LO	Koch	33
KOEHLER	B	C. Schmidt	39
KOEHLER LAGER	B	C. Schmidt	36
KOEHLER PILSENER	B	C. Schmidt	32
KOLONIE BRAU	B	Cold Spring	45
KOOL MULE	ML	C. Schmidt	NR
KREWES	B	Falstaff	45
KRUEGER	B	Falstaff	52
KRUEGER CREAM ALE	A	Falstaff	27
KRUEGER PILSENER	B	Falstaff	59
LEINENKUGEL	B	Leinenkugel	41
LEINIE'S LIGHT	LO	Leinenkugel	27
LIBERTY ALE	A	Anchor	78
LIEBOTSCHANER ALE	A	Lion	37
LIEBOTSCHANER BOCK	BK	Lion	20
LITE	LO	Miller	43
LONE STAR	B	Olympia	35
LONE STAR DRAFT	B	Olympia	44
LONE STAR LIGHT	LO	Olympia	32
LORD CHESTERFIELD ALE	A	Yuengling	20
LOWENBRAU DARK	B	Miller	48
LOWENBRAU LIGHT	B	Miller	54
LUCKY BOCK	BK	Falstaff	40
LUCKY BOCK	BK	General	20
LUCKY DRAFT	B	General	42
LUCKY 50	LO	General	15
LUCKY LAGER	B	Falstaff	44
LUCKY LAGER	B	General	26
LUCKY LITE	LO	Falstaff	29
LUCKY 96 EXTRA LIGHT	LO	General	18
LUDWIG HUDEPOHL OKTOBERFEST BEER	B	Hudepohl	59
LUDWIG HUDEPOHL BOCK	BK	Hudepohl	50
MACHO 1200	B	Schell	35
MAGNA CARTA CREAM ALE	A	Pittsburgh	18
MAGNUM	ML	Miller	18
MARK V	B	Pittsburgh	34
MASTER BREW	B	Walter	14
MASTER'S CHOICE	B	Heileman	35
MATT'S PREMIUM	B	F.X. Matt	32
MAXIMUS SUPER	B	F.X. Matt	57
McSORLEY'S CREAM ALE	A	C. Schmidt	63
MEDALLION	B	Olympia	43
MEISTER BRAU	B	Miller	39
METBREW/METBRAU	NB	Champale	16
METBREW LIGHT	NB	Champale	16
MICHELOB	B	Anheuser-Busch	66
MICHELOB DARK	B	Anheuser-Busch	19
MICHELOB LIGHT	LO	Anheuser-Busch	47
MICKEY'S	ML	Heileman	61
MILLER HIGH LIFE	B	Miller	58
MILLER MALT LIQUOR	ML	Miller	29
MILLER SPECIAL RESERVE	B	Miller	27
MILWAUKEE BRAND	B	Eastern	22
MILWAUKEE BRAND BOCK	BK	Eastern	18
MILWAUKEE BRAND CREAM ALE	A	Eastern	23
MILWAUKEE BRAND ISRAEL EXPORT	B	Eastern	48
MILWAUKEE MALT TONIC	NB	Eastern	14
MILWAUKEE'S BEST	B	Miller	26

MUNICH LIGHT	B	Falstaff	45
MUSTANG	ML	Pittsburgh	51
NARRAGANSETT	B	Falstaff	45
NARRAGANSETT BOCK	BK	Falstaff	26
NARRAGANSETT CREAM ALE	A	Falstaff	15
NARRAGANSETT 96 EXTRA LIGHT	LO	Falstaff	40
NARRAGANSETT PORTER	P	Falstaff	42
NATIONAL BOHEMIAN	B	Heileman	57
NATIONAL PREMIUM	B	Heileman	45
NEW ALBION ALE	A	New Albion	42
NEW ALBION PORTER	P	New Albion	20
NEW ALBION STOUT	S	New Albion	4
NEW AMSTERDAM AMBER	B	Old New York	58
NEUWEILER CREAM ALE	A	C. Schmidt	14
NEUWEILER IX	A	C. Schmidt	34
900 COUNTRY CLUB	ML	General (Pearl)	45
905	B	Heileman	16
905 LIGHT	LO	Pittsburgh	30
NO FRILLS	B	Lion	28
NORTHERN	B	Cold Spring	39
NORTH STAR	B	Cold Spring	31
NUDE	B	Eastern	38
OERTEL'S 92	B	Huber	36
OLD BOHEMIAN	B	Eastern	26
OLD BOHEMIAN ALE	A	Eastern	17
OLD BOHEMIAN BOCK	BK	Eastern	18
OLD BOHEMIAN LIGHT	LO	Eastern	39
OLD CHICAGO	B	Huber	12
OLD CHICAGO DARK	B	Huber	60
OLD CROWN	B	Huber	26
OLD CROWN ALE	A	Huber	32
OLD DUTCH BRAND	B	Pittsburgh	21
OLD ENGLISH 800	ML	Heileman	24
OLD ENGLISH 800	ML	C. Schmidt	15
OLDE PUB	B	C. Schmidt	19
OLD EXPORT	B	Pittsburgh	6
OLD FOGHORN ALE	A	Anchor	69
OLD FROTHINGSLOSH	B	Pittsburgh	42
OLD GERMAN	B	Huber	21
OLD GERMAN	B	Yuengling	42
OLD GERMAN BRAND	B	Eastern	22
OLD GERMAN BRAND	B	Pittsburgh	20
OLD GERMAN MALT BEVERAGE	NB	Eastern	14
OLD HEIDELBRAU	B	Falstaff	26
OLD MILWAUKEE	B	Schlitz	56
OLD MILWAUKEE LIGHT	LO	Schlitz	20
OLD SHAY ALE	A	Jones	17
OLD STYLE BREWERS LAGER	B	C. Schmidt (Brewer's)	30
OLD STYLE BREWERS LAGER	B	C. Schmidt (Forrest)	35
OLD TIMERS	B	Walter	31
OLYMPIA	B	Olympia	50
OLYMPIA GOLD	LO	Olympia	34
ORIGINAL OYSTER HOUSE	B	Pittsburgh	34
ORTLIEB'S	B	C. Schmidt	36
ORTLIEB'S BOCK	BK	C. Schmidt	23
OUR	B	Huber	42
OUR SPECIAL ALE 1978	A	Anchor	45
OUR SPECIAL ALE 1979	A	Anchor	26
OUR SPECIAL ALE 1980	A	Anchor	81
OUR SPECIAL ALE 1981	A	Anchor	63
OUR SPECIAL ALE 1982	A	Anchor	68
OUR SPECIAL ALE 1983	A	Anchor	63
PABST EXTRA LIGHT	LO	Pabst	20
PABST SPECIAL DARK	B	Pabst	42
PACE	RA	Hudepohl	21
PADRE	B	General	29
PEARL	B	General	64
PEARL CREAM ALE	A	General	52
PEARL LIGHT	B	General	24
PEARL LIGHT LAGER	B	General	27

PETER HAND 1891	B	Huber	35
PETER HAND EXTRA LIGHT	LO	Huber	42
PFEIFFER	B	Heileman	26
PHOENIX	B	Koch	12
PICKETT'S LIGHT	LO	Pickett	31
PICKETT'S PREMIUM	B	Pickett	39
PICKWICK ALE	A	Falstaff	35
PIELS	B	Stroh	48
PIELS LIGHT	B	Stroh	45
PIELS REAL DRAFT	B	Stroh	32
PILGRIM'S PRIDE	B	Koch	47
PILSENER CLUB	B	General	41
PILSENER ON CALL (POC)	B	C. Schmidt	36
PINK CHAMPALE	ML	Champale	36
PIPING ROCK	B	Koch	20
PLAYER'S	LO	Miller	14
POINT BOCK	BK	Stevens Point	18
POINT SPECIAL	B	Stevens Point	48
POINT VIEW HOTEL	B	Pittsburgh	28
POLAR CERVEZA	B	Eastern	30
PRIMO	B	Schlitz	24
PRIOR DOUBLE DARK	B	C. Schmidt	87
PRIOR LIGHT	B	C. Schmidt	58
PRIZER	B	C. Schmidt	10
PULASKI PIVO	B	Falstaff	27
RAINIER	B	Heileman	27
RAINIER ALE	A	Heileman	39
RAINIER LIGHT	LO	Heileman	18
RAM'S HEAD ALE	A	C. Schmidt	37
READING	B	C. Schmidt	50
REAL ALE PORTER	P	Real Ale	42
REAL ALE STOUT	S	Real Ale	63
RED WHITE AND BLUE	B	Pabst	42
RED WHITE AND BLUE LIGHT	LO	Pabst	32
REGAL	B	Heileman	52
REGAL BRAU	B	Huber	36
REGAL FAMOUS	B	Pickett	27
REGAL SELECT	B	General	34
REIDENBACH	B	General	27
RHEINGOLD	B	C. Schmidt	37
RHEINGOLD EXTRA LIGHT	LO	C. Schmidt	29
RHEINLANDER	B	Heileman	44
RHEINLANDER BOCK	BK	Huber	68
RHEINLANDER EXPORT	B	Huber	35
RIVER CITY BOCK	BK	River City	72
RIVER CITY DARK	B	River City	50
RIVER CITY GOLD	B	River City	50
ROBIN HOOD CREAM ALE	A	Pittsburgh	40
ROCK & ROLL	B	Dixie	47
ROLLING ROCK	B	Latrobe	50
ROLLING ROCK LIGHT	LO	Latrobe	29
ROSE ALE	ML	Pittsburgh	8
ROYAL AMBER	B	Heileman	74
SAVALOT	B	Lion	18
SCHAEFER	B	Stroh	48
SCHAEFER BOCK	BK	Stroh	20
SCHAEFER CREAM ALE	A	Stroh	31
SCHAEFER LIGHT	LO	Stroh	18
SCHELL DEER BRAND EXPORT	B	Schell	56
SCHELL DEER BRAND EXPORT II	B	Schell	10
SCHELL'S EXPORT LIGHT	LO	Schell	27
SCHELL'S GRAND OLD BEER	B	Schell	38
SCHELL'S HUNTER'S SPECIAL	B	Schell	24
SCHELL'S 1978 XMAS BREW	B	Schell	18
SCHELL'S 1979 BOCK	BK	Schell	31
SCHLITZ	B	Schlitz	39
SCHLITZ LIGHT	LO	Schlitz	25
SCHLITZ MALT LIQUOR	ML	Schlitz	49
SCHOENLING CREAM ALE	A	Schoenling	33
SCHOENLING DRAFT	B*	Schoenling	11

SCHOENLING DRAFT BIG JUG	B	Schoenling	30
SCHOENLING OLD TIME BOCK	BK	Schoenling	26
SCHMIDT	B	Heileman	31
SCHMIDT CLASSIC	B	C. Schmidt	35
SCHMIDT EXTRA SPECIAL	B	Heileman	31
SCHMIDT LIGHT	LO	Heileman	36
SCHMIDT SELECT	NB	Heileman	17
SCHMIDT'S	B	C. Schmidt	60
SCHMIDT'S BAVARIAN	B	C. Schmidt	30
SCHMIDT'S BOCK	BK	C. Schmidt	40
SCHMIDT'S LIGHT	LO	C. Schmidt	17
SCHMIDT'S OKTOBERFEST	B	C. Schmidt	46
SCHWEGMANN	B	Dixie	16
SCOTCH BUY	B	Falstaff	38
SCOTCH BUY LIGHT	LO	Falstaff	36
SEVEN SPRINGS	B	Pittsburgh	48
SGA	B	Heileman	42
SGA GOLD LABEL	B	Pittsburgh	20
SHINER	B	Spoetzl	38
SHINER BOCK	BK	Spoetzl	41
SIERRA	B	Pittsburgh	26
SIERRA NEVADA PALE ALE	A	Sierra Nevada	58
SIERRA NEVADA PORTER	P	Sierra Nevada	57
SIERRA NEVADA STOUT	S	Sierra Nevada	40
SIMON PURE	B	Koch	31
SIR EDWARD STOUT	B	Schoenling	29
SLIM PRICE	B	General	33
SLIM PRICE LIGHT	LO	General	22
SPRING	B	General	15
STAG	B	Heileman	47
STANDARD DRY ALE	A	Eastern	38
STEEL VALLEY	B	Pittsburgh	25
STEGMAIER	B	Lion	27
STEGMAIER LIGHT	LO	Lion	24
STEGMAIER PORTER	P	Lion	21
STEINBRAU	NB	Eastern	6
STEINBRAU	B	General	22
STEINBRAU LIGHT	LO	General	12
STEINBRAU LIGHT NB	NB	Eastern	4
STEINHAUS	B	Schell	18
STENGER	B	HUber	49
STERLING	B	Heileman	45
STERLING LIGHT	LO	Heileman	27
STITE	ML	Heileman	31
STONEY'S	B	Jones	15
STRAUB	B	Straub	63
STROH BOHEMIAN	B	Stroh	43
STROH'S BOCK	BK	Stroh	62
STROH SIGNATURE	B	Stroh	56
STROH'S LIGHT	LO	Stroh	45
SUMMIT	B	Koch	18
TAMALPAIS DARK	B	Franklin	50
TAP	B	Hudepohl	15
TECH LIGHT	B	Pittsburgh	30
TEXAS PRIDE LITE	LO	General	40
TEXAS PRIDE	B	General	40
TEXAS SELECT	NB	General	15
THOUSAND OAKS	B	Thousand Oaks	4
TIGER HEAD ALE	A	C. Schmidt	44
TIME SAVER	B	Falstaff	51
TIVOLI	B	Heileman	23
TOP HAT	B	Schoenling	15
TOPPER	B	Eastern	21
TRI-STAR	NB	Eastern	20
TUBORG DARK	B	Heileman	68
TUBORG GOLD	B	Heileman	56
TUDOR ALE	A	C. Schmidt	25
TUDOR PREMIUM	B	C. Schmidt	31
TWELVE HORSE ALE	A	Genesee	63

2001 VIP	B	Pittsburgh	17
ULTRA LIGHT	LO	Falstaff	30
ULTRA LIGHT	LO	Pittsburgh	20
UTICA CLUB CREAM ALE	A	F.X. Matt	30
UTICA CLUB LIGHT	LO	F.X. Matt	24
UTICA CLUB PILSENER	B	F.X. Matt	17
VALLEY FORGE	B	C. Schmidt	43
VAN LAUTER BAVARIAN	B	Heileman	40
VAN MERRITT	B	Huber	15
WALTER EXTRA LIGHT ALE	A	Walter	17
WALTER'S	B	Walter	19
WALTER'S (Colo.)	B	Walter	36
WEIR BIG 14	B	Pittsburgh	27
WESTERN	B	Cold Spring	45
WFBG RADIO	B	Pittsburgh	27
WHITE LABEL	B	Cold Spring	39
WIEDEMANN BOHEMIAN	B	Heileman	57
WINDJAMMER	B	Koch	46
WISCONSIN CLUB	B	Huber	40
WISCONSIN GOLD LABEL	B	Huber	35
WISCONSIN HOLIDAY	B	Huber	38
WISCONSIN OLD TIMER'S	B	Walter	28
WISCONSIN PREMIUM	B	Heileman	33
WURZBURGER US BOTTLING	B	Anheuser-Busch	46
YUENGLING DARK BREW PORTER	P	Yuengling	32
YUENGLING PREMIUM	B	Yuengling	59
ZODIAC	ML	Huber	15

Canada

BRAND	TYPE	COMPANY	RATING
ALPINE	B	Moosehead	36
ALTA 3.9	LO	Carling	22
AMSTEL	B	Amstel	40
BEER	B	Old Ford	42
BENNETT'S DOMINION	A	Carling	47
BLACK HORSE ALE	A	Carling	51
BLACK HORSE BEER	B	Carling	29
BLENDED OLD STOCK ALE	A	Carling	45
BLUE STAR	B	Labatt	46
BOHEMIAN LAGER	B	Molson	20
BRADING ALE	A	Carling	33
BRADOR	ML	Molson	45
BREW LIGHT	LO	Amstel	21
BUCKEYE	A	Carling	23
BUDWEISER	B	Labatt	48
BULLDOG	B	Old Fort	36
CALGARY EXPORT ALE	A	Carling	8
CALGARY EXPORT	B	Carling	32
CALGARY EXPORT LAGER (domestic)	B	Carling	25
CALGARY STAMPEDE	B	Carling	30
CANADIAN 55	B	Northern	42
CANADIAN GOLD	B	Old Fort	2
CANADIAN NORTHERN	B	Northern	15
CANADIAN RED CAP	A	Carling	37
CARLING BLACK LABEL	B	Carling	33
CARLING PILSENER	B	Carling	27
CARLSBERG	B	Carling	41
CARLSBERG BOCK	BK	Carling	49
CARLSBERG GOLD	ML	Carling	71
CARLSBERG LIGHT	LO	Carling	15
CERVOISE	A	Labatt	29
CHAMPLAIN PORTER	P	Carling	20
CHARRINGTON TOBY	A	Carling	35
CINCI LAGER (domestic)	B	Carling	47
CINCI LAGER (export)	B	Carling	47
COLT .45	B	Carling	18

COLUMBIA	ML	Labatt	35
COOL SPRING	LO	Labatt	27
COY INTERNATIONAL	B	Old Fort	20
DOW BLACK HORSE ALE	A	Carling	22
DOW CREAM PORTER	P	Carling	66
EUROPA 60	NB	ID Foods	NR
GOLD KEG	B	Labatt	58
GOLD PEAK	B	Rocky Mountain	38
GRAND PRIX	A	Labatt	27
GRIZZLY	B	Amstel	53
GUINNESS EXTRA STOUT	S	Labatt	57
HEIDELBERG (Ont.)	B	Carling	12
HEIDELBERG (Que.)	B	Carling	32
HENNINGER EXPORT	B	Amstel	39
HENNINGER MEISTER PILS	B	Amstel	20
INDIA	B	Molson	58
IRON HORSE	ML	Old Fort	44
IRON HORSE (EXPORT)	ML	Old Fort	44
JOCKEY CLUB	B	Labatt	58
JOHN LABATT CLASSIC	B	Labatt	12
JOHN LABATT'S EXTRA STOCK	ML	Labatt	69
KEITH'S INDIA PALE ALE	IPA	Labatt	54
KINGSBEER	B	Carling	39
KOKANEE	B	Labatt	39
KOOTENAY	A	Labatt	48
KRONENBRAU 1308	B	Carling	27
LABATT'S BEER	B	Labatt	39
LABATT'S BLUE DRAFT	B	Labatt	55
LABATT'S CANADIAN ALE	A	Labatt	32
LABATT'S CRYSTAL LAGER	B	Labatt	50
LABATT'S 50	A	Labatt	47
LABATT'S INDIA PALE ALE	IPA	Labatt	33
LABATT'S PILSENER "BLUE"	B	Labatt	34
LABATT'S SPECIAL LITE	LO	Labatt	29
LABATT'S SUPER BOCK	ML	Labatt	35
LAURENTIDE	A	Molson	48
LETHBRIDGE	B	Molson	20
LONDON STOUT	S	Moosehead	52
MAGNUM ALE	A	Carling	41
MOLSON ALE	A	Molson	62
MOLSON CANADIAN	B	Molson	68
MOLSON EXPORT	A	Molson	63
MOLSON EXPORT LIGHT	LO	Molson	29
MOLSON GOLDEN	A	Molson	32
MOLSON LIGHT	LO	Molson	27
MOLSON MALT LIQUOR	ML	Molson	30
MOLSON OKTOBERFEST	B	Molson	42
MOLSON PORTER	B	Molson	65
MOLSON STOCK ALE	A	Molson	33
MOOSEHEAD CANADIAN LAGER	B	Moosehead	50
MOOSEHEAD EXPORT	A	Moosehead	54
MOOSEHEAD GOLDEN LIGHT	LO	Moosehead	29
MOOSEHEAD PALE ALE	A	Moosehead	33
MOOSEHEAD SPECIAL ALE	A	Moosehead	54
NORTHERN ALE	A	Northern	18
O'KEEFE CANADIAN ALE (domestic)	A	Carling	27
O'KEEFE CANADIAN ALE (Maritimes)	A	Carling	39
O'KEEFE CANADIAN ALE	A	Carling	20
O'KEEFE CANADIAN EXPORT ALE	A	Carling	22
O'KEEFE CANADIAN GOLDEN LIGHT	LO	Carling	32
O'KEEFE EXTRA OLD STOCK	ML	Carling	50
O'KEEFE OLD VIENNA	B	Carling	52
OLAND EXPORT ALE	A	Labatt	64
OLAND EXTRA STOUT	S	Labatt	58
OLAND LITE	LO	Labatt	36
OLAND'S OLD SCOTIA ALE (old)	A	Labatt	52
OLAND'S OLD SCOTIA ALE (new)	A	Labatt	50
OLD BLUE	B	Rocky Mountain	29
OLD FORT	B	Old Fort	32

OLD STYLE PILSENER	B	Molson	36
OLD STYLE PILSNER	B	Molson	22
OLD STYLE PILSNER	B	Molson	60
PACIFIC GOLD	B	Old Fort	44
PACIFIC GOLD (domestic)	B	Old Fort	25
RALLYE	A	Carling	42
ROYAL BLUE	B	Labatt	39
ROYAL CANADIAN	B	Old Fort	35
SCHOONER	B	Labatt	32
STANDARD LAGER	B	Carling	34
STEEPLEJACK	B	Rocky Mountain	30
SUPERIOR	B	Northern	21
TEN-PENNY ALE	A	Moosehead	42
TOBY ALE	A	Carling	24
TRAPPER	B	Rocky Mountain	26
TRAPPER MALT LIQUOR	ML	Rocky Mountain	27
TRILIGHT	LO	Carling	14
UNCLE BEN'S MALT LIQUOR	ML	Rocky Mountain	22
VELVET CREAM PORTER	P	Labatt	24
YUKON GOLD	B	Old Fort	36
YUKON GOLD (domestic)	B	Old Fort	46
YUKON GOLD LAGER	B	Old Fort	24

Mexico

BRAND	TYPE	COMPANY	RATING
BOHEMIA ALE	A	Cuauhtemoc	45
BRISA LIGERA	LO	Cuauhtemoc	18
CARTA BLANCA	B	Cuauhtemoc	34
CARTA BLANCA DARK	B	Cuauhtemoc	28
CHIHUAHUA	B	Cruz Blanca	21
CORONA	B	Modelo	54
CORONA EXTRA	B	Modelo	41
CRUZ BLANCA	B	Cruz Blanca	28
DOS EQUIS	B	Moctezuma	54
DOS EQUIS LIGHT	LO	Moctezuma	33
DOS EQUIS SPECIAL LAGER	B	Moctezuma	45
INDIO OSCURA	B	Cuauhtemoc	41
MODELO ESPECIAL	B	Modelo	14
MONTEJO DARK	B	Yucateca	29
MONTEJO PREMIUM	B	Yucateca	29
NEGRA MODELO	B	Modelo	68
NOCHE BUENA	B	Moctezuma	75
PACIFICO CLARA	B	Pacifico	30
SOL ESPECIAL	B	Moctezuma	33
SUPERIOR	B	Moctezuma	32
TECATE	B	Cuauhtemoc	51
TRES EQUIS DARK	B	Moctezuma	18
TRES EQUIS LIGHT	B	Moctezuma	42

Caribbean and Central America

BRAND	TYPE	COUNTRY	RATING
BANKS	B	Jamaica	27
BELIKIN BEER	B	Belize	45
BELIKIN STOUT	B	Belize	32
BREW MASTER'S	B	Puerto Rico	22
CORONA	B	Puerto Rico	33
CORONA CERVEZA	B	Puerto Rico	20
DRAGON	S	Jamaica	50
EBONY	B	Jamaica	26
INDIA	B	Puerto Rico	24
INDIA CERVEZA	B	Puerto Rico	36
PILSENER OF EL SALVADOR	B	El Salvador	34

PRESIDENTE	B	Dominican Republic	41
QUISQUEYA	B	Dominican Rep.	26
RED STRIPE	B	Barbados	18

South America

BRANDS	TYPE	COUNTRY	RATING
BIECKERT ETIQUETA AZUL	B	Argentina	36
BIECKERT PILSEN ESPECIAL	B	Argentina	68
BIECKERT PILSEN ESPECIAL LIVIANA	B	Argentina	32
BRAHMA	B	Brazil	30
BRAHMA BRAZILIAN	B	Brazil	14
BRAHMA CHOPP	B	Brazil	27
CALLAO	B	Peru	56
CARACU	S	Brazil	33
CLAUSEN	B	Colombia	39
CLUB	B	Ecuador	9
CLUB COLOMBIA	B	Colombia	31
CRISTAL	B	Peru	14
INGLESINHA	S	Brazil	23
LEON DE ORO	B	Argentina	58
POLAR	B	Venezuela	46
QUILMES EXPORT	B	Argentina	26
SANTE FE	B	Argentina	26
SKOL	B	Brazil	34
TAQUINA	B	Bolivia	43

Australia and New Zealand

BRAND	TYPE	COUNTRY	RATING
ABBOTS LAGER	B	Australia	26
BIG BARREL	B	Australia	21
BOAGS XXX	A	Australia	24
CARBINE STOUT	S	Australia	45
CARLTON DRAUGHT	B	Australia	47
CARLTON LIGHT	LO	Australia	27
CASCADE DRAUGHT	B	Australia	29
CASCADE SPARKLING BITTER	A	Australia	44
CASCADE SPARKLING PALE	A	Australia	50
CASTLEMAINE BITTER	A	Australia	63
CASTLEMAINE DRAUGHT	B	Australia	18
CASTLEMAINE EXPORT LAGER	B	Australia	18
COOPER BEST EXTRA STOUT	S	Australia	60
COOPER GOLD CROWN	B	Australia	30
COOPER LAGER	B	Australia	40
COOPER'S REAL ALE	A	Australia	47
COURAGE DRAUGHT	B	Australia	42
CREST LAGER	B	Australia	22
DB EXPORT	B	New Zealand	33
DOUBLE BROWN	B	New Zealand	24
FESTIVAL PILSENER	B	Australia	21
FOSTER'S LAGER	B	Australia	60
LEOPARD EXPORT	B	New Zealand	14
LEOPARD LAGER	B	New Zealand	17
LEOPARD STRONG	B	New Zealand	26
MELBOURNE BITTER	B	Australia	36
RESCHS PILSENER	B	Australia	13
SOUTHWARK BITTER	B	Australia	29
SOUTHWARK EXPORT	B	Australia	30
STEINLAGER	B	New Zealand	54
SWAN EXPORT	B	Australia	38
SWAN PREMIUM	B	Australia	58
TASMANIAN LAGER	B	Australia	41

THOS. COOPER STOUT	S	Australia	50
THOS. COOPER ALE	A	Australia	30
TOOHEY'S DRAUGHT	B	Australia	29
TOOHEY'S LAGER	B	Australia	53
TOOHEY'S LITE	LO	Australia	20
TOOTH KB	B	Australia	25
TOOTH SHEAF STOUT	S	Australia	67
TRAK	B	Australia	26
VICTORIA BITTER	A	Australia	33
WEST END BITTER	B	Australia	42
WEST END EXPORT	B	Australia	45

Africa

BRAND	TYPE	COUNTRY	RATING
AMSTEL	B	South Africa	37
CASTLE LAGER	B	South Africa	32
HANSA PILSENER	B	South Africa	44
JULBREW	B	Gambia	NR
LION LAGER	B	South Africa	36
ROGUE	B	South Africa	31

Asia and Oceania

BRAND	TYPE	COUNTRY	RATING
ABC EXTRA STOUT	S	Singapore	53
AMARIT	B	Thailand	30
ANCHOR	B	Singapore	35
ASAHI DRAFT	B	Japan	29
ASAHI LAGER	B	Japan	48
BEERSHEBA	B	Israel	14
BOMBAY	B	India	13
DYNASTY	B	Taiwan	62
EAGLE	B	India	10
FIJI BITTER	B	Fiji	33
GOLDEN EAGLE	B	India	45
GREAT WALL	B	China	35
HINANO	B	Tahiti	30
KINGFISHER	B	India	27
KIRIN	B	Japan	60
KIRIN LIGHT	LO	Japan	25
MACCABEE	B	Israel	35
MON-LEI	B	Hong Kong	22
MURREE EXPORT	B	Pakistan	14
ORIENTAL OB	B	Korea	21
ORION	B	Japan	9
PEKING	B	China	42
RAINMAKER	B	Samoa	30
SAN MIGUEL	B	Indonesia	22
SAN MIGUEL	B	New Guinea	10
SAN MIGUEL	B	Philippines	60
SAN MIGUEL DARK	B	Philippines	78
SAN MIGUEL NEGRA	B	New Guinea	44
SAN MIGUEL PALE PILSEN	B	Philippines	26
SAN MIGUEL SPECIAL DARK	B	Indonesia	76
SAPPORO BLACK	B	Japan	44
SAPPORO DRAFT	B	Japan	12
SAPPORO LAGER	B	Japan	20
SHANGHAI GOLDEN	B	Shanghai	44
SHANGHAI	B	Shanghai	38
SINGHA	B	Thailand	36
SINGHA STOUT	B	Thailand	14
SOUTH PACIFIC (SP)	B	New Guinea	6
SOUTH PACIFIC SPECIAL	B	New Guinea	29
SOVEREIGN	B	India	38
SUN-LIK	B	Hong Kong	47

257

SUNTORY DRAFT	B	Japan	30
TAIWAN	B	Taiwan	22
TAJ MAHAL	B	India	20
TIGER GOLD	B	Singapore	29
TSING-TAO	B	China	36
TSING-TAO PORTER	P	China	38
YUCHUAN	B	China	20

Europe

BRAND	TYPE	COUNTRY	RATING
AASS BOK	BK	Norway	45
AASS EXPORT	B	Norway	57
AASS JULE ØL	B	Norway	62
AASS NORWEGIAN	B	Norway	33
ABBEY DE LEFFE	B	Belgium	29
ABBOT ALE	A	England	12
ADELSHOFFEN	B	France	24
ADELSCOTT	ML	France	48
ADLER BRAU	B	Austria	44
AEGEAN HELLAS	B	Greece	40
AGUILA DORADA	B	Spain	19
AGUILA IMPERIAL	B	Spain	66
ALBANI EXPORT	B	Denmark	41
ALBANI PILSENER	B	Denmark	41
ALBANI PORTER	P	Denmark	75
ALFA LAGER	B	Holland	50
ALPINE AYINGERBRAU	B	England	22
ALTENMÜNSTER	B	Germany	33
ALT SEIDELBRAU	B	Germany	13
AMSTEL LIGHT	LO	Holland	18
ANDECHS	B	Germany	83
ANDREAS	B	Germany	32
ANGEL ALE	A	England	46
ANGEL BEER	B	England	32
ASTRA ALE	A	Germany	48
ASTRA MEISTER BOCK	BK	Germany	30
ATHENIAN	B	Greece	45
ATLAS	B	Greece	33
AUGUSTINER LIGHT	B	Germany	50
AUGUSTINER MAXIMATOR	B	Germany	72
AUSTRIAN GOLD	B	Austria	33
BADGER ALE	A	England	44
BAMBERGER KRONEN	B	Germany	22
BASS PALE ALE	A	England	78
BASS PALE ALE DRAUGHT	A	England	84
BAVARIA LAGER	B	Holland	28
BEAMISH	S	Ireland	18
BEAVER	B	England	NR
BECK'S	B	Germany	62
BECK'S DARK	B	Germany	58
BECKER'S EXPORT	B	Germany	28
BECKER'S PILS	B	Germany	30
BELHAVEN	A	Scotland	31
BELLE-VUE CREAM	L	Belgium	36
BELLE-VUE KRIEK	L	Belgium	33
BERLINER KINDL PILS	B	Germany	30
BERLINER KINDL WEISS	W	Germany	18
BERLINER PILS EXPORT	B	Germany	30
BERLINER WEISS SCHULTHEISS	W	Germany	38
BIG BEN	B	England	41
BIOS	A	Belgium	NR
BIRELL	NB	Switzerland	42
BITBURGER	B	Germany	35
BODDINGTON'S BITTER	B	England	26
BRAND	B	Holland	58
BRASSIN DE GARDE	A	France	60

BREDA	B	Holland	9
BREMER DOM-BRAU	B	Germany	14
BROCK LAGER	B	England	4
BULLDOG	B	England	54
BULLDOG PALE ALE	A	England	26
BURGERBRÄU PILS	B	Germany	36
BUSH BEER STRONG ALE	A	Belgium	NR
CAMPBELL'S CHRISTMAS	A	England	82
CARDINAL	B	Switzerland	75
CARLSBERG ELEPHANT	ML	Denmark	22
CARLSBERG ROYAL LAGER	B	Denmark	54
CARLSBERG SPECIAL DARK	B	Denmark	46
CARLSBERG	B	Denmark	42
CELEBRATOR	BK	Germany	57
CERES	B	Denmark	24
CHARLES WELLS BOMBARDIER ALE	A	England	34
CHARLES WELLS LIGHT ALE	A	England	NR
CHESHIRE ENGLISH PUB	A	England	26
CHIMAY	A	Belgium	32
CLUB WEISSE	W	Germany	63
COURAGE LAGER	B	England	24
CRISTAL	B	Portugal	36
CRYSTALL WÜHRER	B	Italy	50
CUVEE DE L'HERMITAGE	B	Belgium	51
DAB ALT	A	Germany	19
DAB ORIGINAL	B	Germany	48
DAB EXPORT	B	Germany	48
DAB KRAFT PERLE	NB	Germany	8
DAB MEISTER PILS	B	Germany	76
DAHL'S EXPORT	B	Norway	60
DAHL'S PILS	B	Norway	48
DAMM	B	Spain	27
DART MÖRKT STARKOL	B	Sweden	57
DIEKIRCH MALT LIQUOR	ML	Luxembourg	48
DIEKIRCH ML EXCLUSIVE	ML	Luxembourg	26
DIEKIRCH PILS	B	Luxembourg	61
DIESTER'S	A	Belgium	44
DINKELACKER BLACK FOREST	B	Germany	45
DINKELACKER BOCK	BK	Germany	80
DINKELACKER DARK BREW	B	Germany	33
DINKELACKER DARK C.D.	B	Germany	61
DINKELACKER DARK IMPORT	B	Germany	31
DINKELACKER PRIVAT LIGHT	B	Germany	61
DINKELACKER WEIZENKRONE	W	Germany	21
DORTMUNDER HANSA EXPORT	B	Germany	45
DORTMUNDER IMPERIAL	B	Germany	56
DORTMUNDER IMPERIAL ALT	A	Germany	32
DORTMUNDER IMPERIAL OKTOBERFEST	B	Germany	52
DORTMUNDER KRONEN CLASSIC	B	Germany	69
DORTMUNDER KRONEN PILSKRONE	B	Germany	34
DORTMUNDER RITTER BOCK	BK	Germany	76
DORTMUNDER RITTER DARK	B	Germany	45
DORTMUNDER RITTER EXPORT	B	Germany	9
DORTMUNDER RITTER LIGHT	B	Germany	64
DORTMUNDER RITTER PILS	B	Germany	54
DORTMUNDER STIFTS	B	Germany	26
DORTMUNDER UNION BEER	B	Germany	39
DORTMUNDER UNION DARK	B	Germany	36
DORTMUNDER UNION LIGHT	B	Germany	NR
DORTMUNDER UNION MALT LIQUOR	ML	Germany	30
DORTMUNDER UNION PILSENER	B	Germany	30
DORTMUNDER UNION SIEGEL PILS	B	Germany	68
DORTMUNDER UNION SPECIAL	B	Germany	72
DORTMUNDER WESTFALIA EXPORT	B	Germany	29
DORTMUNDER WESTFALIA SPECIAL	B	Germany	29
DOUBLE DIAMOND ALE	A	England	48
DOUBLE DIAMOND PILSENER	B	England	51

259

DOUBLE DRAGON	A	England	39
DREHER EXPORT	B	Italy	33
DREHER FORTE	B	Italy	59
DRESSLER EXPORT	B	Germany	10
DUVEL	A	Belgium	41
EDER	B	Germany	30
EGGER PILS	B	Austria	50
EKU DARK RESERVE	B	Germany	28
EKU HESE-WEIZEN DUNKEL	W	Germany	38
EKU KULMBACHER EXPORT	B	Germany	52
EKU KULMINATOR URTYP HELL 28	B	Germany	45
EKU JUBILÄUMSBIER	B	Germany	72
EKU MAIBOCK	BK	Germany	82
EKU SPECIAL	B	Germany	38
EKU PILS	B	Germany	26
EPHESUS	B	Turkey	35
ERIKOIS	B	Finland	50
ERZQUELL	B	Germany	27
ESTRELLA DORADA	B	Spain	50
EULER LANDPILS	B	Germany	34
EX BIER	NB	Switzerland	14
EXTRACTO DE MALTA	MB	Germany	40
FALCON EXPORT	B	Sweden	24
FARO LAMBIC	L	Belgium	NR
FASSL GOLD	B	Austria	82
FASSL GOLD PILS	B	Austria	26
FELDSCHLOSSEN	B	Switzerland	68
FELINFOEL BITTER	A	England	31
FEST BEER MAISEL	B	Germany	83
FINLANDIA GOLD	B	Finland	74
FINLANDIA LIGHT	B	Finland	26
FISCHER GOLD	B	France	48
FISCHER LA BELLE STRAS-BOURGEOISE	B	France	42
FISCHER PILS	B	France	41
FIX	B	Greece	45
FIX SPEZIAL	B	Greece	21
FORST EXPORT	B	Italy	35
FRYDENLUND'S EXPORT	B	Norway	30
FRYDENLUND'S PILSENER	B	Norway	21
FULLER'S LONDON PRIDE	A	England	30
FULLER'S PALE ALE	A	England	24
FÜRSTENBERG PILSENER	B	Germany	44
FÜRSTENBERG IMPORTED	B	Germany	55
GASTHAUS SPECIAL	B	Germany	38
GILDE EDEL-EXPORT	B	Germany	81
GILDE RATSKELLER	B	Germany	20
GIRAF	ML	Denmark	59
GOLD EAGLE BITTER	A	England	51
GOLD LABEL NO. 1 BARLEY WINE	A	England	18
GOSSER	B	Austria	24
GOSSER EXPORT	B	Austria	47
GOSSER GOLDEN ROCK	B	Austria	20
GRÄNGES	B	Sweden	45
GRÄNGES BLONDE	B	Sweden	54
GREENE KING	A	England	10
GREEN ROOSTER	ML	Denmark	58
GRENZQUELL DARK	B	Germany	48
GRENZQUELL PILSENER	B	Germany	40
GROLSCH	B	Holland	43
GROLSCH LAGER	B	Holland	26
GUEUZE BELLE-VUE	L	Belgium	NR
GUEUZE LAMBIC	L	Belgium	NR
GUINNESS CREAM STOUT	S	Ireland	16
GUINNESS EXTRA STOUT	S	Ireland	60
GUINNESS EXTRA STOUT DRAUGHT	S	Ireland	67
HACKER EDELHELL	B	Germany	67
HACKER PSCHORR DARK	B	Germany	37
HACKER PSCHORR LIGHT	B	Germany	67

HACKER—PSCHORR MAIBOCK	B	Germany	48
HACKER PSCHORR OKTOBERFEST	B	Germany	61
HACKER PSCHORR OKTOBERFEST MÄRZEN	B	Germany	72
HACKER PSCHORR WEISS	W	Germany	57
HANSA EXPORT	B	Norway	35
HANSA FJORD	B	Norway	82
HANSA PILSENER	B	Norway	38
HANSA PILS	B	Norway	42
HARBOE BEAR	ML	Denmark	42
HARBOE GOLD	B	Denmark	37
HARP (USA)	B	Ireland	37
HARP (Canada)	B	Ireland	38
HEINEKEN	B	Holland	65
HEINEKEN LAGER	B	Holland	62
HEINEKEN SPECIAL DARK	B	Holland	68
HEINEKEN SPECIAL DARK DRAUGHT	B	Holland	66
HENNINGER	B	Germany	61
HENNINGER DARK	B	Germany	72
HENNINGER DOPPELBOCK	BK	Germany	78
HENNINGER INTERNATIONAL	B	Germany	17
HENNINGER KAISER	B	Germany	54
HERFORDER PILS	B	Germany	26
HERFORDER PILSNER	B	Germany	22
HERITAGE	A	England	78
HERRENBRÄU LIGHT	B	Germany	30
HERRENBRÄU PILSNER	B	Germany	38
HERRENBRÄU WEIZEN	B	Germany	12
HERRENHAUSEN	B	Germany	45
HOEGAARDEN TRIPLE	A	Belgium	58
HOFBRAU DARK RESERVE	B	Germany	46
HOFBRAU LIGHT RESERVE	B	Germany	45
HOFBRAU OKTOBERFEST	B	Germany	48
HOLSTEN CERVEZA TIGRE	B	Germany	32
HOLSTEN EXPORT	B	Germany	65
HOLSTEN LAGER	B	Germany	30
HORSY	B	Germany	69
HUMMER	B	Germany	26
HURLIMANN STERN/SPEZIAL	B	Switzerland	46
IMPERIAL STOUT	S	Denmark	60
ISENBECK EXPORT	B	Germany	30
ISENBECK EXTRA DRY	B	Germany	62
ISI 08 SPECIAL	NB	Germany	21
ITALA PILSEN	B	Italy	66
ITALA PILSEN GOLD	B	Italy	77
JADRAN	B	Yugoslavia	30
JAEGER	B	Holland	14
JEVER PILSENER	B	Germany	21
JOHN BROWN ALE	A	England	33
JOHN COURAGE EXPORT	B	England	28
KAISER BAVARIA	B	Germany	62
KAISERDOM PILSENER	B	Germany	68
KAISERDOM RAUCHBIER	B	Germany	58
KALBACK	B	Sweden	30
KANTERBRAU	B	France	45
KARJALA EXPORT	B	Finland	54
KARLOVACKO SPECIAL	B	Yugoslavia	24
KARLOVACKO LIGHT	B	Yugoslavia	15
KARLSBRAU	B	Germany	39
KELLERBRAU	B	England	NR
KEO PILSENER	B	Cyprus	19
KIESEL EXPORT	B	Germany	51
KIESEL FESTBIER	B	Germany	63
KIESEL MARZEN	B	Germany	33
KIESEL PERL BOCK	BK	Germany	57
KIESEL PILS	B	Germany	71
KIESEL WEISS	W	Germany	41
KILLIAN'S BIÈRE ROUSSE	A	France	77
KINROSS	A	England	56

261

KLOSTER ALTENBERG	B	Germany	24
KLOSTER PILS	B	Germany	30
KOFF	B	Finland	42
KOFF IMPERIAL	S	Finland	48
KÖNIG-PILSENER	B	Germany	36
KÖNIGSBACHER ALT	A	Germany	46
KÖNIGSBACHER PILS	B	Germany	44
KROMBACHER PILS	B	Germany	48
KRONENBOURG	B	France	34
KRONENBOURG DARK	B	France	15
KRAKUS	B	Poland	47
KULMBACHER MÖNCHSHOF FESTBIER	B	Germany	76
KULMBACHER MÖNCHSHOF OKTOBER	B	Germany	74
KULMBACHER MONKSHOF AMBER LIGHT	B	Germany	72
KULMBACHER MONKSHOF DARK BEER	B	Germany	69
KULMBACHER MONKSHOF DRY LIGHT	B	Germany	59
KULMBACHER MONKSHOF HELLER BOCK	BK	Germany	68
KULMBACHER MONKSHOF KLOSTER BOCK	BK	Germany	75
KULMBACHER MONKSHOF KLOSTER SCHWARZ	B	Germany	75
KULMBACHER REICHELBRÄU	B	Germany	46
KULMBACHER REICHELBRÄU EDELHERB PILS	B	Germany	68
KULMBACHER REICHELBRÄU FRANKISCHES URBIER	B	Germany	62
KULMBACHER SCHWEIZERHOF-BRAU	B	Germany	38
KULMBACHER SCHWEIZERHOF-BRAU BOCK	BK	Germany	87
KUPPER'S KÖLSCH	B	Germany	56
LAMOT PILSOR	B	Belgium	22
LEDERER EXPORT	B	Germany	33
LEDERER EXPORT LIGHT	B	Germany	25
LEEUW	B	Holland	36
LEFFE BLONDE	A	Belgium	46
LEFFE DARK	A	Belgium	73
LEFFE RADIEUSE	A	Belgium	50
LEOPOLD	B	Belgium	12
LIBERO	NB	Switzerland	18
LINDEMAN'S GUEUZE LAMBIC	L	Belgium	NR
LINDEMAN'S KRIEK LAMBIC	L	Belgium	NR
LOBURG	B	Belgium	30
LOHRER	B	Germany	38
LOLLAND/FALSTERS	B	Denmark	23
LOWENBRAU MUNICH DARK	B	Germany	36
LOWENBRAU MUNICH LIGHT	B	Germany	54
LOWENBRAU SWISS SPECIAL LIGHT	B	Switzerland	38
LOWENBRAU ZURICH EXPORT DARK	B	Switzerland	28
LOWENBRAU ZURICH EXPORT LIGHT	B	Switzerland	46
LUTÈCE	A	France	72
MACANDREW'S SCOTCH ALE	A	Scotland	66
MACEWAN'S EDINBURGH ALE	A	Scotland	82
MACEWAN'S MALT LIQUOR	ML	Scotland	45
MACEWAN'S SCOTCH ALE	A	Scotland	70
MACEWAN'S STRONG ALE	A	Scotland	34
MACEWAN'S STRONG MALT LIQUOR	ML	Scotland	71
MACEWAN'S TARTAN ALE	A	Scotland	72
MACKESON STOUT	S	England	80
MACKESON TRIPLE STOUT	S	England	46
MAGNUS	A	Belgium	62
MAISEL BAYRISCH	B	Germany	42
MAISEL EXPORT	B	Germany	42

MAISEL PILSNER	B	Germany	47
MAISEL WEIZEN	W	Germany	29
MAISEL HESE WEISSBIER	W	Germany	20
MANN'S BROWN ALE	A	England	55
MARATHON	B	Greece	45
MARCUS	B	Yugoslavia	22
MARIESTADS FESTIVAL	B	Sweden	33
MAXIMILIAN	BK	Germany	58
METEOR PILS	B	France	29
MORETTI EXPORT	B	Italy	35
MORETTI FRIULANA	B	Italy	32
MORETTI PILSENER	B	Italy	51
MOUSSY	NB	Switzerland	33
MUNICH OKTOBERFEST	B	Germany	45
MURPHY EXPORT	S	Ireland	23
MÜTZIG	B	France	6
NASTRO AZZURRO	B	Italy	26
NEPTUN GOLDEN BROWN	B	Denmark	16
NEPTUN PASKE BRYG	B	Denmark	52
NEPTUN PILSNER	B	Denmark	42
NEPTUN PINSE BRYG	B	Denmark	52
NEWCASTLE BROWN	A	Scotland	65
NIKSICKO PIVO	B	Yugoslavia	16
NORSK	B	Norway	32
OKOCIM FULL LIGHT	B	Poland	42
OKOCIM PORTER	P	Poland	32
OLD BEDFORD ALE	A	England	57
OLD PECULIER	A	England	46
ORANJEBOOM	B	Holland	40
ORIGINAL OKTOBER	B	Germany	42
ORVAL	A	Belgium	34
ORVAL ALE	A	Belgium	12
PADERBORNER LIGHT	LO	Germany	2
PADERBORNER PILSENER	B	Germany	18
PADERBORNER REGULAR	B	Germany	35
PAINE'S PALE ALE	A	England	15
PANACH	B	France	10
PANTHER	NB	France	24
PATRIZIER EDELHELL EXPORT	B	Germany	54
PATRIZIER EXPORT	B	Germany	45
PATRIZIER PILS	B	Germany	29
PAULANER ALT MÜNCHENER DUNKEL	B	Germany	42
PAULANER FEST-BIER	B	Germany	62
PAULANER HELL URTYP EXPORT	B	Germany	52
PAULANER MÜNCHENER MÄRZEN	B	Germany	58
PAULANER OKTOBERFEST	ML	Germany	48
PAULANER PILS	B	Germany	30
PAULANER SALVATOR	B	Germany	58
PAULANER UR-BOCK HELL	BK	Germany	56
PAULANER URTYP 1634	B	Germany	36
PAULANER WEIS'N-MÄRZEN	W	Germany	45
PAULANER WEISSBIER	W	Germany	53
PELFORTH	B	France	54
PERONI BEER	B	Italy	74
PERONI BIRRA	B	Italy	33
PETER'S BRAND	B	Holland	54
PINKUS ALT	A	Germany	10
PINKUS MALZ BIER	MB	Germany	6
PINKUS PILS	B	Germany	23
PINKUS WEIZEN	W	Germany	59
PIPER EXPORT	A	Scotland	25

Sign called the "Ale-Stake."

POPE'S "1880"	B	England	68
PORETTI ORO	B	Italy	15
PORTER 39	P	France	38
PRINZ EXPORT	B	Italy	30
PRIPPS EXPORT	B	Sweden	68
PRIPPS JUBILEE	B	Sweden	56
PSCHORR MUNICH	ML	Germany	13
PUNTIGAM	B	Austria	25
RADEBERGER	B	East Germany	28
RAFFO	B	Italy	12
RED BARREL	B	England	29
RED ERIC	ML	Denmark	NR
RINGNES BOCK	B	Norway	56
RINGNES DARK	B	Norway	42
RINGNES EXPORT	B	Norway	30
RINGNES MALT LIQUOR	ML	Norway	18
RINGNES SPECIAL	B	Norway	66
RIVA 2000	B	Belgium	56
RODENBACH RED BEER	A	Belgium	NR
ROEMER	B	France	36
ROTHENBURG	B	Germany	27
ROYAL DUTCH	B	Holland	12
ROYAL DUTCH KOSHER	B	Holland	14
RUDDLE'S COUNTRY ALE	A	England	24
SAGRES	B	Portugal	6
SAGRES DARK	B	Portugal	46
SAILER PILS	B	Germany	36
SAILER WEISSE (NO YEAST)	W	Germany	57
SAILER WEISSE (WITH YEAST)	W	Germany	41
ST. PAULI GIRL	B	Germany	66
ST. PAULI GIRL DARK	B	Germany	62
ST. SIXTUS ABDY	B	Belgium	45
SAISON REGAL	A	Belgium	NR
SAMUEL SMITH GOLDEN BROWN	A	England	65
SAMUEL SMITH NUT BROWN	A	England	34
SAMUEL SMITH OATMEAL STOUT	S	England	70
SAMUEL SMITH PALE ALE	A	England	77
SAN MARTIN	B	Spain	13
SAN MIGUEL	B	Spain	22
SCANDIA GOLD	B	Denmark	62
SCHAFF FEUERFEST	B	Germany	59
SCHLOSS-BIER	B	Italy	21
SCHOUS	B	Norway	16
SCHUTZ	B	France	15
SCHUTZENBERGER JUBILATOR	B	France	25
SCHWABEN BRÄU	B	Germany	21
SENATOR	BK	Germany	15
SKANSEN	B	France	24
SKI	B	Norway	24
SKOL	B	Holland	22
SLAVIA	B	France	47
SPARTAN	B	Greece	39
SPATEN LIGHT	B	Germany	48
SPATEN DOPPELSPATEN OPTIMA-TOR	B	Germany	70
SPATEN URMÄRZEN OKTOBERFEST	B	Germany	69
SPLÜGEN BOCK	BK	Italy	84
SPLÜGEN DRY	B	Italy	21
SPLÜGEN ORO	B	Italy	24
STAUDER	B	Germany	24
STELLA ARTOIS	B	Belgium	46
STEFFL EXPORT	B	Austria	20
STEINHAUSER	B	Germany	42
STERN PREMIUM	B	Germany	60
STINGO	A	England	30
STRASBRÄU	B	Germany	48
SWINKELS	B	Holland	32
TADDY PORTER	P	England	84
TENNENT'S	B	Scotland	75

TETLEY	A	England	27
THEAKSTON BEST BITTER	A	England	44
"33" EXPORT	B	France	62
"33" EXTRA DRY	B	France	75
"33" RECORD	B	France	62
THOMAS HARDY ALE	A	England	75
THOR	B	Denmark	9
THREE HORSES	B	Holland	9
THREE TOWNS	B	Sweden	46
TOLLY	A	England	38
TRAPPISTES, BIÈRES DES	B	Belgium	23
TRAQUAIR HOUSE	A	England	81
TUBORG	B	Denmark	27
TUCHER	B	Germany	36
TUCHER PILS	B	Germany	33
TÜRMER	B	Germany	26
UNION EXPORT	B	Yugoslavia	45
UNION EXPORT STOUT	S	Yugoslavia	41
UNION SVETLO PIVO	B	Yugoslavia	34
URQUELL	B	Czechoslovakia	65
VAUX DOUBLE MAXIM	A	England	30
VILLACHER GOLD	B	Austria	42
VONDEL TRIPLE	A	Belgium	18
WAGNER BRÄU BOCK	BK	Germany	8
WAGNER BRÄU MÄRZEN	B	Germany	20
WALSHEIM	B	Germany	37
WARD'S ENGLISH ALE	A	England	41
WARD'S GOLDEN ALE	A	England	59
WARSTEINER PREMIUM VERUM	B	Germany	57
WARTECK	NB	Switzerland	26
WATNEY'S	B	England	43
WESTMALLE DUBBEL	A	Belgium	82
WESTMALLE TRIPLE	A	Belgium	65
WHITBREAD BREWMASTER	B	England	30
WHITBREAD PALE	A	England	70
WHITBREAD TANKARD	A	England	62
WIEZE	B	Belgium	68
WORTHINGTON ALE	A	England	65
WORTHINGTON E	B	England	46
WÜNSTER 18	B	Italy	81
WÜNSTER 14	B	Italy	51
WÜRZBURGER BOCK	BK	Germany	59
WÜRZBURGER DARK	B	Germany	59
WÜRZBURGER LIGHT	B	Germany	72
WÜRZBURGER LIGHT (US bottling)	B	Germany	46
WÜRZBURGER OKTOBERFEST	B	Germany	72
X-PERT	B	Holland	28
YOLL DAMM	B	Spain	28
YOUNGER'S KESTREL LAGER	B	England	42
ZIPFER URTYP	B	Austria	45
ZYWIEC	B	Poland	37
ZYWIEC FULL LIGHT	B	Poland	33
ZYWIEC PIAST	B	Poland	31

APPENDIX II
List of Breweries Authorized to Operate in the United States

ARIZONA
Carling National Breweries, Inc.
Division of G. Heileman Brewing
   Co., Inc.
150 So. 12th St.
Phoenix

CALIFORNIA
Anchor Brewing Co.
1705 Mariposa St.
San Francisco

Anheuser-Busch, Inc.
P.O. Box 2113
Los Angeles

Anheuser-Busch, Inc.
3101 Busch Drive
Fairfield

Franklin Brewing Co.
Emeryville

Mendenhall Brewing Ltd.
1560 Mansfield Road
Santa Cruz

Miller Brewing Co.
15801 East First St.
Irwindale

Miller Brewing Co.
319 N. Vernon Avenue
Azusa

New Albion Brewing Co.
20330 Eight Street East
Sonoma

Numano Sake Co.
708 Addison Street
Berkeley

Ozeki San Benito
249 Hillcrest Road
Hollister

Pabst Brewing Co.
P.O. Box 3849
Terminal Annex
Los Angeles

River City Brewing Co.
3508 LaGrande Blvd.
Sacramento 95823

Jos. Schlitz Brewing Co.
P.O. Box 32
Van Nuys

Sierra Nevada Brewing Co.
2539 Gilman Way
Chico 95926

COLORADO
Adolph Coors Co.
Golden

Boulder Beer
15555 N. 83rd Street
Longmont

FLORIDA
Anheuser-Busch, Inc.
111 Busch Drive
Jacksonville

Anheuser-Busch, Inc.
P.O. Box 9245
Sulpher Springs Station
Tampa

Duncan Brewing Co., Inc.
Division of Carling National
   Brewing Co.
   (G. Heileman Brewing Co.,
   Inc.)
202 Gandy Road
Auburndale

Jos. Schlitz Brewing Co.
11111-30th St.
Tampa

GEORGIA
Miller Brewing Co.
405 Cordele Road
Albany

G. Heileman Brewing Co.
Georgia Highway 247 Spur
Perry

HAWAII
Honolulu Sake Brewery & Ice Co.,
   Ltd.
P.O. Box 1266
Honolulu

ILLINOIS
Carling National Breweries, Inc.
Division of G. Heileman Brewing
   Co., Inc.
1201 West "E" St.
Belleville

Pabst Brewing Co.
P.O. Box 3217
Peoria Heights

INDIANA
Falstaff Brewing Corp.
1019-1051 Grant Ave.
Fort Wayne

G. Heileman Brewing Co. of
   Indiana, Inc.
1301 Pennsylvania St.
Evansville

IOWA
Dubuque Star Brewing Co.
East 4th Street Extension
Dubuque

KENTUCKY
The Geo. Wiedemann Brewing Co.
Division of G. Heileman Brewing
   Co., Inc.
601 Columbia St.
Newport

LOUISIANA
Dixie Brewing Co., Inc.
2537 Tulane Ave.
New Orleans

MARYLAND
Carling National Breweries, Inc.
Division of G. Heileman Brewing
   Co., Inc.
4501 Hollins Ferry Road
Baltimore

MICHIGAN
Carling National Breweries, Inc.
926 S. Main St.
Frankenmuth

Geyer Bros. Brewing Co.
415 S. Main St.
Frankenmuth

Real Ale Co., Inc.
320 No. Main
Chelsea 48118

Stroh Brewing Co.
One Stroh Drive
Detroit

MINNESOTA
Cold Spring Brewing Co.
219 North Red River St.
Cold Spring

G. Heileman Brewing Co., Inc.
882 W. 7th St.
St. Paul

Olympia Brewing Co.
707 E. Minnehaha Ave.
St. Paul

August Schell Brewing Co.
South Payne St.
Outlet #400
New Ulm

MISSOURI
Anheuser-Busch, Inc.
721 Pestalozzi St.
St. Louis

NEBRASKA
Falstaff Brewing Corp.
25th Street & Deer Park Blvd.
Omaha

NEW HAMPSHIRE
Anheuser-Busch, Inc.
1000 Daniel Webster Hwy.
Merrimack

NEW JERSEY
Anheuser-Busch, Inc.
200 U.S. Highway 1
Newark

Champale, Inc.
Lalor & Lamberton Sts.
Trenton

Eastern Brewing Corp.
334 N. Washington St.
Hammonton

Pabst Brewing Co.
400 Grove St.
Newark

NEW YORK
Genesee Brewing Co., Inc.
419-445 St. Paul St. and
   14-33 Cataract St.
Rochester

Old New York Beer Co.
809 Washington St.
New York 10014

Fred Koch Brewery
15-25 W. Courtney St.
Dunkirk

Miller Brewing Co.
P.O. Box 200
Owens Road
South Volney

Wm. S. Newman Brewing Co.
32 Learned St.
Albany 12207

F.X. Matt Brewing Co.
811 Edward St.
Utica

NORTH CAROLINA
Miller Brewing Co.
863 E. Meadow Rd.
Eden

Jos. Schlitz Brewing Co.
4791 Schlitz Ave.
Winston-Salem

OHIO
Anheuser-Busch, Inc.
700 East Schrock Rd.
Columbus

Hudepohl Brewing Co.
Fifth & Gest Sts.
Cincinnati

C. Schmidt Brewing Co.
9400 Quincy Ave.
Cleveland

Schoenling Brewing Co.
1625 Central Parkway
Cincinnati

OREGON
Blitz-Weinhard Brewing Co.
Division of G. Heileman Brewing Co.
1133 W. Burnside St.
Portland

PENNSYLVANIA
Jones Brewing Co.
Second St. & B&O RR.
Smithton

Latrobe Brewing Co.
P.O. Box 350
Latrobe

Lion, Inc.
5-6 Hart St.
Wilkes-Barre

Pittsburgh Brewing Co.
3340 Liberty Ave.
Pittsburgh

F&M Schaefer Brewing Co.
P.O. Box 2568
Allentown

C. Schmidt Brewing Co.
127 Edward St.
Philadelphia

Straub Brewery, Inc.
Rear 303 Sorg St.
St. Mary's

D.G. Yuengling & Son, Inc.
S.E. Cor. 5th & Mahantogo Sts.
Pottsville

TENNESSEE
Jos. Schlitz Brewing Co.
5151 Raines Rd.
Memphis

TEXAS
Anheuser-Busch, Inc.
775 Gellhorn Drive
Houston

Lone Star Brewing Co.
Division of G. Heileman Brewing Co.
P.O. Box 2060
San Antonio

Miller Brewing Co.
7001 South Freeway
Fort Worth

Pearl Brewing Co.
   Subsidiary of the General
   Brewing Co.
P.O. Box 1661
San Antonio

Jos. Schlitz Brewing Co.
1400 West Cotton St.
Longview

Spoetzl Brewery, Inc.
603 E. Brewery St.
Shiner

VIRGINIA
Anheuser-Busch, Inc.
2000 Pocahontas Trail
Williamsburg

Champale Products Corp.
710 Washington Ave.
Norfolk

WASHINGTON
Carling National Breweries, Inc.
Division of G. Heileman Brewing
   Co., Inc.
2120 South C. St.
Tacoma

General Brewing Co.
615 Columbia St.
Vancouver

267

Independent Ale Brewing Co.
4620 Leary Way, NW
Seattle

Olympia Brewing Co.
P.O. Box 947
Olympia

Rainier Brewing Co.,
Division of G. Heileman
    Brewing Co., Inc.
3100 Airport Way So.
Seattle

Yakima Brewing & Malting Co.
25 N. Front St.
Yakima

WISCONSIN
G. Heileman Brewing Co., Inc.
1000-1028 S. Third St.
LaCrosse

Jos. Huber Brewing Co.
1200-1206 14th Ave.
Monroe

Jacob Leinenkugel Brewing Co.
1 and 3 Jefferson Ave.
Chippewa Falls

Miller Brewing Co
3939 W. Highland Blvd.
Milwaukee

Pabst Brewing Co.
917 W. Juneau Ave.
Milwaukee

Jos. Schlitz Brewing Co.
235 W. Galena St.
Milwaukee

Stevens Point Beverage Co.
2617 Water St.
Stevens Point

Walter Brewing Co.
318 Elm St.
Eau Claire

GLOSSARY

acidic—having a taste of acid, a predominance of sourness.

acidification—to make or become sour or acid.

adjunct—a thing added to something else, but secondary in importance or not essential; in beer making there are malt adjuncts, such as corn and rice, which are used in place of barley to make a paler and less expensive brew.

aftertaste—a palate sensation that occurs after the beer has been swallowed

ale—probably derived from the Norse *oel,* which originally referred to fermented malt beverages that were not flavored by hops. In the earliest times, all such beverages would have been ale by that definition. When the use of hops as a flavoring agent became prevalent, such hopped brews were identified as beer. At that time both ale and beer were top-fermented and in all ways identical except for the hops. Later, when bottom fermentation came along, terms were revised. Today *beer* usually identifies lager specifically and the entire class of malt beverages in general, whereas the term *ale* applies only to top-fermented brews.

ambient—that which surrounds, as on all sides. The ambient temperature is the temperature of the room, or of the outside air.

aroma—fragrance, usually in a pleasant sense; applied to a beverage, it is the component of the odor that derives from the ingredients of the beverage, as opposed to the bouquet, which is the result of by-products from the fermentation process.

aromatic—of or having an aroma, usually in the sense of being particularly fragrant, sweet or spicy.

astringent—causing contraction or shrinking, as of tissue in the mouth; harsh, severe, stern.

austere—as applied to beer tastes, simple, lacking complexity. (The dictionary-preferred meaning of harsh and severe is not intended herein.)

balance—the feature of a beer concerned with the harmony of various flavors and sensations.

barley—a cereal grass with bearded spikes of flowers, and its seed or grain. Barley is the most suitable cereal grain for making malt beverages; it provides flavor, head, body, and color.

barley wine—a strongly flavored ale that dates back to the ancient Egyptians; today's barley wine is still strong in flavor and alcohol, assertive of both sweetness and bitterness in the nose and the mouth.

barrel—a large wooden cylindrical container with sides that bulge outward and flat ends. Usually made of wooden staves bound with metal bands. Also, a standard of measure for liquids: 31 1/2 gallons in the U.S., 36 imperial gallons in Great Britain, and 42 gallons in the brewing trade.

beer—describes fermented malt beverages in general and bottom-fermented brews in particular. (See also ale.)

beery—that which is typical of beer, as an odor that is generally malty, but having a noticeable level of hops.

bitter—the tangy or sharp taste in beer that results from hops; without the bitterness a beer has no zest, with too much bitterness it is hard and biting.

bock—a strong dark German beer. In America there are a number of so-called bock beers that derive their color and flavor artificially.

body—the mouth-filling property of a beer. Taken at its extreme, stout has a heavy or full body, pale low-calorie beer may be thin or watery.

bouquet—that portion of the odor caused by fermentation. (See also aroma.)

brackish—partly salty, but not necessarily unpleasant.

brasserie—the French word for brewery.

brewer—one who brews; the leading brewer at a brewery is called the brewmaster.

brewery—a brewing plant, a place where beer is made.

brewhouse—archaic term for brewery.

bright—a term used to describe appearance (its clarity and brilliance) and taste (its zest).

Burton—a location in England noted for the quality of its ales.

calorie—the unit of heat needed to raise one kilogram of water one degree Celsius; human body intake and energy expenditure are measured in calories. A twelve-ounce portion of beer has some 150 calories.

caramelize—to turn into caramel, a burnt sugar.

carbon dioxide—CO_2, the ingredient in beer that gives it the bubbles; it comes to the beer either naturally through the fermentation process, through krausening, or through carbonic injection, the artificial charging of the beverage with CO_2 just before it is packaged.

cardboard—a taste or odor that is like wet cardboard. It is most frequently encountered in foreign beers, especially from the Orient. It is caused by oxidation.

cask—a barrel of any size. Brewers' casks come in seven sizes: butt (108 gallons), puncheon (72), hogshead (54), barrel, kilderkin (18), firkin (9), and pin (4 1/2).

269

clarify—clear of particulate matter, either naturally with settling out or artificially with fining agents.

clarity—the degree to which the beer is without particulate matter in solution, ranging from clear to cloudy or (heaven forbid) murky.

clean—fresh; makes your mouth feel refreshed and "clean."

cloying—too sweet or rich; a thick sweetness so intense as to be offensive.

creamy—foamy and bubbly; feel of liquid that is infused with small bubble carbonation. Needs to be accompanied with a good flavor to come off well.

dank—slightly moldy, as the smell in a damp basement.

dextrin—a soluble gummy substance obtained from starch.

dextrose—a crystalline sugar found in plants and animals; in beer it is produced from starch in the conversion of barley into malt.

Dortmunder—style of lager beer much the same as pilsener, developed in Dortmund, Germany.

draught (or draft)—beer drawn from a cask or the act of drawing beer from a cask.

dry—not sweet.

effervescence—a bubbling up, foaming.

enzyme (amylolytic)—an organic substance that converts starch into soluble substances such as sugars.

enzyme (proteolytic)—an organic substance that converts proteins into soluble substances.

fermentation—the breakdown of complex molecules in organic compounds caused by the action of a ferment (such as yeast). In malt beverages, it is the decomposition of sugar into ethyl alcohol and carbon dioxide.

ferruginous—ironlike or like iron rust; in flavor it refers to a taste like spring water with a high iron content or water piped through rusty pipes.

fining—a process of hastening the clarification of a malt beverage (or wine); it usually involves the addition of fining agents such as isinglass, enzymes, gelatin (all coagulants), or bentonite or cellulose (mechanical).

finish—that part of the palate sensation that occurs just before and during swallowing.

flabby—soft and sweet; a derogatory term when speaking of beer.

flavor—that quality of a substance which gives it its characteristic taste taken either singly or in aggregate.

gallon—a liquid measure, four quarts.

green beer—young or immature beer, fresh from its first fermentation, before it has been aged or lagered.

hogshead—a large barrel with a capacity of 100-140 gallons; or a liquid measure of 63 gallons.

hops—the dried ripe cones of the female flowers of a climbing-vine member of the nettle family. The resin or extract from the cones is used for bittering and preserving beer.

India pale ale—a very strong ale of the type produced for British troops serving in India in the past century. It had to be produced very strong so that it could survive the long passage to India, which took over six months and involved equatorial crossings.

kiln—a drying oven (also oast).

krausening—a technique whereby young beer is added to fully aged beer before packaging to accomplish a "natural" infusion of carbon dioxide.

lactic acid—a clear syrupy acid created by the action of microorganisms on sucrose.

lager—the popular name given to today's bottom-fermented beer, which is chill-brewed and stored, or lagered, for proper aging; it derives from the German *lagern,* meaning to store.

logo—short for logotype, a word referring to a trademark, symbol, or design that represents a product or company.

malster—one who controls the malting process.

malt—barley that has been steeped in water to produce sprouting, then kiln-dried.

malt extract—a sticky, sugary substance obtained from malt.

malting process—the process of producing malt from barley.

maltose—malt sugar, produced by the action of diastase of malt on starch.

mash—crushed or ground malt soaked in water for making wort.

mash tun—a large vessel wherein the wort is separated from the grist.

mead—an ancient drink of fermented honey and water.

metallic—of or pertaining to metal. A metallic flavor in a beer could be caused by either its container or a flaw in the brewing process. Sometimes an overage beer will take on metalliclike flavors, even in a bottle.

molecule—the smallest particle of a compound that can exist in a free state.

near-beer—a beerlike beverage brewed either to be nonalcoholic or to have a low alcoholic content (on the order of one-half of one percent).

nose—the total sensation in the nose; the total effect of the beer's odor; the combination of aroma and bouquet.

NR—nonreturnable.

oast—a kiln, especially one for drying hops.

over the hill—too old, gone by, bad tasting because it is overaged.

pablum—an old-time baby cereal consisting of finely ground oatmeal.

package—the container that holds the beer, either a bottle or can. Otherwise beer is on draft, or on tap. Packaged beer is usually pasteurized.

particulate matter—particles held in suspension in the liquid, such as protein matter, dead yeast cells, grain fragments.

pasteurize—to subject to a temperature of 142° to 145° F. for thirty minutes to destroy disease-producing bacteria and to check fermentation.

photosynthesis—the formation of carbohydrates by the action of sunlight.

pilsener—a type of very pale lager beer, so named because the pinnacle of the style was first reached in Pilsen, Czechoslovakia. It is similar to the Dortmunder style of beer.

popular-priced—lower priced and therefore more popular with the consumer, but supposedly less well made than premium beer.

porter—a dark brew; first made in England in the eighteenth century to fill the market for a mixture of ale, beer, and Twopenny, a popular drink of that time and place. Today it is not unlike stout except that it is lighter in body and may be more highly carbonated.

premium—a term used by brewers to indicate the top of their product line. (The term is much abused.)

pub—a business establishment in Great Britain whose principal wares are malt beverages.

quaff—to drink in large drafts.

rack—to fill a container with beer in a brewery.

saccharometer—a form of hydrometer for measuring the amount of sugar in a solution.

saturation—the degree of intensity of a color.

skunky—like the peculiar aroma of a skunk. A beer may smell and taste of skunk, a defect found usually in well-hopped beers and caused, it is believed, by photosynthesis.

spruce beer—a beer (alcoholic or nonalcoholic) made by steeping spruce boughs and fermenting the resulting sugared liquid.

stout—a rich dark brew made from roasted malt, often with the addition of caramelized sugar, and a reasonably high proportion of hops.

swampy—like a swamp, as in the odors of the rotting vegetation frequently encountered in such a damp area.

tangy—strong or penetrating.

tannin—tannic acid; an astringent.

tap—the lever that releases the beer from a tapped keg; to tap, or open, a keg of draft beer; a taproom, a place where draft beer is served.

tavern—a place where alcoholic beverages are sold for consumption on the premises.

tawny—brownish yellow.

texture—the physical "feel" of a beer in the mouth.

tied house—in England, a pub, inn, or restaurant under agreement to buy all its beer from a single brewer. Often owned by the brewer. There are brewery-owned public accommodations all over Europe.

tinny—a metallic taste in beer, as if from the "tin," or can; a term held over from the days when the cans were made of tin and not steel or aluminum.

trub—a protein precipitate which results when the wort is boiled.

vegetal—a vegetablelike nature in aroma or taste, as in raw broccoli or cabbage; frequently used in an unpleasant sense.

vinous—a winy, winelike, fruity in a fermented sense.

Weiss—a type of beer still popular in Berlin. It is white in color, cloudy and foamy, with a very yeasty nose and taste. It is made from wheat, usually not pasteurized. Traditionally it is served in a large wide-bowled stem glass with a dash of raspberry syrup. *Weiss* is German for white.

wort—the solution of malt extract in water.

XXX—a guarantee of quality. Originally, X indicated the number of times that a liquor had been distilled, whereas XXX or XXXX showed it had been run through the maximum number of times that it was meaningful to do so, and therefore had reached its height of strength and purity.

The term was adopted centuries ago to indicate beer quality. It is now greatly abused.

yeast—the ferment, or fermenting agent, which turns the wort into beer. In particular, in beer making the yeast is the strain *Saccharomyces cerevisiae*, or brewer's yeast.

COURTESY THE STROH BREWERY COMPANY

Early photo of Stroh Brewery Company.

BIBLIOGRAPHY

BOOKS

Abel, Bob. *The Book of Beer,* Chicago: Henry Regnery Co., 1976.

Anderson, Sonja and Will. *Beers, Breweries, and Breweriana.* Carmel: 1969.

Anderson, Will. *The Beer Book.* Princeton: Pyne Press, 1973.

Arnold, John P. *Origin and History of Beer and Brewing.* Chicago: Alumni Association of the Wahl-Henius Institute of Fermentology, 1911.

Brewers Association of Canada. *About Beer and the Brewing Industry.* Ottawa: 1965.

Carlsberg Brewing Co. *The Book of Carlsberg.* Copenhagen: 1965.

Dabbs, Robert L., and Harris, David S. *Worldwide Beer Can Collector's Guide.* Independence: World Wide Beer Can Collectors, 1974.

Emerson, Edward R. *Beverages, Past and Present.* New York: G.P. Putnam's Sons, 1908.

Friedrich, Manfred, and Bull, Donald. *The Register of United States Breweries 1876-1976.* Trumbull: Donald Bull, 1976.

Jackson, Michael, ed. *The World Guide to Beer.* Englewood Cliffs: Prentice-Hall, 1977.

Kroll, Wayne L. *Badger Breweries, Past and Present.* Jefferson: 1976.

Kroll, Wayne L. *Wisconsin Breweries and Their Bottles.* Jefferson: 1972.

McWhirter, Norris and Ross. *Guinness Book of World Records.* New York: Ballantine Books, 1977.

Martello, Jack. *Beer Can Collector's Bible.* New York: Ballantine Books, 1977.

Mathias, Peter. *The Brewing Industry in England, 1700-1830.* Cambridge: University Press, 1959.

One Hundred Years of Brewing. Chicago: H.S. Rich & Co., 1903.

Porter, John. *All About Beer.* New York: Doubleday & Co., 1974.

Protz, Roger. *Pulling a Fast One.* London: Pluto Press, 1978.

Robertson, James D. *The Great American Beer Book.* Thornwood: Caroline House, 1978.

Vlantes, Stanley N., ed. *1977 Modern Brewery Age Blue Book.* East Norwalk: MBA Publishing Corp., 1977.

Waldo, Myra. *Beer and Good Food.* Garden City: Doubleday & Co., 1958.

Wallerstein Laboratories. *Bottle Beer Quality.* New York: Wallerstein Co., Inc., 1948.

Weiner, Michael. *The Taster's Guide to Beer.* New York: Macmillan Co., 1977.

Wright, Larry, ed. *The Beer Can.* Matteson: Great Lakes Living Press, 1976.

ENCYCLOPEDIAS

Encyclopedia Britannica (1958), "Beer."

JOURNALS AND MAGAZINES

Abel, Robert. "Beer Is Not a Proletarian Drink." *The Friends of Wine,* July-August 1980.

"America's Oldest Brewery Endures—and Grows." *Brewer's Digest,* February 1980.

"The Anatomy of Light Beer." *Modern Brewery Age.* April 9, 1979.

"BD Visits the Cold Spring Brewing Company in Cold Spring, Minn." *Brewer's Digest,* September 1972.

"BD Visits the Fred Koch Brewery in Dunkirk, N.Y." *Brewer's Digest,* April 1966.

"BD Visits the Hudepohl Brewing Co. in Cincinnati, Ohio." *Brewer's Digest,* July 1971.

"BD Visits the Spoetzl Brewery, Inc., in Shiner, Texas." *Brewer's Digest,* October 1966.

"BD Visits the Straub Brewery in St. Mary's, Pa." *Brewer's Digest,* July 1980.

"Beer Sediments Developed During Shaking Abuse." *Brewer's Digest,* June 1979.

Davies, Charles. "Pint Size." *Weekend Magazine,* 24 September 1977, pp. 4-7.

"Dixie Barrels Ahead." *Brewer's Digest,* January 1981.

Fine, Steven M. "The King of Suds." (Article from unidentified Pittsburgh area newspaper magazine), 1977.

Gray, Malcolm. "A B.C. Return to Real Ale." *MacLean's,* August 15, 1983.

"Hudepohl Scores with Hudy Delight." *Brewer's Digest,* February 1979.

"The Lion Roars." *Brewer's Digest,* September 1980.

"The Lone Star Turnaround." *Brewer's Digest,* August 1980.

"Miller Celebrates 125th Year." *Modern Brewery Age,* April 21, 1980.

"The Nationals Almost Drove Old Dixie Down." *Modern Brewery Age,* February 16, 1981.

"Objective Measurement of the Flavor Quality of Beer." *Brewer's Digest,* December 1977.

"The Ortlieb Renaissance." *Brewer's Digest,* May 1977.

"The Ortlieb Renaissance Continues." *Brewer's Digest,* October 1979.

"Pearl's 'Spunk' Is a Tradition." *Modern Brewery Age,* April 21, 1980.

"Pickett's Revisited." *Brewer's Digest,* August 1977.

"The Pittsburgh Brewing Company Turns It Around." *Brewer's Digest,* March 1980.

"Prinz Brau, Alaska's New Brewery is Banking on State's Future Growth." *Brewer's Digest,* December 1976.

"Putting It All Together." *Canadian Beverage News,* May 1973.

"Quality You Can Taste—Automation in the Production of Beer." *Siemens Review,* July–August 1983.

"A Report on Brasserie de Tahiti." *Brewer's Digest,* February 1981.

"A Report on Henninger Brewery (Ontario), Ltd." *Brewer's Digest,* September 1979.

"Schlitz Raids the Competition." *Business Week,* 21 November 1977, p. 54.

"A Struggle to Stay First in Brewing." *Business Week,* 24 March 1973.

"Tradition Preserved...." *Brewer's Digest,* November 1980.

"A Tradition Reborn." *Brewer's Digest,* November 1979.

"Trouble Brewing." *Newsweek,* 23 July 1973.

"What's Ahead for Pickett." *Brewer's Digest,* October 1980.

NEWSPAPERS

"Decline of Breweries in Wyoming Valley Parallels Trends Reported in Other Sections of State, Nation." *Wilkes-Barre Times Leader,* 12 September 1977.

McGuire, Patrick A. "Rockies' 2d-Largest Brewery Home Brew Gone Big-Time." *Denver Post,* 1 October 1980.

"New Ulm Industry Day." *New Ulm Daily Journal,* 9 September 1974.

Sedlmeyer, Angeline. "The History of the Brewing Industry in Shiner, Texas." *Shiner Gazette,* 29 July 1971.

Tomb, Geoffrey. "Something's Brewing in the Straub Family." *St. Mary's Post Gazette Daily Magazine,* 22 September 1977.

REPORTS

Eckhardt, Fred. *A Treatise of Lager Beers.* Portland: Hobby Winemakers, 1975.

U.S. Department of the Treasury. Bureau of Alcohol, Tobacco & Firearms. *Breweries Authorized to Operate,* July 1980.

Privatbrauerei Dortmunder Kronen, *250 Jahre Familienbesitz—550 Jahre Brautradition.* Dortmund, 1979.

Index